The Nuremberg Nazi Trial

Excerpts From the Testimony of Herman Goering, Albert Speer, Auschwitz Commander Rudolf Hoess, and Others

Red and Black Publishers, St Petersburg, Florida

Excerpted from "Trial of the Major War Criminals Before the International Military Tribunal". Nuremberg, Germany: International Military Tribunal, 1947.

Library of Congress Cataloging-in-Publication Data

The Nuremberg Nazi trial : excerpts from the testimony of Herman Goering, Albert Speer, Auschwitz commander Rudolf Hoess, and others.
    p. cm.
   "Excerpted from "Trial of the Major War Criminals Before the International Military Tribunal". Nuremberg, Germany: International Military Tribunal, 1947."
   ISBN 978-1-934941-95-9
1. Nuremberg Trial of Major German War Criminals, Nuremberg, Germany, 1945-1946. 2. Nuremberg War Crime Trials, Nuremberg, Germany, 1946-1949. 3. Göring, Hermann, 1893-1946. 4. Speer, Albert, 1905-1981. 5. Höss, Rudolf, 1900-1947.
   KZ1176.N85 2010
   341.6'90268--dc22

                                     2010018904

Red and Black Publishers, PO Box 7542, St Petersburg, Florida, 33734
Contact us at: info@RedandBlackPublishers.com
Printed and manufactured in the United States of America

Contents

The London Agreement

August 8, 1945

AGREEMENT by the Government of the UNITED STATES OF AMERICA, the Provisional Government of the FRENCH REPUBLIC, the Government of the UNITED KINGDOM OF GREAT BRITAIN AND NORTHERN IRELAND and the Government of the UNION OF SOVIET SOCIALIST REPUBLICS for the Prosecution and Punishment of the MAJOR WAR CRIMINALS of the EUROPEAN AXIS

WHEREAS the United Nations have from time to time made declarations of their intention that War Criminals shall be brought to justice;

AND WHEREAS the Moscow Declaration of the 30th October 1943 on German atrocities in Occupied Europe stated that those German Officers and men and members of the Nazi Party who have been responsible for or have taken a consenting part in atrocities and crimes will be sent back to the countries in which their abominable deeds were done in order that they may be judged and punished according to the laws of these liberated countries and of the free Governments that will be created therein;

AND WHEREAS this Declaration was stated to be without prejudice to the case of major criminals whose offenses have no particular geographical location and who will be punished by the joint decision of the Governments of the Allies;

NOW THEREFORE the Government of the United States of America, the Provisional Government of the French Republic, the Government of the United Kingdom of Great Britain and Northern Ireland and the Government of the Union of Soviet Socialist Republics (hereinafter called "the Signatories") acting in the interests of all the United Nations and by their representatives duly authorized thereto have concluded this Agreement.

Article 1. There shall be established after consultation with the Control Council for Germany an International Military Tribunal for the trial of war criminals whose offenses have no particular geographical location whether they be accused individually or in their capacity as members of the organizations or groups or in both capacities.

Article 2. The constitution, jurisdiction and functions of the International Military Tribunal shall be those set in the Charter annexed to this Agreement, which Charter shall form an integral part of this Agreement.

Article 3. Each of the Signatories shall take the necessary steps to make available for the investigation of the charges and trial the major war criminals detained by them who are to be tried by the International Military Tribunal. The Signatories shall also use their best endeavors to make available for investigation of the charges against and the trial before the International Military Tribunal such of the major war criminals as are not in the territories of any of the Signatories.

Article 4. Nothing in this Agreement shall prejudice the provisions established by the Moscow Declaration concerning the return of war criminals to the countries where they committed their crimes.

Article 5. Any Government of the United Nations may adhere to this Agreement by notice given through the diplomatic channel to the Government of the United Kingdom, who shall inform the other signatory and adhering Governments of each such adherence.

Article 6. Nothing in this Agreement shall prejudice the jurisdiction or the powers of any national or occupation court established or to be established in any allied territory or in Germany for the trial of war criminals.

Article 7. This Agreement shall come into force on the day of signature and shall remain in force for the period of one year and shall continue thereafter, subject to the right of any Signatory to give, through the diplomatic channel, one month's notice of intention to terminate it. Such termination shall not prejudice any proceedings already taken or any findings already made in pursuance of this Agreement.

IN WITNESS WHEREOF the Undersigned have signed the present Agreement.

DONE in quadruplicate in London this 8th day of August 1945 each in English, French and Russian, and each text to have equal authenticity.

For the Government of the United States of America

Robert H. Jackson

For the Provisional Government of the French Republic

Robert Falco

For the Government of the United Kingdom of Great Britain and Northern Ireland

Jowitt C.

For the Government of the Union of Soviet Socialist Republics

I.   Nikitchenko

A. Trainin

The Nuremberg Charter

I. CONSTITUTION OF THE INTERNATIONAL MILITARY TRIBUNAL

Article 1. In pursuance of the Agreement signed on the 8th day of August 1945 by the Government of the United States of America, the Provisional Government of the French Republic, the Government of the United Kingdom of Great Britain and Northern Ireland and the Government of the Union of Soviet Socialist Republics, there shall be established an International Military Tribunal (hereinafter called "the Tribunal") for the just and prompt trial and punishment of the major war criminals of the European Axis.

Article 2. The Tribunal shall consist of four members, each with an alternate. One member and one alternate shall be appointed by each of the Signatories. The alternates shall, so far as they are able, be present at all sessions of the Tribunal. In case of illness of any member of the Tribunal or his incapacity for some other reason to fulfill his functions, his alternate shall take his place.

Article 3. Neither the Tribunal, its members nor their alternates can be challenged by the prosecution, or by the Defendants or their Counsel. Each Signatory may replace its members of the Tribunal or his alternate for reasons of health or for other good reasons, except that no replacement may take place during a Trial, other than by an alternate.

Article 4

(a) The presence of all four members of the Tribunal or the alternate for any absent member shall be necessary to constitute the quorum.

(b) The members of the Tribunal shall, before any trial begins, agree among themselves upon the selection from their number of a President, and the President shall hold office during the trial, or as may otherwise be agreed by a vote of not less than three members. The principle of rotation of presidency for successive trials is agreed. If, however, a session of the Tribunal takes place on the territory of one of the four Signatories, the representative of that Signatory on the Tribunal shall preside.

(c.) Save as aforesaid the Tribunal shall take decisions by a majority vote and in case the votes are evenly divided, the vote of the President shall be decisive: provided always that convictions and sentences shall only be imposed by affirmative votes of at least three members of the Tribunal.

Article 5. In case of need and depending on the number of the matters to be tried, other Tribunals may be set up; and the establishment, functions, and procedure of each Tribunal shall be identical, and shall be governed by this Charter.

II. JURISDICTION AND GENERAL PRINCIPLES

Article 6. The Tribunal established by the Agreement referred to in Article 1 hereof for the trial and punishment of the major war criminals of the European Axis countries shall have the power to try and punish persons who, acting in the interests of the European Axis countries, whether as individuals or as members of organizations, committed any of the following crimes.

The following acts, or any of them, are crimes coming within the jurisdiction of the Tribunal for which there shall be individual responsibility:

(a) CRIMES AGAINST PEACE: namely, planning, preparation, initiation or waging of a war of aggression, or a war in violation of international treaties, agreements or assurances, or participation in a common plan or conspiracy for the accomplishment of any of the foregoing;

(b) WAR CRIMES: namely, violations of the laws or customs of war. Such violations shall include, but not be limited to, murder, ill-treatment or deportation to slave labor or for any other purpose of civilian population of or in occupied territory, murder or ill-treatment of prisoners of war or persons on the seas, killing of hostages, plunder of public or private property, wanton destruction of cities, towns or villages, or devastation not justified by military necessity;

(c.) CRIMES AGAINST HUMANITY: namely, murder, extermination, enslavement, deportation, and other inhumane acts committed against any civilian population, before or during the war; or persecutions on political, racial or religious grounds in execution of or in connection with any crime within the jurisdiction of the Tribunal, whether or not in violation of the domestic law of the country where perpetrated.

Leaders, organizers, instigators and accomplices participating in the formulation or execution of a common plan or conspiracy to commit any of the foregoing crimes are responsible for all acts performed by any persons in execution of such plan.

Article 7. The official position of defendants, whether as Heads of State or responsible officials in Government Departments, shall not be considered as freeing them from responsibility or mitigating punishment.

Article 8. The fact that the Defendant acted pursuant to order of his Government or of a superior shall not free him from responsibility, but may be considered in mitigation of punishment if the Tribunal determines that justice so requires.

Article 9. At the trial of any individual member of any group or organization the Tribunal may declare (in connection with any act of which the individual may be convicted) that the group or organization of which the individual was a member was a criminal organization.

After the receipt of the Indictment the Tribunal shall give such notice as it thinks fit that the prosecution intends to ask the Tribunal to make such declaration and any member of the organization will be entitled to apply to the Tribunal for leave to be heard by the Tribunal upon the question of the criminal character of the organization. The Tribunal shall have power to allow or reject the application. If the application is allowed, the Tribunal may direct in what manner the applicants shall be represented and heard.

Article 10. In cases where a group or organization is declared criminal by the Tribunal, the competent national authority of any Signatory shall have the right to bring individuals to trial for membership therein before national, military or occupation courts. In any such case the criminal nature of the group or organization is considered proved and shall not be questioned.

Article 11. Any person convicted by the Tribunal may be charged before a national, military or occupation court, referred to in Article 10 of this Charter, with a crime other than of membership in a criminal group or organization and such court may, after convicting him, impose upon him punishment independent of and additional to the punishment imposed by the Tribunal for participation in the criminal activities of such group or organization.

Article 12. The Tribunal shall have the right to take proceedings against a person charged with crimes set out in Article 6 of this Charter in his absence, if he has not been found or if the Tribunal, for any reason, finds it necessary, in the interests of justice, to conduct the hearing in his absence.

Article 13. The Tribunal shall draw up rules for its procedure. These rules shall not be inconsistent with the provisions of this Charter.

III. COMMITTEE FOR THE INVESTIGATION AND PROSECUTION OF MAJOR WAR CRIMINALS

Article 14. Each Signatory shall appoint a Chief Prosecutor for the investigation of the charges against and the prosecution of major war criminals.

The Chief Prosecutors shall act as a committee for the following purposes:

(a) to agree upon a plan of the individual work of each of the Chief Prosecutors and his staff,

(b) to settle the final designation of major war criminals to be tried by the Tribunal,

(c.) to approve the Indictment and the documents to be submitted therewith,

(d) to lodge the Indictment and the accompany documents with the Tribunal,

(e) to draw up and recommend to the Tribunal for its approval draft rules of procedure, contemplated by Article 13 of this Charter. The Tribunal shall have the power to accept, with or without amendments, or to reject, the rules so recommended.

The Committee shall act in all the above matters by a majority vote and shall appoint a Chairman as may be convenient and in accordance with the principle of rotation: provided that if there is an equal division of vote concerning the designation of a Defendant to be tried by the Tribunal, or the crimes with which he shall be charged, that proposal will be adopted which was made by the party which proposed that the particular Defendant be tried, or the particular charges be preferred against him.

Article 15. The Chief Prosecutors shall individually, and acting in collaboration with one another, also undertake the following duties:

(a) investigation, collection and production before or at the Trial of all necessary evidence,

(b) the preparation of the Indictment for approval by the Committee in accordance with paragraph (c) of Article 14 hereof,

(c.) the preliminary examination of all necessary witnesses and of all Defendants,

(d) to act as prosecutor at the Trial,

(e) to appoint representatives to carry out such duties as may be assigned them,

(f) to undertake such other matters as may appear necessary to them for the purposes of the preparation for and conduct of the Trial.

It is understood that no witness or Defendant detained by the Signatory shall be taken out of the possession of that Signatory without its assent.

IV. FAIR TRIAL FOR DEFENDANTS

Article 16. In order to ensure fair trial for the Defendants, the following procedure shall be followed:

(a) The Indictment shall include full particulars specifying in detail the charges against the Defendants. A copy of the Indictment and of all the documents lodged with the Indictment, translated into a language which he understands, shall be furnished to the Defendant at reasonable time before the Trial.

(b) During any preliminary examination or trial of a Defendant he will have the right to give any explanation relevant to the charges made against him.

(c.) A preliminary examination of a Defendant and his Trial shall be conducted in, or translated into, a language which the Defendant understands.

(d) A Defendant shall have the right to conduct his own defense before the Tribunal or to have the assistance of Counsel.

(e) A Defendant shall have the right through himself or through his Counsel to present evidence at the Trial in support of his defense, and to cross-examine any witness called by the Prosecution.

V. POWERS OF THE TRIBUNAL AND CONDUCT OF THE TRIAL

Article 17. The Tribunal shall have the power

(a) to summon witnesses to the Trial and to require their attendance and testimony and to put questions to them

(b) to interrogate any Defendant,

(c.) to require the production of documents and other evidentiary material,

(d) to administer oaths to witnesses,

(e) to appoint officers for the carrying out of any task designated by the Tribunal including the power to have evidence taken on commission.

Article 18. The Tribunal shall

(a) confine the Trial strictly to an expeditious hearing of the cases raised by the charges,

(b) take strict measures to prevent any action which will cause reasonable delay, and rule out irrelevant issues and statements of any kind whatsoever,

(c.) deal summarily with any contumacy, imposing appropriate punishment, including exclusion of any Defendant or his Counsel from some or all further proceedings, but without prejudice to the determination of the charges.

Article 19. The Tribunal shall not be bound by technical rules of evidence. It shall adopt and apply to the greatest possible extent expeditious and nontechnical procedure, and shall admit any evidence which it deems to be of probative value.

Article 20. The Tribunal may require to be informed of the nature of any evidence before it is entered so that it may rule upon the relevance thereof.

Article 21. The Tribunal shall not require proof of facts of common knowledge but shall take judicial notice thereof. It shall also take judicial notice of official governmental documents and reports of the United Nations, including the acts and documents of the committees set up in the various allied countries for the investigation of war crimes, and of records and findings of military or other Tribunals of any of the United Nations.

Article 22. The permanent seat of the Tribunal shall be in Berlin. The first meetings of the members of the Tribunal and of the Chief Prosecutors shall be held at Berlin in a place to be designated by the Control Council for Germany. The first trial shall be held at Nuremberg, and any subsequent trials shall be held at such places as the Tribunal may decide.

Article 23. One or more of the Chief Prosecutors may take part in the prosecution at each Trial. The function of any Chief Prosecutor may be discharged by him personally, or by any person or persons authorized by him.

The function of Counsel for a Defendant may be discharged at the Defendant's request by any Counsel professionally qualified to conduct cases before the Courts of his own country, or by any other person who may be specially authorized thereto by the Tribunal.

Article 24. The proceedings at the Trial shall take the following course:

(a) The Indictment shall be read in court.

(b) The Tribunal shall ask each Defendant whether he pleads "guilty" or "not guilty".

(c.) The prosecution shall make an opening statement.

(d) The Tribunal shall ask the prosecution and the defense what evidence (if any) they wish to submit to the Tribunal, and the Tribunal shall rule upon the admissibility of any such evidence.

(e) The witnesses for the Prosecution shall be examined and after that the witnesses for the Defense. Thereafter such rebutting evidence as may be held by the Tribunal to be admissible shall be called by either the Prosecution or the Defense.

(f) The Tribunal may put any question to any witness and to any defendant, at any time.

(g) The Prosecution and the Defense shall interrogate and may cross-examine any witnesses and any Defendant who gives testimony.

(h) The Defense shall address the court.

(i) The Prosecution shall address the court.

(j) Each Defendant may make a statement to the Tribunal.

(k) The Tribunal shall deliver judgment and pronounce sentence.

Article 25. All official documents shall be produced, and all court proceedings conducted, in English, French and Russian, and in the language of the Defendant. So much of the record and of the proceedings may also be translated into the language of any country in which the Tribunal is sitting, as the Tribunal is sitting, as the Tribunal considers desirable in the interests of the justice and public opinion.

VI. JUDGMENT AND SENTENCE

Article 26. The judgment of the Tribunal as to the guilt or the innocence of any Defendant shall give the reasons on which it is based, and shall be final and not subject to review.

Article 27. The Tribunal shall have the right to impose upon a Defendant, on conviction, death or such other punishment as shall be determined by it to be just.

Article 28. In addition to any punishment imposed by it, the Tribunal shall have the right to deprive the convicted person of any stolen property and order its delivery to the Control Council for Germany.

Article 29. In case of guilt, sentences shall be carried out in accordance with the orders of the Control Council for Germany, which may at any time reduce or otherwise alter the sentences, but may not increase the severity thereof. If the Control Council for Germany, after any Defendant has been convicted and sentenced, discovers fresh evidence which, in its opinion, would found a fresh charge against him, the Council shall report accordingly to the Committee established under Article 14 hereof, for such action as they may consider proper, having regard to the interests of justice.

VII. EXPENSES

Article 30. The expenses of the Tribunal and of the Trials, shall be charged by the Signatories against the funds allotted for maintenance of the Control Council of Germany.

Nuremberg Indictment

INDICTMENT

INTERNATIONAL MILITARY TRIBUNAL

THE UNITED STATES OF AMERICA, THE FRENCH REPUBLIC, THE UNITED KINGDOM OF GREAT BRITAIN AND NORTHERN IRELAND, AND THE UNION OF SOVIET SOCIALIST REPUBLICS

– against –

HERMANN WILHELM GOERING, RUDOLF HESS, JOACHIM VON RIBBENTROP, ROBERT LEY, WILHELM KEITEL, ERNST KALTENBRUNNER, ALFRED ROSENBERG, HANS FRANK, WILHELM FRICK, JULIUS STREICHER, WALTER FUNK, HJALMAR SCHACHT, GUSTAV KRUPP VON BOHLEN UND HALBACH, KARL DOENITZ, ERICH RAEDER, BALDUR VON SCHIRACH, FRITZ SAUCKEL, ALFRED JODL, MARTIN BORMANN, FRANZ VON PAPEN, ARTHUR SEYSS-INQUART, ALBERT SPEER, CONSTANTIN VON NEURATH, and HANS FRITZSCHE, Individually and as Members of Any of the Following Groups or Organizations to which They Respectively Belonged, Namely:

DIE REICHS REGIERUNG (REICH CABINET);

DAS KORPS DER POLITISCHEN LEITER DER NATIONALSOZIALISTISCHEN DEUTSCHEN ARBEITERPARTEI (LEADERSHIP CORPS OF THE NAZI PARTY);

DIE SCHUTZSTAFFELN DER NATIONALSOZIALISTISCHEN DEUTSCHEN ARBEITERPARTEI (commonly known as the "SS") and including *DER SICHERHEITSDIENST* (commonly known as the "SD"); *DIE GEHEIME STAATSPOLIZEI* (SECRET STATE POLICE, commonly known as the "GESTAPO"); *DIE STURM ABTEILUNGEN DER NSDAP* (commonly known as the "SA");

and the GENERAL STAFF and HIGH COMMAND of the GERMAN ARMED FORCES, all as defined in Appendix B.

Defendants.

I. The United States of America, the French Republic, the United Kingdom of Great Britain and Northern Ireland, and the Union of Soviet Socialist Republics by the undersigned, Robert H. Jackson, Francois de Menthon, Hartley Shawcross, and R. A. Rudenko, duly appointed to represent their respective Governments in the investigation of the charges against and the prosecution of the major war criminals, pursuant to the Agreement of London dated 8 August 1945, and the Charter of this Tribunal annexed thereto, hereby accuse as guilty, in the respects hereinafter set forth, of Crimes against Peace, War Crimes, and Crimes against Humanity, and of a Common Plan or Conspiracy to commit those Crimes, all as defined in the Charter of the Tribunal, and accordingly name as defendants in this cause and as indicted on the counts hereinafter set out: HERMANN WILHELM GOERING, RUDOLF HESS, JOACHIM VON RIBBENTROP, ROBERT LEY, WILHELM KEITEL, ERNST KALTENBRUNNER, ALFRED ROSENBERG, HANS FRANK, WILHELM FRICK, JULIUS STREICHER, WALTER FUNK, HJALMAR SCHACHT, GUSTAV KRUPP VON BOHLEN UND HALBACH, KARL DOENITZ, ERICH RAEDER, BALDUR VON SCHIRACH, FRITZ SAUCKEL, ALFRED JODL, MARTIN BORMANN, FRANZ VON PAPEN, ARTHUR SEYSS-INQUART, ALBERT SPEER, CONSTANTIN VON NEURATH and HANS FRITZSCHE, individually and as members of any of the groups or organizations next hereinafter named.

II. The following are named as groups or organizations (since dissolved) which should be declared criminal by reason of their aims and the means used for the accomplishment thereof and in connection with the conviction of such of the named defendants as were members thereof:

DIE REICHSREGIERUNG (REICH CABINET);

DAS KORPS DER POLITISCHEN LEITER DER NATIONALSOZIALISTISCHEN DEUTSCHEN ARBEITERPARTEI (LEADERSHIP CORPS OF THE NAZI PARTY);

DIE SCHUTZSTAFFELN DER NATIONALSOZIALISTISCHEN DEUTSCHEN ARBEITERPARTEI (commonly known as the "SS") and including *DER SICHERHEITSDIENST* (commonly known as the "SD"); *DIE GEHEIME STAATSPOLIZEI* (SECRET STATE POLICE, commonly known as the "GESTAPO"); *DIE STURMABTEILUNGEN DER NSDAP* (commonly known as the "SA"); and the GENERAL STAFF of the HIGH COMMAND of the GERMAN ARMED FORCES.

The identity and membership of the groups or organizations referred to in the foregoing titles are hereinafter in Appendix B more particularly defined.

APPENDIX B

Statement of criminality of Groups and Organizations

The statements hereinafter set forth, following the name of each group or organization named in the Indictment as one which should be declared criminal, constitute matters upon which the prosecution will rely *inter alia* as establishing the criminality of the group or organization:

DIE REICHSREGIERUNG (REICH CABINET)

"*Die Reichsregierung* (Reich Cabinet)" referred to in the Indictment consists of persons who were:

(i) Members of the ordinary cabinet after 30 January 1933, the date on which Hitler became Chancellor of the German Republic. The term "ordinary cabinet" as used herein means the Reich Ministers, i.e., heads of departments of the central Government; Reich Ministers without portfolio; State Ministers acting as Reich Ministers; and other officials entitled to take part in meetings of this cabinet.

(ii) Members of *der Ministerrat fur die Reichsverteidigung* (Council of Ministers for the Defense of the Reich).

(iii) Members of *der Geheimer Kabinettsrat* (Secret Cabinet Council).

Under the Fuehrer, these persons functioning in the foregoing capacities and in association as a group, possessed and exercised legislative, executive, administrative, and political powers and functions of a very high order in the system of German Government. Accordingly, they are charged with responsibility for the policies adopted and put into effect by the Government including those which comprehended and involved the commission of the crimes referred to in Counts One, Two, Three, and Four of the Indictment.

DAS KORPS DER POLITISCHEN LEITER DER NATIONALSOZIALISTISCHEN DEUTSCHEN ARBEITERPARTEI (LEADERSHIP CORPS OF THE NAZI PARTY)

"*Das Korps der Politischen Leiter der Nationalsozialistischen Deutschen Arbeiterpartei* (Leadership Corps of the Nazi Party)" referred to in the Indictment consists of persons who were at any time, according to common Nazi terminology, "*Politischen Leiter*" (Political Leaders) of any grade or rank.

The *Politischen Leiter* comprised the leaders of the various functional offices of the Party (for example, the *Reichsleitung*, or Party Reich Directorate, and the *Gauleitung*, or Party Gau Directorate), as well as the territorial leaders of the Party (for example, the Gauleiter).

The *Politischen Leiter* were a distinctive and elite group within the Nazi Party proper and as such were vested with special prerogatives. They were organized according to the Leadership Principle and were charged with planning, developing and imposing upon their followers the policies of the Nazi Party. Thus the territorial leaders among them were called *Hoheitstrager*, or bearers of sovereignty, and were entitled to call upon and utilize the various Party formations when necessary for the execution of Party policies.

Reference is hereby made to the allegations in Count One of the Indictment showing that the Nazi Party was the central core of the common plan or conspiracy therein set forth. The *Politischen Leiter*, as a major power within the Nazi Party proper, and functioning in the capacities above described and in association as a group, joined in the common plan or conspiracy, and accordingly share responsibility for the crimes set forth in Counts One, Two, Three, and Four of the Indictment.

The prosecution expressly reserves the right to request, at any time before sentence is pronounced, that *Politische Leiter* of subordinate grades or ranks or of other types or classes, to be specified by the Prosecution, be excepted from further proceedings in this Case No. 1, but without prejudice to other proceedings or actions against them.

DIE SCHUTZSTAFFELN DER NATIONALSOZIALISTISCHEN DEUTSCHEN ARBEITERPARTE (COMMONLY KNOWN AS THE SS) INCLUDING DER SICHERHEITSDIENST (COMMONLY KNOWN AS THE SD).

"Die Schutzstaffeln der Nationalsozialistische Deutsche Arbeiterpartei (commonly known as the SST) including *Der Sicherheitsdienst* (commonly known as the SD)" referred to in the Indictment consists of the entire corps of the SS and all offices, departments, services, agencies, branches, formations, organizations, and groups of which it was at any time comprised or which were at any time integrated in it, including but not limited to, the Allgemeine SS, the Waffen SS, the SS Totenkopfverbande, SS Polizei Regimente, and the Sicherheitsdienst des Reichsfuehrers – SS (commonly known as the SD).

The SS, originally established by Hitler in 1925 as an elite section of the SA to furnish a protective guard for the Fuehrer and Nazi Party leaders, became an independent formation of the Nazi Party in 1934 under the leadership of the Reichsfuehrer – SS, Heinrich Himmler. It was composed of voluntary members, selected in accordance with Nazi biological, racial, and political theories, completely indoctrinated in Nazi ideology and pledged to uncompromising obedience to the Fuehrer. After the accession of the Nazi conspirators to power, it developed many departments, agencies, formations, and branches and extended its influence and control over numerous fields of Governmental and Party activity. Through Heinrich Himmler, as Reichsfuehrer – SS and Chief of the German Police, agencies and units of the SS and of the Reich were joined in operation to form a unified repressive police force. The Sicherheitsdienst des Reichsfuehrer – SS (commonly known as the SD), a department of the SS, was developed into a vast espionage and counter-intelligence system which operated in conjunction with the Gestapo and criminal police in detecting, suppressing and eliminating tendencies, groups and individuals deemed hostile or potentially hostile to the Nazi Party, its leaders, principles and objectives, and eventually was combined with the Gestapo and criminal police in a single security police department, the Reich Main Security Office.

Other branches of the SS developed into an armed force and served in the wars of aggression referred to in Counts One and Two of the Indictment. Through other departments and branches the SS controlled the administration of concentration camps and the execution of Nazi racial, biological, and resettlement policies.

Through its numerous functions and activities it served as the instrument for insuring the domination of Nazi ideology and protecting and extending the Nazi regime over Germany and occupied territories. It thus participated in and is responsible for the crimes referred to in Counts One, Two, Three, and Four of the Indictment.

DIE GEHEIME STAATSPOLIZEI (SECRET STATE POLICE, COMMONLY KNOWN AS THE GESTAPO)

"*Die Geheime Staatspolizei* (Secret State Police, commonly known as the Gestapo)" referred to in the Indictment consists of the headquarters, departments, offices, branches, and all the forces and personnel of the *Geheime Staatspolizei* organized or existing at any time after 30 January 1933, including the *Geheime Staatspolizei* of Prussia and equivalent secret or political police forces of the Reich and the components thereof.

The Gestapo was created by the Nazi conspirators immediately after their accession to power, first in Prussia by the Defendant Goering and shortly thereafter in all other states in the Reich. These separate secret and political police forces were developed into a centralized, uniform organization operating through a central headquarters and through a network of regional offices in Germany and in occupied territories. Its officials and operatives were selected on the basis of unconditional acceptance of Nazi ideology, were largely drawn from members of the SS, and were trained in SS and SD schools. It acted to suppress and eliminate tendencies, groups, and individuals deemed hostile or potentially hostile to the Nazi Party, its leaders, principles, and objectives, and to repress resistance and potential resistance to German control in occupied territories. In performing these functions it operated free from legal control, taking any measures it deemed necessary for the accomplishment of its missions.

Through its purposes, activities, and the means it used, it participated in and is responsible for the commission of the crimes set forth in Counts One, Two, Three, and Four of the Indictment.

DIE STURMABTEILUNGEN DER NATIONALSOZIALISTISCHEN DEUTSCHEN ARBEITERPARTEI (COMMONLY KNOWN AS THE SA)

"*Die Sturmabteilungen der Nationalsozialistischen Deutschen Arbeiterpartei* (commonly known as the SA)" referred to in the Indictment was a formation of the Nazi Party under the immediate jurisdiction of the Fuehrer, organized on military lines, whose membership was composed of volunteers serving as political soldiers of the Party. It was one of the earliest formations of the Nazi Party and the original guardian of the National Socialist movement. Founded in 1921 as a voluntary militant formation, it was developed by the Nazi conspirators before their accession to power into a vast private army and utilized for the purpose of creating disorder, and terrorizing and eliminating political opponents. It continued to serve as an instrument for the physical, ideological, and military training of Party members and as a reserve for the German Armed Forces. After the launching of the Wars of Aggression, referred to in Counts One and Two of the Indictment, the SA not only operated as an organization for military training but provided auxiliary police and security forces in occupied territories, guarded prisoner-of-war camps and concentration camps and supervised and controlled persons forced to labor in Germany and occupied territories.

Through its purposes and activities and the means it used, it participated in and was responsible for the commission of the crimes set forth in Counts One, Two, Three, and Four of the Indictment.

GENERAL STAFF AND HIGH COMMAND OF THE GERMAN ARMED FORCES

The "General Staff and High Command of the German Armed Forces" referred to in the Indictment consist of those individuals who between February 1938 and May 1945 were the highest commanders of the Wehrmacht, the Army, the Navy, and the Air Forces. The individuals comprising this group are the persons who held the following appointments:

Oberbefehlshaber der Kriegsmarine (Commander in Chief of the Navy);

Chef (and, formerly, *Chef des Stabes) der Seekriegsleitung* (Chief of Naval War Staff);

Oberbefehlshaber des Heeres (Commander in Chief of the Army);

Chef des Generalstabes des Heeres (Chief of the General Staff of the Army);

Oberbefehlshaber der Luftwaffe (Commander in Chief of the Air Force);

Chef des Generalstabes der Luftwaffe (Chief of the General Staff of the Air Force);

Chef des Oberkommandos der Wehrmacht (Chief of the High Command of the Armed Forces);

Chef des Fuhrungsstabes des Oberkommandos der Wehrmacht (Chief of the Operations Staff of the High Command of the Armed Forces);

Stellvertretender Chef des Fuhrungsstabes des Oberkommandos der Wehrmacht (Deputy Chief of the Operations Staff of the High Command of the Armed Forces);

Commanders – in – Chief in the field, with the status of *Oberbefehlshaber*, of the Wehrmacht, Navy, Army, Air Force.

Functioning in such capacities and in association as a group at the highest level in the German Armed Forces Organization these persons had a major responsibility for the planning, preparation, initiation, and waging of illegal wars as set forth in Counts One and Two of the Indictment and for the War Crimes and Crimes against Humanity involved in the execution of the common plan or conspiracy set forth in Counts Three and Four of the Indictment.

Prosecution's Opening Statement

By American Prosecutor Robert H. Jackson

MR. JUSTICE JACKSON: May it please Your Honors:

The privilege of opening the first trial in history for crimes against the peace of the world imposes a grave responsibility. The wrongs which we seek to condemn and punish have been so calculated, so malignant, and so devastating, that civilization cannot tolerate their being ignored, because it cannot survive their being repeated. That four great nations, flushed with victory and stung with injury stay the hand of vengeance and voluntarily submit their captive enemies to the judgment of the law is one of the most significant tributes that Power has ever paid to Reason.

This Tribunal, while it is novel and experimental, is not the product of abstract speculations nor is it created to vindicate legalistic theories. This inquest represents the practical effort of four of the most mighty of nations, with the support of 17 more, to utilize international law to meet the greatest menace of our times – aggressive war. The common sense of mankind demands that law shall not stop with the punishment of petty crimes by little people. It must also reach men who possess themselves of great power and make deliberate and concerted use of it to set in motion evils which leave no home in the world untouched. It is a cause of that magnitude that the United Nations will lay before Your Honors.

In the prisoners' dock sit twenty-odd broken men. Reproached by the humiliation of those they have led almost as bitterly as by the desolation of those they have attacked, their personal capacity for evil is forever past. It is hard now to perceive in these men as captives the power by which as Nazi leaders they once dominated much of the world and terrified most of it. Merely as individuals their fate is of little consequence to the world.

What makes this inquest significant is that these prisoners represent sinister influences that will lurk in the world long after their bodies have returned to dust. We will show them to be living symbols of racial hatreds, of terrorism and violence, and of the arrogance and cruelty of power. They are symbols of fierce nationalisms and of militarism, of intrigue and war-making which have embroiled Europe generation after generation, crushing its manhood, destroying its homes, and impoverishing its life. They have so identified themselves with the philosophies they conceived and with the forces they directed that any tenderness to them is a victory and an encouragement to all the evils which are attached to their names. Civilization can afford no compromise with the social forces which would gain renewed strength if we deal ambiguously or indecisively With the men in whom those forces now precariously survive.

What these men stand for we will patiently and temperately disclose. We will give you undeniable proofs of incredible events. The catalog of crimes will omit nothing that could be conceived by a pathological pride, cruelty, and lust for power. These men created in Germany, under the "*Fuehrerprinzip*", a National Socialist despotism equaled only by the dynasties of the ancient East. They took from the German people all those dignities and freedoms that we hold natural and inalienable rights in every human being. The people were compensated by inflaming and gratifying hatreds towards those who were marked as "scapegoats". Against their opponents, including Jews, Catholics, and free labor, the Nazis directed such a campaign of arrogance, brutality, and annihilation as the world has not witnessed since the pre-Christian ages. They excited the German ambition to be a "master race", which of course implies serfdom for others. They led their people on a mad gamble for domination. They diverted social energies and resources to the creation of what they thought to be an invincible war machine. They overran their neighbors. To sustain the "master race" in its war-making, they enslaved millions of human beings and brought them into Germany, where these hapless creatures now wander as "displaced persons". At length bestiality and bad faith reached such excess that they aroused the sleeping strength of imperiled Civilization. Its united efforts have ground the German war machine to fragments. But the struggle has left Europe a liberated yet prostrate land where a demoralized society struggles to survive. These are the fruits of the sinister forces that sit with these defendants in the prisoners' dock.

In justice to the nations and the men associated in this prosecution, I must remind you of certain difficulties which may leave their mark on this case. Never before in legal history has an effort been made to bring within the scope of a single litigation the developments of a decade, covering a whole continent, and involving a score of nations, countless individuals, and innumerable events. Despite the magnitude of the task, the world has demanded immediate action. This demand has had to be met, though perhaps at the cost of finished craftsmanship. In my country, established courts, following familiar procedures, applying well-thumbed precedents, and dealing with the legal consequences of local and limited events seldom commence a trial within a year of the event in litigation. Yet less than 8 months ago today the courtroom in which you sit was an enemy fortress in the hands of German SS troops. Less than 8 months ago nearly all our witnesses and documents were in enemy hands. The law had not been codified, no procedures had been established, no tribunal was in existence, no usable courthouse stood here, none of the hundreds of tons of official German documents had been examined, no prosecuting staff had been assembled, nearly all of the present defendants were at large, and the four prosecuting powers had not yet joined in common cause to try them. I should be the last to deny that the case may well suffer from incomplete researches and quite likely will not be the example of professional work which any of the prosecuting nations would normally wish to sponsor. It is, however, a completely adequate case to the judgment we shall ask you to render and its full development we shall be obliged to leave to historians.

Before I discuss particulars of evidence, some general considerations which may affect the credit of this trial in the eyes of the world should be candidly faced. There is a dramatic disparity between the circumstances of the accusers and of the accused that might discredit our work if we should falter, in even minor matters, in being fair and temperate.

Unfortunately the nature of these crimes is such that both prosecution and judgment must be by victor nations over vanquished foes. The worldwide scope of the aggressions carried out by these men has left but few real neutrals. Either the victors must judge the vanquished or we must leave the defeated to judge themselves. After the first World War, we learned the futility of the latter course. The former high station of these defendants, the notoriety of their acts, and the adaptability of their conduct to provoke retaliation make it hard to distinguish between the demand for a just and measured retribution, and the unthinking cry for vengeance which arises from the anguish of war. It is our task, so far as humanly possible, to draw the line between the two. We must never forget that the record on which we judge these defendants today is the record on which history will judge us tomorrow. To pass these defendants a poisoned chalice is to put it to our own lips as well. We must summon such detachment and intellectual integrity to our task that this Trial will commend itself to posterity as fulfilling humanity's aspirations to do justice.

At the very outset, let us dispose of the contention that to put these men to trial is to do them an injustice entitling them to some special consideration. These defendants may be hard pressed but they are not ill used. Let us see what alternative they would have to being tried.

More than a majority of these prisoners surrendered to or were tracked down by the forces of the United States. Could they expect us to make American custody a shelter for our enemies against the just wrath of our Allies? Did we spend American lives to capture them only to save them from punishment? Under the principles of the Moscow Declaration, those suspected war criminals who are not to be tried internationally must be turned over to individual governments for trial at the scene of their outrages. Many less responsible and less culpable American-held prisoners have been and will continue to be turned over to other United Nations for local trial. If these defendants should succeed, for any reason, in escaping the condemnation of this Tribunal, or if they obstruct or abort the trial, those who are American-held prisoners will be delivered to our continental Allies. For these defendants, however, we have set up an International Tribunal and have undertaken the burden of participating in a complicated effort to give them fair and dispassionate hearings. That is the best-known protection to any man with a defense worthy of being heard.

If these men are the first war leaders of a defeated nation to be prosecuted in the name of the law, they are also the first to be given a chance to plead for their lives in the name of the law. Realistically, the

Charter of this Tribunal, which gives them a hearing, is also the source of their only hope. It may be that these men of troubled conscience, whose only wish is that the world forget them, do not regard a trial as a favor. But they do have a fair opportunity to defend themselves — a favor which these men, when in power, rarely extended to their fellow countrymen. Despite the fact that public opinion already condemns their acts, we agree that here they must be given a presumption of innocence and we accept the burden of proving criminal acts and the responsibility of these defendants for their commission.

When I say that we do not ask for convictions unless we prove crime, I do not mean mere technical or incidental transgression of international conventions. We charge guilt on planned and intended conduct that involves moral as well as legal wrong. And we do not mean conduct that is a natural and human, even if illegal cutting of corners, such as many of us might well have committed had we been in the defendants' positions. It is not because they yielded to the normal frailties of human beings that we accuse them. It is their abnormal and inhuman conduct which brings them to this bar.

We will not ask you to convict these men on the testimony of their foes. There is no count in the Indictment that cannot be proved by books and records. The Germans were always meticulous record keepers, and these defendants had their share of the Teutonic passion for thoroughness in putting things on paper. Nor were they without vanity. They arranged frequently to be photographed in action. We will show you their own films. You will see their own conduct and hear their own voices as these defendants re-enact for you, from the screen, some of the events in the course of the conspiracy.

We would also make clear that we have no purpose to incriminate the whole German people. We know that the Party was not put in power by a majority of the German vote. We know it came to power by an evil alliance between the most extreme of the Nazi revolutionists, the most unrestrained of the German reactionaries and the most aggressive of the German militarists. If the German populace had willingly accepted the Nazi program, no Stormtroopers would have been needed in the early days of the Party and there would have been no need for concentration camps or the Gestapo, both of which institutions were inaugurated as soon as the Nazis gained control of the German State. Only after these lawless innovations proved successful at home were they taken abroad.

The German people should know by now that the people of United States hold them in no fear, and in no hate. It is true that Germans have taught us the horrors of modern warfare; the ruin that lies from the Rhine to the Danube shows that we, like our Allies, have not been dull pupils. If we are not awed by German fortitude and proficiency in war, and if we are not persuaded of their political maturity, we do respect their skill in the arts of peace, their technical competence, and the sober, industrious, and self-disciplined character of the masses of the German people. In 1933 we saw the German people recovering prestige in the commercial, industrial, and artistic world after the setback of the last war. We beheld their progress neither with envy nor malice. The Nazi regime interrupted this advance. The recoil of the Nazi aggression has left Germany in ruins. The Nazi readiness to pledge the German word without hesitation and to break it without shame has fastened upon German diplomacy a reputation for duplicity that will handicap it for years. Nazi arrogance has made the boast of the "master race" a taunt that will be thrown at Germans the world over for generations. The Nazi nightmare has given the German name a new and sinister significance throughout the world which will retard Germany a century. The German, no less than the non-German world, has accounts to settle with these defendants.

The fact of the war and the course of the war, which is the central theme of our case, is history. From 9/1/1939, when the German armies crossed the Polish frontier, until 9/1942, when they met epic resistance at Stalingrad, German arms seemed invincible. Denmark and Norway, the Netherlands and France, Belgium and Luxembourg, the Balkans and Africa, Poland and the Baltic States, and parts of Russia, all had been overrun and conquered by swift, powerful, well-aimed blows. That attack on the peace of the world is the crime against international society which brings into international cognizance crimes in its aid and preparation which otherwise might be only internal concerns. It was aggressive war, which the nations of the world had renounced. It was war in violation of treaties, by which the peace of the world was sought to be safeguarded.

This war did not just happen; it was planned and prepared for over a long period of time and with no small skill and cunning. The world has perhaps never seen such a concentration and stimulation of the energies of any people as that enabled Germany 20 years after it was defeated, disarmed, and dismembered to come so near carrying out its plan to dominate Europe. Whatever else we may say of those who were the authors of this war, they did achieve a stupendous work in organization, and our first task is to examine the means by which these defendants and their fellow conspirators prepared and incited Germany to go to war.

In general, our case will disclose these defendants all uniting at some time with the Nazi Party in a plan which they well knew could be accomplished only by an outbreak of war in Europe. Their seizure of the German State, their subjugation of the German people, their terrorism and extermination of dissident elements their planning and waging of war, their calculated and planned ruthlessness in the conduct of warfare, their deliberate and planned criminality toward conquered peoples, all these are ends for which they acted in concert; and all these are phases of the conspiracy, a conspiracy which reached one goal only to set out for another and more ambitious one. We shall also trace for you the intricate web of organizations which these men formed and utilized to accomplish these ends. We will show how the entire structure of offices and officials was dedicated to the criminal purposes and committed to the use of the criminal methods planned by these defendants and their co-conspirators, many of whom war and suicide have put beyond reach.

It is my purpose to open the case, particularly under Count One of the Indictment, and to deal with the Common Plan or Conspiracy to achieve ends possible only by resort to Crimes against Peace, War Crimes, and Crimes against Humanity. My emphasis will not be on individual barbarities and perversions which may have occurred independently of any central plan. One of the dangers ever present is that this Trial may be protracted by details of particular wrongs and that we will become lost in a "wilderness of single instances". Nor will I now dwell on the activity of individual defendants except as it may contribute to exposition of the common plan.

The case as presented by the United States will be concerned with the brains and authority back of all the crimes. These defendants were men of a station and rank which does not soil its own hands with blood. They were men who knew how to use lesser folk as tools. We want to reach the planners and designers, the inciters and leaders without whose evil architecture the world would not have been for so long scourged with the violence, and wracked with the agonies and convulsions, of this terrible war.

The Lawless Road to Power:

The chief instrumentality of cohesion in plan and action was the National Socialist German Workers Party, known as the Nazi Party. Some of the defendants were with it from the beginning. Others joined only after success seemed to have validated its lawlessness or power had invested it with immunity from the processes of the law. Adolf Hitler became its supreme leader or "Fuehrer" in 1921.

On the 2/24/1920, at Munich, it publicly had proclaimed its program (1708 – PS). Some of its purposes would commend themselves to many good citizens, such as the demands for "profit-sharing in the great industries," "generous development of provision for old age," "creation and maintenance of a healthy middle class," "a land reform suitable to our national requirements," and "raising the standard of health." It also made a strong appeal to that sort of nationalism which in ourselves we call patriotism and in our rivals chauvinism. It demanded "equality of rights for the German people in its dealing with other nations, and the abolition of the peace treaties of Versailles and St. Germain." It demanded the "union of all Germans on the basis of the right of self-determination of peoples to form a Great Germany." It demanded "land and territory (colonies) for the enrichment of our people and the settlement of our surplus population." All of these, of course, were legitimate objectives if they were to be attained without resort to aggressive warfare.

The Nazi Party from its inception, however, contemplated war. It demanded the "abolition of mercenary troops and the formation of a national army." It proclaimed that: "In view of the enormous sacrifice of life and property demanded of a nation by every war, personal enrichment through war must be regarded as a crime against the nation. We demand therefore, ruthless confiscation of all war profits."

I do not criticize this policy. Indeed, I wish it were universal. I merely wish to point out that in a time of peace, war was a preoccupation of the Party, and it started the work of making war less offensive to the masses of the people. With this it combined a program of physical training and sports for youth that became, as we shall see, the cloak for a secret program of military training.

The Nazi Party declaration also committed its members to an anti-Semitic program. It declared that no Jew or any person of non-German blood could be a member of the nation. Such persons were to be disfranchised, disqualified for office, subject to the alien laws and entitled to nourishment only after the German population had first been provided for. All who had entered Germany after 8/2/1914 were to be required forthwith to depart, and a non-German immigration was to be prohibited.

The Party also avowed, even in those early days, an authoritarian and totalitarian program for Germany. It demanded creation of a strong central power with unconditional authority, nationalization of all businesses which had been "amalgamated," and a "reconstruction" of the national system of education which "must aim at teaching the pupil to understand the idea of the State (state sociology)." Its hostility to civil liberties and freedom of the press was distinctly announced in these words: "It must be forbidden to publish newspapers which do not conduce to the national welfare. We demand the legal prosecution of all tendencies in art or literature of a kind likely to disintegrate our life as a nation and the suppression of institutions which might militate against the above requirements."

The forecast of religious persecution was clothed in the language of religious liberty, for the Nazi program stated, "We demand liberty for all religious denominations in the State." But, it continues with the limitation, "so far as they are not a danger to it and do not militate against the morality and moral sense of the German race."

The Party program foreshadowed the campaign of terrorism. It announced, "We demand ruthless war upon those whose activities are injurious to the common interests", and it demanded that such offenses be punished with death.

It is significant that the leaders of this Party interpreted this program as a belligerent one, certain to precipitate conflict. The Party platform concluded, "The leaders of the Party swear to proceed regardless of consequences – if necessary, at the sacrifice of their lives – toward the fulfillment of the foregoing points." It is this Leadership Corps of the Party, not its entire membership, that stands accused before you as a criminal organization.

Let us now see how the leaders of the Party fulfilled their pledge to proceed regardless of consequences. Obviously, their foreign objectives, which were nothing less than to undo international treaties and to wrest territory from foreign control, as was most of their internal program, could be accomplished only by possession of the machinery of the German State. The first effort, accordingly, was to subvert the Weimar Republic by violent revolution. An abortive *putsch* at Munich in 1923 landed many of them in jail. A period of meditation which followed produced *Mein Kampf*, henceforth the source of law for the Party workers and a source of considerable revenue to its supreme leader. The Nazi plans for the violent overthrow of the feeble Republic then turned to plans for its capture.

No greater mistake could be made than to think of the Nazi party in terms of the loose organizations which we of the western world call "political parties". In discipline, structure, and method the Nazi Party was not adapted to the democratic process of persuasion. It was an instrument of conspiracy and of coercion. The Party was not organized to take over power in the German State by winning support of a majority of the German people; it was organized to seize power in defiance of the will of the people.

The Nazi Party, under the "*Fuehrerprinzip,*" was bound by an iron discipline into a pyramid, with the Fuehrer, Adolf Hitler, at the top and broadening into a numerous Leadership Corps, composed of overlords of a very extensive Party membership at the base. By no means all of those who may have supported the movement in one way or another were actual Party members. The membership took the Party oath which in effect amounted to an abdication of personal intelligence and moral responsibility. This was the oath: "I vow inviolable fidelity to Adolf Hitler; I vow absolute obedience to him and to the leaders he designates for me." The membership in daily practice followed its leaders with an idolatry and self-surrender more Oriental than Western.

We will not be obliged to guess as to the motives or goal of the Nazi Party. The immediate aim was to undermine the Weimar Republic. The order to all Party members to work to that end was given in a letter from Hitler of 8/24/1931 to Rosenberg, of which we will produce the original. Hitler wrote:

"I am just reading in the *Voelkischer Beobachter*, edition 235/236, page 1, an article entitled 'Does Wirth Intend To Come Over?' The tendency of the article is to prevent on our part a crumbling away from the present form of government. I myself am traveling all over Germany to achieve exactly the opposite. May I therefore ask that my own paper will not stab me in the back with tactically unwise articles...." (047 – PS)

Captured film enables us to present the Defendant Alfred Rosenberg who from the screen will himself tell you the story. The SA practiced violent interference with elections. We have the reports of the SD describing in detail how its members later violated the secrecy of elections in order to identify those who opposed them. One of the reports makes this explanation:

" .... The control was effected in the following way: some members of the election committee marked all the ballot papers with numbers. During the ballot itself, a voters' list was made up. The ballot-papers were handed out in numerical order, therefore it was possible afterwards with the aid of this list to find out the persons who cast 'No' votes or invalid votes. One sample of these marked ballot-papers is enclosed. The marking was done on the back of the ballot-papers with skimmed milk .... " (R – 142)

The Party activity, in addition to all the familiar forms of political contest, took on the aspect of a rehearsal for warfare. It utilized a Party formation, *"Die Sturmabteilungen"*, commonly known as the SA. This was a voluntary organization of youthful and fanatical Nazis trained for the use of violence under semi-military discipline. Its members began by acting as bodyguards for the Nazi leaders and rapidly expanded from defensive to offensive tactics. They became disciplined ruffians for the breaking up of opposition meetings and the terrorization of adversaries. They boasted that their task was to make the Nazi Party "master of the streets". The SA was the parent organization of a number of others. Its offspring include *"Die Schutzstaffeln"*, commonly known as the SS, formed in 1925 and distinguished for the fanaticism and cruelty of its members; *"Der Sicherheitsdienst"*, known as the SD; and *"Die Geheime Staatspolizei"*, the Secret State Police, the infamous Gestapo formed in 1934 after Nazi accession to power.

A glance at a chart of the Party organization is enough to show how completely it differed from the political parties we know. It had its own source of law in the Fuehrer and sub-Fuehrer. It had its own courts and its own police. The conspirators set up a government within the Party to exercise outside the law every sanction that any legitimate state could exercise and many that it could not. Its chain of command was military, and its formations were martial in name as well as in function. They were composed of battalions set up to bear arms under military discipline, motorized corps lying corps, and the infamous "Death Head Corps", which was not misnamed. The Party had its own secret police, its security units its intelligence and espionage division, its raiding forces, and its youth forces. It established elaborate administrative mechanisms to identify and liquidate spies and informers, to manage concentration camps, to operate death vans, and to finance the whole movement Through concentric circles of authority, the Nazi Party, as its leadership later boasted, eventually organized and dominated every phase of German life – but not until they had waged a bitter internal struggle characterized by brutal criminality, we charge here. In preparation for this phase of their struggle, they created a Party police system. This became the pattern and the instrument of the police state which was the first goal in their plan.

The Party formations, including the Leadership Corps of the Party, the SD, the SS, the SA, and the infamous Secret State Police, Gestapo, all these stand accused before you as criminal organizations; organizations which, as we will prove from their own documents, were recruited only from recklessly devoted Nazis, ready in conviction and temperament to do the most violent of deeds to advance the common program. They terrorized and silenced democratic opposition and were able at length to combine with political opportunists, militarists, industrialists, monarchists, and political reactionaries.

On 1/30/1933 Adolf Hitler became Chancellor of the German Republic. An evil combination, represented in the prisoners' dock by its most eminent survivors, had succeeded in possessing itself of the machinery of the German Government, a facade behind which they thenceforth would operate to make a reality of the war of conquest they so long had plotted. The conspiracy had passed into its second phase.

The Consolidation of Nazi Power:

We shall now consider the steps, which embraced the most hideous of Crimes against Humanity, to which the conspirators resorted in perfecting control of the German State and in preparing Germany for the aggressive war indispensable to their ends.

The Germans of the 1920's were a frustrated and baffled people as a result of defeat and the disintegration of their traditional government. The democratic elements, which were trying to govern Germany through the new and feeble machinery of the Weimar Republic, got inadequate support from the democratic forces of the rest of the world, including my country. It is not to be denied that Germany, when worldwide depression was added to her other problems, was faced with urgent and intricate pressures in her economic and political life which necessitated bold measures.

The internal measures by which a nation attempts to solve its problems are ordinarily of no concern to other nations. But the Nazi Program from the first was recognized as a desperate program for a people still suffering the effects of an unsuccessful war. The Nazi Policy embraced ends recognized as attainable only by a renewal and a more successful outcome of war, in Europe. The conspirators' answer to Germany's problems was nothing less than to plot the regaining of territories lost in the First World War and the acquisition of other fertile lands of Central Europe by dispossessing or exterminating those who inhabited them. They also contemplated destroying or permanently weakening all other neighboring peoples so as to win virtual domination over Europe and probably of the world. The precise limits of their ambition we need not define, for it was and is as illegal to wage aggressive war for small stakes as for large ones.

We find at this period two governments in Germany, the real and the ostensible. The forms of the German Republic were maintained for a time, and it was the outward and visible government. But the real authority in the State was outside and above the law and rested in the Leadership Corps of the Nazi Party.

On 2/27/1933, less than a month after Hitler became Chancellor, the Reichstag building was set on fire. The burning of this symbol of free parliamentary government was so providential for the Nazis that it was believed they staged the fire themselves. Certainly when we contemplate their known crimes, we cannot believe they would shrink from mere arson. It is not necessary however, to resolve the controversy as to who set the fire. The significant point is in the use that was made of the fire and of the state of public mind it produced. The Nazis immediately accused the Communist Party of instigating and committing the crime, and turned every effort to portray this single act of arson as the beginning of a communist revolution. Then, taking advantage of the hysteria, the Nazis met this phantom revolution with a real one. In the following December the German Supreme Court with commendable courage and independence acquitted the accused Communists, but it was too late to influence the tragic course of events which the Nazi conspirators had set rushing forward.

Hitler, on the morning after the fire, obtained from the aged and ailing President Von Hindenburg a presidential decree suspending the extensive guarantees of individual liberty contained in the constitution of the Weimar Republic. The decree provided that:

"Sections 114, 115, 117, 118, 123, 124, and 153 of the Constitution of the German Reich are suspended until further notice. Thus, restrictions on personal liberty, on the right of free expression of opinion, including freedom of the press, on the right of assembly and the right of association, and violations of the privacy of postal, telegraphic, and telephonic communications, and warrants for house – searches, orders for confiscations as well as restrictions on property, are also permissible beyond the legal limits otherwise prescribed." (1390 – PS)

The extent of the restriction on personal liberty under the decree of 2/28/1933 may be understood by reference to the rights of the Weimar constitution which were suspended:

"Article 114. The freedom of the person is inviolable. Curtailment or deprivation of personal freedom by a public authority is only permissible on a legal basis."

"Persons who have been deprived of their freedom must be informed at the latest on the following day by whose authority and for what reasons the deprivation of freedom was ordered; opportunity shall be afforded them without delay of submitting objections to their deprivation of freedom."

"Article 115. Every German's home is his sanctuary and is inviolable. Exceptions may only be made as provided by law."

"Article 117. The secrecy of letters and all postal, telegraphic and telephone communications is inviolable. Exceptions are inadmissible except by Reich law."

"Article 118. Every German has the right, within the limits of the general laws, to express his opinions freely in speech, in writing, in print, in picture form, or in any other way. No conditions of work or employment may detract from this right and no disadvantage may accrue to him from any person for making use of this right ...."

"Article 123. All Germans have the right to assemble peacefully and unarmed without giving notice and without special permission."

"A Reich law may make previous notification obligatory for assemblies in the open air, and may prohibit them in case of immediate danger to the public safety."

"Article 124. All the Germans have the right to form associations or societies for purposes not contrary to criminal law. This right may not be curtailed by preventive measures. The same provisions apply to religious associations and societies."

"Every association may become incorporated (*Erwerb der Rechtsfaehigkeit*) according to the provisions of the civil law. The right may not be refused to any association on the grounds that its aims are political, social-political, or religious."

"Article 153. Property is guaranteed by the Constitution. Its content and limits are defined by the laws. Expropriation can only take place for the public benefit and on a legal basis. Adequate compensation shall be granted, unless a Reich law orders otherwise. In the case of dispute concerning the amount of compensation, it shall be possible to submit the matter to the ordinary civil courts, unless Reich laws determine otherwise. Compensation must be paid if the Reich expropriates property belonging to the Lands, Communes, or public utility associations."

"Property carries obligations. Its use shall also serve the common good." (2050 – PS)

It must be said in fairness to Von Hindenburg that the constitution itself authorized him temporarily to suspend these fundamental rights "if the public safety and order in the German Reich are considerably disturbed or endangered." It must also be acknowledged that President Ebert previously had invoked this power.

But the National Socialist coup was made possible because the terms of the Hitler – Hindenburg decree departed from all previous ones in which the power of suspension had been invoked. Whenever Ebert had suspended constitutional guarantees of individual rights, his decree had expressly revived the Protective Custody Act adopted by the Reichstag in 1916 during the previous war. This act guaranteed a judicial hearing within 24 hours of arrest, gave a right to have counsel and to inspect all relevant records, provided for appeal, and authorized compensation from Treasury funds for erroneous arrests.

The Hitler – Hindenburg decree of 2/28/1933 contained no such safeguards. The omission may not have been noted by Von Hindenburg. Certainly he did not appreciate its effect. It left the Nazi police and party formations, already existing and functioning under Hitler, completely unrestrained and irresponsible. Secret arrest and indefinite detention, without charges, without evidence, without hearing, without counsel, became the method of inflicting inhuman punishment on any whom the Nazi police suspected or disliked. No court could issue an injunction, or writ of habeas corpus, or certiorari. The German people were in the hands of the police, the police were in the hands of the Nazi Party, and the Party was in the hands of a ring of evil men, of whom the defendants here before you are surviving and representative leaders.

The Nazi conspiracy, as we shall show, always contemplated not merely overcoming current opposition but exterminating elements which could not be reconciled with its philosophy of the state. It not only sought to establish the Nazi "new order" but to secure its sway, as Hitler predicted, "for a thousand years." Nazis were never in doubt or disagreement as to what these dissident elements were. They were concisely described by one of them, Colonel General Von Fritsch, on 12/11/1938 in these words:

"Shortly after the first war I came to the conclusion that we would have to be victorious in three battles if Germany were to become powerful again: 1. The battle against the working class – Hitler has won this. 2. Against the Catholic Church, perhaps better expressed against Ultramontanism. 3. Against the Jews." (1947 – PS)

The warfare against these elements was continuous. The battle for Germany was but a practice skirmish for the worldwide drive. We have in point of geography and of time two groups of Crimes against Humanity, one within Germany before and during the war, the other in occupied territory during the war. But the two are not separated in Nazi planning. They are a continuous unfolding of the Nazi plan to exterminate peoples and nations which might serve as a focus or instrument for overturning their "new world order" at any time. We consider these Crimes against humanity in this address as manifestations of the one Nazi plan and discuss them according to General Von Fritsch's classification.

1. The Battle against the Working Class:

When Hitler came to power, there were in Germany three groups of trade unions. The General German Trade Union Confederation (ADGB) with 28 affiliated unions, and the General Independent Employees Confederation (AFA) with 13 federated unions together numbered more than 4.5 million members. The Christian Trade Union had over 1.25 million members.

The working people of Germany, like the working people of other nations, had little to gain personally by war. While labor is usually brought around to the support of the nation at war, labor by and large is a pacific, though by no means a pacifist, force in the world. The working people of Germany had not forgotten in 1933 how heavy the yoke of the warlord can be. It was the workingmen who had joined the sailors and soldiers in the revolt of 1918 to end the first World War. The Nazis had neither forgiven nor forgotten. The Nazi program required that this part of the German population not only be stripped of power to resist diversion of its scanty comforts to armament, but also be wheedled or whipped into new and unheard of sacrifices as a part of the Nazi war preparation. Labor must be cowed, and that meant its organizations and means of cohesion and defense must be destroyed.

The purpose to regiment labor for the Nazi Party was avowed by Ley in a speech to workers on 5/2/1933 as follows:

"You may say what else do you want, you have the absolute power. True we have the power, but we do not have the whole people, we do not have you workers 100 per cent, and it is you whom we want; we will not let you be until you stand with us in complete, genuine acknowledgment." (614 – PS)

The first Nazi attack was upon the two larger unions. On 4/21/1933 an order not even in the name of the Government, but of the Nazi Party, was issued by the conspirator Robert Ley as "Chief of Staff of the political organization of the NSDAP," applicable to the Trade Union Confederation and the Independent Employees Confederation. It directed seizure of their property and arrest of their principal leaders. The Party order directed Party organs which we here denounce as criminal associations, the SA and SS, "to be employed for the occupation of the trade union properties, and for the taking into custody of personalities who come into question." And it directed the taking into "protective custody" of all chairmen and district secretaries of such unions and branch directors of the labor bank. (392 – PS)

These orders were carried out on 5/2/1933. All funds of the labor unions, including pension and benefit funds, were seized. Union leaders were sent to concentration camps. A few days later, on 5/10/1933, Hitler appointed Ley leader of the German Labor Front (*Deutsche Arbeitsfront*) which succeeded to the confiscated union funds. The German Labor Front, a Nazi-controlled labor bureau, was set up under Ley to teach the Nazi philosophy to German workers and to weed out from industrial employment all who were backward in their lessons. (1940 – PS) "Factory troops" were organized as an "ideological shock squad within the factor" (1817 – PS). The Party order provided that "outside of the German Labor Front, no other organization (whether of workers or of employees) is to exist." On 6/24/1933 the remaining Christian Trade Unions were seized, pursuant to an order of the Nazi Party signed by Ley.

On 5/19/1933, this time by a government decree, it was provided that "trustees" of labor appointed by Hitler, should regulate the conditions of all labor contracts, replacing the former process of collective bargaining (405 – PS). On 11/30/1934 a decree "regulating national labor" introduced the Fuehrer Principle into industrial relations. It provided that the owners of enterprises should be the "Fuehrer" and the workers should be the followers. The "enterprise-Fuehrer" should "make decisions for employees and laborers in all matters concerning the enterprise" (1861 – PS). It was by such bait that the great German industrialists were induced to support the Nazi cause, to their own ultimate ruin.

Not only did the Nazis dominate and regiment German labor but they forced the youth into the ranks of the laboring people thus led into chains. Under a compulsory labor service decree on 6/26/1935 young men and women between the ages of 18-25 were conscripted for labor (1654 – PS). Thus was the purpose to subjugate German labor accomplished. In the words of Ley, this accomplishment consisted "in eliminating the association character of the trade union and employees' associations, and in its place have substituted the conception 'soldiers of work'." The productive manpower of the German nation was in Nazi control. By these steps the defendants won the battle to liquidate labor unions as potential opposition and were enabled to impose upon the working class the burdens of preparing for aggressive warfare.

Robert Ley, the field marshal of the battle against labor, answered our Indictment with suicide. Apparently he knew no better answer.

2.   The Battle against the Churches:

The Nazi Party always was predominantly anti-Christian in its ideology. But we who believe in freedom of conscience and of religion base no charge of criminality on anybody's ideology. It is not because the Nazis themselves were irreligious or pagan, but because they persecuted others of the Christian faith that they become guilty of crime, and it is because the persecution was a step in the preparation for aggressive warfare that the offense becomes one of international consequence. To remove every moderating influence among the German people and to put its population on a total war footing, the conspirators devised and carried out a systematic and relentless repression of all Christian sects and churches.

We will ask you to convict the Nazis on their own evidence. Martin Bormann, in 6/1941, issued a secret decree on the relation of Christianity and National Socialism. The decree provided:

"For the first time in German history the Fuehrer consciously and completely has the leadership of the people in his own hand. With the Party, its components, and attached units the Fuehrer has created for himself and thereby the German Reich leadership an instrument which makes him independent of the church. All influences which might impair or damage the leadership of the people exercised by the Fuehrer with help of the NSDAP, must be eliminated. More and more the people must be separated from the churches and their organs, the pastors. Of course, the churches must and will, seen from their viewpoint, defend themselves against this loss of power. But never again must an influence on leadership of the people be yielded to the churches. This (influence) must be broken completely and finally."

"Only the Reich Government and by its direction the Party its components, and attached units have a right to leadership of the people. Just as the deleterious influences of astrologers, seers, and other fakers are eliminated and suppressed by the State, so must the possibility of church influence also be totally removed. Not until this has happened, does the State leadership have influence on the individual citizens. Not until then are people and Reich secure in their existence for all the future." (D – 75)

And how the Party had been securing the Reich from Christian influence, will be proved by such items as this teletype from the Gestapo, Berlin, to the Gestapo, Nuremberg, on 7/24/1938. Let us hear their own account of events in Rottenburg.

"The Party on 7/23/1938 from 2100 on carried out the third demonstration against Bishop Sproll. Participants about 2500-3000 were brought in from outside by bus, etc. The Rottenburg populace again did not participate in the demonstration. This town took rather a hostile attitude to the demonstrations. The action got completely out of hand of the Party member responsible for it. The demonstrators stormed the palace, beat in the gates and doors. About 150 to 200 people forced their way into the palace, searched the rooms, threw files out of the windows and rummaged through the beds in the rooms of the palace. One bed was ignited. Before the fire got to the other objects of equipment in the rooms and the palace, the flaming bed could be thrown from the window and the fire extinguished. The Bishop was with Archbishop Groeber of Freiburg and the ladies and gentlemen of his menage in the chapel at prayer. About 25 to 30 people pressed into this chapel and molested those present. Bishop Groeber was taken for Bishop Sproll. He was grabbed by the robe and dragged back and forth. Finally the intruders realized that Bishop Groeber is not the one they are seeking. They could then be persuaded to leave the building. After the evacuation of the palace by the demonstrators I had an interview with Archbishop Groeber who left Rottenburg in the night. Groeber wants to turn to the Fuehrer and Reich Minister of the Interior, Dr. Frick, anew. On the course of the action, the damage done as well as the homage of the Rottenburg populace beginning today for the Bishop I shall immediately hand in a full report, after I am in the act of suppressing counter mass meetings ...."

"In case the Fuehrer has instructions to give in this matter, I request that these be transmitted most quickly...." (848 – PS)

Later, Defendant Rosenberg wrote to Bormann reviewing the proposal of Kerrl as Church Minister to place the Protestant church under State tutelage and proclaim Hitler its supreme head. Rosenberg was opposed, hinting that Nazism was to suppress the Christian Church completely after the war (See also 098 – PS).

The persecution of all pacifist and dissenting sects, such as Jehovah's Witnesses and the Pentecostal Association, was peculiarly relentless and cruel. The policy toward the Evangelical Churches, however, was to use their influence for the Nazis' own purposes. In 9/1933 Mueller was appointed the Fuehrer's representative with power to deal with the "affairs of the Evangelical Church" in its relations to the State. Eventually, steps were taken to create a Reich Bishop vested with power to control this Church. A long conflict followed, Pastor Niemoller was sent to concentration camp, and extended interference with the internal discipline and administration of the churches occurred.

A most intense drive was directed against the Roman Catholic Church. After a strategic concordat with the Holy See, signed in 7/1933 in Rome, which never was observed by the Nazi Party, a long and persistent persecution of the Catholic Church, its priesthood, and its members, was carried out. Church schools and educational institutions were suppressed or subjected to requirements of Nazi teaching inconsistent with the Christian faith. The property of the Church was confiscated and inspired vandalism directed against Church property was left unpunished. Religious instruction was impeded and the exercise of religion made difficult. Priests and bishops were laid upon, riots were stimulated to harass them, and many were sent to concentration camps.

After occupation of foreign soil, these persecutions went on with greater vigor than ever. We will present to you from the files of the Vatican the earnest protests made by the Vatican to Ribbentrop summarizing the persecutions to which the priesthood and the Church had been subjected in this twentieth century under the Nazi regime. Ribbentrop never answered them. He could not deny. He dared not justify.

I now come to "Crimes against the Jews."

3. Crimes against the Jews:

The most savage and numerous crimes planned and committed by the Nazis were those against the Jews. Those in Germany in 1933 numbered about 500,000. In the aggregate, they had made for themselves positions which excited envy, and had accumulated properties which excited the avarice of the Nazis. They were few enough to be helpless and numerous enough to be held up as a menace.

Let there be no misunderstanding about the charge of persecuting Jews. What we charge against these defendants is not those arrogances and pretensions which frequently accompany the intermingling of different peoples and which are likely, despite the honest efforts of government, to produce regrettable crimes and convulsions. It is my purpose to show a plan and design, to which all Nazis were fanatically committed, to annihilate all Jewish people. These crimes were organized and promoted by the Party leadership, executed and protected by the Nazi officials, as we shall convince you by written orders of the Secret State Police itself.

The persecution of the Jews was a continuous and deliberate policy. It was a policy directed against other nations as well as against the Jews themselves. Anti-Semitism was promoted to divide and embitter the democratic peoples and to soften their resistance to the Nazi aggression. As Robert Ley declared in *Der Angriff* on 5/14/1944:

"The second German secret weapon is Anti-Semitism because if it is constantly pursued by Germany, it will become a universal problem which all nations will be forced to consider."

Anti-Semitism also has been aptly credited with being a "spear head of terror." The ghetto was the laboratory for testing repressive measures. Jewish property was the first to be expropriated but the custom grew and included similar measures against anti-Nazi Germans, Poles, Czechs, Frenchmen, and Belgians. Extermination of the Jews enabled the Nazis to bring a practiced hand to similar measures against Poles, Serbs, and Greeks. The plight of the Jew was a constant threat to opposition or discontent among other elements of Europe's population pacifists, conservatives, Communists, Catholics, Protestants, Socialists. It was in fact, a threat to every dissenting opinion and to every non-Nazi's life.

The persecution policy against the Jews commenced with nonviolent measures such as disfranchisement and discriminations against their religion, and the placing of impediments in the way of success in economic life. It moved rapidly to organized mass violence against them, physical isolation in ghettos, deportation, labor mass starvation, and extermination. The Government, the party formations indicted before you as criminal organizations, the Secret State Police, the Army, private and semi-public associations, and "spontaneous" mobs that were carefully inspired from official sources, were all agencies that were concerned in this persecution. Nor was it directed against individual Jews for personal bad citizenship or unpopularity. The avowed purpose was the destruction of the Jewish people as a whole, as an end in itself, as a measure of preparation for war, and as a discipline of conquered peoples.

The conspiracy or common plan to exterminate the Jew was so methodically and thoroughly pursued, that despite the German defeat and Nazi prostration this Nazi aim largely has succeeded. Only remnants of the European Jewish population remain in Germany, in the countries which Germany occupied, and in those which were her satellites or collaborators. Of the 9.6 million Jews who lived in Nazi-dominated Europe, 60% are authoritatively estimated to have perished. 5.7 million Jews are missing from the countries in which they formerly lived, and over 4.5 million cannot be accounted for by the normal death rate nor by immigration; nor are they included among displaced persons. History does not record a crime ever perpetrated against so many victims or one ever carried out with such calculated cruelty.

You will have difficulty, as I have, to look into the faces of these defendants and believe that in this twentieth century human beings could inflict such sufferings as will be proved here on their own countrymen as well as upon their so-called "inferior" enemies. Particular crimes, and the responsibility of defendants for them, are to be dealt with by the Soviet Government's counsel, when committed in the East, and by counsel for the Republic of France when committed in the West. I advert to them only to show their magnitude as evidence of a purpose and a knowledge common to all defendants, of an official plan rather than of a capricious policy of some dual commander, and to show such a continuity of Jewish persecution from the rise of the Nazi conspiracy to its collapse as forbids us to believe that any person could be identified with any part of Nazi action without approving this most conspicuous item in their program.

The Indictment itself recites many evidences of the anti-Semitic persecutions. The Defendant Streicher led the Nazis in anti-Semitic bitterness and extremism. In an article appearing in *Der Stuermer* on 3/19/1942 he complained that Christian teachings have stood in the way of "racial solution of the Jewish question in Europe", and quoted enthusiastically as the twentieth century solution the Fuehrer's proclamation of 2/24/1942 that "the Jew will be exterminated." And on 11/4/1943 Streicher declared in *Der Stuermer* that the Jews "have disappeared from Europe and that the Jewish 'Reservoir of the East' from which the Jewish plague has for centuries beset the people of Europe, has ceased to exist." Streicher now has the effrontery to tell us he is "only a Zionist", he says he wants only to return the Jews to Palestine. But on 5/1942 his newspaper, *Der Stuermer*, had this to say:

"It is also not only a European problem! The Jewish question is a world question! Not only is Germany not safe in the face of the Jews as long as one Jew lives in Europe, but also the Jewish question is hardly solved in Europe so long as Jews live in the rest of the world."

And the Defendant Hans Frank, a lawyer by profession, I say with shame, summarized in his diary in 1944 the Nazi policy thus: "The Jews are a race which has to be eliminated, whenever we catch one, it is his end" (2233 – PS, 3/4/1944, P. 26). And earlier speaking of his function as Governor General of Poland, he confided to his diary this sentiment: "Of course I cannot eliminate all lice and Jews in only a year's time" (2233 – PS, Vol. IV, 1940, P. 1108). I could multiply endlessly this kind of Nazi ranting but I will leave it to the evidence and turn to the fruit of this perverted thinking.

The most serious of the actions against Jews were outside of any law, but the law itself was employed to some extent. There were the infamous Nuremberg decrees of 9/15/1935 (*Reichsgesetzblatt* 1935, Part. I, P. 1146). The Jews were segregated into ghettos and put into forced labor; they were expelled from their professions; their property was expropriated, all cultural life, the press, the theater and schools were prohibited them; and the SD was made responsible for them (212 – PS, 069 – PS). This was an ominous guardianship, as the following order for "The Handling of the Jewish Question" shows:

"The competency of the Chief of the Security Police and Security Service, who is charged with the mission of solving the European Jewish question, extends even to the Occupied Eastern Provinces ...."

"An eventual act by the civilian population against the Jews is not to be prevented as long as this is compatible with the maintenance of order and security in the rear of the fighting troops ...."

"The first main goal of the German measures must be strict Segregation of Jewry from the rest of the population. In the execution of this, first of all is the seizing of the Jewish populace by the introduction of a registration order and similar appropriate measures."

"Then immediately the wearing of the recognition sign consisting of a yellow Jewish star is to be brought about and all rights of freedom for Jews are to be withdrawn. They are to be placed in ghettos and at the same time are to be separated according to sexes. The presence of many more or less closed Jewish settlements in White Ruthenia and in the Ukraine makes this mission easier. Moreover, places are to be chosen which make possible the full use of the Jewish manpower in case labor needs are present ...."

"The entire Jewish property is to be seized and confiscated with exception of that which is necessary for a bare existence. As far as the economical situation permits, the power of disposal of their property is to be taken from the Jews as soon as possible through orders and other measures given by the commissariat, so that the moving of property will quickly cease."

"Any cultural activity will be completely forbidden to the Jew. This includes the outlawing of the Jewish press, the Jewish theaters, and schools."

"The slaughtering of animals according to Jewish rites is also to be prohibited ...." (212 – PS)

The anti-Jewish campaign became furious in Germany following the assassination in Paris of the German Legation Councillor Von Rath. Heydrich, Gestapo head, sent a teletype to all Gestapo and SD offices with directions for handling "spontaneous" uprising anticipated for the nights of 11/9 – 10/1938 so as to aid in destruction of Jewish – owned property and protect only that of Germans. No more cynical document ever came into evidence. Then there is a report by an SS brigade leader, Dr. Stahlecker, to Himmler, which recites that:

"... Similarly, native anti-Semitic forces were induced to start pogroms against Jews during the first hours after capture, though this inducement proved to be very difficult. Following our orders, the Security Police was determined to solve the Jewish question with all possible means and most decisively. But it was desirable that the Security Police should not put in an immediate appearance, at least in the beginning, since the extraordinarily harsh measures were apt to stir even German circles. It had to be shown to the world that the native population itself took the first action by way of natural reaction against the suppression by Jews during several decades and against the terror exercised by the Communists during the preceding period."

"In view of the extension of the area of operations and the great number of duties which had to be performed by the Security Police, it was intended from the very beginning to obtain the co-operation of the reliable population for the fight against vermin, that is mainly the Jews and Communists Beyond our directing of the first spontaneous actions of self-cleansing, which will be reported elsewhere, care had to be taken that reliable people should be put to the cleansing job and that they were appointed auxiliary members of the Security Police."

"... Kovno. To our surprise it was not easy at first to set in motion an extensive pogrom against Jews. Klimatis, the leader of the partisan unit, mentioned above, who was used for this purpose primarily, succeeded in starting a pogrom on the basis of advice given to him by a small advanced detachment acting in Kovno, and in such a way that no German order or German instigation was noticed from the outside. During the first pogrom in the night from 25 to 26 June the Lithuanian partisans did away with more than 1,500 Jews, set fire to several synagogues or destroyed them by other means and burned down a Jewish dwelling district consisting of about 60 houses. During the following nights about 2,300 Jews were made harmless in a similar way. In other parts of Lithuania similar actions followed the example of Kovno, though smaller and extending to the Communists who had been left behind."

"These self-cleansing actions went smoothly because the Army authorities who had been informed showed understanding for this procedure. From the beginning it was obvious that only the first days after the occupation would offer the opportunity for carrying out pogroms. After the disarmament of the partisans the self-cleansing actions ceased necessarily."

"It proved much more difficult to set in motion similar cleansing actions in Latvia...." (L – 180)

Of course, it is self-evident that these "uprisings" were managed by the Government and the Nazi Party. If we were in doubt, we could resort to Streicher's memorandum of 4/14/1939 which says:

"The anti-Jewish action of 11/1938 did not arise spontaneously from the people.... Part of the Party formation been charged with the execution of the anti-Jewish action." (406 – PS)

Jews as a whole were fined a billion Reichsmarks. They were excluded from all businesses, and claims against insurance companies for their burned properties were confiscated, all by decree of the Defendant Goering. (*Reichsgesetzblatt*, 1938, Part I, Pp. 1579 – 82)

Synagogues were the objects of a special vengeance. On 11/10/1938 the following order was given:

"By order of the Group Commander:"

"All Jewish synagogues in the area of Brigade 50 have to be blown up or set afire.... The operation will be carried out in civilian clothing .... Execution of the order will be reported...." (1721 – PS)

Some 40 teletype messages from various police headquarters will tell the fury with which all Jews were pursued in Germany on those awful November nights. The SS troops were turned loose and the Gestapo supervised. Jewish-owned property was authorized to be destroyed. The Gestapo ordered twenty to thirty thousand "well-to-do-Jews" to be arrested. Concentration camps were to receive them. Healthy Jews, fit for labor, were to be taken. (3051 – PS)

As the German frontiers were expanded by war, so the campaign against the Jews expanded. The Nazi plan never was limited to extermination in Germany; always it contemplated extinguishing the Jew in Europe and often in the world. In the West, the Jews were killed and their property taken over. But the campaign achieved its zenith of savagery in the East. The eastern Jew has suffered as no people ever suffered. Their sufferings were carefully reported to the Nazi authorities to show faithful adherence to the Nazi design. I shall refer only to enough of the evidence of these to show the extent of the Nazi design for killing Jews.

If I should recite these horrors in words of my own, you would think me intemperate and unreliable. Fortunately, we need not take the word of any witness but the Germans themselves. I invite you now to look at a few of the vast number of captured German orders and reports that will be offered in evidence, to see what a Nazi invasion meant. We will present such evidence as the report of *Einsatzgruppe* (Action Group) A" of 10/15/1941 which boasts that in overrunning the Baltic States, "Native anti-Semitic forces were induced to start pogroms against the Jews during the first hours after occupation ...." The report continues:

"From the beginning it was to be expected that the Jewish problem in the East could not be solved by pogroms alone."

"In accordance with the basic orders received, however, the cleansing activities of the Security Police had to aim at a complete annihilation of the Jews. Special detachments reinforced by selected units in Lithuania partisan detachments in Latvia units of the Latvian auxiliary police therefore performed extensive executions both in the towns and in rural areas. The actions of the execution detachments were performed smoothly."

"The sum total of the Jews liquidated in Lithuania amounts to 71,105. During the pogroms in Kovno 3800 Jews were eliminated, in the smaller towns about 1200 Jews." "In Latvia, up to now a total of 30,000 Jews were executed. Five hundred were eliminated by pogroms in Riga." (L – 180)

This is a captured report from the Commissioner of Sluzk on 10/30/1941 which describes the scene in more detail. It says:

" ... The first lieutenant explained that the police battalion had received the assignment to effect the liquidation of all Jews here in the town of Sluzk, within two days .... Then I requested him to postpone the action one day. However, he rejected this with the remark that he had to carry out this action everywhere and in all towns and that only two days were allotted for Sluzk. Within these two days, the town of Sluzk had to be cleared of Jews by all means.... All Jews without exception were taken out of the factories and shops and deported in spite of our agreement. It is true that part of the Jews was moved by way of the ghetto where many of them were processed and still segregated by me, but a large part was loaded directly on trucks and liquidated without further delay outside of the town .... For the rest, as regards the execution of the action, I must point out to my deepest regret that the latter bordered already on sadism. The town itself offered a picture of horror during the action. With indescribable brutality on the part of both the German police officers and particularly the Lithuanian partisans, the Jewish people, but also among them White Ruthenians, were taken out of their dwellings and herded together. Everywhere in the town shots were to be heard and in different streets the corpses of shot Jews accumulated. The White Ruthenians were in greatest distress to free themselves from the encirclement. Regardless of the fact that the Jewish people, among whom were also tradesmen, were mistreated in a terribly barbarous way in the face of the White Ruthenian people, the White Ruthenians themselves were also worked over with rubber clubs and rifle butts. There was no question of an action against the Jews any more. It rather looked like a revolution ...."

There are reports which merely tabulate the numbers slaughtered. An example is an account of the work of *Einsatzgruppen* of SIPO and SD in the East, which relates that:

"In Estonia all Jews were arrested immediately upon the arrival the Wehrmacht. Jewish men and women above the age of 16 and capable of work were drafted for forced labor. Jews were subjected to all sorts of restrictions and all Jewish property was confiscated. All Jewish males above the age of 16 were executed, with the exception of doctors and elders. Only 500 of an original 4,500 Jews remained. Thirty – seven thousand, one hundred eighty persons have been liquidated by the SIPO and SD in White Ruthenia during October. In one town, 337 Jewish women were executed for demonstrating a 'provocative attitude.' In another, 380 Jews were shot for spreading vicious propaganda."

And so the report continues, listing town after town, where hundreds of Jews were murdered:

"In Vitebsk 3000 Jews were liquidated because of the danger of epidemics. In Kiev 33,771 Jews were executed on September 29 and 30 in retaliation for some fires which were set off there. In Shitomir 3145 Jews 'had to be shot' because, judging from experience they had to be considered as the carriers of Bolshevik propaganda. In Cherson 410 Jews were executed in reprisal against acts of sabotage; In the territory east of the Dnieper, the Jewish problem was 'solved' by the liquidation of 4891 Jews and by putting the remainder into labor battalions of up to 1000 persons." (R – 102)

Other accounts tell not of the slaughter so much as of the depths of degradation to which the tormentors stooped. For example, we will show the report made to Defendant Rosenberg about the army and the SS in the area under Rosenberg's jurisdiction, which recited the following:

"Details: In presence of SS man, a Jewish dentist has to break all gold teeth and fillings out of mouth of German and Russian Jews before they are executed."

"Men, women and children are locked into barns and burned alive."

"Peasants, women and children are shot on the pretext that they are suspected of belonging to bands." (R – 135)

We of the Western World heard of gas wagons in which Jews and political opponents were asphyxiated. We could not believe it, but here we have the report of 5/16/1942 from the German SS officer Becker to his supervisor in Berlin which tells this story:

"Gas vans in C group can be driven to execution spot, which is generally stationed 10 to 15 kms. from main road, only in dry weather. Since those to be executed become frantic if conducted to this place, such vans become immobilized in wet weather."

"Gas vans in D group were camouflaged as cabin trailers, but vehicles well known to authorities and civilian population which calls them 'death vans'."

"Writer of letter (Becker) ordered all men to keep as far as possible during gassing. Unloading van has 'atrocious spiritual and physical effect' on men and they should be ordered not to participate in such work." (501 – PS)

I shall not dwell on this subject longer than to quote one more sickening document which evidences the planned and systematic character of the Jewish persecutions. I hold a report written with Teutonic devotion to detail, illustrated with photographs to authenticate its almost incredible text, and beautifully bound in leather with the loving care bestowed on a proud work. It is the original report of the SS Brigadier General Stroop in charge of the destruction of the Warsaw Ghetto, and its title page carries the inscription "The Jewish ghetto in Warsaw no longer exists." It is characteristic that one of the captions explains that the photograph concerned shows the driving out of Jewish "bandits"; those whom the photograph shows being driven out are almost entirely women and little children. It contains a day-by-day account of the killings mainly carried out by the SS organization, too long to relate, but let me quote General Stroop's summary:

"The resistance put up by the Jews and bandits could only be suppressed by energetic actions of our troops day and night. The Reichsfuehrer SS ordered, therefore, on 4/23/1943, the cleaning out of the ghetto with utter ruthlessness and merciless tenacity. I, therefore, decided to destroy and burn down the entire ghetto without regard to the armament factories. These factories were systematically dismantled and then burned. Jews usually left their hideouts, but frequently remained in the burning buildings and jumped out of the windows only when the heat became unbearable. They then tried to crawl with broken bones across the street into buildings which were not afire. Sometimes they changed their hideouts during the night into the ruins of burned buildings. Life in the sewers was not pleasant after the first week. Many times we could hear loud voices in the sewers. SS men or policemen climbed bravely through the manholes to capture these Jews. Sometimes they stumbled over Jewish corpses: sometimes they were shot at. Tear gas bombs were thrown into the manholes and the Jews driven out of the sewers and captured. Countless numbers of Jews were liquidated in sewers and bunkers through blasting. The longer the resistance continued the tougher became the members of the Waffen SS, Police and Wehrmacht who always discharged their duties in an exemplary manner. Frequently Jews who tied to replenish their food supplies during the night or to communicate with neighboring groups were exterminated."

"This action eliminated," says the SS commander, "a proved total of 56,065. To that, we have to add the number killed through blasting, fire, etc., which cannot be counted." (1061 – PS)

We charge that all atrocities against Jews were the manifestation and culmination of the Nazi plan to which every defendant here was a party. I know very well that some of these men did take step to spare some particular Jew for some personal reason from the horrors that awaited the unrescued Jew. Some protested that particular atrocities were excessive, and discredited the general policy. While a few defendants may show efforts to make specific exceptions to the policy of Jewish extermination, I have found no instance in which any defendant opposed the policy itself or sought to revoke or even modify it.

Determination to destroy the Jews was a binding force which at all times cemented the elements of this conspiracy. On many internal policies there were differences among the defendants. But there is not one of them who has not echoed the rallying cry of Nazism: '*Deutschland erwache, Juda verrecke!*" (Germany awake, Jewry perish!).

Terrorism and Preparation for War:

How a government treats its own inhabitants generally is thought to be no concern of other governments or of international society. Certainly few oppressions or cruelties would warrant the intervention of foreign powers. But the German mistreatment of Germans is now known to pass in magnitude and savagery any limits of what is tolerable by modern civilization. Other nations, by silence, would take a consenting part in such crimes. These Nazi persecutions, moreover, take character as international crimes because of the purpose for which they were undertaken.

The purpose as we have seen, of getting rid of the influence of free labor, the churches, and the Jews was to clear their obstruction to the precipitation of aggressive war. If aggressive warfare in violation of treaty obligation is a matter of international cognizance the preparations for it must also be of concern to the international. Terrorism was the chief instrument for securing the cohesion of the German people in war purposes. Moreover, the cruelties in Germany served as atrocity practice to discipline the membership of the criminal organization to follow the pattern later in occupied countries.

Through the police formations that are before you, accused criminal organizations, the Nazi Party leaders, aided at some point in their basic and notorious purpose by each of the individual defendants, instituted a reign of terror. These espionage and police organizations were utilized to hunt down every form of opposition and to penalize every nonconformity. These organizations early founded and administered concentration camps; Buchenwald in 1933, Dachau in 1934. But these notorious names were not alone. Concentration camps came to dot the German map and to number scores. At first they met with resistance from some Germans. We have a captured letter from Minister of Justice Guertner to Hitler which is revealing. A Gestapo official had been prosecuted for crimes committed in the camp at Hohnstein, and the Nazi Governor of Saxony had promptly asked that the proceeding be quashed. The Minister of Justice in 6/1935 protested because, as he said "In this camp unusually grave mistreatments of prisoners have occurred at least since summer 1933. The prisoners not only were beaten with whips without cause, similarly as in the Concentration Camp Bredow near Stettin till they lost consciousness, but they were also tortured in other manners, e.g. with the help of a dripping apparatus constructed exclusively for this purpose, under which prisoners had to stand until they were suffering from serious purulent wounds of the scalp ...." (787 – PS)

I shall not take time to detail the ghastly proceedings in these concentration camps. Beatings, starvings, tortures, and killings were routine, so routine that the tormenters became blase and careless. We have a report of discovery that in Ploetzensee one night, 186 persons were executed while there were orders for only 180. Another report describes how the family of one victim received two urns of ashes by mistake.

Inmates were compelled to execute each other. In 1942 they were paid five Reichsmarks per execution, but on 6/27/1942 SS General Gluecks ordered commandants of all concentration camps to reduce this honorarium to three cigarettes. In 1943 the Reich leader of the SS and Chief of German Police ordered the corporal punishments on Russian women to be applied by Polish women and vice versa, but the price was not frozen. He said that as reward, a few cigarettes was authorized. Under the Nazis human life had been progressively devalued, until it finally became worth less than a handful of tobacco, ersatz tobacco. There were, however, some traces of the milk of human kindness. On August 2 an order went from Himmler to the commanders of 14 concentration camps that only German prisoners are allowed to beat other German prisoners (2189 – PS).

Mystery and suspense was added to cruelty in order to spread torture from the inmate to his family and friends. Men and women disappeared from their homes or business or from the streets and no word came of them. The omission of notice was not due to overworked staff; it was due to policy. The Chief of the SD and SIPO reported that in accordance with orders from the Fuehrer anxiety should be created in the minds of the family of the arrested person. (668 – PS) Deportations and secret arrests were labeled, with a Nazi wit which seems a little ghoulish, "Nacht und Nebel," (Night and Fog)

(L – 90, 833 – PS). One of the many orders for these actions gave this explanation:

"The decree carries a basic innovation. The Fuehrer and Commander-in-chief of the Armed Forces commands that crimes of the specified sort committed by civilians of the occupied territories are to be punished by the pertinent courts-martial in the occupied territories only when (a) the sentence calls for the death penalty, and (b) the sentence is pronounced within eight days after the arrest."

"Only when both conditions are met does the Fuehrer and Commander-in-chief of the Armed Forces hope for the desired deterrent effect from the conduct of punitive proceedings in the occupied territories."

"In other cases, in the future, the accused are to be secretly brought to Germany, and the further conduct of the trial carried on here. The deterrent effect of these measures lies (a) in allowing the disappearance of the accused without a trace, (b) therein that no information whatsoever may be given about their whereabouts and their fate." (833 – PS)

To clumsy cruelty, scientific skill was added. "Undesirables" were exterminated by injection of drugs into the bloodstream, by asphyxiation in gas chambers. They were shot with poison bullets, to study the effects. (L – 103)

Then, to cruel experiments the Nazi added obscene ones. These were not the work of underling-degenerates but of master-minds high in the Nazi conspiracy. On 5/20/1942 General Field Marshal Milch authorized SS General Wolff to go ahead at Dachau Camp with so-called "cold experiments"; and four female gypsies were supplied for the purpose. Himmler gave permission to carry on these "experiments" also in other camps. (1617 – PS) At Dachau, the reports of the "doctor" in charge show that victims immersed in cold water until their body temperature was reduced to 28C (82.4 degrees Fahrenheit), when they died immediately (1618 – PS). This was in 8/1942. But the "doctor's" technique improved. By 2/1943 he was able report that 30 persons were chilled to 27 – 29 degrees, their hand and feet frozen white, and their bodies "rewarmed" by a hot bath. But the Nazi scientific triumph was "rewarming with animal heat." The victim, all but frozen to death, was surrounded with bodies of living women until he revived and responded to his environment by having sexual intercourse. (1616 – PS) Here Nazi degeneracy reached its nadir.

I dislike to encumber the record with such morbid tales, but we are in the grim business of trying men as criminals, and these are the things that their own agents say happened. We will show you these concentration camps in motion pictures, just as the Allied armies found them when they arrived, and the measures General Eisenhower had to take to clean them up. Our proof will be disgusting and you will say I have robbed you of your sleep. But these are the things which have turned the stomach of the world and set every civilized hand against Nazi Germany.

Germany became one vast torture chamber. Cries of its victims were heard round the world and brought shudders to civilized people everywhere. I am one who received during this war most atrocity tales with suspicion and scepticism. But the proof here will be so overwhelming that I venture to predict not one word I have spoken will be denied. These defendants will only deny personal responsibility or knowledge.

Under the clutch of the most intricate web of espionage and intrigue that any modern state has endured, and persecution and torture of a kind that has not been visited upon the world in many centuries, the elements of the German population which were both decent and courageous were annihilated. Those which were decent but weak were intimidated. Open resistance, which had never been more than feeble and irresolute, disappeared. But resistance, I am happy to say, always remained, although it was manifest in only such events as the abortive effort to assassinate Hitler on 7/20/1944. With resistance driven underground, the Nazi had the German State in his own hands.

But the Nazis not only silenced discordant voices. They created positive controls as effective as their negative ones. Propaganda organs, on a scale never before known, stimulated the Party and Party formations with a permanent enthusiasm and abandon such as we, democratic people, can work up only for a few days before a general election. They inculcated and practiced the Fuehrer which centralized control of the Party and of the Party-controlled state over the lives and thought of the German people, who are accustomed to look upon the German State, by whomever controlled, with a mysticism that is incomprehensible to my people.

All these controls from their inception were exerted with unparalleled energy and single-mindedness to put Germany on a war footing. We will show from the Nazis' own documents their secret training of military personnel, their secret creation of a military air force. Finally, a conscript army was brought into being. Financiers, economists, industrialists joined in the plan and promoted elaborate alterations in industry and finance to support an unprecedented concentration of resources and energies upon preparations for war. Germany's rearmament so outstripped the strength of her neighbors that in about a year she was able to crush the whole military force of continental Europe, exclusive of that of Soviet Russia, and then to push the Russian armies back to the Volga. These preparations were of a magnitude which surpassed all need of defense, and every defendant, and every intelligent German, well understood them to be for aggressive purposes.

Experiments in Aggression:

Before resorting to open aggressive warfare, the Nazis undertook some rather cautious experiments to test the spirit of resistance of those who lay across their path. They advanced, but only as others yielded, and kept in a position to draw back if they found a temperament that made persistence dangerous.

On 3/7/1936 the Nazis reoccupied the Rhineland and then proceeded to fortify it in violation of the Treaty of Versailles and the Pact of Locarno. They encountered no substantial resistance and were emboldened to take the next step, which was the acquisition of Austria. Despite repeated assurances that Germany had no designs on Austria, invasion was perfected. Threat of attack forced Schuschnigg to resign as Chancellor of Austria and put the Nazi Defendant Seyss-Inquart in his place. The latter immediately opened the frontier and invited Hitler to invade Austria "to preserve order". On March 12th invasion began. The next day, Hitler proclaimed himself Chief of the Austrian State, took command of its armed forces, and a law was enacted annexing Austria to Germany.

Threats of aggression had succeeded without arousing resistance. Fears nevertheless had been stirred. They were lulled by an assurance to the Czechoslovak Government that there would be no attack on that country. We will show that the Nazi Government already had detailed plans for the attack. We will lay before you the documents in which these conspirators planned to create incidents to justify their attack. They even gave consideration to assassinating their own Ambassador at Prague in order to create a sufficiently dramatic incident. They did precipitate a diplomatic crisis which endured throughout the summer. Hitler set September 30th as the day when troops should be ready for action. Under the threat of immediate war, the United Kingdom and France concluded a pact with Germany and Italy at Munich on 9/29/1938 which required Czechoslovakia to acquiesce in the cession of the Sudetenland to Germany. It was consummated by German occupation on 10/1/1938.

The Munich Pact pledged no further aggression against Czechoslovakia, but the Nazi pledge was lightly given and quickly broken. On the 3/15/1939, in defiance of the treaty of Munich itself, the Nazis seized and occupied Bohemia and Moravia, which constituted the major part of Czechoslovakia not already ceded to Germany. Once again the West stood aghast, but it dreaded war, it saw no remedy except war, and it hoped against hope that the Nazi fever for expansion had run its course. But the Nazi world was intoxicated by these unresisted successes in open alliance with Mussolini and in covert alliance with Franco. Then, having made a deceitful, delaying peace with Russia, the conspirators entered upon the final phase of the plan to renew war.

War of Aggression:
I will not prolong this address by detailing the steps leading to the war of aggression which began with the invasion of Poland on 9/1/1939. The further story will be unfolded to you from documents including those of the German High Command itself.

The plans had been laid long in advance. As early as 1935 Hitler appointed the Defendant Schacht to the position of General Deputy for the War Economy (2261 – PS). We have the diary of General Jodl (1780 – PS); the "Plan Otto," Hitler's own order for attack on Austria in case trickery failed (C – 102); the "Plan Green" which was the blueprint for attack on Czechoslovakia (388 – PS); plans for the war in the West (375 – PS, 376 – PS); Funk's letter to Hitler dated 8/25/1939 detailing the long course of economic preparation (699 – PS); Keitel's top – secret mobilization order for 1939 – 1940 prescribing secret steps to be taken during a "period of tension" during which no "'state of war will be publicly declared even if open war measures against the foreign enemy will be taken." This letter order (1639A – PS) is in our possession despite a secret order issued on 3/16/1945, when Allied troops were advancing into the heart of Germany, to burn these plans. We have also Hitler's directive, dated 12/18/1940, for the "Barbarossa Contingency" outlining the strategy of the attack upon Russia (446 –

PS). That plan in the original bears the initials of the Defendants Keitel and Jodl. They were planning the attack and planning it long in advance of the declaration of war. We have detailed information concerning "Case White," the plan for attack on Poland (C – 120). That attack began the war. The plan was issued by Keitel on 4/3/1939. The attack did not come until September. Steps in preparation for the attack were taken by subordinate commanders, one of whom issued an order on June 14, providing that:

"The Commander-in-chief of the Army has ordered the working out of a plan of deployment against Poland which takes in account the demands of the political leadership for the opening of war by surprise and for quick success...."

"I declare it the duty of the commanding generals, the divisional commanders, and the commandants to limit as much as possible the number of persons who will be informed, and to limit the extent of the information, and ask that all suitable measures be taken to prevent persons not concerned from getting information...."

"The operation, in order to forestall an orderly Polish mobilization and concentration, is to be opened by surprise with forces which are for the most part armored and motorized, placed on alert in the neighborhood of the border. The initial superiority over the Polish frontier guards and surprise that can be expected with certainty are to be maintained by quickly bringing up other parts of the Army as well to counteract the marching up of the Polish Army...."

"If the development of the political situation should show that a surprise at the beginning of the war is out of question, because of well-advanced defense preparations on the part of the Polish Army, the Commander-in-chief of the Army will order the opening of the hostilities only after the assembling of sufficient additional forces. The basis of all preparations will be to surprise the enemy...." (2327 – PS)

We have also the order for the invasion of England, signed by Hitler and initialed by Keitel and Jodl. It is interesting that it commences with a recognition that although the British military position is "hopeless," they show not the slightest sign of giving in. (442 – PS)

Not the least incriminating are the minutes of Hitler's meeting with his high advisers. As early as 11/5/1937 Hitler told Defendants Goering, Raeder, and Neurath, among others, that German rearmament was practically accomplished and that he had decided to secure by force, starting with a lightning attack on Czechoslovakia and Austria, greater living space for German Europe no later than 1943 – 1945 and perhaps as early as 1938 (386 – PS). On the 5/23/1939 the Fuehrer advised his staff that:

"It is a question of expanding our living space in the East and of securing our food supplies.... Over and above the natural fertility, thorough-going German exploitation will enormously increase the surplus."

"There is therefore no question of sparing Poland, and we are left with the decision: To attack Poland at the first suitable opportunity. We cannot expect a repetition of the Czech affair. There will be war." (L – 79)

On 8/22/1939 Hitler again addressed members of the High Command, telling them when the start of military operations would be ordered. He disclosed that for propaganda purposes, he would provocate a good reason. "It will make no difference," he announced, "whether this reason will sound convincing or not. After all, the victor will not be asked whether he talked the truth or not. We have to proceed brutally. The stronger is always right." (1014 – PS) On 11/23/1939, after the Germans had invaded Poland, Hitler made this explanation:

". . . For the first time in history we have to fight on only one front, the other front is at present free. But no one can know how long that will remain so. I have doubted for a long time whether I should strike in the East and then in the West. Basically I did not organize the armed forces in order not to strike. The decision to strike was always in me. Earlier or later I wanted to solve the problem. Under pressure it was decided that the East was to be attacked first ...."

We know the bloody sequel. Frontier incidents were staged. Demands were made for cession of territory. When Poland refused, the German forces invaded on 9/1/1939. Warsaw was destroyed; Poland fell. The Nazis, in accordance with plan, moved swiftly to extend their aggression throughout Europe and to gain the advantage of surprise over their unprepared neighbors. Despite repeated and solemn assurances of peaceful intentions, they invaded Denmark and Norway on 4/9/1940; Belgium, The Netherlands and Luxembourg on 5/10/1940; Yugoslavia and Greece on 4/6/1941.

As part of the Nazi preparation for aggression against Poland and her allies, Germany, on 8/23/1939, had entered into a non-aggression pact with Soviet Russia. It was only a delaying treaty intended to be kept no longer than necessary to prepare for its violation. On 6/22/1941, pursuant to long-matured plans, the Nazis hurled troops into Soviet territory without any declaration of war. The entire European world was aflame.

Conspiracy with Japan:

The Nazi plans of aggression called for use of Asiatic allies and they found among the Japanese men of kindred mind and purpose. They were brothers, under the skin.

Himmler records a conversation he had on 1/31/1939 with General Oshima, Japanese Ambassador at Berlin. He wrote:

"Furthermore he (Oshima) had succeeded up to now to send 10 Russians with bombs across the Caucasian frontier. These Russians had the mission to kill Stalin. A number of additional Russians, whom he had also sent across, had been shot at the frontier." (2195 – PS)

On 9/27/1940 the Nazis concluded a German-Italian-Japanese 10-year military and economic alliance by which those powers agreed "to stand by and cooperate with one another in regard to their efforts in Greater East Asia and regions of Europe respectively wherein it is their prime purpose to establish and maintain a new order of things."

On 3/5/1941 a top-secret directive was issued by Defendant Keitel. It stated that the Fuehrer had ordered instigation of Japan's active participation in the war and directed that Japan's military power has to be strengthened by the disclosure of German war experiences and support of a military, economic, and technical nature has to be given. The aim was stated to be to crush England quickly thereby keeping the United States out of the war. (C – 75)

On 3/29/1941 Ribbentrop told Matsuoka, the Japanese Foreign Minister, that the German Army was ready to strike against Russia. Matsuoka reassured Ribbentrop about the Far East. Japan, he reported, was acting at the moment as though she had no interest whatever in Singapore, but intends to strike when the right moment comes. (1877 – PS)

On 4/5/1941 Ribbentrop urged Matsuoka that entry of Japan into the war would "hasten the victory" and would be more in the interest of Japan than of Germany since it would give Japan a unique chance to fulfill her national aims and to play a leading part in Eastern Asia (1882 – PS).

The proofs in this case will also show that the leaders of Germany were planning war against the United States from its Atlantic as well as instigating it from its Pacific approaches. A captured memorandum from the Fuehrer's headquarters, dated 10/29/1940, asks certain information as to air bases and supply and reports further that:

"The Fuehrer is at present occupied with the question of the occupation of the Atlantic islands with a view to the prosecution of war against America at a later date. Deliberations on this subject are being embarked upon here." (376 – PS)

On 12/7/1941, a day which the late President Roosevelt declared "will live in infamy," victory for German aggression seemed certain. The Wehrmacht was at the gates of Moscow. Taking advantage of the situation, and while her plenipotentiaries were creating a diplomatic diversion in Washington, Japan without declaration of war treacherously attacked the United States at Pearl Harbor and the Philippines. Attacks followed swiftly on the British Commonwealth, and The Netherlands in the Southwest Pacific. These aggressions were met in the only way that they could be met, with instant declarations of war and with armed resistance which mounted slowly through many long months of reverse until finally the Axis was crushed to earth and deliverance for its victims was won.

I will now take up the subject of "Crimes in the Conduct of War".

Even the most warlike of peoples have recognized in the name of humanity some limitations on the savagery of warfare. Rules to that end have been embodied in international conventions to which Germany became a party. This code had prescribed certain restraints as to the treatment of belligerents. The enemy was entitled to surrender and to receive quarter and good treatment as a prisoner of war. We will show by German documents that these rights were denied, that prisoners of war were given brutal treatment and often murdered. This was particularly true in the case of captured airmen, often my countrymen.

It was ordered that captured English and American airmen should no longer be granted the status of prisoners of war. They were to be treated as criminals and the Army was ordered to refrain from protecting them against lynching by the populace. (R – 118) The Nazi Government, through its police and propaganda agencies, took pains to incite the civilian population to attack and kill airmen who crash-landed. The order, given by the Reichsfuehrer Himmler on 8/10/1943, directed that: "It is not the task of the police to interfere in clashes between German and English and American flyers who have bailed out". This order was transmitted on the same day by SS *Obersturmbannfuehrer* Brandt of Himmler's personal staff to all senior executive SS and Police officers, with these directions:

"I am sending you the inclosed order with the request that the Chief of the Regular Police and of the Security Police be informed. They are to make this instruction known to their subordinate officers verbally." (R – 110)

Similarly, we will show Hitler's top secret order, dated 10/18/1942, that commandos, regardless of condition, were "to be slaughtered to the last man" after capture (498 – PS). We will how the circulation of secret orders, one of which was signed by Hess, to be passed orally to civilians, that enemy fliers or parachutists were to be arrested or liquidated (062 – PS). By such means were murders incited and directed.

This Nazi campaign of ruthless treatment of enemy forces assumed its greatest proportions in the fight against Russia. Eventually all prisoners of war were taken out of control of the Army and put in the hands of Himmler and the SS (058 – PS). In the East, the German fury spent itself. Russian prisoners were ordered to be branded. They were starved. I shall quote passages from a letter written 2/28/1942 by Defendant Rosenberg to Defendant Keitel:

"The fate of the Soviet prisoners of war in Germany is on the contrary a tragedy of the greatest extent. Of 3.6 million prisoners of war, only several hundred thousand are still able to work fully. A large part of them has starved, or died, because of the hazards of the weather. Thousands also died from spotted fever...."

"The camp commanders have forbidden the civilian population to put food at the disposal of the prisoners, and they have rather let them starve to death...."

"In many cases, when prisoners of war could no longer keep up on the march because of hunger and exhaustion, they were shot before the eyes of the horrified population, and the corpses were left. In numerous camps, no shelter for the prisoners of war was provided at all. They lay under the open sky during rain or snow. Even tools were not made available to dig holes or caves...."

"Finally, the shooting of prisoners of war must be mentioned for instance, in various camps, all the 'Asiatics' were shot". (081 – PS)

Civilized usage and conventions to which Germany was a party had prescribed certain immunities for civilian populations unfortunate enough to dwell in lands overrun by hostile armies. The German occupation forces, controlled or commanded by men on trial before you, committed a long series of outrages against the inhabitants of occupied territory that would be incredible except for captured orders and captured reports which show the fidelity with which those orders were executed.

We deal here with a phase of common criminality designed by the conspirators as part of the common plan. We can appreciate why these crimes against their European enemies were not of a casual character but were planned and disciplined crimes when we get at the reason for them. Hitler told his officers on 8/22/1939 that: "The main objective in Poland is the destruction of the enemy and not the reaching of a certain geographical line" (1014 – PS). The project of deporting promising youth from occupied territories was approved by Rosenberg on the theory that "a desired weakening of the biological force" of the conquered people is being achieved (031 – PS). To Germanize or to destroy was the program Himmler announced, "Either we win over any good blood that we can use for ourselves and give it a place in our people or, gentlemen you may call this cruel, but nature is cruel; we destroy this blood." As to "racially good types" Himmler further advised "Therefore, I think that it is our duty to take their children with us, to remove them from their environment, if necessary by robbing or stealing them" (L – 70). He urged deportation of Slavic children to deprive potential enemies of future soldiers.

The Nazi purpose was to leave Germany's neighbors so weakened that even if she should eventually lose the war, she would still be the most powerful nation in Europe. Against this background, we must view the plan for ruthless warfare, which means a plan for the commission of War Crimes and Crimes against Humanity.

Hostages in large numbers were demanded and killed. Mass punishments were inflicted, so savage that whole communities were extinguished. Rosenberg was advised of the annihilation of three unidentified villages in Slovakia. (970 – PS) In 5/1943 another village of about 40 farms and 220 inhabitants was ordered wiped out. The entire population was ordered shot, the cattle and property impounded, and the order required that "the village will be destroyed totally by fire." (163 – PS) A secret report from Rosenberg's Reich Ministry of Eastern Territory reveals that:

"Food rations allowed the Russian population are so low that they fail to secure their existence and provide only for minimum subsistence of limited duration. The population does not know if they will still live tomorrow. They are faced with death by starvation...."

"The roads are clogged by hundreds of thousands of people, sometimes as many as one million according to the estimate of experts, who wander around in search of nourishment...."

"Sauckel's action has caused unrest among the civilians.... Russian girls were deloused by men, nude photos in forced positions were taken, women doctors were locked into freight cars for the pleasure of the transport commanders, women in night shirts were fettered and forced through the Russian towns to the railroad station, etc. All this material has been sent to the OKH." (1381 – PS)

Perhaps the deportation to slave labor was the most horrible and extensive slaving operation in history. On few other subjects is our evidence so abundant or so damaging. In a speech made on 1/25/1944 the Defendant Frank, Governor General of Poland, boasted, "I have sent 1.3 million Polish workers into the Reich" (05 – PS, P. 2). The Defendant Sauckel reported that "out of the 5 million foreign workers who arrived in Germany not even 200,000 came voluntarily." This fact was reported to the Fuehrer and Defendants Speer, Goering, and Keitel. (R – 24) Children of 10-14 years were impressed into service by telegraphic order of Rosenberg's Ministry for the Occupied Eastern Territories:

"The Command is further charged with the transferring of worthwhile Russian youth between 10-14 years of age, to the Reich. The authority is not affected by the changes connected with the evacuation and transportation to the reception camps of Bialystok, Krajewo, and Olitei. The Fuehrer wishes that this activity be increased even more." (200 – PS)

When enough labor was not forthcoming, prisoners of war were forced into war work in flagrant violation of international conventions (016 – PS) Slave labor came from France, Belgium, Holland, Italy, and the East. Methods of recruitment were violent (R – 124, 018 – PS, 204 – PS). The treatment of these slave laborers was stated in general terms, not difficult to translate into concrete deprivations, in a letter to the Defendant Rosenberg from the Defendant Sauckel, which stated:

"All prisoners of war, from the territories of the West as well as of the East, actually in Germany, must be completely incorporated into the German armament and munition industries. Their production must be brought to the highest possible level...."

"The complete employment of all prisoners of war as well as the use of a gigantic number of new foreign civilian workers, men and women, has become an indisputable necessity for the solution of the mobilization of labor program in this war."

"All the men must be fed, sheltered, and treated in such a way as to exploit them to the highest possible extent at the lowest conceivable degrees of expenditure...." (016 – PS)

In pursuance of the Nazi plan permanently to reduce the living standards of their neighbors and to weaken them physically and economically, a long series of crimes were committed. There was extensive destruction, serving no military purpose, of the property of civilians. Dikes were thrown open in Holland almost at the close of the war not to achieve military ends but to destroy the resources and retard the economy of the thrifty Netherlanders.

There was carefully planned economic syphoning off of the assets of occupied countries. An example of the planning is shown by a report on France dated 12/7/1942 made by the Economic Research Department of the Reichsbank. The question arose whether French occupation costs should be increased from RM15 million per day to RM25 million per day. The Reichsbank analyzed the French economy to determine whether it could bear the burden. It pointed out that the armistice had burdened France to that date to the extent of RM18.5 billion, equaling F370 billion. It pointed out that the burden of these payments within 2 ½ years equaled the aggregate French national income in the year 1940, and that the amount of payments handed over to Germany in the first 6 months of 1942 corresponded to the estimate for the total French revenue for that whole year. The report concluded:

"In any case, the conclusion is inescapable that relatively heavier tributes have been imposed on France since the armistice in 6/1940 than upon Germany after the World War. In this connection, it must be noted that the economic powers of France never equaled those of the German Reich and that the vanquished France could not draw on foreign economic and financial resources in the same degree as Germany after the last World War."

The Defendant Funk was the Reich Minister of Economics and President of the Reichsbank; Defendant Ribbentrop was Foreign

Minister; the Defendant Goering was Plenipotentiary of the Four Year Plan; and all of them participated in the exchange of views of which this captured document is a part. (2149 – PS) Notwithstanding this analysis by the Reichsbank, they proceeded to increase the imposition on France from RM15 million to RM25 million per day.

It is small wonder that the bottom has been knocked out of French economy. The plan and purpose of the thing appears in a letter from General Stuelpnagel, head of the German Armistice Commission, to the Defendant Jodl as early as 9/14/1940 when he wrote, "The slogan 'Systematic weakening of France' has already been surpassed by far in reality" (1756 – PS).

Not only was there a purpose to debilitate and demoralize the economy of Germany's neighbors for the purpose of destroying their competitive position, but there was looting and pilfering on an unprecedented scale. We need not be hypocritical about this business of looting. I recognize that no army moves through occupied territory without some pilfering as it goes. Usually the amount of pilfering increases as discipline wanes. If the evidence in this case showed no looting except of that sort, I certainly would ask no conviction of these defendants for it.

But we will show you that looting was not due to the lack of discipline or to the ordinary weaknesses of human nature. The German organized plundering, planned it, disciplined it, and made it official just as he organized everything else, and then he compiled the most meticulous records to show that he had done the best job of looting that was possible under the circumstances. And we have those records.

The Defendant Rosenberg was put in charge of a systematic plundering of the art objects of Europe by direct order of Hitler dated 1/29/1940 (136 – PS). On the 4/16/1943 Rosenberg reported that up to the 7th of April, 92 railway cars with 2775 cases containing art objects had been sent to Germany; and that 53 pieces of art had been shipped to Hitler direct, and 594 to the Defendant Goering. The report mentioned something like 20000 pieces of seized art and the main locations where they were stored. (015 – PS)

Moreover this looting was glorified by Rosenberg. Here we have 39 leather-bound tabulated volumes of his inventory, which in due time we will offer in evidence. One cannot but admire the artistry of this Rosenberg report. The Nazi taste was cosmopolitan. Of the 9455 articles inventoried, there were included 5255 paintings, 297 sculptures, 1372 pieces of antique furniture, 307 textiles, and 2224 small objects of art. Rosenberg observed that there were approximately 10000 more objects still to be inventoried. (015 – PS) Rosenberg himself estimated that the values involved would cone close to a billion dollars (090 – PS).

I shall not go into further details of the War Crimes and Crimes against Humanity committed by the gangster ring whose leaders are before you. It is not the purpose in my part of this case to deal with the individual crimes. I am dealing with the Common Plan or design for crime and will not dwell upon individual offenses. My task is to show the scale on which these crimes occurred and to show that these are the men who were in the responsible positions and who conceived the plan and design which renders them answerable, regardless of the fact that the plan was actually executed by others.

At length, this reckless and lawless course outraged the world. It recovered from the demoralization of surprise attack, assembled its forces and stopped these men in their tracks. Once success deserted their banners, one by one the Nazi satellites fell away. Sawdust Caesar collapsed. Resistance forces in every occupied country arose to harry the invader. Even at home, Germans saw that Germany was being led to ruin by these mad men, and the attempt on 7/20/1944 to assassinate Hitler, an attempt fostered by men of highest station, was a desperate effort by internal forces in Germany to stop short of ruin. Quarrels broke out among the failing conspirators, and the decline of the Nazi power was more swift than its ascendancy. German Armed Forces surrendered, its Government disintegrated, its leaders committed suicide by the dozen, and by the fortunes of war these defendants fell into our hands. Although they are not, by any means, all the guilty ones, they are survivors among the most responsible. Their names appear over and over in the documents and their faces grace the photographic evidence. We have here the surviving top politicians, militarists, financiers, diplomats, administrators, and propagandists, of the Nazi movement. Who was responsible for these crimes if they were not?

The Law of the Case:
The end of the war and capture of these prisoners presented the victorious Allies with the question whether there is any legal

responsibility on high-ranking men for acts which I have described. Must such wrongs either be ignored or redressed in hot blood? Is there no standard in the law for a deliberate and reasoned judgment on such conduct?

The Charter of this Tribunal evidences a faith that the law is only to govern the conduct of little men, but that even rulers are, as Lord Chief Justice Coke put it to King James, "under God and the law." The United States believed that the law long afforded standards by which a juridical hearing could be conducted to make sure that we punish only the right men and for the right reasons. Following the instructions of the late President Roosevelt and the decision of the Yalta conference, President Truman directed representatives of the United States to formulate a proposed International Agreement, which was submitted during the San Francisco Conference to Foreign Ministers of the United Kingdom, the Soviet Union, and the Provisional Government of France. With many modifications, that proposal has become the Charter of this Tribunal.

But the Agreement which sets up the standards by which these prisoners are to be judged does not express the views of the signatory nations alone. Other nations with diverse but highly respected systems of jurisprudence also have signified adherence to it. These are Belgium, The Netherlands, Denmark, Norway, Czechoslovakia, Luxembourg, Poland, Greece, Yugoslavia, Ethiopia, Australia, Haiti, Honduras, Panama, New Zealand, Venezuela, and India. You judge, therefore, under an organic act which represents the wisdom, the sense of justice, and the will of 21 governments, representing an overwhelming majority of all civilized people.

The Charter by which this Tribunal has its being, embodies certain legal concepts which are inseparable from its jurisdiction and which must govern its decision. These, as I have said, also are conditions attached to the grant of any hearing to defendants. The validity of the provisions of the Charter is conclusive upon us a whether we have accepted the duty of judging or of prosecuting under it, as well as upon the defendants, who can point no other law which gives them a right to be heard at all. My able and experienced colleagues believe, as do I, that it will contribute to the expedition and clarity of this Trial if I expound briefly the application of the legal philosophy of the Charter the facts I have recited.

While this declaration of the law by the Charter is final, it may be contended that the prisoners on trial are entitled to have it applied to their conduct only most charitably if at all. It may be said that this is new law, not authoritatively declared at the time they did the acts it condemns, and that this declaration of the law has taken them by surprise.

I cannot, of course, deny that these men are surprised that this is the law; they really are surprised that there is any such thing as law. These defendants did not rely on any law at all. Their program ignored and defied all law. That this is so will appear from many acts and statements, of which I cite but a few.

In the Fuehrer's speech to all military commanders on 11/23/1939 he reminded them that at the moment Germany had a pact with Russia, but declared: "Agreements are to be kept only as long as they serve a certain purpose." Later in the same speech he announced: "A violation of the neutrality of Holland and Belgium will be of no importance" (789 – PS). A top secret document, entitled "Warfare as a Problem of Organization," dispatched by the Chief of the High Command to all commanders on 4/19/1938 declared that "the normal rules of war towards neutrals may be considered to apply on the basis whether operation of rules will create greater advantages or disadvantages for the belligerents" (L – 211). And from the files of the German Navy Staff, we have a "Memorandum on Intensified Naval War," dated 10/15/1939, which begins by stating a desire to comply with International Law. "However," it continues, "if decisive successes are expected from any measure considered as a war necessity, it must be carried through even if it is not in agreement with international law." (L – 184) International law, natural law, German law, any law at all was to these men simply a propaganda device to be invoked when it helped and to be ignored when it would condemn what they wanted to do. That men may be protected in relying upon the law at the time they act is the reason we find laws of retrospective operations unjust. But these men cannot bring themselves within the reason of the rule which in some systems of jurisprudence prohibits *ex post facto* laws. They cannot show that they ever relied upon international law in any state or paid it the slightest regard.

The third Count of the Indictment is based on the definition of War Crimes contained in the Charter. I have outlined to you the systematic course of conduct toward civilian populations and combat forces which violates international conventions to which Germany was a party. Of the criminal nature of these acts at least, the defendants had, as we shall show, clear knowledge. Accordingly they took pains to conceal their violations. It will appear that the Defendants Keitel and Jodl were informed by official legal advisors that the orders to brand Russian prisoners of war, to shackle British prisoners of war, and to execute commando prisoners were clear violations of international law. Nevertheless, these orders were put into effect. The same is true of orders issued for the assassination of General Giraud and General Weygand, which failed to be executed only because of a ruse on the part of Admiral Canaris, who was himself later executed for his part in the plot to take Hitler's life on 7/20/1944.

The fourth Count of the Indictment is based on Crimes against Humanity. Chief among these are mass killings of countless human beings in cold blood. Does it take these men by surprise that murder is treated as a crime?

The first and second Counts of the Indictment add to these crimes the crime of plotting and waging wars of aggression and as in violation of nine treaties to which Germany was a party. There was a time, in fact, I think the time of the first World War, it could not have been said that war-inciting or war-making was a crime in law, however reprehensible in morals.

Of course, it was, under the law of all civilized peoples, a crime for one man with his bare knuckles to assault another. How did it come that multiplying this crime by a million, and adding firearms to bare knuckles, made it a legally innocent act? The doctrine was that one could not be regarded as criminal for committing the usual violent acts in the conduct of legitimate warfare. The age of imperialistic expansion during the eighteenth and nineteenth centuries added the foul doctrine, contrary to the teachings of early Christian and international law scholars such as Grotius, that all wars are to be regarded as legitimate wars. The sum of these two doctrines was to give war-making a complete immunity from accountability to law.

This was intolerable for an age that called itself civilized. Plain people with their earthy common sense, revolted at such fictions and legalisms so contrary to ethical principles and demanded checks on war immunities. Statesmen and international lawyers at first cautiously responded by adopting rules of warfare designed to make the conduct of war more civilized. The effort was to set legal limits to the violence that could be done to civilian populations and to combatants as well.

The common sense of men after the first World War demanded, however, that the law's condemnation of war reach deeper, and that the law condemn not merely uncivilized ways of waging war, but also the waging in any way of uncivilized wars, wars of aggression. The world's statesmen again went only as far as they were forced to go. Their efforts were timid and cautious and often less explicit than we might have hoped. But the 1920's did outlaw aggressive war.

The re-establishment of the principle that there are unjust wars and that unjust wars are illegal is traceable in many steps. One of the most significant is the Briand-Kellogg Pact of 1928, by which Germany, Italy, and Japan, in common with practically all nations of the world, renounced war as an instrument of national policy, bound themselves to seek the settlement of disputes only by pacific means, and condemned recourse to war for the solution of international controversies. This pact altered the legal status of a war of aggression. As Mr. Stimson, the United States Secretary of State put it in 1932, such a war:

"... is no longer to be the source and subject of rights. It is no longer to be the principle around which the duties, the conduct, and the rights of nations revolve. It is an illegal thing.... By that very act, we have made obsolete many legal precedents and have given the legal profession the task of re-examining many of its codes and treaties."

The Geneva Protocol of 1924 for the Pacific Settlement of International Disputes, signed by the representatives of 48 governments declared that "a war of aggression constitutes ... an international crime." The Eighth Assembly of the League of Nations in 1927, on unanimous resolution of the representatives of 48 member nations including Germany, declared that a war of aggression constitutes an international crime. At the Sixth Pan-American Conference of 1928 the 21 American Republics unanimously adopted a resolution stating that "war of aggression constitutes an international crime against the human species."

A failure of these Nazis to heed, or to understand the force and meaning of this evolution in the legal thought of the world, is not a defense or a mitigation. If anything, it aggravates their offense and makes it the more mandatory that the law they have flouted be vindicated by juridical application to their lawless conduct. Indeed by their own law – had they heeded any law – these principles were binding on these defendants. Article 4 of the Weimar constitution provided that: "The generally accepted rules of international law are to be considered as binding integral parts of the law of the German Reich" (2050 – PS). Can there be any doubt that the outlawry of aggressive war was one of the "generally accepted rules of international law" in 1939?

Any resort to war – to any kind of a war – is a resort to means that are inherently criminal. War inevitably is a course of killings, assaults, deprivations of liberty, and destruction of property. An honestly defensive war is, of course, legal and saves those lawfully conducting it from criminality. But inherently criminal acts cannot be defended by showing that those who committed them were engaged in a war, when war itself is illegal. The very minimum legal consequence of the treaties making aggressive wars illegal is to strip those who incite or wage them of every defense the law ever gave, and to leave war-makers subject to judgment by the usually accepted principles of the law of crimes.

But if it be thought that the Charter, whose declarations concededly bind us all, does contain new law I still do not shrink from demanding its strict application by this Tribunal. The rule of law in the world, flouted by the lawlessness incited by these defendants, had to be restored at the cost to my country of over a million casualties, not to mention those of other nations. I cannot subscribe to the perverted reasoning that society may advance and strengthen the rule of law by the expenditure of morally innocent lives but that progress in the law may never be made at the price of morally guilty lives.

It is true of course, that we have no judicial precedent for the Charter. But international law is more than a scholarly collection of abstract and immutable principles. It is an outgrowth of treaties and agreements between nations and of accepted customs. Yet every custom has its origin in some single act, and every agreement has to be initiated by the action of some state. Unless we are prepared to abandon every principle of growth for international law, we cannot deny that our own day has the right to institute customs and to conclude agreements that will themselves become sources of a newer and strengthened international law. International law is not capable of development by the normal processes of legislation, for there is no continuing international legislative authority. Innovations and revisions in international law are brought about by the action of governments such as those I have cited, designed to meet a change in circumstances. It grows, as did the common law, through decisions reached from time to time in adapting settled principles to new situations. The fact is that when the law evolves by the case method, as did the common law and as international law must do if it is to advance at all, it advances at the expense of those who wrongly guessed the law and learned too late their error. The law, so far as international law can be decreed, had been clearly pronounced when these acts took place. Hence, I am not disturbed by the lack of judicial precedent for the inquiry it is proposed to conduct.

The events I have earlier recited clearly fall within the standards of Crimes, set out in the Charter, whose perpetrators this Tribunal is convened to judge and punish fittingly. The standards for War Crimes and Crimes against Humanity are too familiar to need comment. There are, however, certain novel problems in applying other precepts of the Charter which I should call to your attention.

The Crime against Peace:

A basic provision of the Charter is that to plan, prepare, initiate, or wage a war of aggression, or a war in violation of international treaties, agreements, and assurances, or to conspire or participate in a common plan to do so, is a crime.

It is perhaps a weakness in this Charter that it fails itself define a war of aggression. Abstractly, the subject is full of difficulty and all kinds of troublesome hypothetical cases can be conjured up. It is a subject which, if the defense should be permitted to go afield beyond the very narrow charge in the Indictment, would prolong the Trial and involve the Tribunal in insoluble political issues. But so far as the question can properly be involved in this case, the issue is one of no novelty and is one on which legal opinion has well crystalized.

One of the most authoritative sources of international law on this subject is the Convention for the Definition of Aggression signed at London on 7/3/1933 by Romania, Estonia, Latvia, Poland, Turkey, the Soviet Union, Persia, and Afghanistan. The subject has also been considered by international committees and by commentators whose views are entitled to the greatest respect. It had been little discussed prior to the first World War but has received much attention as international law has evolved its outlawry of aggressive war. In the light of these materials of international law and so far as relevant to the evidence in this case, I suggest that an "aggressor" is generally held to be that state which is the first to commit any of the following actions:

(1) Declaration of war upon another state;

(2) Invasion by its armed forces, with or without a declaration of war, of the territory of another state;

(3) Attack by its land, naval, or air forces, with or without a declaration of war, on the territory, vessels or aircraft of another state; and

(4) Provision of support to armed bands formed in the territory of another state, or refusal, notwithstanding the request of the invaded state, to take in its own territory, all the measures in its power to deprive those bands of all assistance or protection.

And I further suggest that it is the general view that no political military, economic, or other considerations shall serve as an excuse or justification for such actions; but exercise of the right of legitimate self – defense, that is to say, resistance to an act of aggression, or action to assist a state which has been subjected to aggression, shall not constitute a war of aggression.

It is upon such an understanding of the law that our evidence of a conspiracy to provoke and wage an aggressive war is prepared and presented. By this test each of the series of wars begun by these Nazi leaders was unambiguously aggressive.

It is important to the duration and scope of this Trial that we bear in mind the difference between our charge that this war was one of aggression and a position that Germany had no grievances. We are not inquiring into the conditions which contributed to causing this war. They are for history to unravel. It is no part of our task to vindicate the European status quo as of 1933, or as of any other date. The United States does not desire to enter into discussion of the complicated pre-war currents of European politics, and it hopes this trial will not be protracted by their consideration. The remote causations avowed are too insincere and inconsistent, too complicated and doctrinaire to be the subject of profitable inquiry in this trial. A familiar example is to be found in the *Lebensraum* slogan, which summarized the contention that Germany needed more living space as a justification for expansion. At the same time that the Nazis were demanding more space for the German people, they were demanding more German people to occupy space. Every known means to increase the birth rate, legitimate and illegitimate, was utilized. *"Lebensraum"* represented a vicious circle of demand; from neighbors more space, and from Germans more progeny. We do not need to investigate the verity of doctrines which led to constantly expanding circles of aggression. It is the plot and the act of aggression which we charge to be crimes.

Our position is that whatever grievances a nation may have, however objectionable it finds the status quo, aggressive warfare is illegal means for settling those grievances or for altering those conditions. It may be that the Germany of the 1920's and 1930's faced desperate problems, problems that would have warranted the boldest measures short of war. All other methods—persuasion, propaganda, economic competition, diplomacy—were open to an aggrieved country, but aggressive warfare was outlawed. These defendants did make aggressive war, a war in violation of treaties. They did attack and invade their neighbors in order to effectuate a foreign policy which they knew could not be accomplished by measures short of war. And that is as far as we accuse or propose to inquire.

The Law of Individual Responsibility:

The Charter also recognizes individual responsibility on the Part of those who commit acts defined as crimes, or who incite others to do so, or who join a common plan with other persons, groups or organizations to bring about their commission. The principle of individual responsibility for piracy and brigandage, which have long been recognized as crimes punishable under international law, is old and well established. That is what illegal warfare is.

This principle of personal liability is a necessary as well as logical one if international law is to render real help to the maintenance of peace. An international law which operates only on states can be enforced only by war because the most practicable method of coercing a state is warfare. Those familiar with American history know that one of the compelling reasons for adoption of our constitution was that the laws of the Confederation, which operated only on constituent states, were found ineffective to maintain order among them. The only answer to recalcitrance was impotence or war. Only sanctions which reach individuals can peacefully and effectively be enforced. Hence, the principle of the criminality of aggressive war is implemented by the Charter with the principle of personal responsibility. Of course, the idea that a state, any more than a corporation commits crimes, is a fiction. Crimes always are committed only by persons. While it is quite proper to employ the fiction of responsibility of a state or corporation for the purpose of imposing a collective liability, it is quite intolerable to let such a legalism become the basis of personal immunity. The Charter recognizes that one who has committed criminal acts may not take refuge in superior orders nor in the doctrine that his crimes were acts of states. These twin principles working together have heretofore resulted in immunity for practically everyone concerned in the really great crimes against peace and mankind. Those in lower ranks were protected against liability by the orders of their superiors. The superiors were protected because their orders were called acts of state. Under the Charter, no defense based on either of these doctrines can be entertained. Modern civilization puts unlimited weapons of destruction in the hands of men. It cannot tolerate so vast an area of legal irresponsibility. Even the German Military Code provides that: "If the execution of a military order in the course of duty violates the criminal law, then the superior officer giving the order will bear the sole responsibility therefor. However, the obeying subordinate will share the punishment of the participant: (1) if he has exceeded the order given to him, or (2) if it was within his knowledge that the order of his superior officer concerned an act by which it was intended to commit a civil or military crime or transgression." (*Reichsgesetzblatt*, 1926 No. 37, P. 278, Art. 47) Of course, we do not argue that the circumstances under which one commits an act should be disregarded in judging its legal effect. A conscripted private on a firing squad cannot expect to hold an inquest on the validity of the execution. The Charter implies common sense limits to liability just as it places common sense limits upon immunity. But none of these men before you acted in minor parts. Each of them was entrusted with broad discretion and exercised great power. Their responsibility is correspondingly great and may not be shifted to that fictional being, "the State", which cannot be produced for trial, cannot testify, and cannot be sentenced.

The Charter also recognizes a vicarious liability, which responsibility recognized by most modern systems of law, for acts committed by others in carrying out a common plan or conspiracy to which a defendant has become a party. I need not discuss the familiar principles of such liability. Every day in the courts of countries associated in this prosecution, men are convicted for acts that they did not personally commit, but for which they were held responsible because of membership in illegal combinations or plans or conspiracies.

The Political, Police, and Military Organizations:

Accused before this Tribunal as criminal organizations are certain political and police organizations which the evidence will show to have been instruments of cohesion in planning and executing the crimes I have detailed. Perhaps the worst of the movement were the Leadership Corps of the NSDAP, the *Schutzstaffeln* or "SS" and the *Sturmabteilungen* or "SA", and the subsidiary formations which these include. These were the Nazi Party leadership, espionage, and policing groups. They were the real government, above and outside of any law. Also accused as organizations are the Reich Cabinet and the Secret Police, or Gestapo, which were fixtures of the Government but animated solely by the Party.

Except for a late period when some compulsory recruiting was done in the SS, membership in all these militarized organizations was voluntary. The police organizations were recruited from ardent partisans who enlisted blindly to do the dirty work the leaders planned The Reich Cabinet was the governmental facade for Nazi Party Government and in its members legal, as well as actual responsibility was vested for the entire program. Collectively they were responsible for the program in general, individually they were especially responsible for segments of it. The finding which we ask you to make, that these are criminal organizations, will subject members to punishment to be hereafter determined by appropriate tribunals, unless some personal defense, such as becoming a member under threat to person, to family, or inducement by false representation, or the like, be established. Every member will have a chance to be heard in the subsequent forum on his personal relation to the organization, but your finding in this trial will conclusively establish the criminal character of the organization as a whole.

We have also accused as criminal organizations the High Command and the General Staff of the German Armed Forces. We recognize that to plan warfare is the business of professional soldiers in all countries. But it is one thing to plan strategic moves in the event war comes, and it is another thing to plot and intrigue to bring on that war. We will prove the leaders of the German General Staff and of the High Command to have been guilty of just that. Military men are not before you because they served their country. They are here because they mastered it, along with these others, and drove it to war. They are not here because they lost the war, but because they started it. Politicians may have thought of them as soldiers, but soldiers know they were politicians. We ask that the General Staff and the High Command, as defined in the Indictment, be condemned as a criminal group whose existence and tradition constitute a standing menace to the peace of the world.

These individual defendants did not stand alone in crime and will not stand alone in punishment. Your verdict of " guilty" against these organizations will render *prima facie* guilt, as nearly as we can learn, thousands upon thousands of members now in custody of United States forces and of other armies.

The responsibility of this Tribunal:

To apply the sanctions of the law to those whose conduct is found criminal by the standards I have outlined, is the responsibility committed to this Tribunal. It is the first court ever to undertake the difficult task of overcoming the confusion of many tongues and the conflicting concepts of just procedure among diverse systems of law, so as to reach a common judgment. The tasks of all of us are such as to make heavy demands on patience and good will. Although the need for prompt action has admittedly resulted in imperfect work on the part of the Prosecution, four great nations bring you their hurriedly assembled contributions of evidence. What remains undiscovered we can only guess. We could, with witnesses' testimony, prolong the recitals of crime for years; but to what avail. We shall rest the case when we have offered what seems convincing and adequate proof of the crimes charged without unnecessary cumulation of evidence. We doubt very much whether it will be seriously denied that the crimes I have outlined took place. The effort will undoubtedly be to mitigate or escape personal responsibility.

Among the nations which unite in accusing these defendants the United States is perhaps in a position to be the most dispassionate, for, having sustained the least injury, it is perhaps the least animated by vengeance. Our American cities have not been bombed by day and by night, by humans, and by robots. It is not our temples that had been laid in ruins. Our countrymen have not had homes destroyed over their heads. The menace of Nazi aggression, except to those in actual service, has seemed less personal and immediate to us than to

European peoples. But while the United States is not first in rancor, it is not second in determination that forces of law and order be made equal to the task of dealing such international lawlessness as I have recited here.

Twice in my lifetime, the United States has sent its young manhood across the Atlantic, drained its resources, and burdened itself with debt to help defeat Germany. But the real hope and faith that has sustained the American people in these great efforts was that victory for ourselves and our Allies would lay the basis for an ordered international relationship in Europe and would end the centuries of strife on this embattled continent.

Twice we have held back in the early stages of European conflict in the belief that it might be confined to a purely European affair. In the United States, we have tried to build an economy without armament, a system of government without militarism, and a society where men are not regimented for war. This purpose, we know now, can never be realized if the world periodically is to be embroiled in war. The United States cannot, generation after generation, throw its youth or its resources on to the battlefields of Europe to redress the lack of balance between Germany's strength and that of her enemies, and to keep the battles from our shores.

The American dream of a peace-and-plenty economy, as well as the hopes of other nations, can never be fulfilled if those nations are involved in a war every generation so vast and devastating as to crush the generation that fights and burden the generation that follows. But experience has shown that wars are no longer local. All modern wars become world wars eventually. And none of the big nations at least can stay out. If we cannot stay out of wars, our only hope is to prevent wars.

I am too well aware of the weaknesses of juridical action alone to contend that in itself your decision under this Charter can prevent future wars. Judicial action always comes after the event. Wars are started only on the theory and in the confidence that they can be won. Personal punishment, to be suffered only in the event the war is lost, will probably not be a sufficient deterrent to prevent a war where the war-makers feel the chances of defeat to be negligible.

But the ultimate step in avoiding periodic wars, which are inevitable in a system of international lawlessness, is to make statesmen responsible to law. And let me make clear that while this law is first applied against German aggressors, the law includes, and if it is to serve a useful purpose it must condemn aggression by any other nations, including those which sit here now in judgment. We are able to do away with domestic tyranny and violence and aggression by those in power against the rights of their own people only when we make all men answerable to the law. This trial represents mankind's desperate effort to apply the discipline of the law to statesmen who have used their powers of state to attack the foundations of the world's peace and to commit aggressions against the rights of their neighbors.

The usefulness of this effort to do justice is not to be measured by considering the law or your judgment in isolation. This trial is part of the great effort to make the peace more secure. One step in this direction is the United Nations organization, which may take joint political action to prevent war if possible, and joint military action to insure that any nation which starts a war will lose it. This Charter and this Trial, implementing the Kellogg-Briand Pact, constitute another step in the same direction – juridical action of a kind to ensure that those who start a war will pay for it personally.

While the defendants and the prosecutors stand before you as individuals, it is not the triumph of either group alone that is committed to your judgment. Above all personalities there are anonymous and impersonal forces whose conflict makes up much of human history. It is yours to throw the strength of the law back of either the one or the other of these forces for at least another generation. What are the real forces that are contending before you?

No charity can disguise the fact that the forces which these defendants represent, the forces that would advantage and delight in their acquittal, are the darkest and most sinister forces in society; dictatorship and oppression, malevolence and passion, militarism and lawlessness. By their fruits we best know them. Their acts have bathed the world in blood and set civilization back a century. They have subjected their European neighbors to every outrage and torture, every spoliation and deprivation that insolence, cruelty, and greed could inflict. They have brought the German people to the lowest pitch of wretchedness, from which they can entertain no hope of early deliverance. They have stirred hatreds and incited domestic violence on every continent. These are the things that stand in the dock shoulder to shoulder with these prisoners.

The real complaining party at your bar is Civilization. In all countries it is still a struggling and imperfect thing. It does not plead that the United States, or any other country, has been blameless of the conditions which made the German people easy victims to the blandishments and intimidations of the Nazi conspirators.

But it points to the dreadful sequence of aggressions and crimes I have recited, it points to the weariness of flesh, the exhaustion of resources and the destruction of all that was beautiful or useful in so much of the world, and to greater potentialities for destruction in the days to come. It is not necessary among the ruins of this ancient and beautiful city with untold members of its civilian habitants still buried in its rubble, to argue the proposition that to start or wage an aggressive war has the moral qualities of the worst of crimes. The refuge of the defendants can be only their hope that international law will lag so far behind the moral sense of mankind that conduct which is crime in the moral sense must be regarded as innocent in law.

Civilization asks whether law is so laggard as to be utterly helpless to deal with crimes of this magnitude by criminals of this order of importance. It does not expect that you can make war impossible. It does expect that your juridical action will put the forces of international law, its precepts, its prohibitions and, most of all, its sanctions, on the side of peace, so that men and women of good will, in all countries, may have "leave to live by no man's leave, underneath the law."

Testimony of SS General Otto Ohlendorf

Einsatzgruppe D

COLONEL JOHN HARLAN AMEN (Associate Trial Counsel for the United States): May it please the Tribunal, I wish to call as a witness for the Prosecution, Mr. Otto Ohlendorf ...

[Witness Otto Ohlendorf took the stand]

THE PRESIDENT: Otto Ohlendorf, will you repeat this oath after me" "I swear by God the Almighty and Omniscient that I will speak the pure truth and will withhold and add nothing."

[The witness repeated the oath]

COL. AMEN: Will you try to speak slowly and pause between each question and answer.

OTTO OHLENDORF: Yes.

COL. AMEN: Where were you born?

OHLENDORF: In Hohen-Egelsen.

COL. AMEN: How old are you?

OHLENDORF: Thirty-eight years old.

COL. AMEN: When, if ever, did you become a member of the National Socialist Party?

OHLENDORF: 1925.

COL. AMEN: When, if ever, did you become a member of the SA?

OHLENDORF: For the first time in 1926.

COL. AMEN: When, if ever, did you become a member of the SS?

OHLENDORF: I must correct my answer to the previous question. I thought you were asking about my membership in the SS.

COL. AMEN: When did you become a member of the SA?

OHLENDORF: In the year 1925.

COL. AMEN: When, if ever, did you join the SD?

OHLENDORF: In 1936.

COL. AMEN: What was your last position in the SD?

OHLENDORF: Chief of Amt III in the RSHA....

COL. AMEN: Did you tell us for what period of time you continued as chief of Amt III?

OHLENDORF: I was part-time chief of Amt III from 1939 to 1945.

COL. AMEN: Turning now to the designation "Mobile Units" with the army shown in the lower right hand corner of the chart, please explain to the Tribunal the significance of the terms "*Einsatzgruppe*" and "*Einsatzkommando.*"

OHLENDORF: The concept "*Einsatzgruppe*" was established after an agreement between the chiefs of the RSHA, OKW, and OKH, on the seperate use of Sipo units in the operational areas. The concept of "*Einsatzgruppe*" first appeared during the Polish campaign.

The agreement with the OKH and OKW however, was arrived at only before the beginning of the Russian campaign. This agreement specified that a representative of the chief of the Sipo and the SD would be assigned to the army groups, or armies, and that this official would have at his disposal mobile units of the Sipo and the SD in the form of an *Einsatzgruppe*, subdivided into *Einsatzkommandos*. The *Einsatzkommandos* would, on orders from the army group or army, be assigned to the individual army units as needed.

COL. AMEN: State, if you know, whether prior to the campaign against Soviet Russia, any agreement was entered into between the OKW, OKH, and RHSA?

OHLENDORF: Yes, the *Einsatzgruppen* and *Einsatzkommandos*, as I have just described them, were used on the basis of a written agreement between the OKW, OKH, and RHSA.

COL. AMEN: How do you know that there was such a written agreement?

OHLENDORF: I was repeatedly present during the negotiations which Albrecht and Schellenberg conducted with the OKH and OKW; and I also had a written copy of this agreement which was the outcome of these negotiations, in my own hands when I took over the *Einsatzgruppe*.

COL. AMEN: Explain to the Tribunal who Schellenberg was. What position, if any, did he occupy?

OHLENDORF: Schellenberg was, at the end, chief of Amt VI in the RHSA; at the time when he was conducting as the representative of Heydrich, he belonged to the Amt VI.

COL. AMEN: On approximately what date did these negotiations take place?

OHLENDORF: The negotiations lasted several weeks. The agreement must have been reached one or two weeks before the beginning of the campaign.

COL. AMEN: Did you yourself ever see a copy of this written agreement?

OHLENDORF: Yes!

COL. AMEN: Did you ever have occasion to work with this written agreement?

OHLENDORF: Yes!

COL. AMEN: On more than one occasion?

OHLENDORF: Yes; in all questions arising out of the relationship between the *Einsatzgruppen* and the army.

COL. AMEN: Do you know where the original or any copy of that agreement is located today?

OHLENDORF: No.

COL. AMEN: To the best of your knowledge and recollection, please explain to the Tribunal the entire substance of this written agreement.

OHLENDORF: First of all, the agreement stated that *Einsatzgruppen* and *Einsatzkommandos* would be set up and used in the operational areas. This created a precedent, because until that time the army had, on its own responsibility, discharged the tasks which would now fall solely to the Sipo. The second was the regulations as to competence.

COL. AMEN: You're going too fast. What is it that you say the *Einsatzkommandos* did under the agreement?

OHLENDORF: I said this was the relationship between the army and the *Einsatzgruppen* and the *Einsatzkommandos*. The agreement specified that the army groups or armies would be responsible for the movement and the supply of *Einsatzgruppen*, but that instructions for their activities would come from the chief of Sipo and the SD.

COL. AMEN: Let us understand. It is correct that an *Einsatz* group was to be attached to each army group or army?

OHLENDORF: Every army group was to have an *Einsatzgruppe* attached to it. The army group in its turn would then attach the *Einsatzkommandos* to the armies of the army group.

COL. AMEN: And was the army command to determine the area within which the *Einsatz* group was to operate?

OHLENDORF: The operational area of the *Einsatzgruppe* was already determined by the fact that it was attached to a specific army group and therefore moved with it, whereas the operational areas of the *Einsatzkommandos* were fixed by the army group or army.

COL. AMEN: Did the agreement also provide that the army command was to direct the time during which they were to operate?

OHLENDORF: That was included under the heading "movement."

COL. AMEN: And, also, to direct any additional tasks that they were to operate?

OHLENDORF: Yes. Even though the chiefs of Sipo and SD had the right to issue instructions to them on their work, there existed a general agreement that the army was also entitled to issue orders to the *Einsatzgruppen* if the operational situation made it necessary.

COL. AMEN: What did the agreement provide with respect to the attachment of the *Einsatz* group command to this army command?

OHLENDORF: I can't remember whether anything specific was contained in the agreement about that. At any rate a liason man between the army command and the SD was appointed.

COL. AMEN: Do you recall any other provisions of this written agreement?

OHLENDORF: I believe I can state the main contents of that agreement.

COL. AMEN: What position did you occupy with respect to this agreement?

OHLENDORF: From June 1941 to the death of Heydrich in June 1942, I led *Einsatzgruppe* D, and was the representative of the chief of the Sipo and the SD with the 11th Army.

COL. AMEN: And when was Heydrich's death?

OHLENDORF: Heydrich was wounded at the end of May 1942, and died on 4 June 1942.

COL. AMEN: How much advance notice, if any, did you have of the campaign against Soviet Russia?

OHLENDORF: About four weeks.

COL. AMEN: How many *Einsatz* groups were there, and who were their respective leaders?

OHLENDORF: There were four *Einsatzgruppen*, Groups A, B, C, and D. Chief of *Einsatzgruppe* A was Stahlecker; chief of *Einsatzgruppe* B was Nebe; chief of *Einsatzgruppe* C, Dr. Rasche, and later, Dr.Thomas; chief of *Einsatzgruppe* D I myself, and later Bierkamp.

COL. AMEN: To which army was Group D attached?

OHLENDORF: Group D was not attached to any army group but was attached directly to the 11th Army.

COL. AMEN: Where did Group D operate?

OHLENDORF: Group D operated in the southern Ukraine.

COL. AMEN: Will you describe in more detail the nature and extent of the area in which Group D originally operated, naming the cities or territories?

OHLENDORF: The northernmost city was Cernauti; then southward through Mohilev-Podolsk, Yampol, then eastward Zuvalje, Czervind, Melitopol, Mariopol, Taganrog, Rostov, and the Crimea.

COL. AMEN: What was the ultimate objective of Group D?

OHLENDORF: Group D was held in reserve for the Caucasus, for an army group which was to operate in the Caucasus.

COL. AMEN: When did Group D commence to move into Soviet Russia?

OHLENDORF: Group D left Duegen on 21 June and reached Pietra Namsk in Romania in three days. There the first *Einsatzkommandos* were already being demanded by the army, and they immediately set off for the destinations named by the army. The entire *Einsatzgruppe* was put into operation at the beginning of July.

COL. AMEN: You are referring to the 11th Army?

OHLENDORF: Yes.

COL. AMEN: In what respects, if any, were the official duties of the *Einsatz* groups concerned with Jews and Communist commissars?

OHLENDORF: The instructions were that in the Russian operational areas of the *Einsatzgruppen* the Jews, as well as the Soviet political commissars, were to be liquidated.

COL. AMEN: And when you say "liquidated" do you mean "killed"?

OHLENDORF: Yes, I mean "killed".

COL. AMEN: Prior to the opening of the Soviet campaign, did you attend a conference at Pretz?

OHLENDORF: Yes, it was a conference at which the *Einsatzgruppen* and the *Einsatzkommandos* were informed of their tasks and were given the necessary orders.

COL. AMEN: Who was present at that conference?

OHLENDORF: The chiefs of the *Einsatzgruppen* and the commanders of the *Einsatzkommandos* and Streckenbach of the RHSA who transmitted the orders of Heydrich and Himmler.

COL. AMEN: What were those orders?

OHLENDORF: Those were the general orders of the normal work of the Sipo and the SD, and in addition the liquidation order which I have already mentioned.

COL. AMEN: And that conference took place on approximately what date?

OHLENDORF: About three or four days before the mission.

COL. AMEN: So that before you commenced to march into Soviet Russia you received orders at this conference to exterminate the Jews and Communist functionaries in addition to the regular professional work of the Security Police and SD; is that correct?

OHLENDORF: Yes.

COL. AMEN: Did you, personally, have any conversation with Himmler respecting any communication from Himmler to the chiefs of army groups and armies concerning this mission?

OHLENDORF: Yes. Himmler told me that before the beginning of the Russian campaign Hitler had spoken of this mission to a conference of the army groups and the army chiefs – no, not the army chiefs but the commanding generals – and had instructed the commanding generals to provide the necessary support.

COL. AMEN: So that you can testify that the chiefs of the army groups and the armies had been similarly informed of these orders for the liquidation of the Jews and Soviet functionaries?

OHLENDORF: I don't think it is quite correct to put it in that form. They had no orders for liquidation; the order for the liquidation was given to Himmler to carry out, but since this liquidation took place in the operational area of the army group or the armies, they had to be ordered to provide support. Moreover, without such instructions to the army, the activities of the *Einsatzgruppen* would not have been possible.

COL. AMEN: Did you have any other conversation with Himmler concerning this order?

OHLENDORF: Yes, in late summer of 1941 Himmler was in Nikolaiev. He assembled the leaders and men of the *Einsatzkommandos*, repeated to them the liquidation order, and pointed out that the leaders and men who were taking part in the liquidation bore no personal responsibility for the execution of this order. The responsibility was his, alone, and the Führer's.

COL. AMEN: And you yourself heard that said?

OHLENDORF: Yes.

COL. AMEN: Do you know whether this mission of the *Einsatz* group was known to the army group commanders?

OHLENDORF: This order and the execution of these orders were known to the commanding general of the army.

COL. AMEN: How do you know that?

OHLENDORF: Through conferences with the army and through instructions that were given by the army on the execution of the order.

COL. AMEN: Was the mission of the *Einsatz* groups and the agreement between OKW, OKH, and RSHA known to the other leaders in the RSHA?

OHLENDORF: At least some of them knew it, since some of the leaders were also active in the *Einsatzgruppen* and *Einsatzkommandos* in the course of time. Furthermore, the leaders who were dealing with the organization and legal aspects of the *Einsatzgruppen* also knew of it.

COL. AMEN: Most of the leaders came from the RSHA, did they not?

OHLENDORF: Which leaders?

COL. AMEN: Of the *Einsatz* groups?

OHLENDORF: No, one can't say that. The leaders of the *Einsatzgruppen* and *Einsatzkommandos* came from all over the Reich.

COL. AMEN: Do you know whether the mission and the agreement were known to Kaltenbrunner?

OHLENDORF: After his assumption of office Kaltenbrunner had to deal with these questions and consequently must have known details of the *Einsatzgruppen* which were offices of his.

COL. AMEN: Who was the commanding officer of the 11th Army?

OHLENDORF: At first, Riter von Schober; later Von Manstein.

COL. AMEN: Will you tell the Tribunal in what way or ways the command officer of the 11th Army directed or supervised *Einsatz* Group D in carrying out its liquidation activities?

OHLENDORF: An order from the 11th Army was sent to Nikolaiev that liquidations were to take place only at a distance of not less than two hundred kilometers from the headquarters of the commanding general.

COL. AMEN: Do you recall any other occasions?

OHLENDORF: In Simferopol the army command requested the *Einsatzkommandos* in its area to hasten liquidations, because famine was threatening and there was a great housing shortage.

COL. AMEN: Do you know how many persons were liquidated by *Einsatz* Group D under your command?

OHLENDORF: In the year between June 1941 to June 1942 the *Einsatzkommandos* reported ninety thousand people liquidated.

COL. AMEN: Did that include men, women, and children?

OHLENDORF: Yes.

COL. AMEN: On what do you base those figures?

OHLENDORF: On reports sent by the *Einsatzkommandos* to the *Einsatzgruppen*.

COL. AMEN: Were those reports submitted to you?

OHLENDORF: Yes.

COL. AMEN: And you saw them and read them?

OHLENDORF: I beg your pardon?

COL. AMEN: And you saw and read those reports personally?

OHLENDORF: Yes.

COL. AMEN: And it is on those reports that you base the figures you have given the Tribunal?

OHLENDORF: Yes.

COL. AMEN: Do you know how those figures compare with the number of persons liquidated by other *Einsatzgruppen*?

OHLENDORF: The figures which I saw of other *Einsatzgruppen* are considerably larger.

COL. AMEN: That was due to what factor?

OHLENDORF: I believe that to a large extent the figures submitted by the other *Einsatzgruppen* were exaggerated.

COL. AMEN: Did you see reports of liquidations from the other *Einsatz* units from time to time?

OHLENDORF: Yes.

COL. AMEN: And those reports showed liquidations exceeding those of Group D; is that correct?

OHLENDORF: Yes.

COL. AMEN: Did you personally supervise mass executions of these individuals?

OHLENDORF: I was present at two mass executions for purposes of inspection.

COL. AMEN: Will you explain in detail to the Tribunal how an individual mass execution was carried out?

OHLENDORF: A local *Einsatzkommando* attempted to collect all the Jews in its area by registering them. This registration was performed by the Jews themselves.

COL. AMEN: On what pretext, if any, were they rounded up?

OHLENDORF: On the pretext that they were to be resettled.

COL. AMEN: Will you continue?

OHLENDORF: After the registration the Jews were collected at one place; and from there they were later transported to the place of execution, which was, as a rule, an antitank ditch or a natural excavation. The executions were carried out in a military manner, by firing squads under command.

COL. AMEN: In what way were they transported to the place of execution?

OHLENDORF: They were transported to the place of execution in trucks, always only as many as could be executed immediately. In this way it was attempted to keep the span of time from the moment in which the victims knew what was about to happen to them until the time of their actual execution as short as possible.

COL. AMEN: Was that your idea?

OHLENDORF: Yes.

COL. AMEN: And after they were shot what was done with the bodies?

OHLENDORF: The bodies were buried in the antitank ditch or excavation.

COL. AMEN: What determination, if any, was made as to whether the persons were actually dead?

OHLENDORF: The unit leaders or the firing-squad commanders had orders to see to this and, if need be, finish them off themselves.

COL. AMEN: And who would do that?

OHLENDORF: Either the unit leader himself or somebody designated by him.

COL. AMEN: In what positions were the victims shot?

OHLENDORF: Standing or kneeling.

COL. AMEN: What was done with the personal property of the persons executed?

OHLENDORF: All valuables were confiscated at the time of the registration or the rounding up and handed over to the Finance Ministry, either through the RSHA or directly. At first the clothing was given to the population, but in the winter of 1941-42 it was collected and disposed of by the NSV.

COL. AMEN: All their personal property was registered at that time?

OHLENDORF: No, not all of it, only valuables were registered.

COL. AMEN: What happened to the garments which the victims were wearing when they went to the place of execution?

OHLENDORF: They were obliged to take off their outer garments immediately before the execution.

COL. AMEN: All of them?

OHLENDORF: The outer garments, yes.

COL. AMEN: How about the rest of the garments they were wearing?

OHLENDORF: The other garments remained on the bodies.

COL. AMEN: Was that true of not only your group but of the other *Einsatz* groups?

OHLENDORF: That was the order in my *Einsatzgruppe*. I don't know how it was done in other *Einsatzgruppen*.

COL. AMEN: In what way did they handle it.

OHLENDORF: Some of the unit leaders did not carry out liquidations in the military manner, but killed the victims singly by shooting them in the back of the neck.

COL. AMEN: And you objected to that procedure?

OHLENDORF: I was against that procedure, yes.

COL. AMEN: For what reason?

OHLENDORF: Because, both for the victims and for those who carried out the executions, it was, psychologically, an immense burden to bear.

COL. AMEN: Now, what was done with the property collected from the *Einsatzkommandos* from these victims?

OHLENDORF: All valuables were sent to Berlin, to the RSHA or to the Reich Ministry of Finance. The articles which could not be used in the operational area, were disposed of there.

COL. AMEN: For example, what happened to gold and silver taken from the victims?

OHLENDORF: That was, as I have just said, turned over to Berlin, to the Reich Ministry of Finance.

COL. AMEN: How do you know that?

OHLENDORF: I can remember that it was actually handled in that way from Simferopol.

COL. AMEN: How about watches, for example, taken from the victims?

OHLENDORF: At the request of the army, watches were made available to the forces at the front.

COL. AMEN: Were all victims, including the men, women, and children executed in the same manner?

OHLENDORF: Until the spring of 1942, yes. Then an order came from Himmler that in the future women and children were to be killed only in gas vans.

COL. AMEN: How had women and children been killed previously?

OHLENDORF: In the same way as the men – by shooting.

COL. AMEN: What, if anything, was done about burying the victims after they had been executed?

OHLENDORF: The *kommandos* filled the graves to efface the signs of execution, and then labor units of the population leveled them.

COL. AMEN: Referring to the gas vans that you said you received in the spring of 1942, what order did you receive in respect to the use of these vans?

OHLENDORF: These vans were in the future to be used for killing of women and children.

COL. AMEN: Will you explain to the Tribunal the construction of these vans and their appearance?

OHLENDORF: The actual purpose of these vans could not be seen from the outside. They looked like closed trucks, and were so constructed that at the start of the motor, gas was conducted into the van causing death in ten to fifteen minutes.

COL. AMEN: Explain in detail just how one of these vans was used for an execution.

OHLENDORF: The vans were loaded with the victims and driven to the place of burial, which was usually the same as that used for the mass executions. The time needed for transportation was sufficient to insure the death of the victims.

COL. AMEN: How were the victims induced to enter the vans?

OHLENDORF: They were told that they were to be transported to another locality.

COL. AMEN: How was the gas turned on?

OHLENDORF: I am not familiar with technical details.

COL. AMEN: How long did it take to kill the victims ordinarily?

OHLENDORF: About ten to fifteen minutes; the victims were not conscious of what was happening to them.

COL. AMEN: How many people could be killed simultaneously?

OHLENDORF: About fifteen to twenty-five persons. The vans varied in size.

COL. AMEN: Did you receive reports from those persons operating the vans from time to time?

OHLENDORF: I didn't understand the question.

COL. AMEN: Did you receive reports from those who were working on the vans?

OHLENDORF: I received the report that the *Einsatzkommandos* did not willingly use the vans.

COL. AMEN: Why not?

OHLENDORF: Because the burial of the victims was a great ordeal for the members of the *Einsatzkommandos*.

COL. AMEN: Now, will you tell the Tribunal who furnished these vans to the *Einsatz* groups?

OHLENDORF: The gas vans did not belong to the motor pool of the *Einsatzgruppen* but were assigned to the *Einsatzgruppe* as a special unit, headed by the man who had constructed the vans. The vans were assigned to the *Einsatzgruppen* by the RSHA.

COL. AMEN: Were the vans supplied to all of the different *Einsatz* groups?

OHLENDORF: I am not certain. I know only in the case of *Einsatzgruppe* D, and indirectly that *Einsatzgruppe* C also made use of these vans.

COL. AMEN: Referring to your previous testimony, will you explain to the Tribunal why you believe that the type of execution ordered by you, namely, military, was preferable to the shooting-in-the-neck procedure adopted by the other *Einsatz* groups?

OHLENDORF: On the one hand, the aim was that the individual leaders and men should be able to carry out the executions in a military manner acting on orders and should not have to make a decision of their own; it was, to all intents and purposes, an order which they were to carry out. On the other hand, it was known to me that through the emotional excitement of the executions ill treatment could not be avoided, since the victims discovered too soon that they were to be executed and could not therefore endure prolonged nervous strain. And it seemed intolerable to me that individual leaders and men should in consequence be forced to kill a large number of people on their own decision.

COL. AMEN: In what manner did you determine which were the Jews to be executed?

OHLENDORF: That was not part of my task; but the identification of the Jews was carried out by the Jews themselves, since the registration was handled by a Jewish Council of Elders.

COL. AMEN: Did the amount of Jewish blood have anything to do with it?

OHLENDORF: I can't remember the details, but I believe that half-Jews were also considered as Jews.

COL. AMEN: What organization furnished most of the officer personnel of the *Einsatz* groups and *Einsatzkommandos*?

OHLENDORF: I did not understand the question.

COL. AMEN: What organization furnished most of the officer personnel of the *Einsatz* groups?

OHLENDORF: The officer personnel was furnished by the State Police, the Kripo, and, to a lesser extent by the SD.

COL. AMEN: Kripo?

OHLENDORF: Yes, the State Police, the Criminal Police and, to a lesser extent, the SD.

COL. AMEN: Were there any other sources of personnel?

OHLENDORF: Yes, most of the men by the Waffen SS and the *Ordnungspolizie*. The State Police and the Kripo furnished most of the experts and the troops were furnished by the Waffen SS and the *Ordungspolizei*.

COL. AMEN: How about the Waffen SS.

OHLENDORF: The Waffen SS and the *Ordungspolizei* were each supposed to supply the *Einsatzgruppen* with one company.

COL. AMEN: How about the Order Police.

OHLENDORF: The *Ordnungspolizei* also furnished the *Einsatzgruppen* with one company.

COL. AMEN: What was the size of *Einsatz* Group D and its operating area as compared with other *Einsatz* groups?

OHLENDORF: I estimate that *Einsatzgruppen* D was one-half or two-thirds as large as the other *Einsatzgruppen*. That changed in the course of time since some of the *Einsatzgruppen* were greatly enlarged.

COL. AMEN: May it please the Tribunal, relating to organizational matters which I think would clarify some of the evidence which has already been in part received by the Tribunal. But I don't want to take the time of the Tribunal unless they feel that they want any more such testimony. I thought perhaps if any members of the Tribunal had any questions they would ask the witness directly because he is the best informed on these organizational matters of anyone who will be presented in court.

THE PRESIDENT: Colonel Amen, the Tribunal does not think that it is necessary to go further into the organizational questions at this stage, but it is a matter that must be really decided by you because you know what nature of the evidence which you are considering is.

So far as the Tribunal is concerned, they are satisfied at the present stage to leave the matter where it stands, but there is one aspect of the witness's evidence which the Tribunal would like you to investigate, and that is whether the practices by which he has been speaking continued after 1942, and for how long.

COL. AMEN: [To the witness] Can you state whether the liquidation practices that you have described continued after 1942 and, if so, for how long a period of time thereafter?

OHLENDORF: I don't think that the basic order was ever revoked. But I cannot remember the details – at least not with regard to Russia – which would enable me to make concrete statements on this subject. The retreat began very shortly thereafter, so that the operational region of the *Einsatzgruppen* became ever smaller. I do know, however, that other *Einsatzgruppen* with similiar orders had been envisaged for other areas.

COL. AMEN: Your personal knowledge extends up to what date?

OHLENDORF: I know that the liquidation of Jews was prohibited about six months before the end of the war. I also saw a document terminating the liquidation of Soviet commissary but I cannot recall a specific date.

COL. AMEN: Do you know whether in fact it was so terminated?

OHLENDORF: Yes, I believe so.

THE PRESIDENT: The Tribunal would like to know the number of men in your *Einsatz* group.

OHLENDORF: There were about five hundred men in my *Einsatzgruppe*, excluding those who were added to the goup as assistants from the country itself.

COL. AMEN: May it please the Tribunal. The witness is now available to other counsel. I understand that Colonel Pokrovsky has some questions that he wished to ask on behalf of the Soviets.

COLONEL Y. V. POKROVSKY (Deputy Chief Prosecutor for the USSR): The testimony of the witness is important for the clarification of questions in a report on which the Soviet delegation is at present working. Therefore, with the permission of the Tribunal, I would like to put a number of questions to the witness.

[Turning to the witness]

Witness, you said that you were present twice at mass executions. On whose orders were you an inspector at the executions?

OHLENDORF: I was present at the executions on my own iniative.

COL. POKROVSKY: But you said you attended as inspector.

OHLENDORF: I said that I attended for inspection purposes.

COL. POKROVSKY: On your own initiative?

OHLENDORF: Yes.

COL. POKROVSKY: Did one of your chiefs always attend the executions for purposes of inspection?

OHLENDORF: Whenever possible I sent a member of the staff of the *Einsatzgruppen* to witness the executions but this was not always feasible since the *Einsatzgruppen* had to operate over great distances.

COL. POKROVSKY: Why was some person sent for purposes of inspection?

OHLENDORF: Would you please repeat the question?

COL. POKROVSKY: For what purpose was an inspector sent?

OHLENDORF: To determine whether or not my instructions regarding the manner of the execution were actually carried out.

COL. POKROVSKY: Am I to understand that the inspector was to make certain that the execution had actually been carried out?

OHLENDORF: No, it would not be correct to say that. He was to ascertain whether the conditions which I had set for the execution were actually being carried out.

COL. POKROVSKY: What manner of conditions had you in mind?

OHLENDORF: One: exclusion of the public; two: military execution by a firing-squad; three: arrival of transports and carrying out of the liquidation in a smooth manner to avoid unnecessary excitement; four: supervision of the property to prevent looting. There may have been other details that I no longer remember. At any rate, all ill-treatment, whether physical or mental, was to be prevented through these measures.

COL. POKROVSKY: You wished to make sure that what you considered to be an equitable distribution of this property was effected, or did you aspire to complete acquisition of the valuables?

OHLENDORF: Yes.

COL. POKROVSKY: You spoke of ill-treatment. What did you mean by ill-treatment at the executions?

OHLENDORF: If, for instance, the manner in which the executions were carried out caused excitement and disobedience among the victims, so that the *kommandos* were forced to restore order by means of violence.

COL. POKROVSKY: What do you mean by "restore order by means of violence"? What do you mean by supression of the excitement amongst the victims by means of violence?

OHLENDORF: If, as I have already said, in order to carry out the liquidation in an orderly fashion it was necessary, for example, to resort to beating.

COL. POKROVSKY: Was it absolutely necessary to beat the victims?

OHLENDORF: I myself never witnessed it, but I heard of it.

COL. POKROVSKY: From whom?

OHLENDORF: In conversations with members of other *kommandos*.

COL. POKROVSKY: You said that cars, autocars, were used for the executions?

OHLENDORF: Yes.

COL. POKROVSKY: Do you know where, and with whose assistance, the inventor, Becker, was able to put his invention into practice?

OHLENDORF: I remember only that it was done through Amt II of the RSHA; but I can no longer say that with certainty.

COL. POKROVSKY: How many persons were executed in these cars?

OHLENDORF: I did not understand the question.

COL. POKROVSKY: How many persons were executed by means of these cars?

OHLENDORF: I cannot give precise figures, but the number was comparatively small – perhaps a few hundred.

COL. POKROVSKY: You said that mostly women and children were executed in these vans. For what reason?

OHLENDORF: That was a special order from Himmler to the effect that women and children were not to be exposed to the mental strain of the executions; and thus the men of the *kommandos*, mostly married men, should not be compelled to aim at women and children.

COL. POKROVSKY: Did anybody observe the behavior of the persons executed in these vans?

OHLENDORF: Yes, the doctor.

COL. POKROVSKY: Did you know that Becker had reported that death in these vans was particularly agonizing?

OHLENDORF: No. I learned of Becker's reports for the first time from the letter to Rauff, which was shown to me here. On the contrary, I know from the doctor's reports that the victims were not conscious of their impending death.

COL. POKROVSKY: Did any military units – I mean, army units – take part in these mass executions?

OHLENDORF: As a rule, no.

COL. POKROVSKY: And as an exception?

OHLENDORF: I think I remember that in Nikolaiev and in Simferopol a spectator from the Army High Command was present for a short time.

COL. POKROVSKY: For what purpose?

OHLENDORF: I don't know, probably to obtain information personally.

COL. POKROVSKY: Were military units assigned to carry out the executions in these towns?

OHLENDORF: Officially, the army did not assign any units for this purpose; the army as such was actually opposed to the liquidations.

COL. POKROVSKY: But in practice?

OHLENDORF: Individual units occasionally volunteered. However, at the moment I know of no such case among the army itself, but only among units attached to the army (*Heeresgefolge*).

COL. POKROVSKY: You were the man by whose orders people were sent to their death. Were Jews only handed over for execution by the *Einsatzgruppe* or were Communists – "Communist officials" you call them in your instructions – handed over for execution along with the Jews?

OHLENDORF: Yes, activists and political commissars. Mere membership in the Communist Party was not sufficient to persecute or kill a man.

COL. POKROVSKY: Were any special investigations made concerning the part played by persons in the Communist Party?

OHLENDORF: No, I said on the contrary that mere membership of the Communist Party was not, in itself, a determining factor in persecuting or executing a man; he had to have a special political function.

COL. POKROVSKY: Did you have any discussions on the murder vans sent from Berlin and on their use?

OHLENDORF: I did not understand the question.

COL. POKROVSKY: Had you occasion to discuss, with your chiefs and your collegues, the fact that motor vans had been sent to your own particular *Einsatzgruppe* from Berlin for carrying out the executions? Do you remember any such discussion?

OHLENDORF: I do not remember any specific discussion.

COL. POKROVSKY: Had you any information concerning the fact that members of the execution squad in charge of the executions were unwilling to use the vans?

OHLENDORF: I knew that the *Einsatzkommandos* were using the vans.

COL. POKROVSKY: No, I had something else in mind. I wanted to know whether you received reports that members of the execution squads were unwilling to use the vans and preferred other means of execution?

OHLENDORF: That they would rather kill by means of the gas vans than by shooting?

COL. POKROVSKY: On the contrary, that they preferred execution by shooting to killing by means of the gas vans.

OHLENDORF: You have already said the gas van.

COL. POKROVSKY: And why did they prefer execution by shooting to killing in the gas vans?

OHLENDORF: Because, as I have already said, in the opinion of the leader of the *Einsatzkommandos*, the unloading of the corpses was an unnecessary mental strain.

COL. POKROVSKY: What do you mean by "an unnecessary mental strain"?

OHLENDORF: As far as I can remember the conditions at that time – the picture presented by the corpses and probably because certain functions of the body had taken place leaving the corpses lying in filth.

COL. POKROVSKY: You mean to say that the sufferings endured prior to death were clearly visible on the victims? Did I understand you correctly?

OHLENDORF: I don't understand the question; do you mean during the killing in the van?

COL. POKROVSKY: Yes.

OHLENDORF: I can only repeat what the doctor told me, that the victims were not conscious of their death in the van.

COL. POKROVSKY: In that case, your reply to my previous question, that the unloading of the bodies made a very terrible impression on the members of the execution squad, becomes entirely incomprehensible.

OHLENDORF: And, as I said, the terrible impression created by the position of corpses themselves, and probably by the state of the vans which had probably been dirtied and so on.

COL. POKROVSKY: I have no further questions to put to this witness at the present stage of the trial.

THE TRIBUNAL (Gen. Niktchenko): In your testimony you said that the *Einsatz* group had the object of annihilating the Jews and the commissars, is that correct?

OHLENDORF: Yes.

THE TRIBUNAL (Gen. Niktchenko): And in what category did you consider the children? For what reason were the children massacred?

OHLENDORF: The order was that the Jewish population should be totally exterminated.

THE TRIBUNAL (Gen. Niktchenko): Including the children?

OHLENDORF: Yes.

THE TRIBUNAL (Gen. Niktchenko): Were all the Jewish children murdered?

OHLENDORF: Yes.

THE TRIBUNAL (Gen. Niktchenko): But the children of those whom you considered as belonging to the category of commissars, were they also killed?

OHLENDORF: I am not aware that inquiries were ever made after the families of Soviet commmissars.

THE TRIBUNAL (Gen. Niktchenko): Did you send anywhere reports on the executions that the group carried out?

OHLENDORF: Reports on the executions were regularly submitted to the RSHA.

THE TRIBUNAL (Gen. Niktchenko): No, did you personally send any reports on the annihilation of thousands of people which you effected? Did you personally submit any report?

OHLENDORF: The reports came from the *Einsatzkommandos* who carried out the actions, to the *Einsatzgruppe* and the *Einsatzgruppe* informed the RHSA.

THE TRIBUNAL (Gen. Niktchenko): Whom?

OHLENDORF: The reports went to the chief of Sipo personally.

THE TRIBUNAL (Gen. Niktchenko): Personally?

OHLENDORF: Yes, personally.

THE TRIBUNAL (Gen. Niktchenko): What was the name of this police officer? Can you give his name?

OHLENDORF: At that time, Heydrich.

THE TRIBUNAL (Gen. Niktchenko): After Heydrich?

OHLENDORF: I was no longer there then, but that was the standing order.

THE TRIBUNAL (Gen. Niktchenko): I am asking you whether you continued to submit reports after Heydrich's death or not?

OHLENDORF: After Heydrich's death I was no longer in the *Einsatz*, but the reports were, of course, continued.

THE TRIBUNAL (Gen. Niktchenko): Do you know whether the reports continued to be submitted after Heydrich's death or not?

OHLENDORF: Yes.

THE TRIBUNAL (Gen. Niktchenko): Yes?

OHLENDORF: No, the reports...

THE TRIBUNAL (Gen. Niktchenko): Was the order concerning the annihilation of the Soviet people in conformity with the policy of the German government or the Nazi Party or was it against it? Do you understand the question?

OHLENDORF: Yes. One must distinguish here: the order for the liquidation came from the Führer of the Reich, and it was to be carried out by the Reichsführer SS Himmler.

THE TRIBUNAL (Gen. Niktchenko): But was it in conformity with the policy conducted by the Nazi Party and the German government, or was it in contradiction to it?

OHLENDORF: A policy amounts to a practice so that in this respect it was laid down by the Führer. If you were to ask whether this activity was in conformity with the idea of National Socialism, then I would say "no".

THE TRIBUNAL (Gen. Niktchenko): I am talking about the practice.

THE PRESIDENT: I understood you to say that objects of value were taken from the Jewish victims by the Jewish Council of Elders?

OHLENDORF: Yes.

THE PRESIDENT: Did the Jewish Council of Elders settle who were to be killed?

OHLENDORF: That was done in various ways. As far as I remember, the Council of Elders was given the order to collect valuables at the same time.

THE PRESIDENT: So that the Jewish Council of Elders would not know whether or not they were to be killed?

OHLENDORF: Yes.

THE PRESIDENT: Now, a question concerning you personally. From whom did you receive your orders for the liquidation of the Jews and so forth? And in what form?

OHLENDORF: My duty was not the task of liquidation, but I did head the staff which directed the *Einsatzkommandos* in the field, and the *Einsatzkommandos* themselves had already received this order in Berlin on the instructions of Streckenbach, Himmler, and Heydrich. This order was renewed by Himmler at Nikolaiev.

HERR BABEL: You personally were not concerned with the execution of these orders?

OHLENDORF: I led the *Einsatzgruppe,* and therefore I had the task of seeing how the *Einsatzkommandos* executed the orders received.

HERR BABEL: But did you have no scruples in regard to the execution of these orders?

OHLENDORF: Yes, of course.

HERR BABEL: And how is it that they were carried out regardless of these scruples?

OHLENDORF: Because to me it is inconceivable that a subordinate leader should not carry out orders given by the leaders of the state.

HERR BABEL: This is your opinion. But this must have been not only your point of view but also the point of view of the majority of the people involved. Didn't some of the men appointed to execute these orders ask you to be relieved of such tasks?

OHLENDORF: I cannot remember any one concrete case. I excluded some whom I did not consider emotionally suitable for executing these tasks and I sent some of them home.

HERR BABEL: Was the legality of the orders explained to those people under false pretenses?

OHLENDORF: I do not understand your question; since the order was issued by the superior authorities, the question of legality could not arise in the minds of these individuals, for they had sworn obedience to the people who had issued the orders.

HERR BABEL: Could any individual expect to succeed in evading the execution of these orders?

OHLENDORF: No, the result would have been a court martial with a corresponding sentence.

Testimony of Marie Claude Vaillant-Couturier

Auschwitz survivor

MME. VAILLANT-COUTURIER: We saw the unsealing of the cars and the soldiers letting men, women, and children out of them. We then witnessed heart-rending scenes; old couples forced to part from each other, mothers made to abandon their young daughters, since the latter were sent to the camp, whereas mothers and children were sent to the gas chambers. All these people were unaware of the fate awaiting them. They were merely upset at being separated, but they did not know that they were going to their death. To render their welcome more pleasant at this time – June to July 1944 – an orchestra composed of internees, all young and pretty girls dressed in little white blouses and navy blue skirts, played during the selection, at the arrival of the trains, gay tunes such as "The Merry Widow," the "Barcarolle" from "The Tales of Hoffman," and so forth. They were then informed that this was a labor camp and since they were not brought into the camp they saw only the small platform surrounded by flowering plants. Naturally, they could not realize what was in store for them. Those selected for the gas chamber, that is, the old people, mothers, and children, were escorted to a red brick building.

M. DUBOST: These were not given an identification number?

VAILLANT-COUTURIER: No.

DUBOST: They were not tattooed?

VAILLANT-COUTURIER: No. They were not even counted.

DUBOST: You were tattooed?

VAILLANT-COUTURIER: Yes, look. [The witness showed her arm.] They were taken to a red brick building, which bore the letters "Baden," that is to say "Baths." There, to begin with, they were made to undress and given a towel before they went into the so-called shower room. Later on, at the time of the large convoys from Hungary, they had no more time left to play-act or to pretend; they were brutally undressed, and I know these details as I knew a little Jewess from France who lived with her family at the *"Republique"* district.

DUBOST: In Paris?

VAILLANT-COUTURIER: In Paris. She was called "little Marie" and she was the only one, the sole survivor of a family of nine. Her mother and her seven brothers and sisters had been gassed on arrival. When I met her she was employed to undress the babies before they were taken into the gas chamber. Once the people were undressed they took them into a room, which was somewhat like a shower room, and gas capsules were thrown through an opening in the ceiling. An SS man would watch the effect produced through a porthole. At the end of 5 or 7 minutes, when the gas had completed its work, he gave the signal to open the doors; and men with gas masks – they too were internees – went into the room and removed the corpses. They told us that the internees must have suffered before dying, because they were closely clinging to one another and it was very difficult to separate them.

After that a special squad would come to pull out gold teeth and dentures; and again, when the bodies had been reduced to ashes, they would sift them in an attempt to recover the gold.

At Auschwitz there were eight crematories but, as from 1944, these proved insufficient. The SS had large pits dug by the internees, where they put branches, sprinkled with gasoline, which they set on fire. Then they threw the corpses into the pits. From our block we could see after about three-quarters of an hour or an hour after the arrival of a convoy, large flames coming from the crematory, and the sky was lighted up by the burning pits.

One night we were awakened by terrifying cries. And we discovered, on the following day, from the men working in the *Sonderkommando* – the "Gas *Kommando*" – that on the preceding day, the gas supply having run out, they had thrown the children into the furnaces alive.

DUBOST: Can you tell us about the selections that were made at the beginning of winter?

VAILLANT-COUTURIER: During Christmas 1944 – no, 1943, Christmas 1943 – when we were in quarantine, we saw, since we lived opposite Block 25, women brought to Block 25 stripped naked. Uncovered trucks were then driven up and on them the naked women were piled, as many as the trucks could hold. Each time a truck started, the infamous Hessler ran after the truck and with his bludgeon repeatedly struck the naked women going to their death. They knew they were going to the gas chamber and tried to escape. They were massacred. They attempted to jump from the truck and we, from our own block, watched the trucks pass by and heard the grievous wailing of all those women who knew they were going to be gassed. Many of them could very well have lived on, since they were suffering only from scabies and were, perhaps, a little too undernourished.

Since the Jewesses were sent to Auschwitz with their entire families and since they had been told that this was a sort of ghetto and were advised to bring all their goods and chattels along, they consequently brought considerable riches with them. As for the Jewesses from Salonika, I remember that on their arrival they were given picture postcards bearing the post office address of "Waldsee," a place which did not exist; and a printed text to be sent to their families, stating, "We are doing very well here; we have work and we are well treated. We await your arrival." I myself saw the cards in question; and the *Schreiberinnen*, that is, the secretaries of the block, were instructed to distribute them among the internees in order to post them to their families. I know that whole families arrived as a result of these postcards.

[Cross-examination by Dr. Hanns Marx, attorney for Julius Streicher:]

DR. HANNS MARX: Madame Couturier, you declared that you were arrested by the French police?

MME. VAILLANT-COUTURIER: Yes.

MARX: For what reason were you arrested ?

VAILLANT-COUTURIER: Resistance. I belonged to a resistance movement.

MARX: Another question: Which position did you occupy? I mean what kind of post did you ever hold? Have you ever held a post?

VAILLANT-COUTURIER: Where?

MARX: For example, as a teacher?

VAILLANT-COUTURIER: Before the war? I don't quite see what this question has to do with the matter. I was a journalist.

MARX: Yes. The fact of the matter is that you, in your statement, showed great skill in style and expression; and I should like to know whether you held any position such, for example, as teacher or lecturer.

VAILLANT-COUTURIER: No. I was a newspaper photographer.

MARX: How do you explain that you yourself came through these experiences so well and are now in such a good state of health?

VAILLANT-COUTURIER: First of all, I was liberated a year ago; and in a year one has time to recover. Secondly, I was 10 months in quarantine for typhus and I had the great luck not to die of exanthematic typhus, although I had it and was ill for 3 ½ months. Also, in the last months at Ravensbruck, as I knew German, I worked on the Revier roll call, which explains why I did not have to work quite so hard or to suffer from the inclemencies of the weather. On the other hand, out of 230 of us only 49 from my convoy returned alive; and we were only 52 at the end of 4 months. I had the great fortune to return.

MARX: Yes. Does your statement contain what you yourself observed or is it concerned with information from other sources as well?

VAILLANT-COUTURIER: Whenever such was the case I mentioned it in my declaration. I have never quoted anything, which has not previously been verified at the sources and by several persons, but the major part of my evidence is based on personal experience.

MARX: How can you explain your very precise statistical knowledge, for instance, that 700,000 Jews arrived from Hungary?

VAILLANT-COUTURIER: I told you that I have worked in the offices; and where Auschwitz was concerned, I was a friend of the secretary (the *Oberaufseherin*), whose name and address I gave to the Tribunal.

MARX: It has been stated that only 350,000 Jews came from Hungary, according to the testimony of the Chief of the Gestapo, Eichmann.

VAILLANT-COUTURIER: I am not going to argue with the Gestapo. I have good reasons to know that what the Gestapo states is not always true.

MARX: How were you treated personally? Were you treated well?

VAILLANT-COUTURIER: Like the others.

MARX: Like the others? You said before that the German people must have known of the happenings in Auschwitz. What are your grounds for this statement?

VAILLANT-COUTURIER: I have already told you: To begin with there was the fact that when we left, the Lorraine soldiers of the Wehrmacht who were taking us to Auschwitz said to us, "If you knew where you were going, you would not be in such a hurry to get there." Then there was the fact that the German women who came out of quarantine to go to work in German factories knew of these events, and they all said that they would speak about them outside.

Further, the fact that in all the factories where the *Hafflinge* (the internees) worked they were in contact with the German civilians, as also were the *Aufseherinnen*, who were in touch with their friends and families and often told them what they had seen.

MARX: One more question. Up to 1942 you were able to observe the behavior of the German soldiers in Paris. Did not these German soldiers behave well throughout and did they not pay for what they took?

VAILLANT-COUTURIER: I have not the least idea whether they paid or not for what they requisitioned. As for their good behavior, too many of my friends were shot or massacred for me not to differ with you.

MARX: I have no further question to put to this witness.

[The witness left the stand.]

Testimony of Abram Suzkever

Resident of Vilna

SMIRNOV: You stayed in this town for a long time during the German occupation?

SUZKEVER: I stayed there from the first to nearly the last day of the occupation.

SMIRNOV: You witnessed the persecution of the Jews in that city?

SUZKEVER:Yes.

SMIRNOV: I would like you to tell the Court about this.

SUZKEVER: When the Germans seized my city, Vilna, about 80,000 Jews lived in the town. Immediately the so-called *Sonderkommando* was set up at 12 Vilenskaia Street, under the command of Schweichenberg and Martin Weiss. The manhunters of the *Sonderkommandos*, or as the Jews called them, the "*Khapun,*" broke into the Jewish houses at any time of day or night, dragged away the men, instructing them to take a piece of soap and a towel, and herded them into certain buildings near the village of Ponari, about eight kilometers from Vilna. From there hardly one returned. When the Jews found out that their kin were not coming back, a large part of the population went into hiding. However, the Germans tracked them with police dogs. Many were found, and any who were averse to going with them were shot on the spot.

I have to say that the Germans declared that they were exterminating the Jewish race as though legally.

On 8 July an order was issued which stated that all Jews should wear a patch on their back; afterwards they were ordered to wear it on their chest. This order was signed by the commandant of the town of Vilna, Zehnpfennig. But two days later some other commandant named Neumann issued a new order that they should not wear these patches but must wear the yellow Star of David.

SMIRNOV: And what does this yellow Star of David mean?

SUZKEVER: It was a six-pointed patch worn on the chest and on the back, in order to distinguish the Jews from the other inhabitants of the town. On another day they were ordered to wear a blue band with a white star. The Jews did not know which insignia to wear as very few lived in the town. Those who did not wear this sign were immediately arrested and never seen again.

In the first days of August 1941 a German seized me in the Dokumenskaia Street. I was then going to visit my mother. The German said to me, "Come with me, you will act in the circus." As I went along I saw that another German was driving along an old Jew, the old rabbi of this street, Kassel, and a third German was holding a young boy. When we reached the old synagogue on this street I saw that wood was piled up there in the shape of a pyramid. A German drew out his revolver and told us to take off our clothes. When we were naked, he lit a match and set fire to this stack of wood. Then another German brought out of the synagogue three scrolls of the Torah, gave them to us, and told us to dance around this bonfire and sing Russian songs. Behind us stood the three Germans; with their bayonets they forced us toward the fire and laughed. When we were almost unconscious, they left.

I must say that the mass extermination of the Jewish people in Vilna began at the moment when District Commissar Hans Fincks arrived, as well as the referant, or reporter on the Jewish problems, Muhrer. On 31 August, under the direction of District Commissioner Fincks and Muhrer.

THE PRESIDENT: Which year?

SUZKEVER: 1941.

THE PRESIDENT: Go on.

SUZKEVER: Under the direction of Fincks and Muhrer, the Germans surrounded the old Jewish quarter of Vilna, taking in Rudnitskaia and Jewish Streets, Galonsky Alley, the Shabelsky and Strashouna Streets, where some 8 to 10 thousand Jews were living.

I was ill at the time and asleep. Suddenly I felt the lash of a whip on me. When I jumped up from my bed I saw Schweichenberg standing in front of me. He had a big dog with him. He was beating everybody and shouting that we must all run out into the courtyard. When I was out in the courtyard, I saw there many women, children, and aged persons, all the Jews who lived there. Schweichenberg had the *Sonderkommando* surround all this crowd and said that they were taking us to the ghetto. But of course, like all their statements, this was also a lie. We went through the town in columns and were led toward Lutishcheva Prison. All knew that we were going to our death. When we arrived at Lutishcheva Prison, near the so-called Lutishkina market, I saw a whole double line of German soldiers with white sticks standing there to receive us. While we had to pass between them they beat us with sticks. If a Jew fell down, the one next to him was told to pick him up and carry him through the large prison gates which stood open. Near the prison I took to my heels. I swam across the River Vilia and hid in my mother's house.

On 6 September at 6 o'clock in the morning thousands of Germans, led by District Commissar Fincks, by Muhrer, Schweichenberg, Martin Weiss, and others, surrounded the whole town, broke into the Jewish houses, and told the inhabitants to take only that which they could carry off in their hands and get out into the street. Then they were driven off to the ghetto. When they were passing by Wilkomirowskaia Street where I was, I saw the Germans had brought sick Jews from the hospitals. They were all in blue hospital gowns. They were all forced to stand while a German newsreel operator, who was driving in front of the column, filmed this scene.

I must say that not all the Jews were driven into the ghetto. Fincks had set up two ghettos in Vilna. In the first were 29,000 Jews, and in the second some 15,000 Jews. About half the Jewish population of Vilna never reached the ghetto; they were shot on the way. I remember how, when we arrived at the ghetto ...

SMIRNOV: Just a moment, Witness. Did I understand you correctly, that before the ghetto was set up, half the Jewish population of Vilna was already exterminated?

SUZKEVER: Yes, that is right. When I arrived at the ghetto I saw the following scene: Martin Weiss came in with a young Jewish girl. When we went in farther, he took out his revolver and shot her on the spot. The girl's name was Gitele Tarlo.

SMIRNOV: Tell us, how old was this girl?

SUZKEVER: Eleven.

I must state that the Germans organized the ghetto only to exterminate the Jewish population with greater ease. The head of the ghetto was the expert on Jewish questions, Muhrer, and he issued a series of mad orders. For instance, Jews were forbidden to wear watches. The Jews could not pray in the ghetto. When a German passed by, they had to take off their hats but were not allowed to look at him. At the end of December 1941 an order was issued in the ghetto which stated that the Jewish women must not bear children.

SMIRNOV: I would like you to tell us how, or in what form, this order was issued by the German fascists.

SUZKEVER: Muhrer came to the hospital in Street Number 6 and said that an order had come from Berlin to the effect that Jewish women should not bear children and that if the Germans found out that a Jewish woman had given birth, the child would be exterminated.

Towards the end of December in the ghetto my wife gave birth to a child, a boy. I was not in the ghetto at that time, having escaped from one of these so-called "actions." When I came to the ghetto later I found that my wife had had a baby in a ghetto hospital. But I saw the hospital surrounded by Germans and a black car standing before the door. Schweichenberg was standing near the car, and the hunters of the *Sonderkommando* were dragging sick and old people out of the hospital and throwing them like logs into the truck. Among them I saw the well known Jewish writer and editor, Grodnensky, who was also dragged and dumped into this truck.

In the evening when the Germans had left, I went to the hospital and found my wife in tears. It seems that when she had her baby, the Jewish doctors of the hospital had already received the order that Jewish women must not give birth; and they had hidden the baby, together with other newborn children, in one of the rooms. But when this commission with Muhrer came to the hospital, they heard the cries of the babies. They broke open the door and entered the room. When my wife heard that the door had been broken, she immediately got up and ran to see what was happening to the child. She saw one German holding the baby and smearing something under its nose. Afterwards he threw it on the bed and laughed. When my wife picked up the child, there was something black under his nose. When

I arrived at the hospital, I saw that my baby was dead. He was still warm.

Shortly afterwards the second ghetto was liquidated, and the German newspaper in Vilna announced that the Jews from this district had died of an epidemic.

SMIRNOV: Please, Witness, I am interested in the following question: You said that at the beginning of the German occupation 80,000 Jews lived in Vilna. How many remained after the German occupation?

SUZKEVER: After the occupation about 600 Jews remained.

SMIRNOV: Thus, 79,400 persons were exterminated?

SUZKEVER: Yes.

SMIRNOV: Your Honors, I have no further questions to ask of the witness.

THE PRESIDENT: Does any other Chief Prosecutor want to ask any questions?

MAXWELL-FYFE: No questions.

DODD: No questions.

THE PRESIDENT: Does any member of the defendants' counsel wish to ask any questions? No? Then the witness can retire.

[The witness left the stand.]

Cross Examination of Hermann Goering

THE PRESIDENT: Do the Chief prosecutors wish to cross examine?

MR. JUSTICE JACKSON: You are perhaps aware that you are the only living man who can expound to us the true purposes of the Nazi Party and the inner workings of its leadership?

GOERING: I am perfectly aware of that.

MR. JUSTICE JACKSON: You, from the very beginning, together with those who were associated with you, intended to overthrow and later did overthrow, the Weimar Republic?

GOERING: That was, as far as I am concerned, my firm intention.

MR. JUSTICE JACKSON: And, upon coming to power, you immediately abolished parliamentary government in Germany?

GOERING: We found it to be no longer necessary. Also I should like to emphasize the fact that we were moreover the strongest parliamentary party, and had the majority. But you are correct when you say that parliamentary procedure was done away with because the various parties were disbanded and forbidden.

MR. JUSTICE JACKSON: You established the Leadership Principle, which you have described as a system under which authority existed only at the top, and is passed downwards and is imposed on the people below; is that correct?

GOERING: In order to avoid any misunderstanding, I should like once more to explain the idea briefly, as I understand it. In German parliamentary procedure in the past responsibility rested with the highest officials, who were responsible for carrying out the anonymous wishes of the majorities, and it was they who exercised the authority. In the Leadership Principle we sought to reverse the direction, that is, the authority existed at the top and passed downwards, while the responsibility began at the bottom and passed upwards.

MR. JUSTICE JACKSON: In other words, you did not believe in and did not permit government, as we call it, by consent of the governed, in which the people, through their representatives, were the source of power and authority?

GOERING: That is not entirely correct. We repeatedly called on the people to express unequivocally and clearly what they thought of our system, only it was in a different way from that previously adopted and from the system in practice in other countries. We chose the way of a so-called plebiscite. We also took the point of view that even a government founded on the Leadership Principle could maintain itself only if it was based in some way on the confidence of the people. If it no longer had such confidence, then it would have to rule with bayonets, and the Fuehrer was always of the opinion that that was impossible in the long run, to rule against the will of the people.

MR. JUSTICE JACKSON: But you did not permit the election of those who should act with authority by the people, but they were designated from the top downward continuously, were they not?

GOERING: Quite right. The people were merely to acknowledge the authority of the Fuehrer, or, let us say, to declare themselves in agreement with the Fuehrer. If they gave the Fuehrer their confidence then it was their concern to exercise the other functions. Thus, not the individual persons were to be selected according to the will of the people, but solely the leadership itself.

MR. JUSTICE JACKSON: Now, was this Leadership Principle supported and adopted by you in Germany because you believed that no people are capable of self-goverrnment, or because you believed that some may be, not the German people; or that no matter whether some of us are capable of using our own system, it should not be allowed in Germany?

GOERING: I beg your pardon, I did not quite understand the question, but I could perhaps answer it as follows:

I consider the Leadership Principle necessary because the system which previously existed, and which we called parliamentary or democratic, had brought Germany to the verge of ruin. I might perhaps in this connection remind you that your own President Roosevelt, as far as I can recall – I do not want to quote it word for word – declared, "Certain peoples in Europe have forsaken democracy, not because they did not wish for democracy as such, but because democracy had brought forth men who were too weak to give their people work and bread, and to satisfy them. For this reason the peoples have abandoned this system and the men belonging to it." There is much truth in that statement. This system had brought ruin by mismanagement and according to my own opinion, only an organization made up of a strong, clearly defined leadership hierarchy could restore order again. But, let it be understood, not against the will of the people, but only when the people, having in the course of time, and by means of a series of elections, grown stronger and stronger, had expressed their wish to entrust their destiny to the National Socialist leadership.

MR. JUSTICE JACKSON: The principles of the authoritarian government which you set up required, as I understand you, that there be tolerated no opposition by political parties which might defeat or obstruct the policy of the Nazi Party?

GOERING: You have understood this quite correctly. By that time we had lived long enough with opposition and we had had enough of it. Through opposition we had been completely ruined. It was now time to have done with it and to start building up.

MR. JUSTICE JACKSON: After you came to power, you regarded it necessary, in order to maintain power, to suppress all opposition parties?

GOERING: We found it necessary not to permit any more opposition, yes.

MR. JUSTICE JACKSON: And you also held it necessary that you should suppress all individual opposition lest it should develop into a party of opposition?

GOERING: Insofar as opposition seriously hampered our work of building up, this opposition of individual persons was, of course not tolerated. Insofar as it was simply a matter of harmless talk it was considered to be of no consequence.

MR. JUSTICE JACKSON: Now, in order to make sure that you suppressed the parties, and individuals also, you found it necessary to have a secret political police to detect opposition?

GOERING: I have already stated that I considered that necessary just as previously the political police had existed, but on a firmer basis and larger scale.

MR. JUSTICE JACKSON: And upon coming to power you also considered it immediately necessary to establish concentration camps to take care of your incorrigible opponents?

GOERING: I have already stated that the reason for the concentration camps was not because it could be said, "Here are a number of people who are opposed to us and they must be taken into protective custody." Rather they were set up as a lightning measure against the functionaries of the Communist Party who were attacking us in the thousands, and who, since they were taken into protective custody, were not put in prison. But it was necessary, as I said, to erect a camp for them; one, two, or three camps.

MR. JUSTICE JACKSON: But you are explaining, as the high authority of this system, to men who do not understand it very well, and I want to know what was necessary to run the kind of system that you set up in Germany. The concentration camp was one of the things you found immediately necessary upon coming into power, was it not? And you set them up as a matter of necessity? As you saw it?

GOERING: That was faultily translated – it went too fast. But I believe I have understood the sense of your remarks. You asked me if I considered it necessary to establish concentration camps immediately in order to eliminate opposition. Is that correct?

MR. JUSTICE JACKSON: Your answer is "yes," I take it?

GOERING: Yes.

MR. JUSTICE JACKSON: Was it also necessary, in operating this system, that you must not have persons entitled to public trials in independent courts? And you immediately issued an order that your political police would not be subject to court review or to court orders, did you not?

GOERING: You must differentiate between the two categories; those who had committed some act of treason against the new state or those who might be proved to have committed such an act, were naturally turned over to the courts. The others, however, of whom one might expect such acts, but who had not yet committed them, were taken into protective custody, and these were the people who were taken to concentration camps. I am now speaking of what happened at the beginning. Later things changed a great deal. Likewise, if for political reasons – to answer your question – someone was taken into protective custody, that is, purely for reasons of state, this could not be reviewed or stopped by any court. Later, when some people were also taken into protective custody for nonpolitical reasons, people who had opposed the system in some other way, I once, as Prussian Prime Minister and Reich Minister of the Interior, I remember —

MR. JUSTICE JACKSON: Let's omit that. I have not asked for that. If you will just answer my question, we shall save a great deal of time. Your counsel will be permitted to bring out any explanations you want to make.

You did prohibit all court review and considered it necessary to prohibit court review of the causes for taking people into what you called protective custody?

GOERING: That I answered very clearly, but I should like to make an explanation in connection with my answer.

MR. JUSTICE JACKSON: Your counsel will see to that. Now, the concentration camps and the protective custody —

THE PRESIDENT: Mr. Justice Jackson, the Tribunal thinks the witness ought to be allowed to make what explanation he thinks right in answer to this question.

MR. JUSTICE JACKSON: The Tribunal thinks that you should be permitted to explain your answer now, and it will listen to your answers.

THE PRESIDENT: I did not mean that to apply generally to his answers. I meant it to apply to this particular answer.

GOERING: In connection with your question that these cases could not be reviewed by the court, I want to say that a decree was issued through me and Frick jointly to the effect that those who were turned over to concentration camps were to be informed after 24 hours of the reason for their being turned over, and that after 48 hours, or some short period of time, they should have the right to an attorney. But this by no means rescinded my order that a review was not permitted by the courts of a politically necessary measure of protective custody. These people were simply not to be given an opportunity of making a protest.

MR. JUSTICE JACKSON: Protective custody meant that you were taking people into custody who had not committed any crimes but who, you thought, might possibly commit a crime?

GOERING: Yes. People were arrested and taken into protective custody who had not yet committed any crime, but who could be expected to do so if they remained free, just as extensive protective measures are being taken in Germany today on a tremendous scale.

MR. JUSTICE JACKSON: Now, it is also a necessity, in the kind of state that you had, that you have some kind of organization to carry propaganda down to the people and to get their reaction and inform the leadership of it, is it not?

GOERING: The last part of that question has not been intelligibly translated.

MR. JUSTICE JACKSON: Well, you had to have organizations to carry out orders and to carry your propaganda in that kind of state, didn't you?

GOERING: Of course, we carried on propaganda, and for this we had a propaganda organization.

MR. JUSTICE JACKSON: And you carried that on through the Leadership Corps of the Nazi Party, did you not?

GOERING: The Leadership Corps was there, of course, partly to spread our ideas among the people. Secondly, its purpose was to lead and organize the people who made up the Party.

MR. JUSTICE JACKSON: Through your system of Gauleiter and Kreisleiter down to Blockleiter, commands and information went down from the authority, and information as to the people's reactions came back to the leadership, didn't it?

GOERING: That is correct. The orders and commands that were to be given for propaganda or other purposes were passed down the grades as far as necessary. On the other hand, it was a matter of course that the reactions of the broad masses of the people were again transmitted upwards, through the various offices, in order to keep us informed of the mood of the people.

MR. JUSTICE JACKSON: And you also had to have certain organizations to carry out orders, executive organizations, organizations to fight for you if necessary, did you not?

GOERING: Yes, administrative organizations were, of course, necessary. I do not quite understand – organizations to fight what?

MR. JUSTICE JACKSON: Well, if you wanted certain people killed you had to have some organization that would kill them didn't you? Rohm and the rest of them were not killed by Hitler's own hands nor by yours, were they?

GOERING: Rohm – the Rohm affair I explained here clearly – that was a matter of State necessity...

MR. JUSTICE JACKSON: I did not ask you . . .

GOERING: ... and was carried out by the police.

MR. JUSTICE JACKSON: But when it was State necessity to kill somebody, you had to have somebody to do it, didn't you?

GOERING: Yes, just as in other countries, whether it is called secret service or something else, I do not know.

MR. JUSTICE JACKSON: And the SA, the SS, and the SD, organizations of that kind, were the organizations that carried out the orders and dealt with people on a physical level, were they not?

GOERING: The SA never received an order to kill anybody, neither did the SS, not in my time. Anyhow, I had no influence on it. I know that orders were given for executions, namely in the Rohm *Putsch*, and these were carried out by the police, that is, by a State organ.

MR. JUSTICE JACKSON: What police?

GOERING: As far as I recall, through the Gestapo. At any rate, that was the organization that received the order. You see, it was a fight against enemies of the State.

MR. JUSTICE JACKSON: And the SS was for the same purpose, was it not?

GOERING: Not in north Germany at that time; to what extent that was the case in south Germany, where the Gestapo and the SS were still separated, and who carried out the action in south Germany, I do not know.

MR. JUSTICE JACKSON: Well, the SS carried out arrests and carried out the transportation of people to concentration camps, didn't they? You were arrested by the SS, weren't you?

GOERING: Yes, I say, yes; but later.

MR. JUSTICE JACKSON: At what time did the SS perform this function of acting as the executor of the Nazi Party?

GOERING: After the seizure of power, when the police came to be more and more in the hands of Himmler. It is difficult for me to explain to an outsider where the SS or where the Gestapo was active. I have already said that the two of them worked very closely together. It is known that the SS guarded the camps and later carried out police functions.

MR. JUSTICE JACKSON: And carried out other functions in the camps?

GOERING: To what functions do you refer?

MR. JUSTICE JACKSON: They carried out all of the functions of the camps, didn't they?

GOERING: If an SS unit was guarding a camp and an SS leader happened to be the camp commander, then this unit carried out all the functions.

MR. JUSTICE JACKSON: Now, this system was not a secret system. This entire system was openly avowed, its merits were publicly advocated by yourself and others, and every person entering into the Nazi Party was enabled to know the kind of system of government you were going to set up, wasn't he?

GOERING: Every person who entered the Party knew that we embraced the Leadership Principle and knew the fundamental measures we wanted to carry out, so far as they were stated in the program. But not everyone who joined the Party knew down to the last detail what was going to happen later.

MR. JUSTICE JACKSON: But this system was set up openly and was well known, was it not, in every one of its details? As to organization, everybody knew what the Gestapo was, did they not?

GOERING: Yes, everyone knew what the Gestapo was.

MR. JUSTICE JACKSON: And what its program was in general, not in detail?

GOERING: I explained that program clearly. At the very beginning I described that publicly, and I also spoke publicly of the tasks of the Gestapo, and I even wrote about it for foreign countries.

MR. JUSTICE JACKSON: And there was nothing secret about the establishment of a Gestapo as a political police, about the fact that people were taken into protective custody, about the fact that these were concentration camps? Nothing secret about those things, was there?

GOERING: There was at first nothing secret about it at all.

MR. JUSTICE JACKSON: As a matter of fact, part of the effectiveness of a secret police and part of the effectiveness of concentration camp penalties is that the people do know that there are such agencies, isn't it?

GOERING: It is true that everyone knows that if he acts against the state he will end up in a concentration camp or will be accused of high treason before a court, according to the degree of his crime. But the original reason for creating the concentration camps was to keep there such people whom we rightfully considered enemies of the State.

MR. JUSTICE JACKSON: Now, that is the type of government – the government which we have just been describing – the only type of government which you think is necessary to govern Germany?

GOERING: I should not like to say that the basic characteristic of this government and its most essential feature was the immediate setting up of the Gestapo and the concentration camps in order to take care of our opponents, but that over and above that we had set down as our government program a great many far more important things, and that those other things were not the basic principles of our government.

MR. JUSTICE JACKSON: But all of these things were necessary things as I understood you, for purposes of protection?

GOERING: Yes, these things were necessary because of the opponents that existed.

MR. JUSTICE JACKSON: And I assume that that is the only kind of government that you think can function in Germany under present conditions?

GOERING: Under the conditions existing at that time, it was, in my opinion, the only possible form, and it also demonstrated that Germany could be raised in a short time from the depths of misery, poverty, and unemployment to relative prosperity.

MR. JUSTICE JACKSON: Now, all of this authority of the State was concentrated – perhaps I am taking up another subject. Is it the intent to recess at this time?

[The Tribunal recessed until 1400 hours.]

MR. JUSTICE JACKSON: Witness, you have related to us the manner in which you and others co-operated in concentrating all authority in the German State in the hands of the Fuehrer is that right?

GOERING: I was speaking about myself and to what extent I had a part in it.

MR. JUSTICE JACKSON: Is there any defendant in the box you know of who did not co-operate toward that end as far as was possible?

GOERING: That none of the defendants here opposed or obstructed the Fuehrer in the beginning is clear, but I should like to call your attention to the fact that we must always distinguish between different periods of time. Some of the questions that are being put to me are very general and, after all, we are concerned with over 24 to 25 years, if a comprehensive survey is to be made.

MR. JUSTICE JACKSON: Now, I want to call your attention to the fruits of this system. You, as I understand it, were informed in 1940 of an impending attack by the German Army on Soviet Russia?

GOERING: I have explained just how far I was informed of these matters.

MR. JUSTICE JACKSON: You believed an attack not only to be unnecessary, but also to be unwise from the point of view of Germany itself?

GOERING: At that particular time I was of the opinion that this attack should be postponed in order to carry through other tasks which I considered more important.

MR. JUSTICE JACKSON: You did not see any military necessity or an attack at that time, even from the point of view of Germany?

GOERING: Naturally, I was fully aware of Russia's efforts in the deployment of her forces, but I hoped first to put into effect the other strategic measures, described by me, to improve Germany's position. I thought that the time required for these would ward off the critical moment. I well knew, of course, that this critical moment for Germany might come at any time after that.

MR. JUSTICE JACKSON: I can only repeat my question, which I submit you have not answered.

Did you at that time see any military necessity for an attack by Germany on Soviet Russia?

GOERING: I personally believed that at that time the danger had not yet reached its climax, and therefore the attack might not yet be necessary. But that was my personal view.

MR. JUSTICE JACKSON: And you were the Number 2 man at that time in all Germany?

GOERING: It has nothing to do with my being second in importance. There were two conflicting points of view as regards strategy.

The Fuehrer, the Number 1 man, saw one danger, and I, as the Number 2 man, if you wish to express it so, wanted to carry out another strategic measure. If I had imposed my will every time then I would probably have become the Number 1 man. But since the Number 1 man was of a different opinion, and I was only the Number 2 man, his opinion naturally prevailed.

MR. JUSTICE JACKSON: I have understood from your testimony – and I think you can answer this "yes" or "no," and I would greatly appreciate it if you would – I have understood from your testimony that you were opposed, and told the Fuehrer that you were opposed, to an attack upon Russia at that time. Am I right or wrong?

GOERING: That is correct.

MR. JUSTICE JACKSON: Now, you were opposed to it because you thought that it was a dangerous move for Germany to make; is that correct?

GOERING: Yes, I was of the opinion that the moment – and I repeat this again – had not come for this undertaking, and that measures should be taken which were more expedient as far as Germany was concerned.

MR. JUSTICE JACKSON: And yet, because of the Fuehrer system, as I understand you, you could give no warning to the German people; you could bring no pressure of any kind to bear to prevent that step, and you could not even resign to protect your own place in history.

GOERING: These are several questions at once. I should like to answer the first one.

MR. JUSTICE JACKSON: Separate them, if you wish.

GOERING: The first question was, I believe, whether I took the opportunity to tell the German people about this danger. I had no occasion to do this. We were at war, and such differences of opinion, as far as strategy was concerned, could not be brought before the public forum during war. I believe that never has happened in world history. Secondly, as far as my resignation is concerned, I do not wish even to discuss that, for during the war I was an officer, a soldier, and I was not concerned with whether I shared an opinion or not I had merely to serve my country as a soldier.

Thirdly, I was not the man to forsake someone, to whom I had given my oath of loyalty, every time he was not of my way of thinking. If that had been the case there would have been no need to bind myself to him from the beginning. It never occurred to me to leave the Fuehrer.

MR. JUSTICE JACKSON: Insofar as you know, the German people were led into the war, attacking Soviet Russia under the belief that you favored it?

GOERING: The German people did not know about the declaration of war against Russia until after the war with Russia had started. The German people, therefore, had nothing to do with this.

The German people were not asked; they were told of the fact and of the necessity for it.

MR. JUSTICE JACKSON: At what time did you know that the war, as regards achieving the objectives that you had in mind, was a lost war?

GOERING: It is extremely difficult to say. At any rate, according to my conviction, relatively late; I mean, it was only towards the end that I became convinced that the war was lost. Up till then I had always thought and hoped that it would come to a stalemate.

MR. JUSTICE JACKSON: Well, in 11/1941 the offensive in Russia broke down?

GOERING: That is not at all correct. We had reverses because of weather conditions, or rather, the goal which we had set was not reached. The push of 1942 proved well enough that there was no question of a military collapse. Some corps, which had pushed forward, were merely thrown back, and some were withdrawn. The totally unexpected early frost that set in was the cause of this.

MR. JUSTICE JACKSON: You said, "relatively late." The expression that you used does not tell me anything, because I do not know what you regard as relatively late. Will you fix in terms, of events or time, when it was that the conviction came to you that the war was lost?

GOERING: When, after 1/12/1945, the Russian offensive pushed forward to the Oder and at the same time the Ardennes offensive had not penetrated, it was then that I was forced to realize that defeat would probably set in slowly. Up to that time I had always hoped that, on the one side, the position at the Vistula toward the East and, on the other side, the position at the West Wall towards the West, could be held until the flow of the new mass-produced weapons should bring about a slackening of the Anglo-American air war.

MR. JUSTICE JACKSON: Now, will you fix that by date; you told us when it was by events.

GOERING: I just said 1/1945; middle, or end of 1/1945. After that there was no more hope.

MR. JUSTICE JACKSON: Do you want it understood that, as a military man, you did not realize until 1/1945 that Germany could not be successful in the war?

GOERING: As I have already said, we must draw a sharp distinction between two possibilities: First, the successful conclusion of a war, and second, a war which ends by neither side being the victor. As regards a successful outcome, the moment when it was realized that that was no longer possible was much earlier, whereas the realization of the fact that defeat would set in did not come until the time I have just mentioned.

MR. JUSTICE JACKSON: For some period before that, you knew that a successful termination of the war could only be accomplished if you could come to some kind of terms with the enemy; was that not true?

GOERING: Of course, a successful termination of a war can only be considered successful if I either conquer the enemy or, through negotiations with the enemy, come to a conclusion which guarantees me success. That is what I call a successful termination. I call it a draw, when I come to terms with the enemy. This does not bring me the success which victory would have brought but, on the other hand, it precludes a defeat. This is a conclusion without victors or vanquished.

MR. JUSTICE JACKSON: But you knew that it was Hitler's policy never to negotiate and you knew that as long as he was the head of the Government the enemy would not negotiate with Germany, did you not?

GOERING: I knew that enemy propaganda emphasized that under no circumstances would there be negotiations with Hitler. That Hitler did not want to negotiate under any circumstances, I also knew, but not in this connection. Hitler wanted to negotiate if there were some prospect of results; but he was absolutely opposed to hopeless and futile negotiations. Because of the declaration of the enemy in the West after the landing in Africa, as far as I remember, that under no circumstances would they negotiate with Germany but would force on her unconditional surrender, Germany's resistance was stiffened to the utmost and measures had to be taken accordingly. If I have no chance of concluding a war through negotiations, then it is useless to negotiate, and I must strain every nerve to bring about a change by a call to arms.

MR. JUSTICE JACKSON: By the time of 1/1945 you also knew that you were unable to defend the German cities against the air attacks of the Allies, did you not?

GOERING: Concerning the defense of German cities against Allied air attacks, I should like to describe the possibility of doing this as follows: Of itself...

MR. JUSTICE JACKSON: Can you answer my question? Time may not mean quite as much to you as it does to the rest of us. Can you not answer "yes" or "no"? Did you then know, at the same time that you knew that the war was lost, that the German cities could not successfully be defended against air attack by the enemy? Can you not tell us "yes" or "no"?

GOERING: I can say that I knew that, at that time, it was not possible.

MR. JUSTICE JACKSON: And after that time it was well known to you that the air attacks which were continued against England could not turn the tide of war, and were designed solely to effect a prolongation of what you then knew was a hopeless conflict?

GOERING: I believe you are mistaken. After 1/1945 there were no more attacks on England, except perhaps a few single planes, because at that time I needed all my petrol for the fighter planes for defense. If I had had bombers and oil at my disposal, then, of course, I should have continued such attacks up to the last minute as retaliation for the attacks which were being carried out on German cities, whatever our chances might have been.

MR. JUSTICE JACKSON: What about robot attacks? Were there any robot attacks after 1/1945?

GOERING: Thank God, we still had one weapon that we could use. I have just said that, as long as the fight was on, we had to hit back; and as a soldier I can only regret that we did not have enough of these V-1 and V-2 bombs, for an easing of the attacks on German cities could be brought about only if we could inflict equally heavy losses on the enemy.

MR. JUSTICE JACKSON: And there was no way to prevent the war going on as long as Hitler was the head of the German Government, was there?

GOERING: As long as Hitler was the Fuehrer of the German people he alone decided whether the war was to go on. As long as my enemy threatens me and demands absolutely unconditional surrender I fight to my last breath, because there is nothing left for me except perhaps a chance that in some way fate may change, even though it seems hopeless.

MR. JUSTICE JACKSON: Well, the people of Germany who thought it was time that the slaughter should stop had no means to stop it except revolution or assassination of Hitler, had they?

GOERING: A revolution always changes a situation, if it succeeds. That is a foregone conclusion. The murder of Hitler at this time, say 1/1945, would have brought about my succession. If the enemy had given me the same answer, that is, unconditional surrender, and had held out those terrible conditions which had been intimated, I would have continued fighting whatever the circumstances.

MR. JUSTICE JACKSON: There was an attack on Hitler's life on 7/20/1944?

GOERING: Unfortunately, yes.

MR. JUSTICE JACKSON: And there came a time in 1945 when Hitler made a will in Berlin whereby he turned over the presidency of the Reich to your co-defendant, Admiral Doenitz. You know about that?

GOERING: That is correct. I read of this will here.

MR. JUSTICE JACKSON: And in making his will and turning over the Government of Germany to Admiral Doenitz, I call your attention to this statement:

"Goering and Himmler, quite apart from their disloyalty to my person, have done immeasurable harm to the country and the whole nation by secret negotiations with the enemy which they conducted without my knowledge and against my wishes, and by illegally attempting to seize power in the State for themselves."

And by that will he expelled you and Himmler from the Party and from all offices of the State.

GOERING: I can only answer for myself. What Himmler did I do not know.

I neither betrayed the Fuehrer, nor did I at that time negotiate with a single foreign soldier. This will, or this final act of the Fuehrer's, is based on an extremely regrettable mistake, and one which grieves me deeply, that the Fuehrer could believe in his last hours that I could ever be disloyal to him. It was all due to an error in the transmission of a radio report and perhaps to a misrepresentation which Bormann gave the Fuehrer. I myself never thought for a minute of taking over power illegally or of acting against the Fuehrer in any way.

MR. JUSTICE JACKSON: In any event you were arrested and expected to be shot?

GOERING: That is correct.

MR. JUSTICE JACKSON: Now, in tracing the rise of power of the Party you have omitted some such things as, for example the

Reichstag fire of 2/27/1933. There was a great purge following that fire, was there not, in which many people were arrested and many people were killed?

GOERING: I do not know of a single case where a man was killed because of the Reichstag fire, except that of the incendiary, Van der Lubbe, who was sentenced by the court. The other two defendants in this trial were acquitted. Herr Thalmann was not, as you recently erroneously believed, accused; it was the communist representative Torgler. He was acquitted, as was also the Bulgarian, Dimitroff. Relatively few arrests were made in connection with the Reichstag fire. The arrests which you attribute to the Reichstag fire are the arrests of communist functionaries. These arrests, as I have repeatedly stated and wish to emphasize once more, had nothing to do with this fire. The fire merely precipitated their arrest and upset our carefully planned action, thus allowing several of the functionaries to escape.

MR. JUSTICE JACKSON: In other words, you had lists of Communists already prepared at the time of the Reichstag fire, of persons who should be arrested, did you not?

GOERING: We had always drawn up, beforehand, fairly complete lists of communist functionaries who were to be arrested. That had nothing to do with the fire in the German Reichstag.

MR. JUSTICE JACKSON: They were immediately put into execution – the arrests, I mean – after the Reichstag fire?

GOERING: Contrary to my intention of postponing this action for a few days and letting it take place according to plan, thereby perfecting the arrangements, the Fuehrer ordered that same night that the arrests should follow immediately. This had the disadvantage, as I said, of precipitating matters.

MR. JUSTICE JACKSON: You and the Fuehrer met at the fire, did you not?

GOERING: That is right.

MR. JUSTICE JACKSON: And then and there you decided to arrest all the Communists that you had listed?

GOERING: I repeat again that the decision for their arrests had been reached some days before this; it simply meant that on that night they were immediately arrested. I would rather have waited a few days according to plan; then some of the important men would not have escaped.

MR. JUSTICE JACKSON: And the next morning the decree was presented to President Von Hindenburg, suspending the provisions of the constitution which we have discussed here, was it not?

GOERING: I believe so, yes.

MR. JUSTICE JACKSON: Who was Karl Ernst?

GOERING: Karl Ernst — whether his first name was Karl I do not now — was the SA leader of Berlin.

MR. JUSTICE JACKSON: And who was Helldorf?

GOERING: Count Helldorf was the subsequent SA leader of Berlin.

MR. JUSTICE JACKSON: And Heines?

GOERING: Heines was the SA leader of Silesia at that time.

MR. JUSTICE JACKSON: Now, it is known to you, is it not, that Ernst made a statement confessing that these three burned the Reichstag and that you and Goebbels planned and furnished the incendiary materials of liquid phosphorus and petroleum which were deposited by you in a subterranean passage for them to get, which passage led from your house to the Reichstag building? You knew of such a statement, did you not?

GOERING: I do not know of any statement by the SA leader Ernst. But I do know of some fairytale published shortly after in the foreign press by Rohm's chauffeur. This was after 1934.

MR. JUSTICE JACKSON: But there was such a passage from the Reichstag building to your house, was there not?

GOERING: On one side of the street is the Reichstag building, and opposite is the palace of the Reichstag president. The two are connected by a passage along which the wagons run which carry the coke for the central heating.

MR. JUSTICE JACKSON: And, in any event, shortly after this, Ernst was killed without a trial and without a chance to tell his story, was he not?

GOERING: That is not correct. The Reichstag fire was in 2/1933. Ernst was shot on 6/30/1934, because together with Rohm he had planned to overthrow the Government and had plotted against the Fuehrer. He, therefore, had a year and a quarter in which he could have made statements regarding the Reichstag fire, if he had wished to do so.

MR. JUSTICE JACKSON: Well, he had begun to make statements, had he not, and you were generally being accused of burning the Reichstag building? You knew that, did you not? That was the . . .

GOERING: That accusation that I had set fire to the Reichstag came from a certain foreign press. That could not bother me because it was not consistent with the facts. I had no reason or motive for setting fire to the Reichstag. From the artistic point of view I did not at all regret that the assembly chamber was burned – I hoped to build a better one. But I did regret very much that I was forced to find a new meeting place for the Reichstag and, not being able to find one, I had to give up my Kroll Opera House, that is, the second State Opera House, for that purpose. The opera seemed to me much more important than the Reichstag.

MR. JUSTICE JACKSON: Have you ever boasted of burning the Reichstag building, even by way of joking?

GOERING: No. I made a joke, if that is the one you are referring to, when I said that, after this, I should be competing with Nero and that probably people would soon be saying that, dressed in a red toga and holding a lyre in my hand, I looked on at the fire and played while the Reichstag was burning. That was the joke. But the fact was that I almost perished in the flames, which would have been very unfortunate for the German people, but very fortunate for their enemies.

MR. JUSTICE JACKSON: You never stated then that you burned the Reichstag?

GOERING: No. I know that Herr Rauschning said in the book which he wrote, and which has often been referred to here, that I had discussed this with him. I saw Herr Rauschning only twice in my life and only for a short time on each occasion. If I had set fire to the Reichstag, I would presumably have let that be known only to my closest circle of confidants, if at all. I would not have told it to a man whom I did not know and whose appearance I could not describe at all today. That is an absolute distortion of the truth.

MR. JUSTICE JACKSON: Do you remember the luncheon on Hitler's birthday in 1942 at the Kasino, the officers' mess, at the headquarters of the Fuehrer in East Prussia?

GOERING: No.

MR. JUSTICE JACKSON: You do not remember that? I will ask that you be shown the affidavit of General Franz Halder, and I call your attention to his statements which may refresh your recollection. I read it.

"On the occasion of a luncheon on the Fuehrer's birthday in 1942, the people around the Fuehrer turned the conversation to the

Reichstag building and its artistic value. I heard with my own ears how Goering broke into the conversation and shouted: 'The only one who really knows the Reichstag is I, for I set fire to it.' And saying this he slapped his thigh."

GOERING: This conversation did not take place and I request that I be confronted with Herr Halder. First of all I want to emphasize that what is written here is utter nonsense. It says, "The only one who really knows the Reichstag is I." The Reichstag was known to every representative in the Reichstag. The fire took place only in the general assembly room, and many hundreds or thousands of people knew this room as well as I did. A statement of this type is utter nonsense. How Herr Halder came to make that statement I do not know. Apparently that bad memory, which also let him down in military matters, is the only explanation.

MR. JUSTICE JACKSON: You know who Halder is?

GOERING: Only too well.

MR. JUSTICE JACKSON: Can you tell us what position he held in the German Army?

GOERING: He was Chief of the General Staff of the Army, and I repeatedly pointed out to the Fuehrer, after the war started, that he would at least have to find a chief who knew something about such matters.

MR. JUSTICE JACKSON: Now, the Rohm purge you have left a little indefinite. What was it that Rohm did that he was shot? What acts did he commit?

GOERING: Rohm planned to overthrow the Government, and it was intended to kill the Fuehrer also. He wanted to follow it up by a revolution, directed in the first place against the Army, the officers' corps; those groups which he considered to be reactionary.

MR. JUSTICE JACKSON: And you had evidence of that fact?

GOERING: We had sufficient evidence of that fact.

MR. JUSTICE JACKSON: But he was never tried in any court where he would have a chance to tell his story as you are telling yours, was he?

GOERING: That is correct. He wanted to bring about a *Putsch* and therefore the Fuehrer considered it right that this thing should be nipped in the bud – not by a court procedure, but by smashing the revolt immediately.

MR. JUSTICE JACKSON: Were the names of the people who were killed in that purge, following the arrest of Rohm, ever published?

GOERING: Some of the names, yes; but not all of them, I believe.

MR. JUSTICE JACKSON: Who actually killed Rohm? Do you know?

GOERING: I do not know who personally carried out this action.

MR. JUSTICE JACKSON: To what organization was the order given?

GOERING: That I do not know either, because the shooting of Rohm was decreed by the Fuehrer and not by me, for I was competent in north Germany.

MR. JUSTICE JACKSON: And who took into custody those who were destined for concentration camps, and how many were there?

GOERING: The police carried out the arrest of those who were, first of all, to be interrogated, those who were not so seriously incriminated and of whom it was not known whether they were incriminated or not. A number of these people were released very soon, others not until somewhat later. Just how many were arrested in this connection I cannot tell you. The arrests were made by the police.

MR. JUSTICE JACKSON: The Gestapo, you mean?

GOERING: I assume so.

MR. JUSTICE JACKSON: And if Milch testified that he saw 700 or 800 in Dachau in 1935, there must have been a very much larger number arrested, since you say many were released. Do you know the number that were arrested?

GOERING: I state again, I do not know exactly how many were arrested because the necessary arrests, or the arrest of those who were considered as having a part in this, did not go through me. My action ended, so to speak, on the date when the revolt was smashed. I understood Milch a little differently and I sent a note to my counsel in order that it be made clear, through a question whether Milch meant by these 700 people those concerned with the Rohm *Putsch* or whether he meant to say that he saw altogether 700 arrested persons there. That is the way I understood it. But to clarify this statement we should have to question Milch again, for I believe this number of 500, 600, or 700, to be far too high for the total number of people arrested in connection with the Rohm *Putsch*.

MR. JUSTICE JACKSON: Among those who were killed were Von Schleicher and his wife. He was one of your political opponents, was he not?

GOERING: That is right.

MR. JUSTICE JACKSON: And also Erich Klausner, who had been Chief of the Catholic Action of Germany?

GOERING: Klausner was likewise among those who were shot. Actually, it was Klausner's case which caused me, as I stated recently, to ask the Fuehrer to give immediate orders to cease any further action, since, in my opinion, Klausner was quite wrongfully shot.

MR. JUSTICE JACKSON: And Strasser, who had been the former Number 2 man to Hitler and had disagreed with him in 12/1932, Strasser was killed, was he not?

GOERING: Of Strasser it cannot be said that he was Number 2 man after Hitler. He played an extremely important role within the Party before the seizure of power, but he was banned from the Party already before the seizure of power. Strasser participated in this revolt and he was also shot.

MR. JUSTICE JACKSON: And when it got down to a point where there were only two left on the list yet to be killed, you intervened and asked to have it stopped; is that correct?

GOERING: No, that is not entirely correct. I made it fairly clear and should like to repeat briefly that not when there were only two left on the list did I intervene; I intervened when I saw that many were shot who were not concerned with this matter. And when I did so, two persons were left who had taken a very active part, and the Fuehrer himself had ordered that they be shot.

The Fuehrer was particularly furious with one of them, the chief instigator of the action. What I wanted to make clear was that I said to the Fuehrer, "It is better for you to give up the idea of having these two main perpetrators executed, and put an end to the whole thing immediately." That is what I meant.

MR. JUSTICE JACKSON: What date was that? Did you fix the time?

GOERING: Yes, I can give you a definite time. As far as I recall the decisive day was Saturday; on Saturday evening between 6 and 7 o'clock the Fuehrer arrived by plane from Munich. My request to stop the action was made on Sunday, some time between 2 and 3 o'clock in the afternoon.

MR. JUSTICE JACKSON: And what happened to the two men who were left on the list – were they ever brought to trial?

GOERING: No. One, as far as I remember, was taken to a concentration camp, and the other was for the time being placed under a sort of house arrest, if I remember correctly.

MR. JUSTICE JACKSON: Now, going back to the time when you met Hitler; you said that he was a man who had a serious and definite aim, that he was not content with the defeat of Germany and with the Versailles Treaty; do you recall that?

GOERING: I am very sorry, the translation was rather defective and I cannot understand it. Please repeat.

MR. JUSTICE JACKSON: When you met Hitler, as I understand your testimony, you found a man with a serious and definite aim, as you said, in that he was not content with the defeat of Germany in the previous war and was not content with the Versailles Treaty.

GOERING: I think you did not quite understand me correctly here, for I did not put it that way at all. I stated that it had struck me that Hitler had very definite views of the impotency of protest; secondly, that he was of the opinion that Germany must be freed from the dictate of Versailles. It was not only Adolf Hitler; every German, every patriotic German had the same feelings, and I, being an ardent patriot, bitterly felt the shame of the dictate of Versailles, and I allied myself with the man about whom I felt that he perceived most clearly the consequences of this dictate, and that probably he was the man who would find the ways and means to set it aside. All the other talk in the Party about Versailles was, pardon the expression, mere twaddle.

MR. JUSTICE JACKSON: So, as I understand you, from the very beginning publicly and notoriously, it was the position of the Nazi Party that the Versailles Treaty must be set aside and that protest was impotent for that purpose?

GOERING: From the beginning it was the aim of Adolf Hitler and his movement to free Germany from the oppressive fetters of Versailles, that is, not from the whole Treaty of Versailles, but from those terms which were strangling Germany's future.

MR. JUSTICE JACKSON: And to do it by war, if necessary?

GOERING: We did not debate about that at all at the time. We debated only about the foremost condition, that Germany should acquire a different political structure, which alone would enable her to raise objections to this dictate, this one-sided dictate; everybody always called it a peace, whereas we Germans always called it a dictate, and not merely objections, but such objections as would demand consideration.

MR. JUSTICE JACKSON: That was the means, the means was the reorganization of the German State, but your aim was to get rid of what you call the dictate of Versailles.

GOERING: Liberation from these terms of the dictate of Versailles, which in the long run would make German life impossible, was the aim and the intention. But by that we did not go as far as to say, "We want to wage war on our enemies and be victorious." Rather, the aim was to suit the methods to the political events. Those were the basic considerations.

MR. JUSTICE JACKSON: And it was for that end that you and all of the other persons who became members of the Nazi Party gave to Hitler all power to make decisions for them, and agreed, in their oath of office, to give him obedience?

GOERING: Again here are several questions. Question One: The fight against the dictate of Versailles was for me the most decisive factor in joining the Party. For others, perhaps, other points of the program or of the ideology, which seemed more important, may have been more decisive. Giving the Fuehrer absolute powers was not a basic condition for getting rid of Versailles, but for putting into practice our conception of the Leadership Principle. To give him our oath before he became the head of the State was, under the conditions then existing, a matter of course for those who considered themselves members of his select leadership corps. I do not know and I cannot tell exactly, just how the oath was given before the seizure of power; I can only tell you what I myself did. After a certain period of time, when I had acquired more insight into the Fuehrer's personality, I gave him my hand and said: "I unite my fate with yours for better or for worse: I dedicate myself to you in good times and in bad, even unto death." I really meant it, and still do.

MR. JUSTICE JACKSON: If you would answer three or four questions for me "yes" or "no," then I would be quite willing to let you give your entire version of this thing. In the first place, you wanted a strong German State to overcome the conditions of Versailles.

GOERING: We wanted a strong State anyhow, regardless of Versailles; but in order to get rid of Versailles the State had, first of all, to be strong, for a weak State never makes itself heard; that we know from experience.

MR. JUSTICE JACKSON: And the Fuehrer principle you adopted because you thought it would serve the ends of a strong State?

GOERING: Correct.

MR. JUSTICE JACKSON: And this aim, which was one of the aims of the Nazi Party, to modify the conditions of Versailles, was a public and notorious aim in which the people generally joined – it was one of your best means of getting people to join with you, was it not?

GOERING: The dictate of Versailles was such that every German in my opinion, could not help being in favor of its modification, and there is no doubt that this was a very strong inducement for joining the movement.

MR. JUSTICE JACKSON: Now, a number of the men who took part in this movement are not here; and, for the record, there is no doubt in your mind, is there, that Adolf Hitler is dead?

GOERING: I believe there can be no doubt about that.

MR. JUSTICE JACKSON: And the same is true of Goebbels?

GOERING: Goebbels, I have no doubt about that, for I heard from someone whom I trust completely, that he saw Goebbels dead.

MR JUSTICE JACKSON: And you have no doubt of the death of Himmler, have you?

GOERING: I am not certain of that, but I think that you must be certain, since you know much more about it than I, as he died a prisoner of yours. I was not there.

MR. JUSTICE JACKSON: You have no doubt of the death of Heydrich, have you?

GOERING: I am absolutely certain about that.

MR. JUSTICE JACKSON: And probably of Bormann?

GOERING: I am not absolutely certain of this. I have no proof. I do not know, but I assume so.

MR. JUSTICE JACKSON: And those are the chief persons in your testimony, who have been mentioned as being responsible – Hitler for everything, Goebbels for inciting riots against the Jews, Himmler, who deceived Hitler, and Bormann, who misled him about his will?

GOERING: The influence exerted on the Fuehrer varied at different times. The chief influence on the Fuehrer, at least up till the end of 1941 or the beginning of 1942, if one can speak of influence at all, was exerted by me. From then until 1943 my influence gradually decreased, after which it rapidly dwindled. All in all, I do not believe anyone had anything like the influence on the Fuehrer that I had. Next to me, or apart from me, if one can speak of influence at all, Goebbels, with whom the Fuehrer was together quite a good deal, exerted an influence in a certain direction from the very beginning.

This influence wavered for a time and was very slight, and then increased greatly in the last years of the war. Before the seizure of power and during the years immediately following the seizure of power, Hess had a certain influence, but only in regard to his special sphere. Then, in the course of the years, Himmler's influence increased. From the end of 1944 on this influence decreased rapidly. The most decisive influence on the Fuehrer during the war, and especially from about 1942, after Hess went out in 1941 and a year had elapsed, was exerted by Herr Bormann. The latter had, at the end, a disastrously strong influence. That was possible only because the Fuehrer was filled with profound mistrust after 20 July, and because Bormann was with him constantly and reported on and described to him all matters. Broadly speaking these are the persons who had influence at one time or another.

MR. JUSTICE JACKSON: You took over a special intelligence organization in 1933 which was devoted to monitoring the telephone conversations of public officials and others inside and outside of Germany, did you not?

GOERING: I have explained that I had erected a technical apparatus which, as you said, monitored the conversations of important foreigners to and from foreign countries, telegrams and wireless communications which were transmitted not only from Germany to foreign countries, but also from one foreign country to the other through the ether, and which were intercepted. It also monitored telephone conversations within Germany of: (1) all important foreigners; (2) important firms, at times; and (3) persons who for any reason of a political or police nature were to be watched.

In order to prevent any abuse on the part of the police, this department had to obtain my personal permission when it was to listen to telephone conversations. Despite this there could, of course, be uncontrolled tapping of wires at the same time, just as that is technically possible everywhere today.

MR. JUSTICE JACKSON: You kept the results of those reports to yourself, did you not?

GOERING: No; this was the procedure: these reports in which the Foreign Office was interested were released to the Foreign Office. Those reports which were important to the Fuehrer went to the Fuehrer. Those which were important to the military authorities went to the Minister of War, or to the Air Ministry, or to the Ministry of Economy. I or my deputy decided whether a report was important for this or that office. There was a man there whose job and responsibility it was to see that these secret reports were submitted only to the chief. I could, of course, order at any time that this or that report should be exclusively for my knowledge and not be handed on. That was always possible.

MR. JUSTICE JACKSON: You had a good deal of difficulty with other police authorities who wanted to get possession of that organization, did you not?

GOERING: That is correct. The police did strive to get this instrument into their hands. But they did not get it from me, and perhaps they kept a watch of their own here and there. But the decisive control which had to be directed through the Ministry of Posts could technically be ordered only by me.

MR. JUSTICE JACKSON: You have listened to the evidence of the Prosecution against all of the defendants in this case, have you not?

GOERING: Yes.

MR. JUSTICE JACKSON: Is there any act of any of your co-defendants which you claim was not one reasonably necessary to carry out the plans of the Nazi Party?

GOERING: At present those are only assertions by the Prosecution; they are not yet facts which have been proved. In these assertions there are a number of actions which would not have been necessary.

MR. JUSTICE JACKSON: Will you specify which acts, of which defendants, you claim, are beyond the scope of the plans of the Party?

GOERING: That is a very difficult question which I cannot answer straight away and without the data.

DR. STAHMER: I object to this question. I do not believe that this is a question of fact, but rather of judgment, and that it is not possible to give an answer to such a general question.

THE PRESIDENT: Mr. Justice Jackson, the Tribunal thinks that the question is somewhat too wide.

MR. JUSTICE JACKSON: You have said that the program of the Nazi Party was to rectify certain injustices which you considered in the Treaty of Versailles; and I ask you whether it is not a fact that your program went considerably beyond any matter dealt with in that Treaty?

GOERING: Of course, the program contained a number of other points which had nothing to do with the Treaty of Versailles.

MR. JUSTICE JACKSON: I call your attention to a statement in *Mein Kampf* as follows:

"The boundaries of 1914 do not mean anything for the future of the German nation. They did not constitute a defense in the past nor do they constitute a power in the future. They will not give to the German people inner security or ensure their food supply, nor do these boundaries appear to be favorable or satisfactory from a military point of view."

That is all true, is it not?

GOERING: I should like to reread the original passage in *Mein Kampf* in order to determine if it is exactly as you have read it. I assume that it is correct. If so, I can reply that this is the text of a public book and not the Party program.

MR. JUSTICE JACKSON: The first country to be absorbed by Germany was Austria, and it was not a part of Germany before the first World War, and had not been taken from Germany by the Treaty of Versailles; is that correct?

GOERING: For this very reason this point was distinctly separated from Versailles in the program. Austria is directly connected with Versailles only insofar as the right of self-determination, as proclaimed there, was most gravely infringed; for Austria and the purely German population were not allowed the *Anschluss* which they wanted to see accomplished as early as 1918, after the revolution.

MR. JUSTICE JACKSON: The second territory taken by Germany was Bohemia, then Moravia, and then Slovakia. These were not taken from Germany by the Treaty of Versailles, nor were they part of Germany before the first World War.

GOERING: As far as the Sudetenland is concerned the same applies as for Austria. The German representatives of the German Sudetenland likewise sat in the Austrian Parliament, and under their leader, Lottmann, cast the same vote. It is different in the case of the last act, that is, the declaration of the Protectorate. These parts of Czech territory, especially Bohemia and Moravia were not constituent parts of the smaller German Reich before the Treaty of Versailles, but formerly they had been united to the German Reich for centuries. That is an historical fact.

MR. JUSTICE JACKSON: You still have not answered my question, although you answered everything else. They were not taken from you by the Treaty of Versailles, were they?

GOERING: Of course Austria was taken away by the Versailles Treaty and likewise the Sudetenland, for both territories, had it not been for the Treaty of Versailles and the Treaty of St. Gerrnain would have become German territories through the right of the people to self-determination. To this extent they have to do with it.

MR. JUSTICE JACKSON: You have testified, have you not, on interrogation, that it was Hitler's information that the United States would never go to war, even if attacked, and that he counted on the isolationists of that country to keep it out of war?

GOERING: This interrogation must have been recorded entirely incorrectly. That is the very reason why I refused from the beginning to give my oath to these interrogations before I had been able to look carefully at the German transcript and determine whether it had been correctly understood and translated. Only once, and that was on the part of the Russian Delegation, was a completely correct transcript submitted to me. I signed it page by page and thereby acknowledged it. Now, as far as this statement is concerned, I should like to put it right. I said that, at first, the Fuehrer did not believe that America would intervene in the war, and that he was confirmed in this belief by the attitude of the isolationist press, while I, on the contrary, unfortunately feared from the very beginning that America would in any case intervene in the war. Such nonsense – I hope you will excuse me – as to say that America would not come into the war even if she were attacked, you will understand that I could never have uttered, because, if a country is attacked, it defends itself.

MR. JUSTICE JACKSON: Do you know Axel Wennergren?

GOERING: He is a Swede whom I have seen two or three times.

MR. JUSTICE JACKSON: You talked with him about this subject, did you not?

GOERING: About the subject of America's entering the war I can very well have talked with him; it is even probable.

MR. JUSTICE JACKSON: You told him that a democracy could not mobilize and would not fight, did you not?

GOERING: I did not tell him any such nonsense, for we had one democracy as our chief enemy, namely England, and how this democracy would fight we knew from the last World War, and we experienced it again during this war. When I talked with Wennergren the war with England was in full swing.

MR. JUSTICE JACKSON: You have testified on interrogation, if I understand you correctly, that there were at all times two basic ideas in Hitler's mind, either to ally himself with Russia and seek increase in living space through the acquisition of colonies, or to ally himself with Britain and seek acquisition of territories in the East. But in view of his orientation, he would very much have preferred to ally himself with Great Britain, is that true?

GOERING: That is correct. I need only to refer to the book *Mein Kampf*, where these things were set down in thorough detail by Hitler.

MR. JUSTICE JACKSON: Now, as early as 1933 you began a real program to rearm Germany regardless of any treaty limitations, did you not?

GOERING: That is not correct.

MR. JUSTICE JACKSON: All right; tell us when you started.

GOERING: After all the proposals of disarmament which the Fuehrer made were refused, that is, shortly after our withdrawal from the disarmament conference, he made several proposals for a limitation; but, since these were not taken seriously or discussed, he ordered a complete rearmament. At the end of 1933 already certain slight preparations were started by me personally, to the extent that I had made some inconsiderable preparations in regard to the air and had also undertaken a certain militarization of the uniformed police. But that was done by me personally; I bear the responsibility.

MR. JUSTICE JACKSON: Well, then, the militarization of the police auxiliary was not a state affair. It was your personal affair. What do you mean by that?

GOERING: Not the auxiliary police, but the municipal police; that is, there was one uniformed police force which had simply police duty on the streets, and a second which was grouped in formations and was at our disposal for larger operations – not created by us, let it be understood, but existing at the time of the seizure of power. This municipal police, which was grouped in units, uniformed, armed, and housed in barracks, I formed very soon into a strong military instrument by taking these men out of the police service and having them trained more along military lines and giving them machine guns and such things, in addition to their small arms. This I did on my own responsibility. These formations were taken into the Armed Forces as regular Army units when the Armed Forces Law was declared.

MR. JUSTICE JACKSON: I want to ask you some questions from your interrogation of the 10/17/1945. I will first read you the questions and answers as they appear in the interrogations and I shall then ask you whether you gave those answers, and then you can make the explanations if you desire, and I assume you do. The interrogation reads:

"I wanted to ask you today about some of the economic history of the period. When was the armament program first discussed, that is, the rearmament program? What year?

"Answer: Immediately; in 1933.

"Question: In other words, Schacht had assumed the obligation at that time already, to raise funds for the rearmament program?

"Answer: Yes. But, of course, in co-operation with the Minister of Finance.

"Question: During the years 1933-1935, before general conscription came in, naturally, the rearmament was a secret rearmament, was it not?

"Answer: Yes.

"Question: So that money that was used outside of the budget would have to be raised by some secret means not to be known to foreign nations?

"Answer: Yes, unless they could be raised from normal Army funds.

"Question: That is to say, you had a small budget for the standing 100,000 man Army which was open, and the rest of the rearmament had to be from secret sources?

"Answer: Yes."

Were you asked those questions and did you give these answers, in substance?

GOERING: More or less; generally speaking that is correct. I have these remarks to make: Firstly, I was asked when rearmament had been discussed, not when it had been started. It had, of course, been discussed already in the year 1933, because it was clear at once that our government had to do something about it, that is to say, to demand that the others should disarm, and, if they did not disarm, that we should rearm. These things required discussion. The conclusion of the discussion and the formulation into a definite order followed after the failure of our attempts to get other countries to disarm. As soon as we, or rather the Fuehrer, saw that his proposals would not be accepted under any circumstances, a gradual rearmament, of course, began to take place. There was no reason whatsoever why we should inform the world about what we were doing in the way of rearmament. We were under no obligation to do that, nor was it expedient.

Herr Schacht, in the year 1933 at the very beginning, could not raise any funds because at the start he held no office. He was able to do this only at a later date. And here it was understandable that the funds had to be raised through the Minister of Finance and the President of the Reichsbank according to the wishes and the orders of the Fuehrer, especially as we had left no doubt that, if the other side did not disarm, we would rearm. That had already been set down on our Party program since 1921, and quite openly.

MR. JUSTICE JACKSON: Is it not a fact that on the 5/21/1935, by a secret decree, Schacht was named Plenipotentiary for the War Economy?

GOERING: The date – if you will kindly submit the decree to me, then I can tell you exactly. I have not the dates of decrees and laws in my head, especially if they do not have anything to do with me personally; but that can be seen from the decree.

MR. JUSTICE JACKSON: At any event, shortly after he was named, he suggested you as Commissioner for Raw Materials and Foreign Currency, did he not?

GOERING: If Herr Schacht made this suggestion shortly after his appointment, then that appointment could not have taken place until 1936, because not until the summer of 1936 did Herr Schacht, together with the Minister of War, Von Blomberg, make the proposal that I should become Commissioner for Raw Materials and Foreign Currency.

MR. JUSTICE JACKSON: Well, I ask you if you did not give this answer to the American interrogator on the 10/10/1945, referring to Schacht:

"He made the suggestion that I was to become the Commissioner for Raw Materials and Foreign Currency. He had the idea that, in that position, I could give the Minister for Economics and the President of the Reichsbank valuable support."

How did you give that answer, and is that information correct?

GOERING: Will you please repeat.

MR. JUSTICE JACKSON: Referring to Schacht, the record shows that you said:

"He made the suggestion that I was to become the Commissioner for Raw Materials and Foreign Currency. He had the idea that, in that position, I could give the Minister for Economics and the President of the Reichsbank valuable support."

GOERING: That is absolutely correct, with the exception of the word *"Reichstagsprasident;"* that ought to be President of the Reichsbank.

MR. JUSTICE JACKSON: Yes. That is the way I have it.

GOERING: It sounded like *"Reichstagsprasident"* over the earphones.

MR. JUSTICE JACKSON: "Moreover, he was very outspoken in the suggestion that he and Blomberg made, that I should be put in charge of the Four Year Plan. However, Schacht's idea was that I did not know very much about economy, and that he could easily hide behind my back."

GOERING: That I said the other day quite clearly.

MR. JUSTICE JACKSON: Now, from that time on you and Schacht collaborated for some time in preparing a rearmament program, did you not?

GOERING: From that time on I worked together with Schacht in economic matters and covered the whole field of German economy, including the armament program, which of course was a *sine qua non* for the reassumed German military sovereignty.

MR. JUSTICE JACKSON: And you and he had some jurisdictional differences and executed an agreement settling your different spheres of authority, did you not?

GOERING: Yes.

MR. JUSTICE JACKSON: And that was on 7/7/1937, right?

GOERING: On that day a certain proposal for a settlement was made, but this did not lead to anything final being accomplished. That was because of the nature of the two posts and our personalities. Both of us, I, as Delegate for the Four Year Plan, and Herr Schacht, as Minister of Economics and President of the Reichsbank, were able to exercise very great influence on German economy. As Herr Schacht also had a very strong personality and felt his position keenly, and I likewise was not inclined to hide my light under a bushel, whether we were friends or not we could not help getting in each other's way because of this question of authority, and one of us had finally to give in to the other.

MR. JUSTICE JACKSON: And there came a time when he left the Ministry and the Reichsbank?

GOERING: First he resigned from the Reich Ministry of Economy in 11/1937, and, as far as I know, he resigned as President of the Reichsbank at the end of 1938, but I cannot be certain about that date.

MR. JUSTICE JACKSON: There was no disagreement between you and him that the program of rearmament should be carried through, was there? You disagreed only in the methods of doing it?

GOERING: I assume that Herr Schacht also, as a good German, was, of course, ready to put all his strength at the disposal of Germany's rearmament, in order that Germany should be strong; and therefore differences could have occurred only in regard to methods, for neither Herr Schacht nor I was arming for a war of aggression.

MR. JUSTICE JACKSON: And after he left the rearmament work he remained as a Minister without Portfolio and sat in the Reichstag for some time, did he?

GOERING: That is correct. The Fuehrer wished it because, I believe, he wanted in this way to express his recognition of Herr Schacht.

MR. JUSTICE JACKSON: And do you recall the time when you considered the calling up of 15-year-olds, the conscription of 15-year-olds?

GOERING: During the war you mean?

MR. JUSTICE JACKSON: Yes.

GOERING: It was a question of Air Force auxiliaries, that is correct. They were 15- or 16-year-olds, I do not remember exactly which, and were called in as Air Force auxiliaries.

MR. JUSTICE JACKSON: I will ask that you be shown Document Number 3700 – PS and ask you whether you received from Schacht the letter of which that is a carbon copy.

[The document was handed to the witness.]

GOERING: Yes, I certainly did receive that letter. The year is not given here; that is missing in the copy.

MR. JUSTICE JACKSON: Could you fix, approximately, the date of its receipt?

GOERING: It says here 3rd of November, but from the incidents described on the other side, I assume it must be 1943. On this copy the year, strangely enough, is not given, but I believe it was in the year 1943, I received this letter.

MR. JUSTICE JACKSON: Did you reply to Document 3700 – PS? Did you reply to this letter?

GOERING: I cannot say that today with certainty – possibly.

MR. JUSTICE JACKSON: Now, the Four Year Plan had as its purpose to put the entire economy in a state of readiness for war, had it not?

GOERING: I have explained that it had two tasks to fulfill. 1) to safeguard German economy against crises, that is to say, to make it immune from export fluctuations, and, as regards food, from harvest fluctuations, as far as possible; and 2) to make it capable of withstanding a blockade, that is to say, in the light of experiences in the first World War, to put it on such a basis that in a second World War a blockade would not have such disastrous consequences. That the Four Year Plan in this respect was a basic prerequisite for the entire building-up and expansion of the armament industry goes without saying. Without it the rearmament industry could not have been shaped in this way.

MR. JUSTICE JACKSON: To get a specific answer, if possible did you not say in a letter to Schacht, dated the 12/18/1936, that you saw it to be your task, using these words "within 4 years to put the entire economy in a state of readiness for war"? Did you say that or did you not?

GOERING: Of course I said that.

MR. JUSTICE JACKSON: Now, do you recall the report of Blomberg in 1937 in which, and you may examine if you wish Document Number C-175, in which he starts his report by saying:

"The general political position justifies the supposition that Germany need not expect an attack from any side."

GOERING: That may have been quite possible at that moment. I took a most reassuring view of the German situation in 1937.

It was after the Olympic games and at that time the general situation was extraordinarily calm. But that had nothing to do with the fact that I felt obliged, quite apart from passing fluctuations from a calmer to a more tense atmosphere, to make German economy ready for war and proof against crises or blockades, for exactly 1 year later incidents of a different nature occurred.

MR. JUSTICE JACKSON: Well now, does not Blomberg continue: "Grounds for this are, in addition to the lack of desire for war in almost all nations, particularly the Western Powers, the deficiencies in the preparedness for war of a number of states, and of Russia in particular"?

That was the situation in 1937, was it not?

GOERING: That is the way Herr Von Blomberg saw the situation. Concerning the readiness for war in Russia, Herr Von Blomberg in the same way as all those representatives of our Reichswehr mentality, was always really mistaken in contrast to the opinion pressed in other quarters with regard to Russian armaments. This is merely the opinion of Herr Von Blomberg, not the Fuehrer's, not mine, and not the opinion of other leading people.

MR. JUSTICE JACKSON: That, however, was the report of the Commander-in-chief of the Armed Forces on the 6/24/1937, was it not?

GOERING: That is correct.

MR. JUSTICE JACKSON: You organized, 1 month later, the Hermann Goering Works?

GOERING: Right.

MR. JUSTICE JACKSON: And the Hermann Goering Works were concerned with putting Germany in the condition of readiness for war, were they not?

GOERING: No, that is not right. The Hermann Goering Works were at first concerned solely with the mining of German iron ore in the region of Salzgitter and in a district in the Oberpfalz, and, after the annexation, with the iron ore works in Austria. The Hermann Goering Works first established exclusively mining and refining plants for this ore and foundries. Only much later steel works and rolling mills were added, that is to say, an industry.

MR. JUSTICE JACKSON: The Hermann Goering Works were a part of the Four Year Plan, were they not?

GOERING: That is right.

MR. JUSTICE JACKSON: And you have already said that the Four Year Plan had as its purpose to put the economy in a state of readiness for war; and the Hermann Goering Works were organized to exploit ore mining and iron smelting resources and to carry the process through to completed guns and tanks, were they not?

GOERING: No, that is not correct; the Hermann Goering Works had at first no armament works of their own, but merely produced, as I again repeat, the basic product, steel, crude steel.

MR. JUSTICE JACKSON: Well, at all events, you continued your efforts and on the 11/8/1943, you made a speech describing those efforts to the Gauleiter in the Fuehrer building at Iunih, is that right?

GOERING: I do not know the exact date, but about that time I made a short speech, one of a series of speeches, to the Gauleiter about the air situation, as far as I remember, and also perhaps about the armament situation. I do not remember the words of that speech, since I was never asked about it until now; but the facts are correct.

MR. JUSTICE JACKSON: Well, let me remind you if you used these terms, refreshing your recollection:

"Germany, at the beginning of the war, was the only country in the world possessing an operative, fighting air force. The other countries had split their air fleets up into army and navy air fleets and considered the air arm primarily as a necessary and important auxiliary of the other branches of the forces. In consequence, they lacked the instrument which is alone capable of dealing concentrated and effective blows, namely, an operative air force. In Germany we had gone ahead on those lines from the very outset, and the main body of the Air Force was disposed in such a way that it could thrust deeply into the hostile areas with strategic effect while a lesser portion of the air force, consisting of Stukas and, of course, fighter planes, went into action on the front line in the battlefields. You all know what wonderful results were achieved by these tactics and what superiority we attained at the very beginning of the war through this modern kind of air force."

GOERING: That is entirely correct; I certainly did say that, and what is more, I acted accordingly. But in order that this be understood and interpreted correctly, I must explain briefly:

In these statements I dealt with two separate opinions on air strategy, which are still being debated today and without a decision having been reached. That is to say: Should the air force form an auxiliary arm of the army and the navy and be split up to form a constituent part of the army and the navy, or should it be a separate branch of the armed forces? I explained that for nations with a very large navy it is perhaps understandable that such a division should be made. From the very beginning, thank God, we made the correct, consistent decision to build up a strong – I emphasize the word "strong" – and independent Air Force along with the Army and the Navy; and I described how we passed from a tentative air force to an operative air force. As an expert I am today still of the opinion that only an operative air force can have a decisive effect. I have also explained in regard to two- and four-engine bombers, that at first I was quite satisfied with the two-engine bombers because, firstly, I did not have four-engine bombers; and secondly, the operational radius of the two-engine bombers was wide enough for the enemy with whom we had to deal at that time. I further pointed out that the main reason for the swift ending of the campaign in Poland and in the West was the effect of the Air Force. So that is quite correct.

MR. JUSTICE JACKSON: I remind you of the testimony of the witness Milch, sworn on your behalf, as to a subject on which I have not heard you express yourself. He said: "I had the impression that already at the time of the occupation of the Rhineland, he, Goering, was worried lest Hitler's policy should lead to war."

Do you remember that?

GOERING: Yes.

MR. JUSTICE JACKSON: And was it true or false? True or mistaken, perhaps, I should say.

GOERING: No, I did not want a war and I thought the best way to avoid a war was to be strongly armed according to the well known adage, "He who has a strong sword has peace."

MR. JUSTICE JACKSON: Well, you are still of that opinion?

GOERING: I am of that opinion today, now that I see the entanglements more than ever.

MR. JUSTICE JACKSON: And it is true, as Milch said, that you were worried that Hitler's policies would lead to war at the time of the occupation of the Rhineland?

GOERING: Excuse me, I just understood you to ask whether it is also my opinion today that only a nation that is strongly armed can maintain peace. That is what I meant to answer with my last statement.

If you are connecting this question to the statement of Milch, that I was worried lest the policy of the Fuehrer might lead to war, I should like to say that I was worried lest war might come; and if possible I wanted to avoid it, but not in the sense that the policy of the Fuehrer would lead to it, because the Fuehrer also desired to carry out his program by agreements and diplomatic action.

In regard to the occupation of the Rhineland I was somewhat worried at the time about the reactions; all the same, it was necessary.

MR. JUSTICE JACKSON: And when nothing happened, the next step was Austria?

GOERING: The one has nothing to do with the other. I never had any misgivings about Austria leading to a war, as I had with the Rhineland occupation, for in the case of the Rhineland occupation I could well imagine that there might be repercussions. But how there could be any repercussions from abroad over the union of two brother nations of purely German blood was not clear to me, especially since Italy, who always pretended that she had a vital interest in a separate Austria, had somewhat changed her ideas. It could not have mattered in the least to England and France nor could they have had the slightest interest in this union. Therefore I did not see the danger of its leading to a war.

MR. JUSTICE JACKSON: I ask you just a few questions about Austria. You said that you and Hitler had felt deep regret about the death of Dollfuss, and I ask you if it is not a fact that Hitler put up a plaque in Vienna in honor of the men who murdered Dollfuss, and went and put a wreath on their graves when he was there. Is that a fact? Can you not answer that question with "yes" or "no"?

GOERING: No, I cannot answer it with either "yes" or "no," if I am to speak the truth according to my oath. I cannot say 'Yes, he did it," because I do not know; I cannot say, "No, he did not do it," because I do not know that either. I want to say that I heard about this event here for the first time.

MR. JUSTICE JACKSON: Now, in 6/1937, Seyss-Inquart came to you and State Secretary Keppler, and you had some negotiations.

GOERING: Yes.

MR. JUSTICE JACKSON: And it was Seyss-Inquart's desire to have an independent Austria, was it not?

GOERING: As far as I remember, yes.

MR. JUSTICE JACKSON: And Keppler was the man who was sent by Hitler to Vienna at the time of the *Anschluss* and who telegraphed to Hitler not to march in, do you recall?

GOERING: Yes.

MR. JUSTICE JACKSON: That is the telegram that you characterized as impudent and senseless from the man who was on the spot, and who had negotiated earlier with Seyss-Inquart, do you recall that?

GOERING: I did not characterize the telegram with this word which has just been translated to me in German, that is "impudent." I said that this telegram could no longer have any influence and was superfluous, because the troops were already on the move and had their order; the thing was already underway.

MR. JUSTICE JACKSON: You had demanded that Seyss-Inquart be made Chancellor? Is that right?

GOERING: I did not desire that personally, but it arose out of the circumstance that at that time he was the only man who could assume the Chancellorship because he was already in the Government.

MR. JUSTICE JACKSON: Now, did Seyss-Inquart become Chancellor of Austria with the understanding that he was to surrender his country to Germany, or did you lead him to believe that he would be independent, have an independent country?

GOERING: I explained the other day that even at the time when I left by plane the next morning, the Fuehrer himself had still not made up his mind as to whether the union with Austria should not be brought about by means of a joint head of state. I also said that I personally did not consider this solution far-reaching enough and that I was for an absolute, direct, and total *Anschluss*.

I did not know exactly what Seyss-Inquart's attitude was at this time. Nevertheless I feared that his attitude was rather in the direction of continued separation with co-operation, and did not go as far as my attitude in the direction of a total *Anschluss*.

Therefore I was very satisfied when this total *Anschluss* crystallized in the course of the day.

MR. JUSTICE JACKSON: I respectfully submit that the answers are not responsive, and I repeat the question.

Did Seyss-Inquart become Chancellor of Austria with an understanding that he would call in the German troops and surrender Austria to Germany, or did you lead him to believe that he could continue an independent Austria?

GOERING: Excuse me, but that is a number of questions which I cannot answer simply with "yes" or "no."

If you ask me, "Did Seyss-Inquart become Chancellor according to Hitler's wishes and yours?" – yes.

If you then ask me, "Did he become Chancellor with the understanding that he should send a telegram for troops to march in?" – I say, "No," because at the time of the Chancellorship there was no question of his sending us a telegram.

If you ask me, thirdly, "Did he become Chancellor on the understanding that he would be able to maintain an independent Austria?" – then I have to say again that the final turn of events was not clear in the Fuehrer's mind on that evening.

That is what I tried to explain.

MR. JUSTICE JACKSON: Is it not true that you suspected that he might want to remain as independent as possible, and that that was one of the reasons why the troops were marched in?

GOERING: No. Excuse me, there are two questions: I strongly suspected that Seyss-Inquart wanted to be as independent as possible. The sending of troops had nothing at all to do with that suspicion; not a single soldier would have been needed for that. I gave my reasons for the sending of the troops.

MR. JUSTICE JACKSON: But it was never intimated to Seyss-Inquart that Austria would not remain independent until after – as you put it – the Fuehrer and you were in control of Austria's fate? Is that a fact?

GOERING: That was certainly not told him beforehand by the Fuehrer. As far as I was concerned, it was generally known that I desired it, and I assume that he knew of my attitude.

MR. JUSTICE JACKSON: Now, you have stated that you then in conversation with Ribbentrop in London, stressed that no ultimatum had been put to Seyss-Inquart, and you have said that legally that was the fact.

GOERING: I did not say "legally," I said "diplomatically."

MR. JUSTICE JACKSON: I ask to have your attention called to Document Number 3575 – PS (Exhibit Number USA – 781) which is the minutes of the Reich Defense Council of 11/18/1938, with you presiding.

I call your attention that the "meeting consisted solely of a 3-hour lecture by the Field Marshal. No decision took place."

Is that correct?

[Document 3575 – PS was submitted to the defendant.]

GOERING: I have to read it first, this is the first time I have seen the document.

MR. JUSTICE JACKSON: You did not know when you testified yesterday that we had this document, did you? Would you kindly answer that question?

GOERING: I have not seen this document before. I have to look at it first. It says here: "Notes on the Session of the Reich Defense Council on 11/18/1938."

The Reich Defense Council, as it was described here, comprise few people. Here there were present, however, all Reich ministers and state secretaries, also the commanders-in-chief of the Army and the Navy, the chiefs of the General Staff, of the three branches of the Armed Forces, Reichsleiter Bormann for the Deputy of the Fuehrer, General Daluege, SS Gruppenfuehrer Heydrich, the Reich Labor Fuehrer, the Price Commissioner, the President of the Reich Labor Office, and others.

When I gave my testimony I was thinking only of the Reich Defense Council as such. This is dealing with the Reich Defense Council within the framework of a large assembly. Nevertheless I was not thinking of that; this concerns, over and beyond the Reich Defense Council, an assembly that was much larger than that provided for under the Reich Defense Council.

MR. JUSTICE JACKSON: I call your attention to the fact that the "Field Marshal stated it to be the task of the Reich Defense Council to correlate all the forces of the nation for accelerated building up of German armament."

Do you find that?

GOERING: Yes, I have it now.

MR. JUSTICE JACKSON: The second paragraph?

GOERING: Yes.

MR. JUSTICE JACKSON: Under II, "The Physical Task: The assignment is to raise the level of armament from a current index of 100 to one of 300."

GOERING: Yes.

DR. SIEMERS: I cannot quite see the reason why it repeatedly happens that the Defense does not receive documents that are discussed in Court and that are submitted to the Court. The document now discussed is also not known to us, at least not to me. During the last few days I have noticed that several times documents were suddenly presented by the Prosecution without any effort having been made to inform us of their existence.

MR. JUSTICE JACKSON: That is perfectly true, and I think every lawyer knows that one of the great questions in this case is credibility, and that if we have, in cross-examination, to submit every document before we can refer to it in cross-examination after we hear their testimony, the possibilities of useful cross-examination are destroyed.

Now, of course, he did not know; and we have had the experience of calling document after document to their attention, always to be met with some explanation, carefully arranged and read here from notes. No defendant has ever had better opportunity to prepare his case than these defendants, and I submit that cross-examination of them should not be destroyed by any requirement that we submit documents in advance.

THE PRESIDENT: Did you wish to say something?

DR. SIEMERS: Yes. I should like to make two points. First, I am entirely agreed if Mr. Justice Jackson wants to make use of the element of surprise. I should merely be thankful if the Defense then were also permitted to use the element of surprise. Yet we have been told heretofore that we must show every document we want to submit weeks ahead of time, so that the Prosecution has several weeks to form an opinion on it.

Secondly, if the element of surprise is being used, I believe that at least we, as Defense Counsel, should not be given this surprise at the moment when the document is submitted to the Court and to the witness. I have at this moment neither today's documents nor the documents of the previous days.

THE PRESIDENT: What you have just said is entirely inaccurate. You have never been compelled to disclose any documents which you wished to put to a witness in cross-examination. This is cross-examination and therefore it is perfectly open to Counsel for the Prosecution to put any document without disclosing it beforehand; just as Defense Counsel could have put any document to witnesses called on behalf of the Prosecution, if they had wished to do so, in cross-examination.

I am sure that if counsel for the defendants wish to re-examine upon any such document as this, a copy of it will be supplied to them for that purpose.

The Tribunal now rules that this document may be put to the witness now.

DR. SIEMERS: Does the Defense also have the opportunity, now that it is known to the entire Court, of receiving the document?

THE PRESIDENT: Yes, certainly.

DR. SIEMERS: I should be thankful if I could have a copy now.

MR. JUSTICE JACKSON: I am frank to say I do not know whether we have adequate copies to furnish them to all the Defense Counsel now.

THE PRESIDENT: Maybe you have not, but you can let them have one or more copies.

MR. JUSTICE JACKSON: But I do not think we should furnish copies until the examination with reference to that document is completed, that is to say —

THE PRESIDENT: Yes, Dr. Dix.

DR. DIX: I should like to make one request that at least the technical possibilities that at least the counsel of these defendants who are being cross-examined also be given the document that is submitted to the defendant, so that they are in a position, just as the Tribunal is, to follow the examination.

If Justice Jackson says that it is his opinion that it would be right for the defense counsel – in this case my colleague Stahmer to receive this document only after the examination – in this case of Goering – has ended, I beg earnestly, in the interest of the dignity and prestige of the Defense, to take objection to this suggestion of Justice Jackson's. I do not believe that he means by that to insinuate that the Defense Counsel would be able – having these documents in its hands at the same time as the Tribunal and at the same time as the witness – somehow through signs or otherwise to influence the defendant and thereby disturb the cross-examination by Mr. Justice Jackson, or by the prosecutor. Mr. Justice Jackson certainly did not mean that, but one might draw that conclusion.

I therefore make this request: If in the cross-examination, for the purpose of the cross-examination, in view of the altogether justified element of surprise, a document is presented to a witness that at the same time is presented to the Tribunal, that at least a copy of this document be given at the same time to the defense counsel, the defense counsel concerned, either the one who has called the witness or the one whose defendant is in the witness box, so that he can have some idea of what the witness is being confronted with, for Goering could read this document, but Dr. Stahmer could not. In other words, he was not in a position to follow the next part of Mr. Justice Jackson's cross-examination. That is certainly not intended, and would certainly not be fair, and I should therefore like to ask Mr. Justice Jackson to reply to my suggestion, and my application, in order to arrive at an understanding and thereby to relieve the Tribunal of the decision on a question that to me seems self-evident.

THE PRESIDENT: Mr. Justice Jackson, the Tribunal is inclined to think – the Tribunal certainly thinks – that you are perfectly right, that there is no necessity at all, as I have already stated, to disclose the document to the defendants before you use it in cross-examination. But, at the time you use it in cross-examination is there any objection to handing a copy of it to the counsel for the defendant who is being cross-examined?

JUSTICE JACKSON: In some instances it is physically impossible because of our situation in reference to these documents. A good many of these documents have come to us very lately. Our photostatic facilities are limited.

THE PRESIDENT: I am not suggesting that you should hand it to all of them, but only to Dr. Stahmer.

DR. JUSTICE JACKSON: If we have copies, I have no objection to doing that, but if we do not have them in German – our difficulty has always been to get German copies of these documents.

DR. DIX: May I say something else. If it is not possible in German, then it should at least be possible in English, for one English copy will certainly be available. Furthermore, if it is a question of German witnesses, such as Goering, the document will be shown him in German anyhow; it will certainly be shown the witness in German. I believe that will surely be possible.

[Dr. Siemers approached the lectern.]

THE PRESIDENT: We do not really need to hear more than one counsel on this sort of point. I have already ruled upon your objection, which was that the document should be produced before hand, but the Tribunal has already ruled that objection should be denied.

DR. SIEMERS: Mr. President, I am sorry. My motion was that the Defense Counsel should receive these documents at the same time the Tribunal does. I am not of the opinion expressed by Dr. Dix, that only one defense counsel should receive it. If it is a report regarding the Reich Defense Council, then it is a document important to several defendants. One copy is therefore not sufficient, but each defense counsel must have one. I believe that Mr. Justice Jackson...

THE PRESIDENT: But not at this moment. There are, as we all know, the very greatest difficulties in producing all these documents, and extraordinary efforts have been made by the Prosecution and the Translating Division to supply the defendants with documents, and with documents in German, and it is not necessary that every member of the Defense Counsel have these documents at the time the witness is being cross-examined. I am sure the Prosecution will do everything it can to let you have the documents in due course – any document that is being used.

In the opinion of the Tribunal it is perfectly sufficient if one copy of the document is supplied to the counsel for the witness who is being cross-examined. As I say, the Prosecution will doubtless let you have copies of these documents in due course.

You are appearing for the Defendant Raeder, and the Defendant Raedfer, I am afraid, at the present rate will not be in the witness.

DR. SIEMERS: The result of that is that the defense counsel who is not momentarily concerned, cannot understand the cross examination. As to the technical question, I ask the Court to consider that I cannot follow Justice Jackson on this technical point. The document is mimeographed by means of a stencil. In mimeographing it makes no difference at all whether 20, 40, 80, or 150 copies are produced. It makes no difference from the point of view of time except perhaps 4 or 5 minutes. I consider for this reason that one can hardly refer to technical difficulties in this matter.

THE PRESIDENT: Counsel for the Prosecution will consider what you say, but no rule has been made by the Tribunal that every document should be supplied to every counsel during cross examination.

GOERING: I should like to say again in regard to the document that this is not...

MR. JUSTICE JACKSON: May I respectfully ask that the witness be instructed to answer the question and reserve his explanations until his counsel takes him on. Otherwise, this cross-examination cannot successfully be conducted, in the sense of being reasonable in time.

THE PRESIDENT: I have already explained, on several occasions, that it is the duty of defendants when they are in the witness box, and the duty of witnesses, to answer questions directly, if they are capable of being answered directly, in the affirmative or in the negative; and if they have any explanation to make afterwards, they can make it after answering the question directly.

MR. JUSTICE JACKSON: I call your attention to Item 3, under II. "Finances," reading as follows:

"Very critical situation of the Reich Exchequer. Relief initially through the milliard imposed on the Jews and through profits accruing to the Reich from the Aryanization of Jewish enterprises."

You find that in the minutes, do you not?

GOERING: Yes, that is there.

MR. JUSTICE JACKSON: And you find the minutes signed by Woermann, do you not?

GOERING: No, that is not true. I beg your pardon? Here on the photostat Woermann has signed it, that is not Bormann. I know Bormann's signature well, it is quite different.

MR. JUSTICE JACKSON: I said Woermann.

GOERING: Woermann, yes.

MR. JUSTICE JACKSON: All right, my poor pronunciation. Well, as it not a fact that you set up a working committee under the Reich Defense Council which did meet from time to time and did carry on certain work?

GOERING: I have already explained recently: That was the committee of departmental chiefs.

MR. JUSTICE JACKSON: And I call your attention to Document Number EC – 405, minutes of a meeting of the Working Committee of the Reich Defense Council, Meeting Number 10.

GOERING: I understood the President to say before that when I have answered the question, I can add an explanation that seems necessary to me. Now that I have clearly answered your question with regard to the first document, I want to stress once again that this was not a meeting of the closed Reich Defense Council but a general calling together of all ministers, state secretaries and numerous other persons. And that I began my statements as follows:

"I. Organization of the Reich Defense Council: The Reich Defense Council was already, by decision of the Cabinet of 1933-1934, called into being; but it has never met. Through the Reich Defense Law of 9/4/1938 it was re-established. The Chairman is the Fuehrer, who has appointed General Field Marshal Goering his permanent deputy."

Concerning the Reich Defense Council, about which we have been talking, consisting of Schacht – or rather of the triumvirate – it is attested here in writing once more, as I have correctly said, that this Council never met. I ask to have the question about the second document repeated, as I have forgotten it.

MR. JUSTICE JACKSON: You testified that the movement into the Rhineland had not been planned in advance.

GOERING: Only a short time in advance, I emphasized.

MR. JUSTICE JACKSON: How long?

GOERING: As far as I recall, at the most 2-3 weeks.

MR. JUSTICE JACKSON: Now, I call your attention to the minutes of the 10th meeting of the Working Committee of the Reich Defense Council, Document Number EC – 405 toward the end of that document, the discussion on 6/26/1935, which reads as follows...

GOERING: May I ask what page? This document is very long and is new to me. What page, please, otherwise I shall have to read the whole document.

MR. JUSTICE JACKSON: Turn to the last paragraph and we will work backwards.

"Commitment to writing of directives for mobilization purposes is permissible only insofar as it is absolutely necessary for the smooth execution of the measures provided for the demilitarized zone. Without exception such material must be kept in safes."

Do you find that part?

GOERING: This document that has been handed to me contains alternating statements of various individuals, that is, a dialogue. May I ask once more . . . The last paragraph contains nothing of what you have stated, apparently there must be a difference between the German and English texts. The last paragraph here is altogether irrelevant. Where, please, am I to read in the document?

MR. JUSTICE JACKSON: Do you find the third paragraph from the end? If my document is correct; we have got the same document.

GOERING: You must tell me who was speaking, for different persons speak here.

[The place in the document was indicated to the defendant.]

Now it has been shown to me. Under the name Jodl; I have to read through it first.

MR. JUSTICE JACKSON: Do you find this:

"The demilitarized zone requires special treatment. In his speech of 5/24/1935 and in other statements, the Fuehrer and Reich Chancellor declared that the stipulations of the Versailles Treaty and the Locarno Pact regarding the demilitarized zone would be observed."

Do you find this?

GOERING: Yes.

MR. JUSTICE JACKSON: And do you find the next paragraph,

"Since at present international entanglements must be avoided under all circumstances, all urgently needed preparations may be made. The preparations as such, or their planning, must be kept in strictest secrecy in the zone itself as well as in the rest of the Reich."

Do you find this?

GOERING: Yes.

MR. JUSTICE JACKSON: And you also find, "These preparations include in particular" – a) and b) are not important to my present question – "c) Preparation for the liberation of the Rhine."

GOERING: Oh, no, here you have made a great mistake. The original phrase – and this alone is the point in question – is: "c) Preparation for the clearing of the Rhine" It is a purely technical preparation that has nothing at all to do with the liberation of the

Rhineland – Here it says, first, mobilization measures for transportation and communications, then "c) Preparation for the clearing of the Rhine," that is, in case of mobilization preparations the Rhine is not to be overburdened with freighters, tugboats, et cetera, but the river has to be clear for military measures. Then it continues: "d) Preparation for local defense," et cetera. Thus you see, it figures among small quite general, ordinary and usual preparations for mobilization. The phrase used by the Prosecution . . .

MR. JUSTICE JACKSON: Mobilization, exactly.

GOERING: That, if you remember, I stressed clearly in my statement, that in the demilitarized zone general preparations for mobilization were made. I mentioned the purchase of horses, et cetera. I wanted only to point out the mistake regarding "clearing of the Rhine," which has nothing to do with the Rhineland, but only with the river.

MR. JUSTICE JACKSON: Well, those preparations were preparations for armed occupation of the Rhineland, were they not?

GOERING: No, that is altogether wrong. If Germany had become involved in a war, no matter from which side, let us assume from the East, then mobilization measures would have had to be carried out for security reasons throughout the Reich, in this event even in the demilitarized Rhineland; but not for the purpose of occupation, of liberating the Rhineland.

MR. JUSTICE JACKSON: You mean the preparations were not military preparations?

GOERING: Those were general preparations for mobilization, such as every country makes, and not for the purpose of the occupation of the Rhineland.

MR. JUSTICE JACKSON: But were of a character which had to be kept entirely secret from foreign powers?

GOERING: I do not think I can recall reading beforehand the publication of the mobilization preparations of the United States.

MR. JUSTICE JACKSON: Well, I respectfully submit to the Tribunal that this witness is not being responsive, and has not been in his examination, and that it is . . .

[The defendant interposed a few words which were not recorded.]

It is perfectly futile to spend our time if we cannot have responsive answers to our questions.

[The defendant interposed a few words which were not recorded.]

We can strike these things out. I do not want to spend time doing that, but this witness, it seems to me, is adopting, and has adopted in the witness box and in the dock, an arrogant and contemptuous attitude toward the Tribunal which is giving him the trial which he never gave a living soul, nor dead ones either.

I respectfully submit that the witness be instructed to make notes, if he wishes, of his explanations, but that he be required to answer my questions and reserve his explanations for his counsel to bring out.

THE PRESIDENT: I have already laid down the general rule which is binding upon this defendant as upon other witnesses.

MR. JUSTICE JACKSON: If the Tribunal please, the last question which I asked last night referring to mobilization preparations in the Rhineland, as shown in the official transcript, was this: "But of a character which had to be kept entirely secret from foreign powers?" The answer was: "I do not believe I can recall the publication of the preparations of the United States for mobilization."

Now, representing the United States of America, I am confronted with these choices – to ignore that remark and allow it to stand for people who do not understand our system; or to develop, at considerable expense of time, its falsity; or to answer it in rebuttal. The difficulty arises from this, Your Honor, that if the witness is permitted to volunteer statements in cross-examination there is no opportunity to make objection until they are placed on the record. Of course, if such an answer had been indicated by a question of counsel, as I respectfully submit would be the orderly procedure, would have been objection, the Tribunal would have been in a position to discharge its duty under the Charter and I would have been in a position to have shortened the case by not having that remark placed.

The Charter in Article 18 provides that the Tribunal shall rule out irrelevant issues and statements of any kind whatsoever. We are squarely confronted with that question; we cannot discharge those duties if the defendant is to volunteer these statements without questions which bring them up. I respectfully submit that, if the ruling of the Tribunal that the defendant may volunteer questions of this kind is to prevail, the control of these proceedings is put in the hands of this defendant, and the United States has been substantially denied its right of cross-examination under the Charter, because cross-examination cannot be effective under this kind of procedure. Since we cannot anticipate, we cannot meet..

THE PRESIDENT: I quite agree with you that any reference to the United States' secrecy with reference to mobilization is entirely irrelevant and that the answer ought not to have been made, but the only rule which the Tribunal can lay down as a general rule is the rule – already laid down – that the witness must answer if possible "yes" or "no," and that he may make such explanations as may be necessary after answering questions directly in that way and that such explanations must be brief and not be speeches. As far as this particular answer goes, I think it is entirely irrelevant.

MR. JUSTICE JACKSON: I must, of course, bow to the ruling of the Tribunal, but it is to the second part, I quite recall the admonition of the Court that there shall be answers "yes" or "no. This witness, of course, pays not the slightest attention to that, and I must say I cannot blame him; he is pursuing his interests. But we have no way of anticipating, and here we are confronted with this statement in the record, because when these statements are volunteered they are in the record before the Tribunal can rule upon them and I have no opportunity to make objections, and the Tribunal have no opportunity to rule. And it puts, as I said before the control of these proceedings in the hands of the defendant, if he first makes the charges and then puts it up to us to ignore them or answer them by long cross-examination in rebuttal; and I think the specific charge made against the United States of America from the witness stand presents that.

Your Honor now advises the United States that it is an improper answer, but it is in the record and we must deal with it. I respectfully submit that unless we have...

THE PRESIDENT: What exactly is the motion you are making? Are you asking the Tribunal to strike the answer out of the record?

MR. JUSTICE JACKSON: Well, no; in a Trial of this kind, where propaganda is one of the purposes of the defendant, striking out does no good after the answer is made, and Goering knows that as well as I. The charge has been made against the United States and it is in the record. I am now moving that this witness be instructed that he must answer my questions "yes" or "no" if they permit an answer, and that the explanation be brought out by his counsel in a fashion that will permit us to make objections, if they are irrelevant, and to obtain rulings of the Tribunal, so that the Tribunal can discharge its functions of ruling out irrelevant issues and statements of any kind whatsoever. We must not let the Trial degenerate into a bickering contest between counsel and the witness. That is not what the United States would expect me to participate in. I respectfully suggest that if he can draw any kind of challenge . . .

THE PRESIDENT: Are you submitting to the Tribunal that the witness has to answer every question "yes" or "no" and wait until he is re-examined for the purpose of making any explanations at all?

MR. JUSTICE JACKSON: I think that is the rule of cross examination under ordinary circumstances. The witness, if the question permits it, must answer, and if there are relevant explanations they should be reserved until later.

Now let me come back to the specific problem I have right here this morning. Here is an answer given which the Tribunal now rules is irrelevant – but we have no opportunity to object to it. The Tribunal had no opportunity to rule upon it. The witness asks, "Did you ever hear of the United States publishing its plan of mobilization?" Of course, we would have objected. The difficulty is that the Tribunal loses control of these proceedings if the defendant, in a case of this kind where we all know propaganda is one of the purposes of the defendant, is permitted to put his propaganda in, and then we have to meet it afterwards. I really feel that the United States is deprived of the opportunity of the technique of cross-examination if this is the procedure.

THE PRESIDENT: Surely it is making too much of a sentence the witness has said, whether the United States makes its orders for mobilization public or not. Surely that is not a matter of very great importance. Every country keeps certain things secret. Certainly it would be much wiser to ignore a statement of that sort. But as to the general rule, the Tribunal will now consider the matter. I have already laid down what I believe to be the rule, and I think with the assent of the Tribunal, but I will ascertain...

MR. JUSTICE JACKSON: Let me say that I agree with Your Honor that as far as the United States is concerned we are not worried by anything the witness can say about it – and we expected plenty. The point is, do we answer these things or leave them, apart from the control of the Trial? And it does seem to me that this is the beginning of this Trial's getting out of hand, if I may say so, if we do not have control of this situation. I trust the Tribunal will pardon my earnestness in presenting this. I think it is a very vital thing.

THE PRESIDENT: I have never heard it suggested that the Counsel for the Prosecution have to answer every irrelevant observation made in cross-examination.

MR. JUSTICE JACKSON: That would be true in a private litigation, but I trust the Court is not unaware that outside of this courtroom is a great social question of the revival of Nazism and that one of the purposes of the Defendant Goering – I think he would be the first to admit – is to revive and perpetuate it by propaganda from this Trial now in process.

THE PRESIDENT: Yes, Doctor Stahmer?

DR. STAHMER: I just wanted to explain the following: An accusation has been made as if we intended to make propaganda here for Nazism, or in some other direction. I do not think this accusation is justified. Neither do I believe that the defendant intended to make an accusation against the United States. I think we have to consider the question that was put to him. That is, it was pointed out to him by the Prosecution that this document which was submitted to him was marked "secret." Then he stated that he had never heard that a document of that kind would have been made public in the United States. If instead of the U.S.A – he had said any other nation, then the remark would have been considered harmless.

In my opinion the answer was quite justified. The witness should be given the possibility not only to answer "yes" or "no," but to give reasons for his answer, as ruled by the Court.

THE PRESIDENT: Mr. Justice Jackson, the Tribunal considers that the rule which it has laid down is the only possible rule and that the witness must be confined strictly to answering the question directly where the question admits of a direct answer, and that he must not make his explanation before he gives a direct answer but, after having given a direct answer to any question which admits of a direct answer, he may make a short explanation; and that he is not to be confined simply to making direct answers "yes" or "no," and leaving the explanation until his counsel puts it to him in his re-examination.

As to this particular observation of the defendant, the defendant ought not to have referred to the United States, but it is a matter which I think you might well ignore.

MR. JUSTICE JACKSON: I shall bow to the ruling, of course.

I wish to make a statement to the Tribunal about one of the documents. At the conclusion of the session yesterday we were considering Document Number EC – 405. The Defendant Goering challenged the use of a word which he said should have been translated "clearance" rather than "liberation." We have since had the translation checked and find that the defendant is correct. This document was introduced under Exhibit Number GB – 160 on the 9th of January, at Page 2396 of the Tribunal's records (Volume V, Page 28), and since it has already been received in evidence and it is before the Tribunal, we think it incumbent upon the Prosecution to make that correction now for the record.

[Turning to the witness.] You stated yesterday that the minutes of the Reich Defense Council with which you were presented were not minutes of a meeting of the Reich Defense Council as such?

GOERING: Yes, I said that.

MR. JUSTICE JACKSON: And your testimony, notwithstanding that document, still stands, I take it, that the Reich Defense Council never met?

GOERING: I said that also, yes.

MR. JUSTICE JACKSON: I now ask to have you shown a document which has just come into our possession, the minutes of the second session of the Reich Defense Council. I should have said, just come to us for translation. We have not had it translated; we just discovered it among our great collection of documents.

THE PRESIDENT: Could Doctor Stahmer have a copy in English or not?

MR. JUSTICE JACKSON: We have not even had a chance to get it into English. I do not know what it says except that it is the minutes of their meeting. We have a photostat.

[Turning to the witness.] Are those not the minutes of the second meeting of the Reich Defense Council held on the 6/23/1939?

GOERING: I must read it first.

MR. JUSTICE JACKSON: I call your attention to the fact that the chairman is Minister President General Field Marshal Goering. You will find that on Page 1.

GOERING: I have never disputed that. It was fixed by law. This deals with the second Reich Defense Council, not the first one. Besides, I was not present at this meeting; and I point out that on the left is a list of the authorities who took part in the meeting, and in my case it says "Minister President Field Marshal Goering," and on the right, as representative for him, "State Secretary Korner and State Secretary Neumann." But I shall have to look through the document first in order to find out whether I took part personally.

MR. JUSTICE JACKSON: Does it not say on Page 1, directly under the place of meeting, "Chairman: Minister President Goering"?

GOERING: Yes. I have to read it first.

MR. JUSTICE JACKSON: Do you deny the authenticity of those minutes?

GOERING: I have not looked them through yet.

It seems to be an absolutely authentic copy of the minutes; I admit that. But here again we are dealing with a meeting not as I said when answering my counsel, of the Reich Defense Council but of a larger meeting in which many other departments participated and it is a matter of the second Reich Defense Council, which was set up after 1938, not a secret council such as was the case from 1933-1938.

MR. JUSTICE JACKSON: In other words, in interpreting your testimony, we must understand that, when you say there was n meeting of the Reich Defense Council, you mean only that there were no meetings at which no other people were present?

GOERING: No, that is not correct. There were two Reich defense laws concerning the Reich Defense Council, which I tried to explain in my statement: the Secret Council of 1933-1938, which was not made public, and the Reich Defense Council which was created 1933 and converted into the Ministerial Council in 1939; the latter held meetings which were in no way confined to its own members.

MR. JUSTICE JACKSON: Then you say that this was not the Defense Council that met under the ban of secrecy?

GOERING: The Prosecution want me to answer first with "yes" or "no." It is hard to answer this question with "yes" or "no." I assert that the Secret Defense Council, which was not made public and which arose out of a meeting of ministers in 1933, never met. After 1938 a new Reich defense law created a new council. At that time it was clear that our military sovereignty had already been declared. This first council, which the Prosecution called the secret one, never met, and the document of yesterday proved that.

MR. JUSTICE JACKSON: Will you refer to Page 19 of this document, please, and tell me whether one of the very things with which this meeting concerned itself was not the lifting of the secrecy ban from the Reich defense law?

GOERING: No, that is not the way it reads here. If I may translate it, the last point on the agenda: Consequences resulting from the lifting of the secrecy ban on the Reich defense law and measures to expedite procedures have already been dealt with by a letter from the

Reich Defense Committee on 26 June: "Consequences resulting from the lifting of the secrecy ban with a view to expediting written communications."

MR. JUSTICE JACKSON: You have stated that on the Jewish question, some of the members of the government were more radical than you. Would you state who these were?

GOERING: Broadly speaking, when we took over the government, we only demanded their removal from political and other leading positions in the State.

MR. JUSTICE JACKSON: That is not what I asked you.

THE PRESIDENT: That is not a direct answer to the question. The question was that you said some members of the government were more radical toward Jews than you were. Would you tell us which of the members of the government were more radical than you were?

GOERING: Excuse me, I did not understand the question to mean who were more radical, but in what way they were more radical. If you ask who, then I would say that those were primarily Minister Goebbels and Himmler.

MR. JUSTICE JACKSON: Do you also include your co-defendant, Streicher, as more radical than you?

GOERING: Yes, but he was not a member of the government.

MR. JUSTICE JACKSON: He was the Gauleiter, was he not, of this very territory in which we are sitting.

GOERING: That is correct; but he had very little or no influence in government measures.

MR. JUSTICE JACKSON: What about Heydrich?

GOERING: Heydrich was subordinate to Himmler. If I said Himmler, I, of course, include Heydrich.

MR. JUSTICE JACKSON: Heydrich is then included in the list the more radical ones to whom you refer?

GOERING: That is right; yes.

MR. JUSTICE JACKSON: What about Bormann?

GOERING: It was only during the later years that I observed at Bormann was becoming more radical. I do not know anything about his attitude in the beginning.

MR. JUSTICE JACKSON: Now, I want to review with you briefly what the Prosecution understands to be public acts taken by you in reference to the Jewish question. From the very beginning you regarded the elimination of the Jews from the economic life of

Germany as one phase of the Four Year Plan under your jurisdiction, did you not?

GOERING: The elimination, yes; that is partly correct. The elimination as far as the large industries were concerned, because there were continual disturbances due to the fact that there were large industries, also armament industries, still partly under Jewish directors, or with Jewish shareholders, and that gave rise to a certain anxiety among the lower ranks.

MR. JUSTICE JACKSON: Now, do I understand that you want he Tribunal to believe that all you were concerned about was the big Jewish enterprises? That is the way you want to be understood?

GOERING: I was not at first disturbed by the small stores. They did not come into the Four Year Plan.

MR. JUSTICE JACKSON: When did you become disturbed by the small stores?

GOERING: When trade had to be limited, it was pointed out that this could be done first by closing the Jewish stores.

MR. JUSTICE JACKSON: Now, let us go through the public acts which you performed on the Jewish question. First, did you proclaim the Nuremberg Laws?

GOERING: As President of the Reichstag, yes. I have already stated that.

MR. JUSTICE JACKSON: What date was that?

GOERING: 1935, I believe; here in Nuremberg, in September.

MR. JUSTICE JACKSON: That was the beginning of the legal measures taken against the Jews, was it not?

GOERING: That was a legal measure.

MR. JUSTICE JACKSON: That was the first of the legal measures taken by your government against the Jews, was it not?

GOERING: No, I believe the removal from office was before.

MR. JUSTICE JACKSON: When was that?

GOERING: I could not state the exact date, but I believe that happened in 1933.

MR. JUSTICE JACKSON: Then on the first day of 12/1936, you promulgated an act making it a death penalty for Germans to transfer property abroad or leave it abroad; the property of a culprit to be forfeited to the State, and the People's Court given jurisdiction to prosecute, did you not?

GOERING: That is correct; the "Decree Governing Restriction on Foreign Currency." That is to say, whoever had an account in a foreign country without permission of the government.

MR. JUSTICE JACKSON: Then, your third public act was on 4/22/1938 when you published penalties for veiling the character of a Jewish enterprise within the Reich, was it not?

GOERING: Yes.

MR. JUSTICE JACKSON: Then on 7/28/1939, you, Hermann Goering, published certain prescriptions on the competence of the courts to handle those matters by the decree, did you not?

GOERING: Please, would you kindly read the law to me? I cannot recall it.

MR. JUSTICE JACKSON: I will not take time reading it. Do you deny that you published the *Reichsgesetzblatt* law, 1939, found on Page 1370, referring to the competence of the courts to handle penalties against Jews? If you do not remember, say so.

GOERING: Yes, I say that I cannot remember the law. If it is in the *Reichsgesetzblatt* and bears my name, then, of course, it is so; but I do not remember the contents.

MR. JUSTICE JACKSON: Now, on 4/26/1938 you, under the Four Year Plan, published a decree providing for the registration of Jewish property and provided that Jews inside and outside Germany must register their property, did you not?

GOERING: I assume so. I no longer remember it, but if you have the decree there, and if it is signed by me, there cannot be any doubt.

MR. JUSTICE JACKSON: On 4/26/1938 you published a decree under the Four Year Plan, did you not, that all acts of disposal of Jewish enterprises required the permission of the authorities?

GOERING: That I remember.

MR. JUSTICE JACKSON: Then you published on 11/12/1938 a decree, also under the Four Year Plan, imposing a fine of a RM1 billion for atonement on all Jews?

GOERING: I have already explained that all these decrees at that time were signed by me, and I assume responsibility for them.

MR. JUSTICE JACKSON: Well, I am asking you if you did not sign that particular decree? I am going to ask you some further questions about it later.

GOERING: Yes.

MR. JUSTICE JACKSON: Then on the 11/12/1938, you also signed a decree that, under the Four Year Plan, all damage caused to

Jewish property by the riots of 1938 must be repaired immediately by the Jews, and at their own expense; and their insurance claims were forfeited to the Reich. Did you personally sign that law?

GOERING: I did sign a similar law. Whether it was exactly the same as you have just read, I could not say.

MR. JUSTICE JACKSON: You do not disagree that that was the substance of the law, do you?

GOERING: No.

MR. JUSTICE JACKSON: And on the 11/12/1938, did you not also personally sign a decree, also under the Four Year Flan, that Jews may not own retail stores, or engage independently in handicrafts or offer goods, or services, for sale at markets, fairs, or exhibitions; or act as leaders of enterprises or as members of cooperatives? Do you recall all of that?

GOERING: Yes. Those are all parts of the decrees for the elimination of Jewry from economic life.

MR. JUSTICE JACKSON: Then, on the 2/21/1939, you personally signed a decree, did you not, that the Jews must render all objects of precious metals and jewels purchased, to the public office within 2 weeks?

GOERING: I do not remember that, but without doubt, that is correct.

MR. JUSTICE JACKSON: I refer to Volume I of the *Reichsgesetzblatt*, 1939, Page 282. You have no recollection of that?

GOERING: I have not the *Reichsgesetzblatt* in front of me now but if there is a decree in the *Reichsgesetzblatt*, or a law signed with my name, then I signed that law and decreed it.

MR. JUSTICE JACKSON: Did you not also, on the 3/3/1939, sign a further decree concerning the period within which items of jewelry must be surrendered by Jews – *Reichsgesetzblatt* Volume I, 1939, Page 387?

GOERING: I assume that was the decree for the execution of the decree for surrender previously mentioned. A law sometimes requires regulations and decrees for execution consequent upon the law. Taken together, this is one single measure.

MR. JUSTICE JACKSON: Did you not also sign personally a decree under the Four Year Plan, of the 17th of September 1940 ordering the sequestration of Jewish property in Poland?

GOERING: Yes, as I stated before, in that part of Poland which, I may say, as an old German province, was to return to Germany.

MR. JUSTICE JACKSON: Did you not also, on the 11/30/1940, personally sign a decree which provided that the Jews should receive no compensation for damages caused by enemy attacks or by German forces, and did you not sign that in the capacity of President of the Reich Defense Council? I refer to the *Reichsgesetzblatt*, Volume I, 1940, Page 1547.

GOERING: If you have it there before you, then it must be correct.

MR. JUSTICE JACKSON: You have no recollection of that?

GOERING: Not of all the separate laws and decrees. That is impossible.

MR. JUSTICE JACKSON: Then, it was you, was it not, who signed, on the 7/31/1941, a decree asking Himmler, and the Chief of Security Police and the SS Gruppenfuehrer Heydrich to make the plans for the complete solution of the Jewish question?

GOERING: No, that is not correct. I know that decree very well.

MR. JUSTICE JACKSON: I ask to have you shown Document 710, Exhibit Number USA – 509.

THE PRESIDENT: Is that 710 – PS?

MR. JUSTICE JACKSON: 710 – PS, Your Honor.

[Turning to the witness.] That document is signed by you, is it not?

GOERING: That is correct.

MR. JUSTICE JACKSON: And it is addressed to the Chief of the Security Police and the Security Service, and to SS Gruppenfuehrer Heydrich, isn't it?

GOERING: That is also correct.

MR. JUSTICE JACKSON: I am not certain whether the entire thing has been read into the record, but I think it should be; and, that we may have no difficulty about the translation of this, you correct me if I am wrong:

"Completing the task that was assigned to you on the 1/24/1939..."

GOERING: Here is a mistake already. It says: "Complementing' not "completing" the task which has been assigned to you.

MR. JUSTICE JACKSON: Very well, I will accept that; ". . . which dealt with arriving at a thorough furtherance of emigration and evacuation, a solution of the Jewish problem, as advantageously as possible, I hereby charge you with making all necessary preparations in regard to organizational and financial matters for bringing about a complete solution of the Jewish question in the German sphere of influence in Europe."

Am I correct so far?

GOERING: No, that is in no way correctly translated.

MR. JUSTICE JACKSON: Give us your translation of it?

GOERING: May I read it as it is written here?

"Complementing the task which was conferred upon you already on 1/24/1939, to solve the Jewish problem by means of emigration and evacuation in the best possible way according to present conditions, I charge you herewith to make all necessary preparations as regards organizational, factual, and material matters...."

Now comes the decisive word which has been mistranslated: "for total solution," not "for a final solution."

". . . for a total solution of the Jewish question within the area of German influence in Europe. Should these come within the competence of other governmental departments, then such departments are to co-operate."

"I charge you further to submit to me as soon as possible a general plan showing the organizational and material measures for reaching the desired total solution of the Jewish question.... Complementing the task assigned to you on 1/24/1939...."

That was at a time when there was no war or prospect of a war.

MR. JUSTICE JACKSON: Now are you reporting the instrument or are you making an explanation?

GOERING: I wanted to add an explanation to the quotation and just to point out the date.

MR. JUSTICE JACKSON: Yes. Well, I just did not want it to appear that it was a part of the instrument. The last that is contained in the instrument is:

"I charge you furthermore to send me, before long, an overall plan concerning the organizational, factual, and material measures necessary for the accomplishment of the desired solution of the Jewish question."

Is that not a substantially accurate translation of your order to Heydrich and Himmler?

GOERING: To Heydrich and the other government departments which had anything to do with it. That can be seen from the first part of the letter, the last sentence.

MR. JUSTICE JACKSON: Let us have no misunderstanding about this translation now. This letter was directed to the Chief of the

Security Police and the Security Service, and SS Gruppenfuehrer Heydrich. We are right about that, are we not?

GOERING: That is correct, but I have to make an explanation in connection with that.

MR. JUSTICE JACKSON: All right.

GOERING: The reason I sent this letter to him was that, by the decree of 1/24/1939, Heydrich, or it may have been Himmler, had been given the task of dealing with the emigration of the Jews. Therefore, this was the government department concerned, and it was to the department which had been given the task that I had to apply concerning all material and economic matters arising therefrom.

MR. JUSTICE JACKSON: Yes. And you ordered all other governmental agencies to co-operate with the Security Police and the SS in the final solution of the Jewish question, did you not?

GOERING: There is nothing about the SS here, only about the *Sicherheitspolizei*, a governmental agency. The fact that Heydrich was SS Gruppenfuehrer had no direct bearing on it, because it was sent to the Chief of the Security Police – mentioning his rank as SS Gruppenfuehrer Heydrich.

MR. JUSTICE JACKSON: And mentioning his rank in the SS was just superfluous and has nothing to do with the case?

GOERING: I have to explain that. For instance, if I write to the Commander-in-chief of the Army, then I write: "To the Commander-in-chief of the Army, Colonel General or Field Marshal Von Brauchitsch." And if I write to the Chief of the Security Police, then I must address it: "To the Chief of the Security Police, SS Gruppenfuihrer Heydrich." That was his rank and his title. However that does not mean that the SS had anything to do with it.

MR. JUSTICE JACKSON: Now, at the time that you issued this order you had received complete reports as to the 1938 riots and Heydrich's part in them, hadn't you?

GOERING: At that time I had no knowledge of Heydrich's part in the riots – only Heydrich's report on the riots, for which I had asked.

MR. JUSTICE JACKSON: All right. Now we will show you Document Number 3058 – PS, in evidence as Exhibit Number USA – 508.

[Document 3058 – PS was submitted to the witness.]

That is the report written by Heydrich which you say you had received, and it is dated 11/11/1938, is it not?

GOERING: That is correct.

MR. JUSTICE JACKSON: And it recited to you the looting of Jewish shops, the arrest of 174 persons for looting, the destruction of 815 shops, 171 dwellings set on fire or destroyed, and that this indicated only a fraction of the actual damage caused; 191 synagogues were set on fire, and another 76 completely destroyed; in addition, 11 parish halls, cemetery chapels, and similar buildings were set on fire, and 3 more completely destroyed; 20000 Jews were arrested; also, 7 Aryans and 3 foreigners – the latter were arrested for their own safety; 36 deaths were reported, and the seriously injured were also numbered at 36. Those killed and injured are Jews. One Jew is still missing. The Jews killed include 1 Polish national, and those injured include 2 Poles.

You had that report on or about the 11/11/1938, did you not?

GOERING: That is correct. That is the report mentioned by me and which I had asked the police to supply, because I wanted to know what had happened up to then.

MR. JUSTICE JACKSON: Exactly. And the note was made at the top of it, The General Field Marshal has been informed and no steps are to be taken." Was it not?

GOERING: That is not quite correct. It says here, "General Field Marshal has taken note. No steps are to be taken by any other Office, because I myself wanted to take them.

MR. JUSTICE JACKSON: Now, you know that that is not true, do you not, that steps were to be taken by some other office? I put it to you squarely whether you are telling this Tribunal the truth when you say that no steps were to be taken by anyone else.

GOERING: This is a note by my staff department, that nothing was to be done by that quarter, because I said I was going to deal with it personally. In fact I went straight to the Fuehrer with this report.

MR. JUSTICE JACKSON: All right. Did you receive a report from the Chief Party Judge of the Nazi Party, dated Munich, the 2/13/1939, concerning the proceedings taken by the Party in these matters?

GOERING: That is correct. I received that report much later.

MR. JUSTICE JACKSON: And at the time you appointed – I withdraw the question. It is obvious from the dates of the documents. You acknowledged the receipt of that document, did you not, to Party member Buch?

GOERING: That is also correct.

MR. JUSTICE JACKSON: And the only proceedings that were taken about these riots were those taken by the Party Court, were they not?

GOERING: Not quite; some were brought before the law courts. That is in the report also.

MR. JUSTICE JACKSON: I ask that he be shown the report, which is Document 3063 – PS. It is not in evidence. Since the document apparently has not been brought here, I will ask you from your recollection.

GOERING: I know it fairly well.

MR. JUSTICE JACKSON: I thought so.

GOERING: No, because it has been submitted to me before, here.

MR. JUSTICE JACKSON: Yes, it has not been kept from you. Now, in the first place, the Party Court reported that it was probably understood – I quote – "by all of the Party leaders present from oral instructions of the Reich Propaganda Director, that the Party should not appear outwardly as the originator of the demonstrations, but in reality should organize and execute them." Was that the report of the Party Court?

GOERING: The Party Court, as a result of its investigation established that the Propaganda Chief, Dr. Goebbels, had given these directives. May I ask, if we are dealing with a report dated March or maybe April?

MR. JUSTICE JACKSON: The 2/13/1939, is the date.

GOERING: Yes, that is correct; that is the result of investigations after the incidents.

MR. JUSTICE JACKSON: That is right. Now, as a result of the riots, did the Court, the Party Court, not also report this to you: that the Supreme Party Court has reserved itself the right to investigate the killings, also the severe mistreatment and moral aims and will request the Fuehrer to drop proceedings against any person whom the Party Court did not find guilty of excesses?

GOERING: That is correct.

MR. JUSTICE JACKSON: And the Party Court was made up of Gauleiter and Group Leaders of the Party?

GOERING: The Party Court changed. I cannot say just now, without having the document, who made up the Party Court at that time. I see that I am being given the document.

MR. JUSTICE JACKSON: I call your attention to Page 4, toward the bottom, where the report says, "Gauleiter and Group Leaders of the branches served as jurors at the trials and decisions."

GOERING: Yes, it was a matter of course that the jurors of the Party Court were always taken from these categories according to their importance. I wanted only to say I did not know which persons were taking part here.

MR. JUSTICE JACKSON: Now, the Party Court found five persons guilty of offenses, did they not? Number 1, a Party member, was guilty of a moral crime and race violation and he was expelled. Is that right?

GOERING: And turned over to the penal court. That is what it says in the last sentence.

MR. JUSTICE JACKSON: That is right. Another Party member, Case Number 2, was suspected of race violation and expelled from the Nazi Party.

GOERING: Expelled for suspected race violation and theft, and turned over to the ordinary court.

MR. JUSTICE JACKSON: Yes; and Number 2, Gustav, was expelled from the Party and SA for theft. Right?

GOERING: You are at Number 3?

MR. JUSTICE JACKSON: I have Number 2, Gustav, the first name mentioned.

GOERING: Gustav is the first name – Gerstner – yes, for theft, also turned over to the ordinary court for suspected race violation.

MR. JUSTICE JACKSON: Now, Number 3 dealt with two expulsions of Party members on the grounds of moral crimes against a Jew, and they are now held in protective custody. Right?

GOERING: Expelled from the NSDAP and taken into protective custody; they were also turned over to the civil court later. I know that very well.

MR. JUSTICE JACKSON: Now, we come to Cases 4 and 5, the first of which was a man, a Party member and SA member, who was reprimanded and declared unfit to hold office for 3 years because of a disciplinary offense, namely, for killing the Jewish couple Selig, contrary to order. Is that right?

GOERING: That is correct.

MR. JUSTICE JACKSON: And in the last of these cases the offender was reprimanded and declared unfit to hold office for 3 years for shooting a 16-year-old Jew, contrary to orders after completion of the drive. Is that right?

GOERING: That is correct.

MR. JUSTICE JACKSON: We now come to the cases of the killing of Jews, where proceedings were suspended or minor punishments pronounced. I will not go through those in detail, but it is a fact that only minor punishments were pronounced by the Supreme Court of the Party for the killing of Jews, were they not?

GOERING: Yes, that is correct.

MR. JUSTICE JACKSON: I now ask you to turn to Page 8.

GOERING: One moment please.

MR. JUSTICE JACKSON: I call your attention to the language in regard to Cases 3 to 16.

GOERING: Which page, please?

MR. JUSTICE JACKSON: Nine, I believe it is. The Supreme Party Court asks the Fuehrer to quash the proceedings in the State criminal courts.

GOERING; To quash them, to beat them down, that does not mean *suppress*. A penal proceeding can be *"niedergeschlagen."* In Germany that is a different thing from "suppress."

MR. JUSTICE JACKSON: Well, you give us your version of it and tell us what it is. What does beating down a proceeding mean? Does it mean that it has ended?

GOERING: That is what it means, but it can only be ordered by an office which has authority to do it; that is to say, the Fuehrer can at any time "beat down" a proceeding by way of an amnesty. The Cabinet could at any time pass a resolution to "beat down" a proceeding – suppressing it would have been illegal. In Germany, *"niedergeschlagen"* is a legal term meaning "to suspend."

MR. JUSTICE JACKSON: And one further question. It was also reported to you, was it not, in that report – I refer to Page 11:

"The public down to the last man realize that political drives, like those of 9 November, were organized and directed by the Party, whether this is admitted or not. When all the synagogues burned down in one night, it must have been organized in some way and can only have been organized by the Party."

That also was in the report of the Supreme Party Court, was it not?

GOERING: I have not found it yet. It is not the same page as mine.

MR. JUSTICE JACKSON: Let us find it and not have any mistake about it. Page 11. I should think it would be at the very bottom of Page 10, perhaps, where it starts.

GOERING: Yes, I have just found it.

MR. JUSTICE JACKSON: Did I give a reasonably correct translation of it?

GOERING: That is correct.

THE PRESIDENT: Would that be a convenient time to break it off? Before we break off, will you offer in evidence these documents that you have been putting to the witness? Those which are not already in evidence?

MR. JUSTICE JACKSON: Yes, they should be, Your Honor, I will do that.

THE PRESIDENT: I think Document 3575 – PS may have been offered yesterday, but not strictly offered in evidence; and Document 3063 – PS today; and one other document the number of which I have not got.

MR. JUSTICE JACKSON: I appreciate very much your calling my attention to it.

MR. JUSTICE JACKSON: [Turning to the witness.] Now, the *Volkischer Beobachter* of the 3/12/1933 quotes a speech of yours delivered at Essen on the 3/11/1933, including the following – and I refresh your recollection by calling it to your attention:

"I am told that I must employ the police. Certainly I shall employ the police, and quite ruthlessly, whenever the German people are hurt; but I refuse the notion that the police are protective troop for Jewish stores. No, the police protect whoever comes into Germany legitimately, but it does not exist for the purpose of protecting Jewish usurers." Did you say that?

GOERING: When did you say that was?

MR. JUSTICE JACKSON: Did you say that on the 3/11/1933 in a speech at Essen, either that, or that in substance?

GOERING: That is correct, but the circumstances were different. Before I answer, I would like to ask whether you have finished with the document in the book that was submitted to me previously. I gave no explanation and will ask my counsel to have me questioned later in regard to that document.

MR. JUSTICE JACKSON: That is satisfactory.

After the riots of November 9th and 10th, you have testified that you called a meeting on the 12th of November and ordered all officials concerned to be present, and that the Fuehrer had insisted on Goebbels being present.

GOERING: Yes, all chiefs of the economic departments.

MR. JUSTICE JACKSON: Could you tell us who was there in addition to yourself and Goebbels?

GOERING: As far as I recall, the following were there for the purpose of reporting: The Chief of the Secret State Police, concerning the events, the Minister of Economy, the Minister of Finance, the Minister of the Interior...

MR. JUSTICE JACKSON: Will you please state their names so that there will not be any mistake about who was there at that time.

GOERING: I can quote only from memory. There were present to draw up a report: The leader of the Secret State Police in Berlin, Heydrich; the Minister of the Interior, Dr. Frick; Dr. Goebbels you have mentioned already; the then Minister of Economy, Funk, was there; the Finance Minister, Count Schwerin von Krosigk; and Fischbock from Austria.

Those are the only names I can recall at present, but there may have been a few others there too.

MR. JUSTICE JACKSON: Part of the time, Hilgard, representing the insurance companies, was also present, was he not?

GOERING: He was summoned and waited there. His views were asked on special questions.

MR. JUSTICE JACKSON: Now, you have been shown the stenographic minutes of that meeting which are in evidence as Exhibit Number USA – 261, being Document Number 1816 – PS, have you not, in your interrogation?

GOERING: Yes.

MR. JUSTICE JACKSON: I will ask that they be shown to you, and now, so that we may have no misunderstanding about the translations.

You opened the meeting with this statement. I will read it: "Gentlemen..." I think perhaps we had better be clear about which meeting it was. This is the meeting held on the 11/12/1938 at the office of the Reich Air Ministry. That is correct, is it not?

GOERING: Yes, that is correct.

MR. JUSTICE JACKSON: You opened the meeting:

"Gentlemen, today's meeting is of a decisive nature. I have received a letter written OD the Fuehrer's orders by the Stabsleiter of the Fuehrer's Deputy, Bormann, requesting that the Jewish question be now, once and for all, coordinated and solved one way or another."

Is that correct?

GOERING: Yes, that is correct.

MR. JUSTICE JACKSON: Further down, I find this:

"Gentlemen, I have had enough of these demonstrations. They do not harm the Jews, but finally devolve on me, the highest authority for the German economy. If today a Jewish shop is destroyed, if goods are thrown into the street, the insurance company will pay the Jew for the damages so that he does not suffer any damage at all. Furthermore, consumer goods, goods belonging to the people, are destroyed. If, in the future, demonstrations occur – and on occasion they may be necessary – then I ask that they be so directed that we do not cut our own throats."

Am I correct?

GOERING: Yes, quite correct.

MR. JUSTICE JACKSON: Skipping two or three paragraphs, I come to this...

GOERING: But the supplement has been omitted.

MR. JUSTICE JACKSON: Well, you can supplement it any way you want to.

GOERING: "...then I ask that they be so directed that we do not cut our own throats. For it is absurd to empty and set fire to a Jewish store, when a German insurance company has to cover the damage, and the goods which I sorely need are burned. I might as well take and burn the raw materials when they come in."

MR. JUSTICE JACKSON: That is right. You read any part of it that you want to as we go along, in addition to what I read.

"I am not going to tolerate a situation in which the German insurance companies are the ones to suffer. To prevent this, I will use my authority and issue a decree. In this, of course, I ask for the support of the competent government agencies, so that everything shall be settled properly and the insurance companies will not be the ones who suffer.

"But another problem immediately emerges: It may be that these insurance companies have re-insurance in foreign countries. If there are such re-insurances, I would not want to give them up, because they bring in foreign exchange. The matter must be looked into. For that reason, I have asked Mr. Hilgard from the insurance company to attend, since he is best qualified to tell us to what extent the insurance companies are covered by re-insurance against such damage. I would not want to give this up under any circumstances. "

Is that correct?

GOERING: That is absolutely correct.

MR. JUSTICE JACKSON: "I do not want to leave any doubt, gentlemen, as to the purpose of today's meeting. We have not come together merely to talk again, but to make decisions; and I earnestly ask the competent departments to take trenchant measures for the Aryanizing of German economy and to submit them to me as far as is necessary."

GOERING: That is correct.

MR. JUSTICE JACKSON: I then skip a considerable portion, unless there is more that you wish to put in, and come to this statement:

"The State Trustee will estimate the value of the business and decide what amount the Jew shall receive. Naturally, this amount is to be fixed as low as possible. The State Trustee will then transfer the business to Aryan ownership. The aim is thus accomplished, inasmuch as the business is transferred to the right ownership and its goodwill and balance sheet remain unimpaired.

"Then the difficulties begin. It is easily understandable that attempts will be made on a large scale to get Party members into all these stores and thus give them some compensation. I have witnessed terrible things in the past; little chauffeurs of Gauleiter have profited so much by these transactions that they have raked in half a million. You gentlemen know it. Is that correct?"

And they assented.

GOERING: Yes, I said that.

MR. JUSTICE JACKSON: Would you care to read anything further in connection with that?

GOERING: Perhaps only the next sentence:

"These are, of course, things which are not permissible, and I shall not hesitate to deal ruthlessly with such underhand dealings. If a prominent person is involved I shall go straight to the Fuehrer and report these dirty tricks quite impartially."

MR. JUSTICE JACKSON: That is, if any individual was attempting to profit by Jewish possessions – is that what you meant?

GOERING: By Aryanization.

MR. JUSTICE JACKSON: I will quote another portion:

"In other words, it must be an ordinary business transaction. One sells his business and another buys it. If there are Party members among the would-be purchasers, they are to be given preference if they fulfill the same conditions. First of all should come those who have suffered damage. After that preference should be given on grounds of Party membership."

I will skip a line or two:

"This Party member should have a chance to buy the business for as cheap a price as possible. In such a case, the State will not receive the full price, but only the amount the Jew received."

Is that correct?

GOERING: Just a moment, please, I believe you skipped something.

MR. JUSTICE JACKSON: Yes, we did. If you want to put it in, you may read it.

GOERING: No, I want to put it quite briefly, so that it will not take too long. I said what you have already said, that all things being equal, the Party member is to be given preference, the first on the list being the member who suffered prejudice by having his business license cancelled because he was a Party member. Then follows the paragraph which you read and which is correct.

MR. JUSTICE JACKSON: Now, you then speak at considerable length of the method by which you intended to Aryanize Jewish businesses, is that right?

GOERING: Yes.

MR. JUSTICE JACKSON: And then you take up the Aryanization of Jewish factories.

GOERING: Yes.

MR. JUSTICE JACKSON: You speak of the smaller factories first.

GOERING: Yes.

MR. JUSTICE JACKSON: Have you found the place where you speak of the factories?

GOERING: Yes, I have found it.

MR. JUSTICE JACKSON: I quote.

"Now the factories. With regard to the smaller and medium sized ones, two things will have to be made clear: First, which are the factories for which I have no use, and which can be shut down? Could they not be put to another use? If not, these factories are to be pulled down. Second, if the factory should be needed, it will be turned over to Aryans in the same manner as the stores."

That is correct, isn't it?

GOERING: Yes.

MR. JUSTICE JACKSON: Do you care to say any more on that subject?

GOERING: No, those are the basic elements for the laws.

MR. JUSTICE JACKSON: Now, I call your attention to the Second paragraph, starting, "Take now the larger factories." Do you find that?

GOERING: Yes.

MR. JUSTICE JACKSON: Dealing with the larger factories, do you not say the solution is very simple, that the factory can be compensated in the same manner as the stores, that is, at a rate which we shall determine, and the Trustee shall take over the Jew's interest, as well as his shares, and in turn sell or transfer them to he State as he thinks fit.

GOERING: That means any one who has any interest in the factories will receive compensation, according to the scale laid down by us.

MR. JUSTICE JACKSON: And the reparation will be turned over to the State Trustee, will it not?

GOERING: Yes, to the State Trustee. The matter was simply is: The Jew relinquished his ownership and received bonds. That was to be settled by the Trustee through 3% bonds.

MR. JUSTICE JACKSON: Well, we will pass on to where you deal with the foreign Jews, do you recall that?

GOERING: Yes.

MR. JUSTICE JACKSON: At that point a representative of the Foreign Office claimed the right to participate on behalf of the Foreign Minister, is that right?

GOERING: Yes.

MR. JUSTICE JACKSON: Well, now, we will pass on to the point of the conversation between yourself and Heydrich.

GOERING: Just a moment, please. Part of the minutes are missing. All right. I have found the place where Heydrich is mentioned for the first time.

MR. JUSTICE JACKSON: You inquired how many synagogues were actually burned, and Heydrich replied, "Altogether there were

101 synagogues destroyed by fire, 76 synagogues demolished, and 7,500 stores destroyed in the Reich." Have I quoted that correctly?

GOERING: Yes.

MR. JUSTICE JACKSON: Well, then Dr. Goebbels interposed "I am of the opinion that this is our chance to dissolve the synagogues." And then you have a discussion about the dissolving of the synagogues, have you not?

GOERING: By Dr. Goebbels, yes.

MR. JUSTICE JACKSON: Then, Dr. Goebbels raised the question of Jews traveling in railway trains?

GOERING: Yes.

MR. JUSTICE JACKSON: Let me know if I quote correctly the dialogue between you and Dr. Goebbels on that subject. Dr. Goebbels said:

"Furthermore, I advocate that Jews be banned from all public places where they might cause provocation. It is still possible for a Jew to share a sleeper with a German. Therefore, the Reich Ministry of Transport must issue a decree ordering that there shall be separate compartments for Jews. If this compartment is full, then the Jews cannot claim a seat. They can only be given separate compartments after all Germans have secured seats. They must not mix with the Germans; if there is no more room, they will have to stand in the corridor."

Is that right?

GOERING: Yes, that is correct.

MR. JUSTICE JACKSON: "Goering: I think it would be more sensible to give them separate compartments.

"Goebbels: Not if the train is overcrowded.

"Goering: Just a moment. There will be only one Jewish coach. If that is filled up the other Jews will have to stay at home.

"Goebbels: But suppose there are not many Jews going, let us say, on the long-distance express train to Munich. Suppose there are two Jews on the train, and the other compartments are overcrowded; these two Jews would then have a compartment to themselves. Therefore, the decree must state, Jews may claim a seat only after all Germans have secured a seat.

"Goering: I would give the Jews one coach or one compartment, and should a case such as you mention arise, and the train be overcrowded, believe me, we will not need a law. He will be kicked out all right, and will have to sit alone in the toilet all the way." Is that correct?

GOERING: Yes. I was getting irritated when Goebbels came with his small details when important laws were being discussed. I refused to do anything. I issued no decrees or laws in this connection. Of course, today, it is very pleasant for the Prosecution to bring it up, but I wish to state that it was a very lively meeting at which Goebbels made demands which were quite outside the economic sphere, and I used these expressions to give vent to my feelings.

MR. JUSTICE JACKSON: Then Goebbels, who felt very strongly about these things, said that Jews should stand in the corridor, and you said that they would have to sit in the toilet. That is the way you said it?

GOERING: No, it is not. I said that they should have a special compartment; and when Goebbels still was not satisfied, and harped on it, I finally told him, "I do not need a law. He can either sit in the toilet or leave the train." These are utterances made in this connection which, however, have nothing to do with the world-wide importance of the great conflict.

MR. JUSTICE JACKSON: Let us go down to where Goebbels brings up the subject of the German forests.

GOERING: Just a moment. Yes. It starts where Goebbels asked for a decree which would prevent Jews from going to German holiday resorts. To which I replied "Give them their own." And then he suggested that it would have to be considered whether we should give them their own resorts, or place some German bathing places at their disposal, but not the best ones so that people might say: "You allow the Jews to get fit by using our bathing resorts." The question must also be considered whether it was necessary to forbid the Jews to go into the German forests. Herds of Jews are today running around in Grunewald; that is a constant provocation – and so on. Then when he broke in again, I replied very sharply, 'It would be better to put a certain part of the forest at the disposal of the Jews," as he wanted them out of the whole of the forests. Then I made the remark which seems to be of so much interest.

MR. JUSTICE JACKSON: Let us have that remark. Is it not correct you did state:

"We will give the Jews a certain part of the forest, and Alpers will see to it that the various animals, which are damnably like the Jews –

the Elk too has a hooked nose – go into the Jewish enclosure and settle down among them."

Is that what you said?

GOERING: Yes, I said it, but it should be linked up with the whole atmosphere of the meeting. Goebbels comes back on it again in the next sentence and says he considers my attitude provoking. I too can say I was provoked by his insistence on unimportant things, when such far-reaching and decisive matters were being discussed.

MR. JUSTICE JACKSON: Now, you come to the point where you ask Mr. Hilgard from the insurance company to come in. Can you find that?

GOERING: Yes.

MR. JUSTICE JACKSON: Then you made a statement to Mr. Hilgard when he came in.

"The position is as follows: Because of the justified anger of the people against the Jews, the Reich has suffered a certain amount of damage. Windows have been broken, goods damaged and people hurt; synagogues have been burned, and so forth I suppose many of the Jews are also insured against damage committed by public disorder?

"Hilgard: Yes.

"Goering: If that is so, the following situation arises. The people in their justified anger meant to harm the Jews, but it is the German insurance companies which have to compensate the Jews for the damage. The thing is simple enough. I have only to issue a decree to the effect that damage resulting from these riots shall not have to be paid by the insurance companies."

Is that what you said?

GOERING: Yes, I said all that.

MR. JUSTICE JACKSON: Hilgard then outlined three kinds of insurance He pointed out that at least as far as plate glass insurance was concerned, the majority of the sufferers were Aryans who owned buildings and that, as a rule, the Jews only rented them. Is that right?

GOERING: Yes, those are the details of the discussion.

MR. JUSTICE JACKSON: And Hilgard said:

"May I draw your attention to the following facts: Plate glass is not manufactured by the Bohemian glass industry, but is entirely in the hands of the Belgian glass industry. In my estimation the damage amounts to 6 millions, that is to say, under the insurance policies, we shall have to pay the owners who for the most part are Aryans, about 6 millions compensation for the glass."

THE PRESIDENT: Mr. Justice Jackson, before you pass from that page, in the third paragraph, just for the sake of accuracy, it appears that the name "Mr. Hilgard" is wrongly placed, does it not, because he seems both to put the question and to answer it.

MR. JUSTICE JACKSON: Well, I think that is . . .

THE PRESIDENT: Probably the Defendant Goering put the question. It is the third paragraph on my page.

MR. JUSTICE JACKSON: I take the minutes to read that when Hilgard appeared, Goering addressed him as "Mr. Hilgard."

THE PRESIDENT: Yes, I see.

MR. JUSTICE JACKSON: But it is correct, as Your Honor suggests.

GOERING: I wish to point out what was said before concerning like broken glass. Goebbels said: "The Jews must pay for the damage," and I said, "It is no use, we have no raw material, it is all foreign glass. That will require foreign currency. It is like asking for the moon." Then Hilgard comes with the discussions just mentioned.

MR. JUSTICE JACKSON: Yes, and Hilgard pointed out that: Incidentally the amount of damage equals about half a year's production of the whole of the Belgian glass industry. We believe that the manufacturers will take 6 months to deliver the glass."

Do you recall that?

GOERING: Yes.

MR. JUSTICE JACKSON: Well, passing down, you come to a point at which Hilgard tells you about a store on Unter den Linden which was attacked. Can you find that?

GOERING: He said, "The biggest incident is the case of Margraf, 3 Unter den Linden." Isn't that so?

MR. JUSTICE JACKSON: That is right.

GOERING: Yes.

MR. JUSTICE JACKSON: "The damage reported to us amounts to 1.7 million because the store was completely ransacked." Is that right?

GOERING: Yes.

MR. JUSTICE JACKSON: "Goering: Daluege and Heydrich, you just get me these jewels by large-scale raids." Is that the order you gave?

GOERING: Yes, of course, so that the stolen goods should be brought back.

MR. JUSTICE JACKSON: Brought back to you, not to the Jews.

GOERING: Not to me personally, I beg your pardon, that is quite clear.

MR. JUSTICE JACKSON: Brought back to the State – you did not intend to return them to the Jews?

GOERING: It does not say that here. The main thing is, that they should be brought back.

MR. JUSTICE JACKSON: "We are trying to get the loot back " as Heydrich put it, is that right? And you added, "And the jewels?"

GOERING: If a large jewelry shop is plundered, something must be done about it because with these valuables a great deal of trouble could be caused. Therefore, I ordered raids to be carried out to have these things, as well as other stolen goods, brought back. When a business was Aryanized, its stock was also transferred to the new owner. The main point, however, was that action should be taken against those who had stolen and plundered, and in fact 150 had already been arrested.

MR. JUSTICE JACKSON: And Heydrich went on to report on the method of these raids after you reminded him to bring back, to get the jewels.

"It is difficult to say. Some of the articles were thrown into the street and picked up. The same happened with the furriers. For example, in the Friedrichstrasse in the district of Police Station C. There the crowd naturally rushed to pick up mink and skunk furs, et cetera. It will be very difficult to recover them. Even children filled their pockets just for the fun of the thing. It is suggested that the Hitler Youth should not be employed on such actions without the Party's consent. Such things are very easily destroyed."

GOERING: Yes, so it says.

MR. JUSTICE JACKSON: And Daluege then suggests:

"The Party should issue an order to the effect that the police must immediately be notified if the neighbor's wife – everybody knows his neighbor very well – has a fur coat remodeled or somebody is seen wearing a new ring or bracelet. We should like the Party to assist in this matter."

GOERING: This is absolutely correct.

MR. JUSTICE JACKSON: Now, Hilgard objected to your plan of releasing the insurance companies from paying the claims, did he not?

GOERING: Yes, this is also correct.

MR. JUSTICE JACKSON: And he gave the reasons:

"Hilgard: If I may give the reasons for my objection, the point is that we do a large international business. Our business has a sound international basis, and in the interests of the foreign exchange position in Germany we cannot allow the confidence in the German insurance business to be shaken. If we were now to refuse to fulfill commitments entered into by legal contracts it would be a blot on the escutcheon of the German insurance business.

"Goering: But it would not be if I were to issue a decree or a law."

Am I quoting correct?

GOERING: Yes, and in Hilgard's reply – and that is the reply I wanted to come to – he pointed out that the insurance companies could not get out of paying claims unless a law provided for it. If the sovereign state passes a law to the effect that the insurance sums must be forfeited to the state, then the insurance companies are no longer under any obligation.

MR. JUSTICE JACKSON: Now, I suggest to you that that is correct, but that even though you proposed to issue a decree absolving the German insurance companies, the companies insisted on meeting their obligations; and then Heydrich interposed and said: "By all means, let them pay the claims and when payment is made it will be confiscated. Thus we will save our face." Correct?

GOERING: Heydrich said that, but I issued a law.

MR. JUSTICE JACKSON: Did you not then say:

"One moment. They will have to pay in any case because Germans suffered damage. There will, however, be a law forbidding them to make direct payments to Jews. They will also have to make payment for damage suffered by Jews, not to the Jews, but to the Minister of Finance.

"Hilgard: Aha."

GOERING: I have just said so.

MR. JUSTICE JACKSON: You accepted Heydrich's suggestion, which was quite contrary to the one you made?

GOERING: No, I did not accept Heydrich's suggestion, but I issued a law to the effect that insurance money due to Jews must be paid to the Minister of Finance, as I did not agree with Heydrich that money should be paid out and then surreptitiously confiscated. I went about it in a legal way and was not afraid to make the necessary law and to take the responsibility for the claims to be paid to the State, that is, to the Minister of Finance.

MR. JUSTICE JACKSON: Well, the Tribunal will judge for itself, we have the evidence.

Now, Hilgard, representing the insurance companies, then raised the question that the amount of glass insurance premium was very important, that glass insurance was the companies' greatest asset "but the amount of the damage now caused is twice as high as in an ordinary year," and he pointed out that the whole of the profits of the German insurance companies would be absorbed, did he not?

GOERING: Yes.

MR. JUSTICE JACKSON: And also the question of the number of the stores destroyed – Heydrich reported 7,500, is that right?

GOERING: Yes.

MR. JUSTICE JACKSON: Now, I call your attention to the following conversation.

Who, by the way, was he?

GOERING: Daluege was the leader of the *Schutzpolizei.*

MR. JUSTICE JACKSON: "One question has still to be discussed. Most of the goods in the stores were not the property of the shopkeepers but were on consignment from other firms which had supplied them. Now the unpaid invoices are being sent in by these firms, which are certainly not all Jewish, but Aryan, in respect to these goods on consignment.

"Hilgard: We will have to pay for them too.

"Goering: I wish you had killed 200 Jews instead of destroying such valuables.

"Heydrich: There were 35 killed."

Do I read that correctly?

GOERING: Yes, this was said in a moment of bad temper and excitement.

MR. JUSTICE JACKSON: Spontaneously sincere, wasn't it?

GOERING: As I said, it was not meant seriously. It was the expression of spontaneous excitement caused by the events, and by the destruction of valuables, and by the difficulties which arose Of course, if you are going to bring up every word I said in the course of 25 years in these circles, I myself could give you instances of even stronger remarks.

MR. JUSTICE JACKSON: Then Funk interposed to discuss the foreign exchange point, did he not? He contributed to the discussion, did he not, for a while? I will not bother to go into it.

GOERING: Yes, but not everything is put down in the minutes, which are not clear on this point. I regret the minutes are incomplete. That is strange.

MR. JUSTICE JACKSON: I join you in that.

Hilgard returned again to the subject of the profit of the insurance companies, did he not?

GOERING: Yes, of course.

MR. JUSTICE JACKSON: And you made this statement, did you not?

"The Jew must report the damage. He will get the insurance money, but it will be confiscated. The final result will be that the insurance companies will gain something, as not all damages will have to be made good. Hilgard, you can consider yourself damned lucky".

"Hilgard: I have no reason for that. The fact that we shall not have to pay for all the damage is called a profit.

"Goering: Just a moment. If you are legally bound to pay 5 millions and all of a sudden an angel, in my somewhat corpulent shape, appears before you and tells you you may keep 1 million, hang it, is this not a profit? I should like to go 50-50 with you or whatever you call it. I only have to look at you, your whole body exudes satisfaction. You are getting a big rake-off."

Am I quoting correctly?

GOERING: Yes, of course, I said all that.

MR. JUSTICE JACKSON: [To the witness.] I would like to call your attention again to the Exhibit USA – 261, Document 1816 – PS. Would you turn to Part 5, where you were speaking of Margraf's jewels that disappeared?

GOERING: That is going back to something already dealt with.

MR. JUSTICE JACKSON: Yes, for a time, to Part 5. I call your attention to your statement as follows:

"Now we come to the damage sustained by the Jew, the disappearance of the jewels at Margraf's, et cetera. Well, they are gone and he will not get them refunded. He is the one who has to suffer the damage. Any of the jewels which may be returned by the police will belong to the State."

Do you find that?

GOERING: Yes, that is correct, but on the basis of the laws he was compensated for that.

MR. JUSTICE JACKSON: Now, there was a representative of Austria present at this meeting, was there not?

GOERING: Yes.

MR. JUSTICE JACKSON: And I ask you to turn to his statement in reference to conditions in Austria, a page or so farther on.

GOERING: Yes.

MR. JUSTICE JACKSON: And I ask you whether he did not report to your meeting as follows:

"Your Excellency, in this matter, we have already a very complete plan for Austria. There are 12000 Jewish workshops and 5000 Jewish retail shops in Vienna. Even before the National Socialist revolution we already had, concerning these 17000 shops, a definite plan for dealing with all tradesmen. Of the 12000 workshops about 10000 were to be closed definitely ..."

GOERING: The interpreter did not follow . . .

MR. JUSTICE JACKSON: Do you find it?

GOERING: I have found it, but the interpreter has not.

MR. JUSTICE JACKSON: "Regarding this total of 17000 stores, of the shops of the 12000 artisans, about 10000 were to be closed definitely and 2000 were to be kept open. Four thousand of the 5000 retail stores were to be closed and 1000 kept open, that is, were to be Aryanized. According to this plan, 3000-3500 of the total of 17000 stores would be kept open, all others closed. This was decided following investigations in every single branch and according to local needs, in agreement with all competent authorities, and is ready for publication as soon as we shall receive the law which we requested in September. This law shall empower us to withdraw licenses from artisans quite independently of the Jewish question. That would be quite a short law.

"Goering: I shall have this decree issued today."

GOERING: Of course. This concerns a law for the curtailment of the heavy retail trade which, even apart from the Jewish question, would have reduced the number of retailers. That can be seen from the minutes.

MR. JUSTICE JACKSON: Very well, let us go on a little further. Do you mean to inform the Tribunal that this did not apply to Jewish shops; that it had no connection with the Jewish question?

GOERING: I have said that independently of the Jewish question, in view of the overfilled retail trade, a limitation of the number of tradesmen would have followed, and that it can be seen from the following statement by Mr. Fischbock, which you have read, that I asked for a law which would authorize us to withdraw licenses, without any connection with the Jewish question. That would be a brief law. Whereupon I answered, "I will issue the decree today."

MR. JUSTICE JACKSON: Now, if you will . . .

GOERING: Naturally, above all, Jewish stores were to be eliminated, as I said in the beginning.

MR. JUSTICE JACKSON: Please go on down two paragraphs to where this was reported:

"But I do not believe that there will be 100 stores, probably fewer — and thus, by the end of the year, we would have liquidated all the recognized Jewish-owned businesses.

"Goering: That would be excellent.

"Fischbock: . . . "

GOERING: Yes, yes, that was the import of that meeting.

MR. JUSTICE JACKSON: "Fischbock: Out of 17000 stores 12000-14000 would be shut down and the remainder Aryanized or handed over to the Trustee's office, which belongs to the State.

"Goering: I have to say that this proposal is grand. This way the whole affair in Vienna, one of the Jewish capitals so to speak, would be wound up by Christmas or by the end of the year.

"Funk: We can do the same thing here. I have prepared a law elaborating that. Effective 1/1/1939, Jews shall be prohibited from operating retail stores and wholesale establishments, as well as independent workshops. They shall be further prohibited from keeping employees, or offering any ready-made products on the market; from advertising or receiving orders. Whenever a Jewish shop is operated the police shall shut it down.

"From 1/1/1939 a Jew can no longer be head of an enterprise, as stipulated in the law for the organization of national labor of 1/20/1934. If a Jew has a leading position in an establishment without being the head of the enterprise, his contract may be declared void within 6 weeks by the head of the enterprise. With the expiration of this period all claims of the employee, including all claims to maintenance, become invalid. That is always very disagreeable and a great danger. A Jew cannot be a member of a corporation. Jewish members of corporations will have to be retired by 12/31/1938. A special authorization is unnecessary. The competent ministers of the Reich are being authorized to issue the provision necessary for execution of this law.

"Goering: I believe we can agree with this law."

GOERING: Yes.

MR. JUSTICE JACKSON: Now I ask you to pass a considerable dialogue relating to the Vienna situation; and I call your attention to the point at which Funk inquires of you:

"Why should the Jew not be allowed to keep bonds?

"Goering: Because in that way he would actually be given a share."

GOERING: Yes, that was the purpose, to get him out of the enterprise. If he kept the bonds, on the basis of his rights as stockholder he still had an interest in the enterprise, and on the basis of ownership of stocks his will would still carry weight in the enterprise.

MR. JUSTICE JACKSON: You turned Funk's suggestion down that the Jews be allowed to keep bonds?

GOERING: Yes. I replaced the bonds with securities.

MR. JUSTICE JACKSON: Well, we will pass several more pages of debate, unless there is something you want to call attention to; and I come to the point where Heydrich is stating his position. I call your attention to this dialogue:

"Heydrich: At least 45000 Jews were made to leave the country by legal measures.

"Goering: . . . "

GOERING: One moment, please. I find it now.

MR. JUSTICE JACKSON: "At least 45000 Jews were made to leave the country by legal measures.

"Goering: How was this possible?"

And then Heydrich tells you that: " . . .through the Jewish — societies we extracted a certain amount of money from the rich Jews who wanted to emigrate. By paying this amount and an additional sum in foreign currency they made it possible for a number of poor Jews to leave. The problem was not to make the rich Jews leave but to get rid of the Jewish mob."

Is that correct?

GOERING: One moment. I do not find it here yet, but generally that is correct, yes.

MR. JUSTICE JACKSON: Pass on a little further. Heydrich is making suggestions and says:

"As for the isolating, I would like to make a few proposals regarding police measures, which are important also because of their psychological effect on public opinion.

"For example, anybody who is Jewish according to the Nuremberg Laws will have to wear a certain badge. That is a possibility which will facilitate many other things. I see no danger of excesses, and it will make our relationship with the foreign Jews easier.

"Goering: A uniform?

"Heydrich: A badge. In this way we could put an end to foreign Jews being molested who do not look different from ours.

"Goering: But my dear Heydrich, you will not be able to avoid the creation of ghettos on a very large scale in all the cities.

"They will have to be created."

Is that what you said?

GOERING: I said that. At that time the problem was also to get the Jews together in certain parts of the cities and in certain streets because on the basis of the tenancy regulations there was no other possibility, and if the wearing of badges was to be made obligatory each individual Jew could have been protected.

MR. JUSTICE JACKSON: Now, passing further in the discussion I call your attention to this warning from Heydrich about those measures which have been discussed:

"Goering: Once we have a ghetto, we could determine what stores ought to be there and we would be able to say, 'You, Jew so and so, together with so and so, shall take care of the delivery of goods,' then a German wholesale firm will be ordered to deliver the goods for this Jewish store. The store would then not be a retail shop but a co-operative store, a co-operative society for Jews.

"Heydrich: All these measures will eventually lead to the institution of a ghetto. I must say: nowadays one should not want to set up a ghetto, but these measures, if carried through as outlined here, will automatically drive the Jews into a ghetto."

Did Heydrich give that warning?

GOERING: Here it says so, yes, but it can be seen from the following discussion that I said: "Now comes that which Goebbels mentioned before, compulsory renting. Now the Jewish tenants will come together." It was a question of the Jewish tenants drawing together in order to avoid the disagreeable results which arose from reciprocal subletting.

MR. JUSTICE JACKSON: You have omitted that Funk also remarked at this point that "Jews will have to stand together. What are million? Every one will have to stand up for the next fellow. Alone he will starve."

Do you find that?

GOERING: Yes. But in another part of these minutes it is stated very clearly: "One cannot let the Jews starve, and therefore the necessary measures must be taken."

MR. JUSTICE JACKSON: Toward the close of that meeting you said the following, didn't you?

"I demand that German Jewry as a whole shall, as a punishment for the abominable crimes, et cetera, make a contribution of RM1 billion. That will work. The pigs will not commit a second murder so quickly. Incidentally, I would like to say again that I would not like to be a Jew in Germany."

GOERING: That was correct, yes.

MR. JUSTICE JACKSON: Were you joking about that too?

GOERING: I have told you exactly what led to the fine of RM1 billion.

MR. JUSTICE JACKSON: You pointed out that the chauffeurs of Gauleiter must be prevented from enriching themselves through the Aryanization of Jewish property, right?

GOERING: Yes.

MR. JUSTICE JACKSON: We will now take up the subject of art.

I call your attention to Document 141–PS, Exhibit Number USA–308. That is the decree establishing priorities on the claim for Jewish art property. Do you recall that?

GOERING: That has been mentioned several times, and I have recently spoken about it in detail.

MR. JUSTICE JACKSON: The order was issued as here stated was it not?

GOERING: Yes, certainly; I emphasized that.

MR. JUSTICE JACKSON: In Paragraph 5 reference is made to art objects that are suitable to be given to French museums, and which were to be sold by auction. The profit from this auction was to be given to the French State for the benefit of war widows and children. You say that this was never done?

GOERING: I did not say that this never happened. That was not my intention in that decree.

MR. JUSTICE JACKSON: Well, I am asking you if it ever has been done.

GOERING: As far as Paragraph 5 is concerned, I cannot say. I can only refer to the payments mentioned in Paragraph 2 – the things that I pointed out – which I had effected after an estimate, and I said the other day that this amount was kept in readiness and that I repeatedly asked into which account it should be paid. And among the object destined to go into the collection which I was to make, I had every single item valued.

MR. JUSTICE JACKSON: Where was this amount kept?

GOERING: In my bank, under the name "Art Funds."

MR. JUSTICE JACKSON: In what bank?

GOERING: It was – I cannot say for sure, there were several banks – in which bank exactly the art fund was deposited, I cannot say. I would have to have the documents here for that.

MR. JUSTICE JACKSON: In the several interrogations you have never been able to point out where that fund is, have you?

GOERING: I cannot say, but you would only have to question my secretary who kept account of all the funds; she can tell you quite accurately.

MR. JUSTICE JACKSON: This order, 141 – PS, was carried out by the Rosenberg Special Staff (*Einsatzstab*), wasn't it?

GOERING: Yes.

MR. JUSTICE JACKSON: Did you know who carried it out who actually was there? Did you know Turner?

GOERING: I did not understand the name.

MR. JUSTICE JACKSON: Did you know Mr. Turner?

GOERING: I know a certain Turner, who, however, had nothing to do with the *Einsatzstab*, the Rosenberg Special Staff and who as far as I know, was in Yugoslavia.

MR. JUSTICE JACKSON: Wasn't State Counsellor Turner in Paris in connection with the art collections?

GOERING: I repeat again so that no error is possible, you said Turner, T – u – r – n – e – r, or Korner, K – o – r – n – e – r?

MR. JUSTICE JACKSON: Turner.

GOERING: Korner?

MR. JUSTICE JACKSON: T – u – r – n – e – r.

GOERING: Turner – I do not know whether he had anything to do with Rosenberg's *Einsatzstab*.

MR. JUSTICE JACKSON: But you knew him, did you not?

GOERING: Yes.

MR. JUSTICE JACKSON: And did you know a Dr. Bunjes?

GOERING: Bunjes, B – u – n – j – e – s, yes.

MR. JUSTICE JACKSON: You knew him?

GOERING: Yes.

MR. JUSTICE JACKSON: He had to do with captured or confiscated Jewish art treasures, did he not?

GOERING: I do not believe that Dr. Bunjes had anything to do with that. He was competent in a different field of art – but the *Einsatzstab* Rosenberg and certain departments of the military administration, had something to do with it.

MR. JUSTICE JACKSON: I will ask to have you shown, so that you can follow me, to refresh your memory, Document 2523 – PS, Exhibit Number USA – 783, a letter from Dr. Bunjes, and ask you if this refreshes your recollection of certain events.

"On Tuesday, 2/4/1941, at 1830 hours I was ordered for the first time to report to the Reich Marshal at the Quai d'Orsay. Field Commander Von Behr of the *Einsatzstab* Rosenberg was present. It is, of course, difficult to describe in words the cordial atmosphere in which the conversation was held."

Do you recall such a meeting?

GOERING: No, it was not important enough for me to remember it, but I do not deny it, in any case.

MR. JUSTICE JACKSON: We shall see if this refreshes your recollection:

"The Reich Marshal dropped the subject for the time being and asked for the report of the present state of the seizure of Jewish art property in the occupied western territories. On this occasion he gave Herr Von Behr the photographs of those objects of art that the Fuehrer wants to bring into his possession. In addition, he gave Herr Von Behr the photographs of those objects of art that the Reich Marshal wants to acquire for himself."

GOERING: I cannot follow here.

MR. JUSTICE JACKSON: You mean you do not find these words, or you do not recall the events?

GOERING: No, I have not found the passage yet, and I would like to have a little time to see the context of this letter, which was neither written by me nor addressed to me.

MR. JUSTICE JACKSON: Let me call your attention to a further paragraph of it and see if it does not refresh your recollection:

"On Wednesday, 2/5/1941, I was ordered to the Jeu de Paume by the Reich Marshal. At 1500 o'clock, the Reich Marshal, accompanied by General Hanesse, Herr Angerer, and Herr Hofer, visited the exhibition of Jewish art treasures newly set up there."

GOERING: Yes, I have already stated before that at Jeu de Paume I selected the art treasures which were exhibited there. That is right.

MR. JUSTICE JACKSON: That is right; now we are getting there. "Then, with me as his guide, the Reich Marshal inspected the exhibited art treasures and made a selection of those works of art which were to go to the Fuehrer, and those which were to be placed in his own collection.

"During this confidential conversation, I again called the Reich Marshal's attention to the fact that a note of protest had been received from the French Government against the activity of the *Einsatzstab* Rosenberg, with reference to the Hague Rules on Land Warfare recognized by Germany at the Armistice of Compiegne and I pointed out that General Von Stulpnagel's interpretation of the manner in which the confiscated Jewish art treasures are to be treated, was apparently contrary to the Reich Marshal's interpretation. Thereupon the Reich Marshal asked for a detailed explanation and gave the following orders:

"'First, it is my orders that you have to follow. You will act directly according to my orders. The art objects collected in the Jeu de Paume are to be loaded on a special train immediately and taken to Germany by order of the Reich Marshal. These art objects which are to go into the Fuehrer's possession and those art objects which the Reich Marshal claims for himself, will be loaded on two railroad cars which will be attached to the Reich Marshal's special train, and upon his departure for Germany, at the beginning of next week, will be taken along to Berlin. Feldfuehrer Von Behr will accompany the Reich Marshal in his special train on the journey to Berlin.'

"When I made the objection that the jurists would probably be of a different opinion and that protests would most likely be made by the military commander in France, the Reich Marshal answered, saying verbatim as follows, 'Dear Bunjes let me worry about that; I am the highest jurist in the State.'

"The Reich Marshal promised to send from his headquarters by courier to the Chief of the Military Administrative District of Paris on Thursday, 6 February, the written order for the transfer to Germany of the confiscated Jewish art treasures."

Now, does that refresh your memory?

GOERING: Not in the least, but it is not at all in contradiction to what I have said with respect to the art treasures, with the exception of one sentence. It is pure nonsense that I should have said that I was the highest jurist in the state because that, thank God, I was not. That is something which Mr. Bunjes said, and I cannot be held responsible for every statement which anyone may have made to somebody else without my having any possibility of correcting it. As for the rest, it corresponds to the statement I made recently.

MR. JUSTICE JACKSON: Now, the art objects then were loaded on cars and shipped to Berlin, were they not?

GOERING: A part of them, yes.

MR. JUSTICE JACKSON: I now call your attention to, and ask to have you shown, Document 014 – PS, Exhibit Number USA – 784. Now, I ask you to refresh your recollection by following this report to he Fuehrer with me, and tell me if this conforms with your testimony:

"I report the arrival..."

GOERING: I would like to point out that this report did not come from me.

MR. JUSTICE JACKSON: I understand that. I am asking if it is right or wrong.

"I report the arrival of the principal shipment of ownerless Jewish treasures of art at the salvage point Neuschwanstein by special train on Saturday the 15th of this month. It was secured by my *Einsatzstab*, in Paris. The special train, arranged for by Reich Marshal Hermann Goering, comprised 25 express baggage cars filled with the most valuable paintings, furniture, Gobelin tapestries, works of artistic craftmanship, and ornaments. The shipment consisted mainly of the most important parts of the collections of Rothschild, Seligmann" – and half a dozen others.

Have you found that and is it correct?

GOERING: I do not know whether this is correct, since the report did not come from me. The only thing which I can remember is that I was asked by the *Einsatzstab* to see to it that a sufficient number of special cars, box cars was put at their disposal to ship the art treasures, since Jeu de Paume was not a safe place in case of air attacks. Neuschwanstein lies south of Munich. This concerns the objects destined for the Fuehrer.

I should like, however, to refer to the next sentence of this document, which was not written by me. It goes as follows:

"The confiscation actions of my *Einsatzstab* were begun in 10/1940 in Paris according to your order, my Fuehrer."

That coincides with what I have said in my previous statements.

MR. JUSTICE JACKSON: And would you care to read further?

GOERING: You mean where it says:

"Besides this special train, the main art objects selected by the Reich Marshal – mainly from the Rothschild collection – had previously been shipped in two special cars to Munich and were there put into the air raid shelter of the Fuehrerhaus."

They are those most precious works of art which I had designated for the Fuehrer, and which were to be sent, at the wish of the Fuehrer, to the air raid shelter. This had nothing to do directly with my affairs, but I did not dispute the fact, and I have explained it in detail.

MR. JUSTICE JACKSON: When you were examined by the American Foreign Assets Commission, you estimated your art objects as having a value, at the time you turned them over to the government, of 50 million Reichsmark, as I recall it. Am I right?

GOERING: That is not quite correct. The Commission insisted a valuation, and the discussion continued a long time backwards and forward. I expressly told the Commission that I could not assess the value because I did not have the objects in hand nor a list of them and I could not quote them from memory; furthermore, that the estimates were subject to fluctuation depending on the one hand upon the prices art lovers might pay and, on the other, upon the actual market value. Since I did not see a copy of the minutes, in spite of my pleas, and especially as minutes of this nature often give rise to misunderstandings, I can only acknowledge the records which I have signed.

MR. JUSTICE JACKSON: Well, do you question this fact? "When I gave the news to the Minister of Finance I estimated the value at that time at 50 million marks." Did you say that or did you not?

GOERING: I cannot estimate the value. I only told the Finance Minister that the entire collection, including my own, would be turned over to the State. And since I know my passion for collecting, I thought that it was quite possible that something might suddenly happen to me, and that as I had put my entire fortune into these works of art, the entire collection might possibly become State, that is, public property, and my family would thus be deprived of every means of subsistence. I therefore asked him to provide for a pension or some compensation for my family. That was the negotiation with the Finance Minister, to which he can testify.

MR. JUSTICE JACKSON: What proportion of your art collection was acquired after 1933?

GOERING: I did not understand the question.

MR. JUSTICE JACKSON: What proportion of your art collection was acquired after 1933?

GOERING: That I could not say in detail – quite a number of pictures and statues.

MR. JUSTICE JACKSON: Now, you have claimed that some part of your art collection you bought?

GOERING: Certainly.

MR. JUSTICE JACKSON: And in connection with that some inquiry was made into your financial transactions, was there not?

GOERING: I do not know who made the inquiries.

MR. JUSTICE JACKSON: Well, you were asked, were you not, your receipt of RM7.276 million from the Reemtsma cigarette factory?

GOERING: No, I was never asked about that.

MR. JUSTICE JACKSON: You were never asked about it?

GOERING: No, neither about the amount nor about the cigarette factory, nor anything else.

MR. JUSTICE JACKSON: Let me refresh your recollection about that. Did you not tell them and did you not tell Colonel Amen in interrogations that this money was given to you by this cigarette factory and that their back taxes were canceled?

GOERING: No, I even denied that their back taxes were ever canceled. I remember now that the question was put to me in a different connection. A sum of money was set aside for the so-called Hitler Fund, and this amount the Fuehrer put at my disposal for general cultural tasks.

MR. JUSTICE JACKSON: By the cigarette factory?

GOERING: Not by the cigarette factory; a number of businesses then subscribed to the Adolf Hitler Fund, and Mr. Reemtsma gave me this sum from the fund in the course of the years, after agreement with the Fuehrer. A part of it was allotted to the State theaters, other part for building up art collections, and other cultural expenditure.

MR. JUSTICE JACKSON: Now, you were interrogated on the 12/2/1945 by the External Assets Branch of the United States Investigation of Cartels and External Assets, were you not?

GOERING: May I first say explicitly that I had been asked whether I would be ready to make any statements about it, and was told that these statements would in no way be connected with this Trial. Therefore the presence of my defense counsel would not be necessary. This was expressly told me, and was repeated to me by the prison authorities, and before the interrogation it was again confirmed to me that these statements should in no way be brought in in connection with this Trial. However, that is all the same to me. You may produce them as far as I am concerned. But because of the method employed, I desire to have this made known here.

DR. STAHMER: I protest against the use of the statements for the reason that has just been given by the witness. I myself sometime ago – I think it was around Christmas – was asked by, I believe, members of the United States Treasury whether they could interrogate the Defendant Goering on questions of property, adding expressly that I did not have to be present at the interrogation because this had nothing to do with the Trial, and would not be used for it.

MR. JUSTICE JACKSON: I am not able either to affirm or deny and therefore I will not pursue this subject further at this time. I do not believe that any stipulation was made that these facts should not be gone into. I was not informed of it, and if there has been of course, it would be absurd.

[Turning to the witness.] Now, you were asked about receiving some art objects from Monte Cassino.

GOERING: Yes.

MR. JUSTICE JACKSON: I ask you if it is not the fact that an altar statue taken from the Cassino Abbey was brought and delivered to you, and that you expressed great appreciation for it.

GOERING: I am glad to be able to clarify this also. After the monastery of Monte Cassino had been completely destroyed by shelling and had been defended by a paratroop division, a delegation arrived one day bringing along a statue of some saint, entirely worthless from an artistic point of view, as a souvenir of this destroyed monastery. I thanked the men and showed the statue to the curator of my art collection, and he also considered the statue as of absolutely no value. It then remained in the box and was put away somewhere. The other...

THE PRESIDENT: I do not think this is coming through sufficiently loud for the shorthand writers to hear.

GOERING: The rest of the art treasures from Monte Cassino according to my knowledge, were shipped in the following manner: A large part, especially those objects which belonged to the old monastery itself, was sent to the Vatican. I must assume this from the fact that the abbot of the monastery sent me and my division a letter written in Latin in which he expressed his extreme gratitude for this action.

Secondly, as far as I remember, the art treasures from the museum in Naples, which were at Monte Cassino, were for the greater part sent by us to Venice and there turned over to the Italian Government. Some pictures and statues were brought to Berlin, and there they were turned over to me. On the very same day I gave the list to the Fuehrer, and some time later also the objects themselves which were in my air raid shelter, so that he could negotiate about the matter with Mussolini. I did not keep a single one of these objects for my own collection. If my troops had not intervened, these priceless art treasures, which were stored in Monte Cassino and belonged to the monastery there, would have been entirely destroyed by enemy bombardment, that is to say, by the British-American attackers. Thus they have been saved.

MR. JUSTICE JACKSON: Now, you say of no value – no substantial value?

GOERING: That is even now my conviction, and I depended, above all, on the judgment of my experts. I never took this statue out of its packing case. It did not interest me. On the other hand, I wanted to say a few words of thanks to the men who brought it.

MR. JUSTICE JACKSON: The labor shortage in the Reich was becoming acute by 11/1941, was it not?

GOERING: That is correct.

MR. JUSTICE JACKSON: And you yourself gave the directives for the employment of Russian prisoners of war, did you not?

GOERING: Employment for what?

MR. JUSTICE JACKSON: For war industry – tanks, artillery pieces, airplane parts.

GOERING: That is correct.

MR. JUSTICE JACKSON: That was at the conference of the 11/7/1941, that you gave that order, was it not?

GOERING: At what conference that was I could not tell you; I issued these directives only in a general way.

MR. JUSTICE JACKSON: And the directive was that Russian prisoners of war should be selected in collecting camps beyond the Reich border, and should be transported as rapidly as possible and employed in the following order of priority: mining, railroad maintenance, war industry – tanks, artillery pieces, airplane parts, agriculture, building industry, et cetera. You gave that order, did you not?

GOERING: If I have signed it, the order is from me. I do not remember details.

THE PRESIDENT: What was the number of that, Mr. Jackson?

MR. JUSTICE JACKSON: I ask to have you shown Document Number 1193 – PS.

GOERING: I have not seen it yet.

[Document 1193 – PS was submitted to the witness.]

This document, which you have just mentioned . . .

MR JUSTICE JACKSON: I did not get the answer.

GOERING: Excuse me. I have just received a document about the use of Russian troops. Is that the document of which you speak?

MR. JUSTICE JACKSON: That is right. I call your attention to the fact that it is referred to as an annex in the letter signed by Goering.

GOERING: I want to point out that this document is not signed by me, but by Korner, which, however, does not diminish my responsibility.

MR. JUSTICE JACKSON: Well, you do not question that on the 11/7/1941, you gave the order, as Korner reports it, do you, in the document referred to as 1193 – PS?

GOERING: I said only that it was not signed by me but by Korner and here even a still younger official, a Regierungsrat, and I wanted only to explain that this was my field and that therefore I assume responsibility. But I have not read it through yet. This deals with directives and outlines which I gave in general and which were then filled in and revised by the department concerned, whereby naturally not every word or every sentence written here was said or dictated by myself. But that does not alter the fact that I bear the responsibility for it, even if I did not know it in detail, or would have perhaps formulated it differently. But the general directives were given by me and implemented accordingly by the lesser authorities.

MR. JUSTICE JACKSON: You also gave the order, did you not, that 100,000 men were to be taken from among the French prisoners of war not yet employed in armament industry? Gaps in manpower resulting therefrom will be filled by Soviet prisoners of war. The transfer of the above-named French prisoners of war is to be accomplished by October the 1st. You gave the order, did you not?

GOERING: That is correct. Here we deal primarily with the fact that a large part of French skilled workers who were prisoners of war were turned into free workers on condition that they worked in the German armament industry. The shortages which occurred at their previous places of work at that time, where they had worked as prisoners of war, were to be remedied by Russian prisoners of war, because I considered it pointless that qualified skilled industrial workers should be employed in agriculture, for instance, or in an other field not corresponding to their abilities. Thus there was an incentive in the fact that these people could become free workers instead of remaining prisoners of war, if they would agree to these conditions. The directives were given by me.

SIR DAVID MAXWELL-FYFE (British prosecutor): I want to ask you first some questions about the matter of the British Air Force officers who escaped from Stalag Luft III. Do you remember that you said in giving your evidence that you knew this incident very completely and very minutely? Do you remember saying that?

GOERING: No – that I had received accurate knowledge; not that I had accurate knowledge – but that I received it.

SIR DAVID MAXWELL-FYFE: Let me quote your own words, as they were taken down, "I know this incident very completely, very minutely, but it came to my attention, unfortunately, at a later period of time." That is what you said the other day, is that right?

GOERING: Yes, that is what I meant; that I know about the incident exactly, but only heard of it 2 days later.

SIR DAVID MAXWELL-FYFE: You told the Tribunal that you were on leave at this time, in the last period of 3/1944, is that right?

GOERING: Yes, as far as I remember I was on leave in March until a few days before Easter.

SIR DAVID MAXWELL-FYFE: And you said, "As I can prove." I want you to tell the Tribunal the dates of your leave.

GOERING: I say again, that this refers to the whole of March – I remember it well – and for proof I would like to mention the people who were with me on this leave.

SIR DAVID MAXWELL-FYFE: What I want to know is, when you were on leave.

GOERING: Here, in the vicinity of Nuremberg.

SIR DAVID MAXWELL-FYFE: So you were within easy reach of the telephone from the Air Ministry or, indeed, from Breslau if you were wanted?

GOERING: I would have been easily accessible by phone if someone wanted to communicate with me.

SIR DAVID MAXWELL-FYFE: I want you to help me with regard to one or two other dates of which you have spoken. You say: "I heard 1 or 2 days later about this escape." Do you understand, Witness, that it is about the escape I am asking you, not about the shooting, for the moment; I want to make it quite clear.

GOERING: It is clear to me.

SIR DAVID MAXWELL-FYFE: Did you mean by that, that you heard about the actual escape 1 or 2 days after it happened?

GOERING: Yes.

SIR DAVID MAXWELL-FYFE: Did you hear about it from the office of your adjutant or from your director of operations?

GOERING: I always heard these things through my adjutant. Several other escapes had preceded this one.

SIR DAVID MAXWELL-FYFE: Yes, that's right. There had been a number of escapes from this camp.

GOERING: I cannot tell you exactly whether they were from this camp. Shortly before several big escapes had taken place which I always heard of through the office of my adjutant.

SIR DAVID MAXWELL-FYFE: I want you to tell the Tribunal another date: You say that on your return from leave your chief of staff made a communication to you. Who was your chief of staff?

GOERING: General Korten was chief of staff at that time.

SIR DAVID MAXWELL-FYFE: Can you tell us the date at which he made this communication to you?

GOERING: No, I cannot tell you that exactly. I believe I discussed his incident with my chief of staff later, telling him what I had already heard about it from other sources.

SIR DAVID MAXWELL-FYFE: Who was the first to tell you about it?

Was it your chief of staff who told you about the shootings? Do you mean that some one else had told you about shooting?

GOERING: I cannot say exactly now whether I heard about the shooting from the chief of staff, or from other sources. But in any event I discussed this with the chief of staff.

SIR DAVID MAXWELL-FYFE: What was the date that you talked about it with your chief of staff?

GOERING: I cannot tell you the date exactly from memory, but it must have been around Easter.

SIR DAVID MAXWELL-FYFE: That would be just about the end of March, wouldn't it?

GOERING: No. It might have been at the beginning of April, the first half of April.

SIR DAVID MAXWELL-FYFE: And then you had an interview with Himmler, you have told us?

GOERING: Yes, I talked with Himmler about this.

SIR DAVID MAXWELL-FYFE: Can you fix that?

GOERING: Of course I cannot establish this date with certainty. I saw Himmler, and, at the first opportunity after I had heard about this incident, spoke to him about it.

SIR DAVID MAXWELL-FYFE: So that you can't fix the date in relation to your coming back from leave, or the interview with your chief of staff, or any other date, or Easter?

GOERING: Without any documents it is, as I said, impossible for me today to fix the date. I can only mention the approximate period of time; and that I have done.

SIR DAVID MAXWELL-FYFE: You said the other day that you could prove when you were on leave. Am I to take it that you haven't taken the trouble to look up what your leave dates were?

GOERING: I have already said the 28th or the 29th of March. I cannot tell you. For proof others perhaps can fix this date more definitely. I know only that I was there in March.

SIR DAVID MAXWELL-FYFE: Witness, will it be perfectly fair to you if I take the latest of your dates, the 29th of March, to work on?

GOERING: It would be more expedient if you would tell me when Easter was that year, because I do not recall it. Then it will be easier for me to specify the dates, because I know that a few days before Easter I returned to Berchtesgaden in order to pass these holidays with my family.

SIR DAVID MAXWELL-FYFE: A few days before Easter you went back to Berchtesgaden?

GOERING: Yes.

SIR DAVID MAXWELL-FYFE: So you had come back on leave some day before that. Before you went to Berchtesgaden you had come back from your March leave?

GOERING: Berchtesgaden was then at the same time the headquarters of the Fuehrer. I returned from my leave to Berchtesgaden and with my return my leave ended, because I returned to duty. The return to Berchtesgaden was identical with the termination of my leave.

SIR DAVID MAXWELL-FYFE: Well, I can't give you Easter offhand, but I happen to remember Whitsuntide was the 28th of May, so that Easter would be early, somewhere about the 5th of April. So that your leave would finish somewhere about the end of March, maybe the 26th or the 29th; that is right, isn't it?

Now, these shootings of these officers went on from the 25th of March to the 13th of April; do you know that?

GOERING: I do not know that exactly.

SIR DAVID MAXWELL-FYFE: You may take that from me because there is an official report of the shooting, and I want to be quite fair with you. Only 49 of these officers were shot on the 6th of April, as far as we can be sure, and one was shot either on the 13th of April or later. But the critical period is the end of March, and we may take it that you were back from leave by about the 29th of March.

I just want you to tell the Tribunal this was a matter of great importance, wasn't it? Considered a matter of great importance?

GOERING: It was a very important matter.

SIR DAVID MAXWELL-FYFE: General Milch – I beg pardon – Field Marshal Milch has said that it was a matter which would require the highest authority, and I think you have said that you know it was Hitler's decision that these officers should be shot. Is that so?

GOERING: The question did not come through clearly.

SIR DAVID MAXWELL-FYFE: It was Hitler's decision that these officers should be shot?

GOERING: That is correct; and I was later notified that it was Hitler's decree.

SIR DAVID MAXWELL-FYFE: I want you just to remember one other thing, that immediately it was published, the British Foreign Secretary, Mr. Eden, at once said that Great Britain would demand justice of the perpetrators of these murders – do you remember that?

GOERING: I cannot remember the speech to the House of Commons given by Eden. I myself do not know the substance of this speech even today. I just heard that he spoke in Parliament about this incident.

SIR DAVID MAXWELL-FYFE: I want you to tell the Tribunal just who the persons in your ministry involved were. I will tell you; I think it would be shorter in the end. If you disagree you can correct me.

The commandant of Stalag Luft III was Oberst Von Lindeiner of your service, was he not?

GOERING: That is quite possible. I did not know the names of all these commandants. There was a court martial against him and that was because the escape was possible. He was not connected with the shootings.

SIR DAVID MAXWELL-FYFE: No, but he was commandant of the camp, and I suppose you had to review and confirm the proceedings of the *Zentralluftwaffengericht* which convicted him and sentenced him to a year's imprisonment for neglect of duty. That would come to you, wouldn't it? Wouldn't that come to you for review?

GOERING: No, only if larger penalties were involved. One year imprisonment would not come to my attention. But I know, and I would like to certify, that court proceedings were taken against him for neglect of duty at the time of the escape.

SIR DAVID MAXWELL-FYFE: In 5/1943, Inspectorate Number 17 had been interposed between the Luftwaffe and the Prisoners of War Organization of the OKW, the *Kriegsgefangenenwesen*; do you remember that?

GOERING: I do not know the details about inspection nor how closely it concerned the Prisoners of War Organization of the OKW, or how it was otherwise.

SIR DAVID MAXWELL-FYFE: I want to remind you of who your own officers were. You understand, Witness, that your own officers are involved in this matter. I want to remind you who they were.

Was the head of Inspectorate 17 Major General Grosch of the Luftwaffe?

GOERING: Major General Grosch is of the Luftwaffe.

SIR DAVID MAXWELL-FYFE: You told the Tribunal the other day – I am quoting your own words – that you knew from information, you knew this incident very completely and very minutely. You are now telling the Tribunal you don't know whether Major General Grosch was head of Inspectorate Number 17 of the Luftwaffe?

GOERING: That is irrelevant. I told the High Tribunal that I heard an accurate account of the incident of the shooting of these airmen, but that has no connection with General Grosch and his inspectorate, for he did not participate in the shooting.

SIR DAVID MAXWELL-FYFE: I will show you that connection in one minute if you will just answer my questions. Was Grosch's second in command Oberst Welder; do you remember that?

GOERING: I do not know the particulars of the organization for inspection of prisoner-of-war camps, nor the leaders, nor what positions they held. At least not by heart. I would like to emphasize again, so that there will be no confusion, that when I said I knew about this matter, I mean that I knew how the order was issued and that the people were shot, that I came to know all about this but not as far as this was related to inspections, possibilities of flight, et cetera.

SIR DAVID MAXWELL-FYFE: And did General Grosch, as head of Inspectorate 17, have to report to General Forster, your director of operations at the Luftwaffe Ministerium?

GOERING: That I cannot tell you without having the diagram of the subordinate posts before me. General Forster was, I believe at that time, head of the Luftwehr, or a similar designation, in the ministry. I concerned myself less with these matters, because they were not directly of a tactical, strategic, or of an armament nature. But it is quite possible and certain that he belonged to this department.

SIR DAVID MAXWELL-FYFE: I put it to you quite shortly, and if you don't know I will leave it for the moment. Did you know Major General Von Graevenitz was head of the Defendant Keitel's department, the *Kriegsgefangenenwesen*, that dealt with prisoners of war?

GOERING: I first heard about General Graevenitz here for this department did not directly concern me. I could not know all of these military subordinate commanders in their hundreds and thousands of departments.

SIR DAVID MAXWELL-FYFE: So I take it that you did not know Colonel, now General Westhoff, of the department under Von Graevenitz?

GOERING: Westhoff I never saw at all, and he did not belong to the Luftwaffe.

SIR DAVID MAXWELL-FYFE: I am not suggesting that Von Graevenitz and Westhoff belonged to the Luftwaffe. I wanted to make it clear that I was suggesting they belonged to General Keitel's organization.

GOERING: I did not know either; and I did not know what posts they occupied.

SIR DAVID MAXWELL-FYFE: Up to that time you still had a considerable influence in the Reich, didn't you?

GOERING: At this time no longer. This no longer concerns 1944.

SIR DAVID MAXWELL-FYFE: But you were still head of the Luftwaffe and head of the Air Ministry, weren't you?

GOERING: Yes, I was.

SIR DAVID MAXWELL-FYFE: And you had, as head of the Luftwaffe and head of the Air Ministry, been responsible for six prisoner-of-war camps for the whole of the war up to that time, hadn't you?

GOERING: How many prisoner-of-war camps I do not know. But of course I bear the responsibility for those which belonged to my ministry.

SIR DAVID MAXWELL-FYFE: To the Air Force?

GOERING: Yes, those which were subordinate to the Air Force.

SIR DAVID MAXWELL-FYFE: You knew about the general plan for treatment of prisoners of war, which we have had in evidence as the "*Aktion Kugel*" plan, didn't you?

GOERING: No. I knew nothing of this action. I was not advised of it.

SIR DAVID MAXWELL-FYFE: You were never advised of *Aktion Kugel*?

GOERING: I first heard of *Aktion Kugel* here; saw the document and heard the expression for the first time. Moreover no officer of the Luftwaffe ever informed me of such a thing; and I do not believe that a single officer was ever taken away from the Luftwaffe camps. A report to this effect was never presented to me, in any case.

SIR DAVID MAXWELL-FYFE: You know what *Aktion Kugel* was: That escaped officers and noncommissioned officers, other than British and American, were to be handed over to the police and taken to Mauthausen, where they were shot by the device of having a gun concealed in the measuring equipment when they thought they were getting their prison clothes. You know what "*Aktion Kugel*" is, don't you?

GOERING: I heard of it here.

SIR DAVID MAXWELL-FYFE: Are you telling the Tribunal that you did not know that escaped prisoners of war who were picked up by the police were retained by the police and taken to Mauthausen?

GOERING: No, I did not know that. On the contrary, various prisoners who escaped from my camps were caught again by the police; and they were all brought back to the camps; this was the first case where this to some extent did not take place.

SIR DAVID MAXWELL-FYFE: But didn't you know that Colonel Welder, as second in command of your ministry's inspectorate, issued a written order a month before this, in 2/1944, that prisoners of war picked up by the Luftwaffe should be delivered back to their camp, and prisoners of war picked up by the police should be held by them and no longer counted as being under the protection of the Luftwaffe; didn't you know that?

GOERING: No. Please summon this colonel to testify if he ever made a report of that nature to me, or addressed such a letter to me.

SIR DAVID MAXWELL-FYFE: Well, of course I cannot tell whether your ministry was well run or not. But he certainly issued the order, because he says so himself.

GOERING: Then he must say from whom he received this order.

SIR DAVID MAXWELL-FYFE: I see. Well, he says that he issued this order, and you know as well as I do that prisoners of war is a thing that you have got to be careful about, because you have got a protecting power that investigates any complaint; and you never denounced the Convention and you had the protecting power in these matters all through the war, had you not? That is right, isn't it?

GOERING: That is correct, but I take the liberty to ask who gave him this order, whether he received this order from me.

SIR DAVID MAXWELL-FYFE: Well, he would not get it direct from you. I do not think you had ever met him, had you? He would get it from Lieutenant General Grosch, wouldn't he?

GOERING: Then Grosch should say whether he received such an order from me. I never gave such an order.

SIR DAVID MAXWELL-FYFE: I see. So you say that you had never heard – this was 3 ½ years after the beginning of the war and you had never heard that any escaped prisoners of war were to be handed over to the police. Is that what you ask the Tribunal to believe?

GOERING: To any offenses or police, I believe gave any order the extent that escaped prisoners of war committed crimes, they were of course turned over to them. But I wish to testify before the Court that I never ordered that they should be handed over to the police or sent to concentration camps merely because they had attempted to break out or escape, nor did I ever know that such measures were taken.

SIR DAVID MAXWELL-FYFE: This is my last question: I want to make it quite clear, Witness, that I am referring to those who had escaped, who had got away from the confines of the camp and were recaptured by the police. Didn't you know that they were handed over to the police?

GOERING: No. Only if they had committed crimes while fleeing, such as murder and so on. Such things occurred.

SIR DAVID MAXWELL-FYFE: Witness, do you remember telling me last night that the only prisoners of war handed over to the police were those guilty of crimes or misdemeanors?

GOERING: I did not express myself that way. I said if the police apprehended prisoners of war, those who had committed a crime during the escape, as far as I know, were detained by the police and were not returned to the camp. To what extent the police kept prisoners of war, without returning them to a camp, I was able to gather from interrogations and explanations here.

SIR DAVID MAXWELL-FYFE: Would you look at Document D – 569? Would you look first at the top left-hand corner, which shows that it is a document published by the Oberkommando der Wehrmacht?

GOERING: The document which I have before me has the following heading at the top left-hand corner: "The Reichsfuehrer SS," and the subheading: "Inspector of Concentration Camps."

SIR DAVID MAXWELL-FYFE: It is a document dated the 11/22/1941. Have you got it?

GOERING: Yes, I have it now.

SIR DAVID MAXWELL-FYFE: Now, look at the left-hand bottom corner, as to distribution. The second person to whom it is distributed is the Air Ministry and Commander-in-chief of the Air Force on 11/22/1941. That would be you.

GOERING: That's correct. I would like to make the following statement in connection with this...

SIR DAVID MAXWELL-FYFE: Just for a moment. I would like you to appreciate the document and then make your statement upon it. I shall not stop you. I want you to look at the third sentence in Paragraph 1. This deals with Soviet prisoners of war, you understand. The third sentence says:

"If escaped Soviet prisoners of war are returned to the camp in accordance with this order, they have to be handed over to the nearest post of the Secret State Police, in any case."

And then Paragraph 2 deals with the special position – if they commit crimes, owing to the fact that:

"...at present these misdemeanors on the part of Soviet prisoners of war are particularly frequent, due most likely to living conditions still being somewhat unsettled, the following temporary regulations come into force. They may be amended later. If a Soviet prisoner of war commits any other punishable offense then the commandant of the camp must hand the guilty man over to the head of the Security Police."

Do I understand this document to say that a man who escapes will be handed over to the Security Police? You understand this document says a man who escapes will be handed over to the Secret Police, a man who commits a crime, as you mentioned, will be headed over to the Security Police. Wasn't that the condition obtained from 1941 up to the date we are dealing with in 3/1944?

GOERING: I would like to read the few preceding paragraphs that no sentences are separated from their context.

SIR DAVID MAXWELL-FYFE: My Lord, while the witness is reading the document, might I go over the technical matter of the arrangement of exhibits? When I cross-examined Field Marshal Slecking I put in three documents, UK – 66, which becomes Exhibit 274, D – 39, which becomes GB – 275; TC – 91, which becomes GB – 276; This document will become GB – 277.

[Turning to the witness.] Have you had an opportunity of reading it, Witness?

GOERING: Yes, I have.

SIR DAVID MAXWELL-FYFE: Then I am right, am I not, that Soviet prisoners of war who escaped were to be, after their return to the camp, handed over to the Secret State Police. If they committed a crime, they were to be handed over to the Security Police, isn't that right?

GOERING: Not exactly correct. I would like to point to the third sentence in the first paragraph. There it says, "If a prisoner-of-war is in the vicinity, then the man who is recaptured is to be transported there."

SIR DAVID MAXWELL-FYFE: But read the next sentence, "If a Soviet prisoner of war is returned to the camp" – that is in accordance with this order which you have just read – "he has to be handed to the nearest service station of the Secret State Police." Your own sentence.

GOERING Yes, but the second paragraph which follows gives an explanation of frequent criminal acts of Soviet prisoners of war, et cetera, committed at that time. You read that yourself; that is connected with this Paragraph Number 1. But this order was given by itself and it was distributed to the Army, the Air Force and the Navy. And I would like to give the explanation of its distribution. In this war there were not only hundreds, but thousands of current orders which were issued by superiors to subordinate officers and were transmitted to various departments. That does not mean that each of these thousands of orders was submitted to the Commander-in-chief; only the most decisive and most important were shown to him. The others went from department to department. Thus it is that this order from the Chief of the High Command was signed by a subordinate department, and not by the Chief of the High Command himself.

SIR DAVID MAXWELL-FYFE: This order would be dealt with by your prisoner-of-war department in your ministry, wouldn't it?

GOERING: This department, according to the procedure adopted for these orders, received the order, but no other department received it.

SIR DAVID MAXWELL-FYFE: I think the answer to my question must be "yes." It would be dealt with by the prisoner-of-war department – your ministry. Isn't that so?

GOERING: I would say yes.

SIR DAVID MAXWELL-FYFE: It is quicker, you see, if you say "yes" in the beginning; do you understand?

GOERING: No; it depends upon whether I personally have read the order or not, and I will then determine as to my responsibility.

SIR DAVID MAXWELL-FYFE: Well now, the escape...

THE PRESIDENT: You were not asked about responsibility; you were asked whether it would be dealt with by your prisoner-of-war department.

SIR DAVID MAXWELL-FYFE: Now, the escape about which I am asking you took place on the night of the 24th to the 25th of March. I want you to have that date in mind. The decision to murder these young officers must have been taken very quickly, because the first murder which actually took place was on the 26th of March. Do you agree with that? It must have been taken quickly?

GOERING: I assume that this order, as I was informed later, was given immediately, but it had no connection with this document.

SIR DAVID MAXWELL-FYFE: No, no; we are finished with that document; we are going into the murder of these young men The *Grossfahndung* – a general hue and cry, I think, would be the British translation – was also issued at once in order that these men should be arrested; isn't that so?

GOERING: That is correct. Whenever there was an escape, and such a large number of prisoners escaped, automatically in the whole Reich, a hue and cry was raised, that is, all authorities had to be on the lookout to recapture the prisoners.

SIR DAVID MAXWELL-FYFE: So that in order to give this order to murder these men, and for the *Grossfahndung*, there must have been a meeting of Hitler, at any rate with Himmler or Kaltenbrunner, in order that that order would be put into effect; isn't that so?

GOERING: That is correct. According to what I heard, Himmler was the first to report this escape to the Fuehrer.

SIR DAVID MAXWELL-FYFE: Now, General Westhoff, who was in Defendant Keitel's *Kriegsgefangenenwesen*, in his prisoner-of-war setup, says this, that "On a date, which I think was the 26th, Keitel said to him, 'This morning Goering reproached me in the presence of Himmler for having let some more prisoners of war escape. It was unheard of.'"

Do you say that General Westhoff is wrong?

GOERING: Yes. This is not in accordance with the facts. General Westhoff is referring to a statement of Field Marshal Keitel. This utterance in itself is illogical, for I could not accuse Keitel because he would not draw my attention to it, as the guarding was his responsibility and not mine.

SIR DAVID MAXWELL-FYFE: One of the Defendant Keitel's officers dealing with this matter was a general inspector, General Rottich. I do not know if you know him.

GOERING: No.

SIR DAVID MAXWELL-FYFE: Well, General Westhoff, as one could understand, is very anxious to assure everyone that his senior officer had nothing to do with it, and he goes on to say this about General Rottich:

"He was completely excluded from it by the fact that these matters were taken out of his hands. Apparently at that conference with the Fuehrer in the morning, that is to say, the conference between Himmler, Field Marshal Keitel, and Goering, which took place in the Fuehrer's presence, the Fuehrer himself always took a hand in these affairs when officers escaped."

You say that is wrong? You were at no such conference?

GOERING: I was not present at this conference, neither was General Westhoff; he is giving a purely subjective view, not the facts of the case.

SIR DAVID MAXWELL-FYFE: So that we find that – you think that – Westhoff is wrong? You see, Westhoff, he was a colonel at this time, I think, and now he finishes as a major general, and he asks that the senior officers be asked about it; he says this: "It should be possible to find out that Himmler made the suggestion to the Fuehrer – to find that out from Goering who was present at the conference." Again and again Westhoff, who after all is a comparatively junior officer, is saying that the truth about this matter can be discovered from his seniors. You say that it cannot.

GOERING: I would not say that. I would like just to say that General Westhoff was never present for even a moment, therefore he cannot say, I know or I saw that Reich Marshal Goering was present. He is assuming it is so, or he may have heard it.

SIR DAVID MAXWELL-FYFE: What he says is, you know, that Keitel blamed him, as I have read to you; that Keitel went on to say to him at General Von Graevenitz', "Gentlemen, the escapes must stop. We must set an example. We shall take very severe measures. I am only telling you that, that the men who have escaped will be shot; probably the majority of them are dead already." You never heard anything of that?

GOERING: I was neither present at the Keitel – Westhoff – Graevenitz conversation nor at the Fuehrer – Himmler conversation. As far as I know General Westhoff will be testifying here. Moreover, Field Marshal Keitel will be able to say whether I was there or not.

Testimony of Rudolf Hoess

Commandant of Auschwitz

DR. KAUFFMANN: With the agreement of the Tribunal, I now call the witness Hoess.

[The witness Hoess took the stand.]

THE PRESIDENT: Stand up. Will you state your name?

HOESS (Witness): Rudolf Franz Ferdinand Hoess.

THE PRESIDENT: Will you repeat this oath after me: "I swear by God, the Almighty and Omniscient, that I will speak the pure truth, and will withhold and add nothing.

[The witness repeated the oath in German.]

THE PRESIDENT: Will you sit down?

DR. KAUFFMANN: Witness, your statements will have far-reaching significance. You are perhaps the only one who can throw some light upon certain hidden aspects, and who can tell which people gave the orders for the destruction of European Jewry, and can further state how this order was carried out and to what degree the execution was kept a secret.

THE PRESIDENT: Dr. Kauffmann, will you kindly put questions to the witness.

DR. KAUFFMANN: Yes.

[Turning to the witness.] From 1940 to 1943, you were the Commander of the camp at Auschwitz. Is that true?

HOESS: Yes.

DR. KAUFFMANN: And during that time, hundreds of thousands of human beings were sent to their death there. Is that correct?

HOESS: Yes.

DR. KAUTFFMANN: Is it true that you, yourself, have made no exact notes regarding the figures of the number of those victims because you were forbidden to make them?

HOESS: Yes, that is correct.

DR. KAUFFMANN: Is it furthermore correct that exclusively one man by the name of Eichmann had notes about this, the man who had the task of organizing and assembling these people?

HOESS: Yes.

DR. KAUFFMANN: Is it furthermore true that Eichmann stated to you that in Auschwitz a total sum of more than 2 million Jews had been destroyed?

HOESS: Yes.

DR. KAUFFMANN: Men, women, and children?

HOESS: Yes.

DR. KAUFFMANN: You were a participant in the World War?

HOESS: Yes.

DR. KAUFFMANN: And then in 1922, you entered the Party?

HOESS: Yes.

DR. KAUFFMANN: Were you a member of the SS?

HOESS: Since 1934.

DR. KAUFFMANN: Is it true that you, in the year 1924, were sentenced to a lengthy term of hard labor because you participated in a so-called political murder?

HOESS: Yes.

DR. KAUFFMANN: And then at the end of 1934, you went to the concentration camp of Dachau?

HOESS: Yes.

DR. KAUFFMANN: What task did you receive?

HOESS: At first, I was the leader of a block of prisoners and then I became clerk and finally, the administrator of the property of prisoners.

DR. KAUFFMANN: And how long did you stay there?

HOESS: Until 1938.

DR. KAUFFMANN: What job did you have from 1938 on and where were you then?

HOESS: In 1938 I went to the concentration camp at Sachsenhausen where, to begin with, I was adjutant to the commander and later on I became the head of the protective custody camp.

DR. KAUFFMANN: When were you commander at Auschwitz?

HOESS: I was commander at Auschwitz from May 1940 until December 1943.

DR. KAUFFMANN: What was the highest number of human beings, prisoners, ever held at one time at Auschwitz?

HOESS: The highest number of internees held at one time at Auschwitz, was about 140,000 men and women.

DR. KAUFFMANN: Is it true that in 1941 you were ordered to Berlin to see Himmler? Please state briefly what was discussed.

HOESS: Yes. In the summer of 1941 I was summoned to Berlin to Reichsfuhrer SS Himmler to receive personal orders. He told me something to the effect – I do not remember the exact words – that the Fuhrer had given the order for a final solution of the Jewish question. We, the SS, must carry out that order. If it is not carried out now then the Jews will later on destroy the German people. He had chosen Auschwitz on account of its easy access by rail and also because the extensive site offered space for measures ensuring isolation.

DR. KAUFFMANN: During that conference did Himmler tell you that this planned action had to be treated as a secret Reich matter?

HOESS: Yes. He stressed that point. He told me that I was not even allowed to say anything about it to my immediate superior Gruppenfuhrer Glácks. This conference concerned the two of us only and I was to observe the strictest secrecy.

DR. KAUFFMANN: What was the position held by Glácks whom you have just mentioned?

HOESS: Gruppenfuhrer Glácks was, so to speak, the inspector of concentration camps at that time and he was immediately subordinate to the Reichsfuhrer.

DR. KAUFFMANN: Does the expression "secret Reich matter" mean that no one was permitted to make even the slightest allusion to outsiders without endangering his own life?

HOESS: Yes, "secret Reich matter" means that no one was allowed to speak about these matters with any person and that everyone promised upon his life to keep the utmost secrecy.

DR. KAUFFMANN: Did you happen to break that promise?

HOESS: No, not until the end of 1942.

DR. KAUFFMANN: Why do you mention that date? Did you talk to outsiders after that date?

HOESS: At the end of 1942 my wife's curiosity was aroused by remarks made by the then-Gauleiter of Upper Silesia, regarding happenings in my camp. She asked me whether this was the truth and I admitted that it was. That was my only breach of the promise I had given to the Reichsfuhrer. Otherwise I have never talked about it to anyone else.

DR. KAUFFMANN: When did you meet Eichmann?

HOESS: I met Eichmann about 4 weeks after having received that order from the Reichsfuhrer. He came to Auschwitz to discuss the details with me on the carrying out of the given order. As the Reichsfuhrer had told me during our discussion, he had instructed Eichmann to discuss the carrying out of the order with me and I was to receive all further instructions from him.

DR. KAUFFMANN: Will you briefly tell whether it is correct that the camp of Auschwitz was completely isolated, describing the measures taken to insure as far as possible the secrecy of carrying out of the task given to you.

HOESS: The Auschwitz camp as such was about 3 kilometers away from the town. About 20,000 acres of the surrounding country had been cleared of all former inhabitants, and the entire area could be entered only by SS men or civilian employees who had special passes. The actual compound called "Birkenau," where later on the extermination camp was constructed, was situated 2 kilometers from the Auschwitz camp. The camp installations themselves, that is to say, the provisional installations used at first were deep in the woods and could from nowhere be detected by the eye. In addition to that, this area had been declared a prohibited area and even members of the SS who did not have a special pass could not enter it. Thus, as far as one could judge, it was impossible for anyone except authorized persons to enter that area.

DR. KAUFFMANN: And then the railway transports arrived. During what period did these transports arrive and about how many people, roughly, were in such a transport?

HOESS: During the whole period up until 1944 certain operations were carried out at irregular intervals in the different countries, so that one cannot speak of a continuous flow of incoming transports. It was always a matter of 4 to 6 weeks. During those 4 to 6 weeks two to three trains, containing about 2,000 persons each, arrived daily. These trains were first of all shunted to a siding in the Birkenau region and the locomotives then went back. The guards who had accompanied the transport had to leave the area at once and the persons who had been brought in were taken over by guards belonging to the camp.

They were there examined by two SS medical officers as to their fitness for work. The internees capable of work at once marched to Auschwitz or to the camp at Birkenau and those incapable of work were at first taken to the provisional installations, then later to the newly constructed crematoria.

DR. KAUFFMANN: During an interrogation I had with you the other day you told me that about 60 men were designated to receive these transports, and that these 60 persons, too, had been bound to the same secrecy described before. Do you still maintain that today?

HOESS: Yes, these 60 men were always on hand to take the internees not capable of work to these provisional installations and later on to the other ones. This group, consisting of about ten leaders and subleaders, as well as doctors and medical personnel, had repeatedly been told, both in writing and verbally, that they were bound to the strictest secrecy as to all that went on in the camps.

DR. KAUFFMANN: Were there any signs that might show an outsider who saw these transports arrive, that they would be destroyed or was that possibility so small because there was in Auschwitz an unusually large number of incoming transports, shipments of goods and so forth?

HOESS: Yes, an observer who did not make special notes for that purpose could obtain no idea about that because to begin with not only transports arrived which were destined to be destroyed but also other transports arrived continuously, containing new internees who were needed in the camp. Furthermore, transports likewise left the camp in sufficiently large numbers with internees fit for work or exchanged prisoners.

The trains themselves were closed, that is to say, the doors of the freight cars were closed so that it was not possible, from the outside, to get a glimpse of the people inside. In addition to that, up to 100 cars of materials, rations, et cetera, were daily rolled into the camp or continuously left the workshops of the camp in which war material was being made.

DR. KAUFFMANN: And after the arrival of the transports were the victims stripped of everything they had? Did they have to undress completely; did they have to surrender their valuables? Is that true?

HOESS: Yes.

DR. KAUFFMANN: And then they immediately went to their death?

HOESS: Yes.

DR. KAUFFMANN: I ask you, according to your knowledge, did these people know what was in store for them?

HOESS: The majority of them did not, for steps were taken to keep them in doubt about it and suspicion would not arise that they were to go to their death. For instance, all doors and all walls bore inscriptions to the effect that they were going to undergo a delousing operation or take a shower. This was made known in several languages to the internees by other internees who had come in with earlier transports and who were being used as auxiliary crews during the whole action.

DR. KAUFFMANN: And then, you told me the other day, that death by gassing set in within a period of 3 to 15 minutes. Is that correct?

HOESS: Yes.

DR. KAUFFMANN: You also told me that even before death finally set in, the victims fell into a state of unconsciousness?

HOESS: Yes. From what I was able to find out myself or from what was told me by medical officers, the time necessary for reaching unconsciousness or death varied according to the temperature and the number of people present in the chambers. Loss of consciousness took place within a few seconds or a few minutes.

DR. KAUFFMANN: Did you yourself ever feel pity with the victims, thinking of your own family and children?

HOESS: Yes.

DR. KAUFFMANN: How was it possible for you to carry out these actions in spite of this?

HOESS: In view of all these doubts which I had, the only one and decisive argument was the strict order and the reason given for it by the Reichsfuhrer Himmler.

DR. KAUFFMANN: I ask you whether Himmler inspected the camp and convinced himself, too, of the process of annihilation?

HOESS: Yes. Himmler visited the camp in 1942 and he watched in detail one processing from beginning to end.

DR. KAUFFMANN: Does the same apply to Eichmann?

HOESS: Eichmann came repeatedly to Auschwitz and was intimately acquainted with the proceedings.

DR. KAUFFMANN: Did the Defendant Kaltenbrunner ever inspect the camp?

HOESS: No.

DR. KAUFFMANN: Did you ever talk with Kaltenbrunner with reference to your task?

HOESS: No, never. I was with Obergruppenfuhrer Kaltenbrunner on only one single occasion.

DR. KAUFFMANN: When was that?

HOESS: That was one day after his birthday in the year 1944.

DR. KAUFFMANN: And what was the subject of that conference which you have just mentioned?

HOESS: It concerned a report from the camp at Mauthausen on the so-called nameless internees and their engagement in armament industry. Obergruppenfuhrer Kaltenbrunner was to make a decision on the matter. For that reason I came to him with the report from the commander at Mauthausen but he did not make a decision telling me he would do so later.

DR. KAUFFMANN: Regarding the location of Mauthausen, will you please state in which district Mauthausen is situated. Is that Upper Silesia or is it the Government General?

HOESS: Mauthausen . . .

DR. KAUFFMANN: Auschwitz, I beg your pardon, I made a mistake. I mean Auschwitz.

HOESS: Auschwitz is situated in the former state of Poland. Later, after 1939, it was incorporated in the province of Upper Silesia.

DR. KAUFFMANN: Is it right for me to assume that administration and feeding of concentration camps were exclusively under the control of the Main Economic and Administrative Office?

HOESS: Yes.

DR. KAUFFMANN: A department which is completely separated from the RSHA?

HOESS: Quite correct.

DR. KAUFFMANN: And then from 1943 until the end of the war, you were one of the chiefs in the Inspectorate of the Main Economic and Administrative Office?

HOESS: Yes, that is correctly stated.

DR. KAUFFMANN: Do you mean by that, that you are particularly well informed on everything occurring in concentration camps regarding the treatment and the methods applied?

HOESS: Yes.

DR. KAUFFMANN: I ask you, therefore, first of all, whether you have any knowledge regarding the treatment of internees, whether certain methods became known to you according to which they were tortured and cruelly treated? Please formulate your statement according to periods, up to 1939 and after 1939.

HOESS: Until the outbreak of war in 1939, the situation in the camps regarding feeding, accommodations, and treatment of internees, was the same as in any other prison or penitentiary in the Reich. The internees were treated severely, but methodical beatings or ill-treatments were out of the question. The Reichsfuhrer gave frequent orders that every SS man who laid violent hands on an internee would be punished; and several times SS men who did ill-treat internees were punished.

Feeding and billeting at that time were on the same basis as those of other prisoners under legal administration.

The accommodations in the camps during those years were still normal because the mass influxes at the outbreak of the war and during the war had not yet taken place. When the war started and when mass deliveries of political internees arrived, and, later on, when prisoners who were members of the resistance movements arrived from the occupied territories, the construction of buildings and the extensions of the camps could no longer keep pace with the number of incoming internees. During the first years of the war this problem could still be overcome by improvising measures; but later, due to the exigencies of the war, this was no longer possible, since there were practically no building materials any more at our disposal. And, furthermore, rations for the internees were again and again severely curtailed by the provincial economic administration offices.

This then led to a situation where internees in the camps no longer had the staying power to resist the now gradually growing epidemics.

The main reason why the prisoners were in such bad condition towards the end of the war, why so many thousands of them were found sick and emaciated in the camps, was that every internee had to be employed in the armament industry to the extreme limit of his forces. The Reichsfuhrer constantly and on every occasion kept this goal before our eyes, and also proclaimed it through the Chief of the Main Economic and Administrative Office, Obergruppenfuhrer Pohl, to the concentration camp, commanders and administrative leaders during the so-called commanders' meetings.

Every commander was told to make every effort to achieve this. The aim was not to have as many dead as possible or to destroy as many internees as possible; the Reichsfuhrer was constantly concerned with being able to engage all forces available in the armament industry.

DR. KAUFFMANN: There is no doubt that the longer the war lasted, the larger became the number of the ill-treated and tortured inmates. Whenever you inspected the concentration camps did you not learn something of this state of affairs through complaints, et cetera, or do you consider that the conditions which have been described are more or less due to excesses?

HOESS: These so-called ill-treatments and this torturing in concentration camps, stories of which were spread everywhere among the people, and later by the prisoners that were liberated by the occupying armies, were not, as assumed, inflicted methodically, but were excesses committed by individual leaders, subleaders, and men who laid violent hands on internees.

DR. KAUFFMANN: Do you mean you never took cognizance of these matters?

HOESS: If in any way such a case came to be known, then the perpetrator was, of course, immediately relieved of his post or transferred somewhere else. So that, even if he were not punished for lack of evidence to prove his guilt, even then, he was taken away from the internees and given another position.

DR. KAUFFMANN: To what do you attribute the particularly bad and shameful conditions, which were ascertained by the entering Allied troops, and which to a certain extent were photographed and filmed?

HOESS: The catastrophic situation at the end of the war was due to the fact that, as a result of the destruction of the railway network and of the continuous bombing of the industrial plants, care for these masses – I am thinking of Auschwitz with its 140,000 internees – could no longer be assured. Improvised measures, truck columns, and everything else tried by the commanders to improve the situation were of little or no avail; it was no longer possible. The number of the sick became immense. There were next to no medical supplies; epidemics raged everywhere. Internees who were capable of work were used over and over again. By order of the Reichsfuhrer, even half-sick people had to be used wherever possible in industry. As a result every bit of space in the concentration camps which could possibly be used for lodging was overcrowded with sick and dying prisoners.

DR. KAUFFMANN: I am now asking you to look at the map which is mounted behind you. The red dots represent concentration camps. I will first ask you how many concentration camps as such existed at the end of the war?

HOESS: At the end of the war there were still 13 concentration camps. All the other points which are marked here on the map mean so-called labor camps attached to the armament industry situated there. The concentration camps, of which there are 13 as I have already said, were the center and the central point of some district, such as the camp at Dachau in Bavaria, or the camp of Mauthausen in Austria; and all the labor camps in that district were under the control of the concentration camp. That camp had then to supply these outside camps, that is to say, they had to supply them with workers, exchange the sick inmates and furnish clothing; the guards, too, were supplied by the concentration camp.

From 1944 on, the supplying of food was almost exclusively a matter of the individual armament industries in order to give the prisoners the benefit of the wartime supplementary rations.

DR. KAUFFMANN: What became known to you about so-called medical experiments on living internees?

HOESS: Medical experiments were carried out in several camps. For instance, in Auschwitz there were experiments on sterilization carried out by Professor Klaubert and Dr. Schumann; also experiments on twins by SS medical officer Dr. Mengele.

DR. KAUFFMANN: Do you know the medical officer Dr. Rascher?

HOESS: In Dachau he was a medical officer of the Luftwaffe who carried out experiments, on internees who had been sentenced to death, about the resistance of the human body to cold and in high pressure chambers.

DR. KAUFFMANN: Can you tell whether such experiments carried out within the camp were known to a large circle?

HOESS: Such experiments, just like all other matters, were, of course, called "secret Reich matters." However, it could not be avoided that the experiments became known since they were carried out in a large camp and must have been seen in some way by the inmates. I cannot say, however, to what extent the outside world learned about these experiments.

DR. KAUFFMANN: You explained to me that orders for executions were received in the camp at Auschwitz, and you told me that until the outbreak of war such orders were few, but that later on they became more numerous. Is that correct?

HOESS: Yes. There were hardly any executions until the beginning of the war – only in particularly serious cases. I remember one case in Buchenwald where an SS man had been attacked and beaten to death by internees, and the internees were later hanged.

DR. KAUFFMANN: But during the war – and that you will admit – the number of executions increased, and not inconsiderably.

HOESS: That had already started with the beginning of the war.

DR. KAUFFMANN: Was the basis for these execution orders in many cases a legal sentence of German courts?

HOESS: No. Orders for the executions carried out in the camps came from the RSHA.

DR. KAUFFMANN: Who signed the orders for executions which you received? Is it correct that occasionally you received orders for executions which bore the signature "Kaltenbrunner," and that these were not the originals but were teleprints; which therefore had the signature in typewritten letters?

HOESS: It is correct. The originals of execution orders never came to the camps. The original of these orders either arrived at the Inspectorate of the Concentration Camps, from where they were transmitted by teletype to the camps concerned, or, in urgent cases, the RSHA sent the orders directly to the camps concerned, and the Inspectorate was then only informed, so that the signatures in the camps were always only in teletype.

DR. KAUFFMANN: So as to again determine the signatures, will you tell the Tribunal whether the overwhelming majority of all execution orders either bore the signature of Himmler or that of Muller in the years before the war and until the end of the war.

HOESS: Only very few teletypes which I have ever seen came from the Reichsfuhrer and still fewer from the Defendant Kaltenbrunner. Most of them, I could say practically all, were signed "Signed Muller."

DR. KAUFFMANN: Is that the Muller with whom you repeatedly talked about such matters as you stated earlier?

HOESS: Gruppenfuhrer Muller was the Chief of Department IV in the RSHA. He had to negotiate with the Inspectorate about all matters connected with concentration camps.

DR. KAUFFMANN: Would you say that you went to see the Gestapo Chief Muller because you, on the strength of your experience, were of the opinion that this man because of his years of activities was acting almost independently?

HOESS: That is quite right. I had to negotiate all matters regarding concentration camps with Gruppenfuhrer Muller. He was informed on all these matters, and in most cases he would make an immediate decision.

DR., KAUFFMANN: Well, so as to have a clear picture, did you ever negotiate these matters with the defendant?

HOESS: No.

DR. KAUFFMANN: Did you learn that towards the end of the war concentration camps were evacuated? And, if so, who gave the orders?

HOESS: Let me explain. Originally there was an order from the Reichsfuhrer, according to which camps, in the event of the approach of the enemy or in case of air attacks, were to be surrendered to the enemy. Later on, due to the case of Buchenwald, which had been reported to the Fuhrer, there was – no, at the beginning of 1945, when various camps came within the operational sphere of the enemy, this order was withdrawn. The Reichsfuhrer ordered the Higher SS and Police Leaders, who in an emergency case were responsible for the security and safety of the camps, to decide themselves whether an evacuation or a surrender was appropriate.

Auschwitz and Gross-Rosen were evacuated. Buchenwald was also to be evacuated, but then the order from the Reichsfuhrer came through to the effect that on principle no more camps were to be evacuated. Only prominent inmates and inmates who were not to fall into Allied hands under any circumstances were to be taken away to other camps. This also happened in the case of Buchenwald. After Buchenwald had been occupied, it was reported to the Fuhrer that internees had armed themselves and were carrying out plunderings in the town of Weimar. This caused the Fuhrer to give the strictest order to Himmler to the effect that in the future no more camps were to fall into the hands of the enemy, and that no internees capable of marching would be left behind in any camp.

This was shortly before the end of the war, and shortly before northern and southern Germany were cut. I shall speak about the Sachsenhausen camp. The Gestapo chief, Gruppenfuhrer Muller, called me in the evening and told me that the Reichsfuhrer had ordered that the camp at Sachsenhausen was to be evacuated at once. I pointed out to Gruppenfuhrer Muller what that would mean. Sachsenhausen could no longer fall back on any other camp except perhaps on a few labor camps attached to the armament works that were almost filled up anyway. Most of the internees would have to be sheltered in the woods somewhere. This would mean countless thousands of deaths and, above all it would be impossible to feed these masses of people. He promised me that he would again discuss these measures with the Reichsfuhrer He called me back and told me that the Reichsfuhrer had refused and was demanding that the commanders carry out his orders immediately.

At the same time Ravensbruk was also to be evacuated in the same manner but it could no longer be done. I do not know to what extent camps in southern Germany were cleared, since we, the Inspectorate, no longer had any connections with southern Germany.

DR. KAUFFMANN: It has been maintained here—and this is my last question—that the Defendant Kaltenbrunner gave the order that Dachau and two auxiliary camps were to be destroyed by bombing or with poison. I ask you, did you hear anything about this; if not, would you consider such an order possible?

HOESS: I have never heard anything about this, and I do not know anything either about an order to evacuate any camps in southern Germany, as I have already mentioned. Apart from that, I consider it quite impossible that a camp could be destroyed by this method.

DR. KAUFFMANN: I have no further questions.

THE PRESIDENT: Do any of the defendants' counsel want to ask any questions?

DR. MERKEL: Witness, did the State Police, as an authority of the Reich, have anything to do with the destruction of Jews in Auschwitz?

HOESS: Yes, insofar as I received all my orders as to the carrying out of that action from the Obersturmfuhrer Eichmann.

DR. MERKEL: Was the administration of concentration camps under the control of the Main Economic and Administrative Office?

HOESS: Yes.

DR. MERKEL: You said already that you had nothing to do with the RSHA.

HOESS: No.

DR. MERKEL: Please, will you emphasize, therefore, that the Gestapo as such had nothing to do with the administration of the camps or the accommodation, feeding, and treatment of the internees, but that this was exclusively a matter for the Main Economic and Administrative Office?

HOESS: Yes, that is quite correct.

DR. MERKEL: How do you explain it then that you, nevertheless, discussed different questions concerning concentration camps with Muller?

HOESS: The RSHA, or rather Amt IV, had the executive power for the directing of all internees into camps, classification into the camp grades 1, 2, 3, and furthermore, the punishments which were to be carried out on the part of the RSHA. Executions, the accommodation, of special internees, and all questions which might ensue therefrom were also taken care of by the RSHA or Amt IV.

DR. MERKEL: When was this Main Economic and Administrative Office created?

HOESS: The Main Economic and Administrative Office existed since 1933 under various names. The Inspectorate of Concentration Camps was, however, subordinated only to this Main Economic and Administrative Office since the year 1941.

DR. MERKEL: Then these concentration camps were from the very beginning under the control of this Main Economic and Administrative Office, that is to say the SS and not the State Police.

HOESS: Yes.

DR. MERKEL: You mentioned the name of Dr. Rascher a while ago. Do you know this doctor personally?

HOESS: Yes.

DR. MERKEL: Do you know that Dr. Rascher before beginning his work at Dachau had become a member of the SS?

HOESS: No, I know nothing about that. I only know that later he – I still saw him in the uniform of an Air Force medical officer. Later he was supposed to have been taken over into the SS, but I did not see him again.

DR. MERKEL: I have no further questions. Thank you very much.

HERR LUDWIG BABEL (Counsel for SS): Witness, at the beginning of your examination you stated that when you were ordered to the Reichsfuhrer SS Himmler, he told you that the carrying out of this order of the Fuhrer was to be left to the SS and that the SS had been ordered to do it. What is to be understood under this general title SS?

HOESS: According to the explanations of the Reichsfuhrer, this could only mean the men guarding the concentration camps. According to the nature of the order only concentration camp crews and not the Waffen SS could be concerned with the carrying out of this task.

HERR BABEL: How many members of the SS were assigned to concentration camps, and which units did they belong to?

HOESS: Toward the end of the war there were approximately 35,000 SS men and in my estimation approximately 10,000 men from the Army, Air Force, and the Navy detailed to the labor camps for guard duties.

HERR BABEL: What were the tasks of these guards? As far as I know, the duties varied. First, there was the actual guarding and then there was a certain amount of administrative work within the camp.

HOESS: Yes, that is correct.

HERR BABEL: How many guards were there within the camps for, let us say, 1,000 internees?

HOESS: You cannot estimate it in that way. According to my observations about 10 percent of the total number of guarding personnel were used for internal duties, that is to say, administration and supervision of internees within the camp, including the medical personnel of the camp.

HERR BABEL: So that 90 percent were therefore used for the exterior guarding, that is to say, for watching the camp from watch towers and for escorting the internees on work assignments.

HOESS: Yes.

HERR BABEL: Did you make any observations as to whether there was any ill-treatment of prisoners to a greater or lesser degree on the part of those guards, or whether the ill-treatment was mainly to be traced back to the so-called Kapos?

HOESS: If any ill-treatment of prisoners by guards occurred – I myself have never observed any – then this was possible only to a very small degree since all officers in charge of the camps took care that as few SS men as possible had direct contact with the inmates, because in the course of the years the guard personnel had deteriorated to such an extent that the standards formerly demanded could no longer be maintained.

We had thousands of guards who could hardly speak German, who came from all lands as volunteers and joined these units, or we had older men, between 50 and 60, who lacked all interest in their work, so that a camp commander had to watch constantly that these men fulfilled even the lowest requirements of their duties. It is obvious that there were elements among them who would ill-treat internees, but this ill-treatment was never tolerated.

Besides, it was impossible to have these masses of people directed at work or when in the camp by SS men only; therefore, inmates had to be assigned everywhere to direct the other prisoners and set them to work. The internal administration of the camp was almost completely in their hands. Of course a great deal of ill-treatment occurred which could not be avoided because at night there were hardly any members of the SS in the camps. Only in specific cases were SS men allowed to enter the camp, so that the internees were more or less exposed to these Kapos.

HERR BABEL: You have already mentioned regulations which existed for the guards, but there was also a standing order in each camp. In this camp order certainly punishment was provided for internees who violated the camp rules. What punishment was provided?

HOESS: First of all, transfer to a penal company (*Strafkompanie*), that is to say, harder work and restricted accommodations; next, detention in the cell block, detention in a dark cell; and in very serious cases, chaining or strapping. Punishment by strapping was prohibited in the year 1942 or 1943 – I cannot say exactly when – by the Reichsfuhrer. Then there was the punishment of standing at the camp gate over a rather long period, and finally corporal punishment.

However, no commander could decree this corporal punishment on his own authority. He could only apply for it. In the case of men, the decision came from the Inspector of Concentration Camps Gruppenfuhrer Schmidt, and where women were concerned, the Reichsfuhrer reserved the decision exclusively for himself.

HERR BABEL: It may also be known to you that for members of the SS, too, there were two penal camps which sometimes were called concentration camps, namely, Dachau and Danzig-Matzkau.

HOESS: That is right.

HERR BABEL: Were the existing camp regulations and the treatment of members of the SS who were put in such camps different from the regulations applying to the other concentration camps?

HOESS: Yes, these two detention camps were not under the Inspectorate for Concentration Camps, but they were under an SS and

Police court. I myself have neither inspected nor seen these two camps.

HERR BABEL: So that you know nothing about the standing orders relating to those camps?

HOESS: I know nothing about them.

HERR BABEL: I have no further questions to the witness.

FLOTTENRICHTER OTTO KRANZBAHLER (Counsel for Defendant Doenitz): Witness, you just mentioned that members of the Navy were detailed to guard concentration camps.

HOESS: Yes.

FLOTTENRICHTER KRANZBAHLER: Were these concentration camps, or were they labor camps?

HOESS: They were labor camps.

FLOTTENRICHTER KRANZBAHLER: Are labor camps barracks camps of the armament industries?

HOESS: Yes, if they were not accommodated in the actual factories themselves.

FLOTTENRICHTER KRANZBAHLER: I have been informed that soldiers who were to be assigned for guard duty at labor camps were given over to the SS.

HOESS: That is only partially correct. A part of these men – I do not recall the figures – was taken over into the SS. A part was returned to the original unit, or exchanged. Exchanges were continually taking place.

FLOTTENRICHTER KRANZBAHLER: Thank you.

COL. AMEN: If the Tribunal please, first I would like to submit, on behalf of our British Allies, a series of exhibits pertaining to the Waffen-SS, without reading them. It is merely statistical information with respect to the number of Waffen-SS guards used at the concentration camps.

I ask that the witness be shown Documents D – 745 (a – b), D – 746 (a – b),' D – 747, D – 748, D – 749 (b), and D – 750, one of them being a statement of this witness.

[The documents were submitted to the witness.1

Witness, you made the statement, D – 749 (b), which has been handed to you?

HOESS: Yes.

COL. AMEN: And you are familiar with the content of the others?

HOESS: Yes.

COL. AMEN: And you testify that those figures are true and correct?

HOESS: Yes.

COL. AMEN: Very good. Those will become Exhibit Number USA – 810.

Witness, from time to time did any high Nazi officials or functionaries visit the camp at Mauthausen or Dachau while you were there?

HOESS: Yes.

COL. AMEN: Will you state the names of such persons to the Tribunal please?

HOESS: I remember that in 1935 all the Gauleiters inspected Dachau guided by Reichsfuhrer Himmler. I do not remember them individually.

COL. AMEN: Do you recall any of the ministers having visited either of those camps while you were there?

HOESS: Do you mean by this the inspection tour of 1935?

COL. AMEN: At any time while you were at either of those concentration camps.

HOESS: In 1938 Minister Frick was at Sachsenhausen.

COL. AMEN: Do you recall any other ministers who were there at any time?

HOESS: Not at Sachsenhausen, but at Auschwitz, the Minister of Justice.

COL. AMEN: Who was he?

HOESS: Thierack.

COL. AMEN: And who else? Do you recall any others?

HOESS: Yes, but, I do not remember the name for the moment.

COL. AMEN: Well, who?

HOESS: I have already stated that in the record, but at the moment I cannot recall the name.

COL. AMEN: All right. You have testified that many of the execution orders were signed by Muller. Is that correct?

HOESS: Yes.

COL. AMEN: Is it not a fact that all of those execution orders to which you testified were signed by . . .

DR. STEINBAUER: Pardon me, Mr. President, documents have been submitted and the witness is being questioned about the contents. The Defense is not in a position to follow the Prosecution because we do not know the contents of these documents. I request that we receive copies of them.

THE PRESIDENT: Haven't copies of these documents been handed to the defendants?

COL. AMEN: Yes, so I understood. We have copies here. However, five German copies have been distributed.

THE PRESIDENT: Well, the matter can be looked into.

COL. AMEN: Witness, I was asking you about these execution orders which you testify were signed by Muller. Do you understand?

HOESS: Yes.

COL. AMEN: Is it not a fact that all of these execution orders which you testify were signed by Muller were also signed by order of, or as representative of, the Chief of the RSHA, Kaltenbrunner?.

HOESS: Yes. That was on the copies that I had in the originals. Afterwards, when I was employed at Oranienburg, it said underneath, "I. V. Muller"; "in Vertretung Muller" (as representative, Muller).

COL. AMEN: In other words Muller was merely signing as the representative of the Chief of the RSHA, Kaltenbrunner? Is that not correct?

HOESS: I must assume so.

COL. AMEN: And, of course, you know that Muller was a subordinate of the Chief of the RSHA, Kaltenbrunner.

HOESS: Yes.

COL. AMEN: Witness, you made an affidavit, did you not, at the request of the Prosecution?

HOESS: Yes.

COL. AMEN: I ask that the witness be shown Document 3868 – PS, which will become Exhibit USA – 819.

[The document was submitted to the witness.]

COL. AMEN: You signed that affidavit voluntarily, Witness?

HOESS: Yes.

COL. AMEN: And the affidavit is true in all respects?

HOESS: Yes.

COL. AMEN: This, if the Tribunal please, we have in four languages.

[Turning to the witness.] Some of the matters covered in this affidavit you have already told us about in part, so I will omit some parts of the affidavit. If you will follow along with me as I read, please. Do you have a copy of the affidavit before you?

HOESS: Yes.

COL. AMEN: I will omit the first paragraph and start with Paragraph 2:

"I have been constantly associated with the administration of concentration camps since 1934, serving at Dachau until 1938; then as Adjutant in Sachsenhausen from 1938 to 1 May 1940, when I was appointed Commandant of Auschwitz. I commanded Auschwitz until 1 December 1943, and estimate that at least 2,500,000 victims were executed and exterminated there by gassing and burning, and at least another half million succumbed to starvation and disease making a total dead of about 3,000,000. This figure represents about 70 or 80 percent of all persons sent to Auschwitz as prisoners, the remainder having been selected and used for slave labor in the concentration camp industries; included among the executed and burned were approximately 20,000 Russian prisoners of war (previously screened out of prisoner-of-war cages by the Gestapo) who were delivered at Auschwitz in Wehrmacht transports operated by regular Wehrmacht officers and men. The remainder of the total number of victims included about 100,000 German Jews, and great numbers of citizens, mostly Jewish, from Holland, France, Belgium, Poland, Hungary, Czechoslovakia, Greece, or other countries. We executed about 400,000 Hungarian Jews alone at Auschwitz in the summer of 1944."

That is all true, Witness?

HOESS: Yes, it is.

COL. AMEN: Now I omit the first few lines of Paragraph 3 and start in the middle of Paragraph 3:

". . . prior to establishment of the RSHA, the Secret State Police Office (Gestapo) and the Reich Office of Criminal Police were responsible for arrests, commitments to concentration camps, punishments and executions therein. After organization of the RSHA all of these functions were carried on as before, but pursuant to orders signed by Heydrich as Chief of the RSHA. While Kaltenbrunner was Chief of RSHA orders for protective custody, commitments, punishment, and individual executions were signed by Kaltenbrunner or by Muller, Chief of the Gestapo, as Kaltenbrunner's deputy."

THE PRESIDENT: Just for the sake of accuracy, the last date in Paragraph 2, is that 1943 or 1944?

COL. AMEN: 1944, I believe. Is that date correct, Witness, at the close of Paragraph 2, namely, that the 400,000 Hungarian Jews alone at Auschwitz in the summer of 1944 were executed? Is that 1944 or 1943?

HOESS: 1944. Part of that figure also goes back to 1943; only a part. I cannot give the exact figure; the end was 1944, autumn of 1944.

COL. AMEN: Right.

"4. Mass executions by gassing commenced during the summer of 1941 and continued until fall 1944. 1 personally supervised executions at Auschwitz until first of December 1943 and know by reason of my continued duties in the Inspectorate of Concentration Camps, WVHA, that these mass executions continued as stated above. All mass executions by gassing took place under the direct order, supervision, and responsibility of RSHA. I received all orders for carrying out these mass executions directly from RSHA." Are those statements true and correct, Witness?

HOESS: Yes, they are.

COL. AMEN: "5. On 1 December 1943 1 became Chief of Amt 1 in Amt Group D of the WVHA, and in that office was responsible for co-ordinating all matters arising between RSHA and concentration camps under the administration of WVHA. I held this position until the end of the war. Pohl, as Chief of WVHA, and Kaltenbrunner, as Chief of RSHA, often conferred personally and frequently communicated orally and in writing concerning concentration camps. . . ."

You have already told us about the lengthy report which you took to Kaltenbrunner in Berlin, so I will omit the remainder of Paragraph 5.

"6. The 'final solution' of the Jewish question meant the complete extermination of all Jews in Europe. I was ordered to establish extermination facilities at Auschwitz in June 1941. At that time, there were already in the General Government three other extermination camps: Belzek, Treblinka, and Wolzek. These camps were under the *Einsatzkommando* of the Security Police and SD. I visited Treblinka to find out how they carried out their exterminations. The camp commandant at Treblinka told me that he had liquidated 80,000 in the course of one-half year. He was principally concerned with liquidating all the Jews from the Warsaw Ghetto. He used monoxide gas, and I did not think that his methods were very efficient. So when I set up the extermination building at Auschwitz, I used Cyklon B, which was a crystallized prussic acid which we dropped into the death chamber from a small opening. It took from 3 to 15 minutes to kill the people in the death chamber, depending upon climatic conditions. We knew when the people were dead because their screaming stopped. We usually waited about one-half hour before we opened the doors and removed the bodies. After the bodies were removed our special *Kommandos* took off the rings and extracted the gold from the teeth of the corpses."

Is that all true and correct, Witness?

HOESS: Yes.

COL. AMEN: Incidentally, what was done with the gold which was taken from the teeth of the corpses, do you know?

HOESS: Yes.

COL. AMEN: Will you tell the Tribunal?

HOESS: This gold was melted down and brought to the Chief Medical Office of the SS at Berlin.

COL. AMEN:

"7 Another improvement we made over Treblinka was that we built our gas chamber to accommodate 2,000 people at one time whereas at Treblinka their 10 gas chambers only accommodated 200 people each. The way we selected our victims was as follows: We had two SS doctors on duty at Auschwitz to examine the incoming transports of prisoners. The prisoners would be marched by one of the doctors who would make spot decisions as they walked by. Those who were fit for work were sent into the camp. Others were sent immediately to the extermination plants. Children of tender years were invariably exterminated since by reason of their youth they were unable to work. Still another improvement we made over Treblinka was that at Treblinka the victims almost always knew that they were to be exterminated and at Auschwitz we endeavored to fool the victims into thinking that they were to go through a delousing process. Of course, frequently they realized our true intentions and we sometimes had riots and difficulties due to that fact. Very frequently women would hide their children under the clothes, but of course when we found them we would send the children in to be exterminated. We were required to carry out these exterminations in secrecy but of course the foul and nauseating stench from the continuous burning of bodies permeated the entire area and all of the people living in the surrounding communities knew that exterminations were going on at Auschwitz."

Is that all true and correct, Witness?

HOESS: Yes.

COL. AMEN: Now, I will omit Paragraphs 8 and 9, which have to do with the medical experiments as to which you have already testified.

"10. Rudolf Mildner was the chief of the Gestapo at Katowice . . . from approximately March 1941 until September 1943. As such, he frequently sent prisoners to Auschwitz for incarceration or execution. He visited Auschwitz on several occasions. The Gestapo court, the SS Standgericht, which tried persons accused of various crimes, such as escaping prisoners of war, et cetera, frequently met within Auschwitz, and Mildner often attended the trial of such persons, who usually were executed in Auschwitz following their sentence. I showed Mildner through the extermination plant at Auschwitz and he was directly interested in it since he had to send the Jews from his territory for execution at Auschwitz.

"I understand English as it is written above. The above statements are true; this declaration is made by me voluntarily and without compulsion; after reading over the statement I have signed and executed the same at Nuremberg, Germany, on the fifth day of April 1946."

Now I ask you, Witness, is everything which I have read to you true to your own knowledge?

HOESS: Yes.

COL. AMEN: That concludes my cross-examination, except for one exhibit that our British allies would like to have in, which is a summary sheet of the exhibits which I introduced at the commencement of the cross-examination. That will be Exhibit Number USA – 810. It is a summary of the earlier exhibits that I put in with respect to the Waffen-SS at the commencement of my cross-examination.

Now, I understand, Your Lordship, that both the Soviet and the French delegations have one or two questions which they consider peculiar to their country which they would like to put to this witness.

THE PRESIDENT: General Rudenko, you will remember that the Tribunal was assured by Counsel for the Prosecution that, so far as witnesses were concerned, with the exception of one or two particular defendants, the Prosecution would have only one cross-examination and now, since that assurance was given, this is the second instance when the Prosecution have desired to have more than one cross-examination.

GEN. RUDENKO: This is correct, Mr. President, that the Prosecution did make that statement; however, the Prosecution reserved the right to do otherwise on certain occasions when deemed necessary. Since, in this case, the Prosecution represent four different states, occasions do arise when each of the prosecutors feels that he has the right to ask the defendant or witnesses individual questions particularly interesting to his own country.

THE PRESIDENT: Will you indicate the nature of the questions which the Soviet Prosecution desire to put? I mean the subjects upon which they are. I don't mean the exact questions but the subject.

GEN. RUDENKO: Yes, I understand. Colonel Pokrovsky, who intends to ask the questions, will report on the subject to the Tribunal.

COL. POKROVSKY: May I report to you, Mr. President, that the questions of interest to the Soviet Prosecution are those dealing specifically with the annihilation of millions of Soviet citizens and some details connected with that annihilation. At the request of the French Prosecution, and in order to clarify the contents I would also like to ask two or three questions connected with the documents which in due course were submitted as Document F − 709(a) to the Tribunal by the French Prosecution. This is really all there is; however, these questions do have great importance for us.

THE PRESIDENT: Colonel Pokrovsky, the Tribunal, as has just been stated, made the rule, with the assent of the Prosecutors, that in the case of the witnesses there should be one cross-examination. There is nothing in the Charter which expressly gives to the Prosecution the right for each prosecutor to cross-examine and there is, on the other hand, Article 18 which directs the Tribunal to take strict measures to prevent any action which will cause unreasonable delay, and, in the opinion of the Tribunal in the present case, the subject has been fully covered and the Tribunal therefore think it right to adhere to the rules which they have laid down in this case. They will therefore not hear any further cross-examination.

Do you wish to re-examine, Dr. Kauffmann?

DR. KAUFFMANN: I will be very brief.

Witness, in the affidavit which was just read, you said under Point 2 that "at least an additional half million died through starvation and disease." I ask you, when did this take place? Was it towards the end of the war or was this fact observed by you already at an earlier period?

HOESS: No, it all goes back to the last years of the war, that is beginning with the end of 1942.

DR. KAUFFMANN: Under Point 3, do you still have the affidavit before you?

HOESS: No.

DR.KAUFFMANN: May I ask that it be given to the witness again?

[The document was returned to the witness.]

Under Point 3, at the end you state that orders for protective custody, commitments, punishments, and special executions were signed by Kaltenbrunner or Muller, Chief of the Gestapo, as Kaltenbrunner's deputy. Thus, do you wish to contradict what you stated previously?

HOESS: No, this only completes what I said over and again. I read only a few decrees signed by Kaltenbrunner; most of them were signed by Muller.

DR. KAUFFMANN: Under Point 4, at the end, you state:

"All mass executions through gassing took place under the direct order, supervision, and responsibility of RSHA. I received all orders for carrying out these mass executions directly from RSHA."

According to the statements which you previously made to the Tribunal, this entire action came to you directly from Himmler through Eichmann, who had been personally delegated. Do you maintain that now as before?

HOESS: Yes.

DR.KAUFFMANN: With this last sentence under Point 4, do you wish to contradict what you testified before?

HOESS: No. I always mean regarding mass executions, Obersturmbannfuhrer Eichmann in connection with the RSHA.

DR. KAUFFMANN: Under Point 7, at the end, you state – I am not going to read it – you were saying that even though exterminations took place secretly, the population in the surrounding area noticed something of the extermination of people. Did not, at an earlier period of time – that is, before the beginning of this special extermination action – something of this nature take place to remove people who had died in a normal manner in Auschwitz?

HOESS: Yes, when the crematoria had not yet been built we burned in large pits a large part of those who had died and who could not be cremated in the provisional crematoria of the camp; a large number – I do not recall the figure anymore – were placed in mass graves and later also cremated in these graves. That was before the mass executions of Jews began.

DR. KAUFFMANN: Would you agree with me if I were to say that from the described facts alone, one could not conclusively prove that this was concerned with the extermination of Jews?

HOESS: No, this could in no way be concluded from that. The population . . .

THE PRESIDENT: What was your question about?

DR. KAUFFMANN: My question was whether one could assume from the established facts at the end of Paragraph 7 that this concerned the so-called extermination of Jews. I tied this question to the previous answer of the witness. It is my last question.

THE PRESIDENT: The last sentence of Paragraph 7 is with reference to the foul and nauseating stench. What is your question about that?

DR. KAUFFMANN: Whether the population could gather from these things that an extermination of Jews was taking place.

THE PRESIDENT: That really is too obvious a question, isn't it? They could not possibly know who it was being exterminated.

DR. KAUFFMANN: That is enough for me. I have no further questions.

DR. PANNENBECKER: I ask the Tribunal's permission to ask a few supplementary questions, for during cross-examination the witness stated that the Defendant Frick had visited the concentration camps Sachsenhausen and Oranienburg in 1938.

Witness, when an inspection of the concentration camp of Oranienburg took place at that time, 1937-38, was there any evidence at all of atrocities?

HOESS: No.

DR. PANNENBECKER: Why not?

HOESS: Because there was no question of atrocities at that time.

DR. PANNENBECKER: Is it correct that at that period of time the concentration camp at Oranienburg was still a model of order and that agricultural labor was the main occupation? .

HOESS: Yes, that is right. However, work was mainly done in workshops, in wood-finishing workshops.

DR. PANNENBECKER: Can you give me any details as to what was shown at that time at such an official visit?

HOESS: Yes. The visiting party was shown through the prisoners' camp proper, inspected the quarters, the kitchen, the hospital, and then all the administrative buildings; above all the workshops, where the inmates were employed.

DR. PANNENBECKER: At that time were the quarters and the hospitals already overcrowded?

HOESS: No, at that time they were normally filled.

DR. PANNENBECKER: How did these quarters look?

HOESS: At that period of time, living quarters looked the same as the barracks of a training ground. The internees still had bed-clothing and all necessary hygienic facilities. Everything was yet in the best of order.

DR. PANNENBECKER: That is all. I have no further questions.

THE TRIBUNAL (Mr. Francis Biddle, Member for the United States): Witness, what was the greatest number of labor camps existing at any one time?

HOESS: I cannot give the exact figure but in my estimation there were approximately 900.

THE TRIBUNAL (Mr. Biddle): What was the population of these 900?

HOESS: I am not able to say that either; the population varied. There were camps with 100 internees and camps with 10,000 internees. Therefore, I cannot give any figure of the total number of people who were in these labor camps.

THE TRIBUNAL (Mr. Biddle): Under whose administration were the labor camps? Under what offices?

HOESS: These labor camps, as far as the guarding, direction, and clothing were concerned, were under the control of the Economic and Administration Main Office. All matters dealing with labor output and the supplying of food were attended to by the armament industries which employed these internees.

THE TRIBUNAL (Mr. Biddle): And at the end of the war were the conditions in those labor camps similar to those existing in the concentration camps as you described them before?

HOESS: Yes. Since there no longer was any possibility of bringing ill internees to the main camps, there was much overcrowding in these labor camps and the death rate very high.

THE PRESIDENT: The witness can retire.

[The witness left the stand.]

Cross-examination of Albert Speer

Minister of Armaments

THE PRESIDENT: Do any of the other defendants' counsel want to ask questions? Then, do the Prosecution wish to cross-examine?

MR. JUSTICE ROBERT H. JACKSON (Chief of Counsel for the United States): Defendant, your counsel divided your examination into two parts which he described first as your personal responsibilities, and secondly as the political part of the case, and I will follow the same division.

You have stated a good many of the matters for which you were not responsible, and I want to make clear just what your sphere of responsibility was.

You were not only a member of the Nazi Party after 1932, but you held high rank in the Party, did you not?

SPEER: Correct.

MR. JUSTICE JACKSON: And what was the position which you held in the Party?

SPEER: I have already mentioned that during my pre-trial interrogations. Temporarily in 1934 I became a department head in the German Labor Front and dealt with the improvement of labor conditions in German factories. Then I was in charge of public works on the staff of Hess. I gave up both these activities in 1941. Notes of the conference I had with Hitler about this are available. After

2/8/1942 I automatically became Todt's successor in the central office for technical matters in the Reichsleitung of the NSDAP.

MR. JUSTICE JACKSON: And what was your official title?

SPEER: Party titles had just been introduced, and they were so complicated that I cannot tell you at the moment what they were. But the work I did there was that of a department chief in the *Reichsleitung* of the NSDAP. My title was *Hauptdienstleiter* or something of the kind.

MR. JUSTICE JACKSON: In the 1943 directory it would appear that you were head of the "*Hauptamt fur Technik.*"

SPEER: Yes.

MR. JUSTICE JACKSON: And your rank appears to be "*Oberbefehlsleiter*"?

SPEER: Yes, that is quite possible.

MR. JUSTICE JACKSON: Which as I understand corresponds roughly to a lieutenant general in the army?

SPEER: Well, compared to the other tasks I had it was very little.

MR. JUSTICE JACKSON: And you attended Party functions from time to time and were informed in a general way as to the Party program, were you not?

SPEER: Before 1942 I joined in the various Party rallies here in Nuremberg because I had to take part in them as an architect, and of course besides this I was generally present at official Party meetings or Reichstag sessions.

MR. JUSTICE JACKSON: And you heard discussed, and were generally familiar with, the program of the Nazi Party in its broad outlines, were you not?

SPEER: Of course.

MR. JUSTICE JACKSON: You there is some question as to just what your relation to the SS was. Will you tell me whether you were a member of the SS?

SPEER: No, I was not a member of the SS.

MR. JUSTICE JACKSON: You filled out an application at one time, or one was filled out for you, and you never went through with it, I believe, or something of that sort.

SPEER: That was in 1943 when Himmler wanted me to get a high rank in the SS. He had often wanted it before when I was still an architect. I got out of it by saying that I was willing to be an ordinary SS man under him because I had already been an SS man before. Thereupon, Gruppenfuhrer Wolff provisionally filled out an application form and wanted to know what my previous SS activities had been in 1932. It came up during his inquiries that in those days I was never registered as a member of the SS, and because of this they did not insist on my joining as I did not want to become a new member now.

MR. JUSTICE JACKSON: And why did you not want to be a member of the SS, which was after all one of the important Party formations?

SPEER: No, I became well known for turning down all these honorary ranks. I did not want them because I felt that one should only hold a rank where one had responsibility.

MR. JUSTICE JACKSON: And you did not want any responsibility in the SS?

SPEER: I had too little contact with the SS, and did not want any responsibility in that connection.

MR. JUSTICE JACKSON: Now there has been some testimony about your relation to concentration camps, and, as I understand it, you have said to us that you did use and encourage the use of forced labor from the concentration camps.

SPEER: Yes, we did use it in the German armament industry.

MR. JUSTICE JACKSON: And I think you also recommended that persons in labor camps who were slackers be sent to the concentration camps, did you not?

SPEER: That was the question of the so-called "*Bummelanten,*" and by that name we meant workers who did not get to their work on time or who pretended to be ill. Severe measures were taken against such workers during the war, and I approved of these measures.

MR. JUSTICE JACKSON: In fact, in the 10/30/1942 meeting of the Central Planning Board you brought the subject up in the following terms, did you not:

"We must also discuss the slackers. Ley has ascertained that the sick list decreases to one-fourth or one-fifth in factories where doctors are on the staff who examine the sick men. There is nothing to be said against SS and Police taking drastic steps and putting those known to be slackers into concentration camp factories. There is no alternative. Let it happen several times, and the news will soon get around."

That was your recommendation?

SPEER: Correct.

MR. JUSTICE JACKSON: In other words, the workmen stood in considerable terror of concentration camps, and you wanted to take advantage of that to keep them at their work, did you not?

SPEER: It is certain that concentration camps had a bad reputation with us, and the transfer to a concentration camp, or threat of such a possibility, was bound to reduce the number of absentees in the factories right from the beginning. But at that meeting, as I already said yesterday, there was nothing further said about it. It was one of the many remarks one can make in wartime when one is upset.

MR. JUSTICE JACKSON: However, it is very clear, and if I misinterpret you I give you the chance to correct me, that you understood the very bad reputation that the concentration camp had among the workmen and that the concentration camps were regarded as being much more severe than the labor camps as places to be in.

SPEER: That is correct. I knew that. I did not know, of course, what I have heard during this Trial, but the other thing was a generally known fact.

MR. JUSTICE JACKSON: Well, it was known throughout Germany, was it not, that the concentration camps were pretty tough places to be put?

SPEER: Yes, but not to the extent which has been revealed in this Trial.

MR. JUSTICE JACKSON: And the bad reputation of the concentration camp, as a matter of fact, was a part of its usefulness in making people fearful of being sent there, was it not?

SPEER: No doubt concentration camps were a means, a menace used to keep order.

MR. JUSTICE JACKSON: And to keep people at work?

SPEER: I would not like to put it in that way. I assert that a great number of the foreign workers in our country did their work quite voluntarily once they had come to Germany.

MR. JUSTICE JACKSON: Well, we will take that up later. You used the concentration camp labor in production to the extent that you were required to divide the proceeds of the labor with Himmler, did you not?

SPEER: That I did not understand.

MR. JUSTICE JACKSON: Well, you made an agreement finally with Himmler that he should have 5 percent, or roughly 5 percent, of the production of the concentration camp labor while you would get for your work 95 percent?

SPEER: No, that is not quite true.

MR. JUSTICE JACKSON: Well, tell me how it was. That is what the documents indicate, if I read them aright.

SPEER: Yes, it is put that way in the Fuhrer minutes, but I should like to explain the meaning to you. Himmler, as I said yesterday wanted to build factories of his own in his concentration camps. Then he would have been able to produce arms without any outside control, which Hitler, of course, knew. The 5 percent arms production which was to have been handed to Himmler was to a certain extent a compensation for the fact that he himself gave up the idea of building factories in the camps. From the psychological point of view it was not so simple for me to get Himmler to give up this idea when he kept on reminding Hitler of it. I was hoping that he would be satisfied with the 5 percent arms production we were going to give him. Actually this 5 percent was never handed over. We managed things quietly with the Operations Staff of the OKW and with General Buhle, so that he never got the arms at all.

MR. JUSTICE JACKSON: Well, I am not criticizing the bargain, you understand. I don't doubt you did very well to get 95 percent, but the point is that Himmler was using, with your knowledge, concentration camp labor to manufacture arms, or was proposing to do so, and you wanted to keep that production within your control?

SPEER: Could the translation come through a bit clearer? Would you please repeat that?

MR. JUSTICE JACKSON: You knew at this time that Himmler was using concentration camp labor to carry on independent industry and that he proposed to go into the armament industry in order to have a source of supply of arms for his own SS?

SPEER: Yes.

MR. JUSTICE JACKSON: You also knew the policy of the Nazi Party and the policy of the Government towards the Jews, did you not?

SPEER: I knew that the National Socialist Party was anti-Semitic, and I knew that the Jews were being evacuated from Germany.

MR. JUSTICE JACKSON: In fact, you participated in that evacuation, did you not?

SPEER: No.

MR. JUSTICE JACKSON: Well, I gather that impression from Document L – 156, Exhibit RF – 1522, a letter from the Plenipotentiary for the Allocation of Labor which is dated 3/26/1943, which you have no doubt seen. You may see it again, if you wish. In which he says...

SPEER: I know it.

MR. JUSTICE JACKSON: "At the end of February, the Reichsfuhrer SS, in agreement with myself and the Reich Minister for armaments and munitions, for reasons of state security, has removed from their places of work all Jews who were still working freely and not in camps, and either transferred them to a labor corps or collected them for removal." Was that a correct representation of your activity?

SPEER: No.

MR. JUSTICE JACKSON: Will you tell me what part you had in that? There is no question that they were put into labor corps or collected for removal, is there?

SPEER: That is correct.

MR. JUSTICE JACKSON: Now you say you did not do it, so will you tell me who did?

SPEER: It was a fairly long business. When, in 2/1942, I took over my new office, the Party was already insisting that Jews who were still working in armament factories should be removed from them. I objected at the time, and managed to get Bormann to issue a circular letter to the effect that these Jews might go on being employed in armament factories and that Party offices were prohibited from accusing the heads of these firms on political grounds because of the Jews working there. It was the Gauleiter who made such political accusations against the heads of concerns, and it was mostly in the Gau Saxony and in the Gau Berlin. So after this the Jews could remain in these plants.

Without having any authority to do so, I had had this circular letter from the Party published in my news sheet to heads of factories and had sent it to all concerned, so that I would in any case receive their complaints if the Party should not obey the instruction. After that the problem was left alone, until September or October of 1942. At that time a conference with Hitler took place, at which Sauckel also was present. At this conference Hitler insisted emphatically that the Jews must now be removed from the armament firms, and he gave orders for this to be done, this will be seen from a Fuhrer protocol which has been preserved. In spite of this we managed to keep the Jews on in factories and it was only in 3/1943, as this letter shows, that resistance gave way and the Jews finally did have to get out.

I must point out to you that, as far as I can remember, it was not yet a question of the Jewish problem as a whole, but in the years 1941 and 1942 Jews had gone to the armament factories to do important war work and have an occupation of military importance; they were able to escape the evacuation which at that time was already in full swing. They were mostly occupied in the electrical industry, and Geheimrat Bucher, of the electrical industry that is AEG and Siemens, no doubt lent a helping hand in order to get the Jews taken on there in greater numbers. These Jews were completely free and their families were still in their homes.

The letter by Gauleiter Sauckel you have before you was not, of course submitted to me; and Sauckel says that he himself had not seen it. But it is certainly true that I knew about it before action was taken; I knew because the question had to be discussed as to how one should get replacements. It is equally certain, though, that I also protested at the time at having skilled labor removed from my armament industries because, apart from other reasons, it was going to make things difficult for me.

MR. JUSTICE JACKSON: That is exactly the point that I want to emphasize. As I understand it, you were struggling to get manpower enough to produce the armaments to win a war for Germany.

SPEER: Yes.

MR. JUSTICE JACKSON: And this anti-Semitic campaign was so strong that it took trained technicians away from you and disabled you from performing your functions. Now, isn't that the fact?

SPEER: I did not understand the meaning of your question.

MR. JUSTICE JACKSON: Your problem of creating armaments to win the war for Germany was made very much more difficult by this anti-Jewish campaign which was being waged by others of your codefendants.

SPEER: That is a certainty; and it is equally clear that if the Jews who were evacuated had been allowed to work for me, it would have been a considerable advantage to me.

THE PRESIDENT: Mr. Justice Jackson, has it been proved who signed that document, L – 156? It has got a signature apparently on it.

MR. JUSTICE JACKSON: There is a signature on it, I believe the plenipotentiary general for the employment of labor is my thought on it. We will look at that.

THE PRESIDENT: Perhaps the defendant could tell what the signature is.

[The document was shown to the defendant.]

SPEER: I do not know the man. Yes, he must be one of the smaller officials in the offices of the Plenipotentiary for Labor, because I knew all the immediate associates of Sauckel personally no; I beg your pardon, the document comes from the Regierungsprasident in Koblenz, as I see here. Then it is an assistant in the Government District of Koblenz, whom of course I did not know.

MR. JUSTICE JACKSON: In any event, there is no question about the statement as you have explained it?

SPEER: No.

MR. JUSTICE JACKSON: Now I want to ask you about the recruiting of forced labor. As I understand it, you know about the deportation of 100000 Jews from Hungary for subterranean airplane factories, and you told us in your interrogation of 10/18/1945 that you made no objection to it. That is true, is it not?

SPEER: That is true, yes.

MR. JUSTICE JACKSON: And you told us also, quite candidly, on that day that it was no secret to you that a good deal of the manpower brought in by Sauckel was brought in by illegal methods. That is also true, is it not?

SPEER: I took great care at the time to notice what expression the interrogating officer used; he used the expression "they came against their wish"; and that I confirmed.

MR. JUSTICE JACKSON: Did you not say that it was no secret to you that they were brought in an illegal manner? Didn't you add that yourself?

SPEER: No, no. That was certainly not so.

MR. JUSTICE JACKSON: Well, in any event, you knew that at the Fuhrer conference in August of 1942 the Fuhrer had approved of all coercive measures for obtaining labor if they couldn't be obtained on a voluntary basis, and you knew that that program was carried out. You, as a matter of fact, did not give any particular attention to the legal side of this thing, did you? You were after manpower; isn't that the fact?

SPEER: That is absolutely correct.

MR. JUSTICE JACKSON: And whether it was legal or illegal was not your worry?

SPEER: I consider that in view of the whole war situation and of our views in general on this question it was justified.

MR. JUSTICE JACKSON: Yes, it was in accordance with the policy of the Government, and that was as far as you inquired at the time, was it not?

SPEER: Yes. I am of the opinion that at the time I took over my office, in 2/1942, all the violations of international law, which are now brought up against me, had already been committed.

MR. JUSTICE JACKSON: And you don't question that you share a certain responsibility for that program for bringing in, whether it is a legal responsibility or not, in fact, for bringing in this labor against its will? You don't deny that, do you?

SPEER: The workers were brought to Germany largely against their will, and I had no objection to their being brought to Germany against their will. On the contrary, during the first period, until the autumn of 1942, I certainly also took some pains to see that as many workers as possible should be brought to Germany in this manner.

MR. JUSTICE JACKSON: You had some participation in the distribution of this labor, did you not, as among different plants, different industries, that were competing for labor?

SPEER: No. That would have to be explained in more detail. I do not quite understand it like that.

MR. JUSTICE JACKSON: Well, you finally entered into an agreement with Sauckel, did you not, in reference to the distribution of the labor after it reached the Reich?

SPEER: That was arranged according to the so-called priority grades. I had to tell Sauckel, of course, in which of my programs labor was needed most urgently. But that sort of thing was dealt with by general instructions.

MR. JUSTICE JACKSON: In other words, you established the priorities of different industries in their claim for the labor when it came into the Reich?

SPEER: That was a matter of course; naturally that had to be done.

MR. JUSTICE JACKSON: Yes. Now, as to the employment of prisoners of war, you, whatever disagreement there may be about the exact figures, there is no question, is there, that prisoners of war were used in the manufacture of armament?

SPEER: No, only Russian prisoners of war and Italian military internees were used for the production of arms. As for the use of French and other prisoners of war in this production I had several conferences with Keitel on the subject. And I must tell you that Keitel always adopted the view that these prisoners of war could not be used in violation of the Geneva Prisoner of War Convention. I can claim that on the strength of this fact I no longer used my influence to see that these prisoners of war should be used in armament industries in violation of the Geneva Convention. The conception, of course, "production of arms" is very much open to argument. It always depends on what position one takes, whether you have a wide conception of "armaments" or a narrow one.

MR. JUSTICE JACKSON: Well, you succeeded to Dr. Todt's organization, and you had all the powers that he had, did you not?

SPEER: Yes.

MR. JUSTICE JACKSON: And one of his directives was dated 10/31/1941, a letter from the OKW which is in evidence here as Exhibit 214, Document EC – 194, which provides that the deputies of the Reich Minister for arms and munitions are to be admitted to prisoner-of-war camps for the purpose of selecting skilled workers. That was among your powers, was it not?

SPEER: No. That was a special action which Dr. Todt introduced on the strength of an agreement with the OKW. It was dropped later, however.

MR. JUSTICE JACKSON: Now, on 4/22/1943, at the thirty-sixth meeting of this Planning Board, you made this complaint, did you not, Herr Speer? Quoting:

"There is a statement showing in what sectors the Russian POW's have been distributed, and this statement is quite interesting. It shows that the armament industry only received 30 percent. I always complained about that." That is correct, is it not?

SPEER: I believe that has been wrongly translated. It should not say "munitions industry"; it should say, "The armament industry received 30 percent."

MR. JUSTICE JACKSON: I said "armament."

SPEER: Yes. But this is still no proof that these prisoners of war were employed in violation of the Geneva Prisoner of War Convention, because in the sector of the armament industry there was ample room to use these workers for production articles which, in the sense of the Geneva Prisoner of War Agreement, were not armament products. However, I believe that in the case of the Russian prisoners of war, there was not the same value attached to strict observance of the Geneva Convention as in the case of prisoners from western countries.

MR. JUSTICE JACKSON: Is it your contention that the prisoners were not used? I now speak of French prisoners of war that French prisoners of war were not used in the manufacture of materials which directly contributed to the war, or is it your contention that although they were used it was legal under the Geneva Convention?

SPEER: As far as I know, French prisoners of war were not used contrary to the rules of the Convention. I cannot check that, because my office was not responsible for controlling the conditions of their employment. During my numerous visits to factories, I never noticed that any prisoner of war from the western territories was working directly on armament products.

MR. JUSTICE JACKSON: Just tell exactly what French prisoners of war did do by way of manufacture. What were they working on?

SPEER: That I cannot answer. I already explained yesterday that the allotment of prisoners of war, or foreign workers, or German workers to a factory was not a matter for me to decide, but was carried out by the labor office, together with the Stalag, when it was a question of prisoners of war. I received only a general survey of the total number of workers who had gone to the factories, and so I could get no idea of what types of labor were being employed in each individual factory. So I cannot give a satisfactory answer to your question.

MR. JUSTICE JACKSON: Now let us take the 50000 skilled workers that you said yesterday you removed and put to work in a different location, that Sauckel complained about. What did you put them to work at?

SPEER: Those were not prisoners of war.

MR. JUSTICE JACKSON: Let us take those workers. What were you doing with them?

SPEER: Those workers had been working on the Atlantic Wall. From there they were transferred to the Ruhr to repair the two dams which had been destroyed by an air attack. I must say that the transfer of these 50000 workers took place without my knowledge, and the consequences of bringing 50000 workers from the West into Germany amounted to a catastrophe for us on the Atlantic Wall. It meant that more than one-third of all the workers engaged on the Atlantic Wall left because they, too, were afraid they might have to go to Germany. That is why we rescinded the order as quickly as possible, so that the French workers on the Atlantic Wall should have confidence in us. This fact will show you that the French workers we had working for the Organization Todt were not employed on a coercive basis, otherwise they could not have left in such numbers when they realized that under certain circumstances they, too, might be taken to

Germany. So these measures taken with the 50,000 workers from the Organization Todt in France were only temporary and were revised later. It was one of those mistakes which can happen if a minister gives a harsh directive and his subordinates begin to carry it out by every means in their

MR. JUSTICE JACKSON: Are you familiar with Document EC – 60, which reports that the labor organization of Todt had to recruit its manpower by force?

SPEER: At the moment I cannot recollect it.

MR. JUSTICE JACKSON: I beg your pardon?

SPEER: At this moment I cannot recollect it. Could I see the document?

MR. JUSTICE JACKSON: Yes, if you would like to. I just remind you that the evidence is to the contrary of your testimony on that subject.

Page 42, the paragraph which reads:

"Unfortunately the assignments for the Organization Todt on the basis of Article 52 of the Hague Convention on Land Warfare have for some time decreased considerably, because the larger part of the manpower allocated does not turn up. Consequently further compulsory measures must be employed. The prefect and the French labor exchanges co-operate quite loyally, it is true, but they have not sufficient authority to carry out these measures."

SPEER: I think that I have perhaps not understood correctly. I do not deny that a large number of the people working for the Organization Todt in the West had been called up and came to their work because they had been called up, but we had no means whatsoever of keeping them there by force. That is what I wanted to say. So if they did not want to work, they could leave again; and then they either joined the resistance movement or went into hiding somewhere else.

MR. JUSTICE JACKSON: Very well. But this calling-up system was a system of compulsion, was it not?

SPEER: It was the calling-up of French workers for service in the Reich or in France. But here again I must add something. This report is dated 6/1943. In 10/1943 the whole of the Organization Todt was given the status of a "blocked factory" and thereby received the advantages which other blocked factories had. I explained that sufficiently yesterday. Because of this, the Organization Todt had large offers of workers who went there voluntarily, unless, of course, you see direct coercion in the pressure put on them through the danger of their transfer to Germany, and which led them to the Organization Todt or the blocked factories.

MR. JUSTICE JACKSON: Were they kept in labor camps?

SPEER: That is the custom in the case of such building work.

The building sites were far away from any villages, and so workers' camps were set up to accommodate the German and foreign workers. But some of them were also accommodated in villages, as far as it was possible to accommodate them there. I do not think that on principle they were only meant to be accommodated in camps, but I cannot tell you that for certain.

THE PRESIDENT: Has the document been introduced before?

MR. JUSTICE JACKSON: I was just going to give it to you. The document from which I have quoted is United States Exhibit 892.

Now, leaving the question of the personal participation in this . . .

THE PRESIDENT: Is it new, Mr. Justice Jackson?

MR. JUSTICE JACKSON: No, it has been in.

THE PRESIDENT: It has been in before?

MR. JUSTICE JACKSON: I am told that I am wrong about that, and that it is new. 892 is a new number

[Turning to the defendant.] Leaving the part of your personal participation in this program...

THE PRESIDENT: Could you tell us what the document is and where it comes from? I see it is EC – 60; so it must be captured. But ...

MR. JUSTICE JACKSON: It is one of the economic documents. It is a very large document.

THE PRESIDENT: Could you tell us what it is or who signed it? It is a very long document, apparently, is it?

MR. JUSTICE JACKSON: It is a long document, and it is a report of the Oberfeldkommandant L – I – L – L – E is the name of the signer.

Now, coming to the question...

THE PRESIDENT: Let me look at the document, will you?

You see, Mr. Justice Jackson, my attention has been drawn to the point that as far as the record is concerned, we have only this extract which you read. We have not got the date, and we do not have the signature, if any, on the document.

MR. JUSTICE JACKSON: I was merely refreshing his recollection to get out the facts, and I was not really offering the document for its own sake. I will go into more detail about it, if Your Honor wishes. There is a great deal of irrelevant material in it.

THE PRESIDENT: If you do not want to offer it, then we need not bother about it.

MR. JUSTICE JACKSON: A great part of it is not relevant.

THE PRESIDENT: Yes.

MR. JUSTICE JACKSON: The quotation is adequately verified.

THE PRESIDENT: In that case you may refer to it without the document being used. Then we need not have the document identified as an exhibit.

MR. JUSTICE JACKSON: [Turning to the defendant.] Leaving the question of your personal participation in these matters and coming to the questions dealt with in the second part of your examination, I want to ask you about your testimony concerning the proposal to denounce the Geneva Convention.

You testified yesterday that it was proposed to withdraw from the Geneva Convention. Will you tell us who made those proposals?

SPEER: This proposal, as I already testified yesterday, came from Dr. Goebbels. It was made after the air attack on Dresden, but before this, from the autumn of 1944 on, Goebbels and Ley had often talked about intensifying the war effort in every possible way, so that I had the impression that Goebbels was using the attack on Dresden and the excitement it created merely as an excuse to renounce the Geneva Convention.

MR. JUSTICE JACKSON: Now, was the proposal made at that time to resort to poison gas warfare?

SPEER: I was not able to make out from my own direct observations whether gas warfare was to be started, but I knew from various associates of Ley's and Goebbels' that they were discussing the question of using our two new combat gases, Tabun and Sarin. They believed that these gases would be of particular efficacy, and they did in fact produce the most frightful results. We made these observations as early as the autumn of 1944, when the situation had become critical and many people were seriously worried about it.

MR. JUSTICE JACKSON: Now, will you tell us about these two gases and about their production and their effects, their qualities, and the preparations that were made for gas warfare?

SPEER: I cannot tell you that in detail. I am not enough of an expert. All I know is that these two gases both had a quite extraordinary effect, and that there was no respirator, and no protection against them that we knew of. So the soldiers would have been unable to protect themselves against this gas in any way. For the manufacture of this gas we had about three factories, all of which were undamaged and which until 11/1944 were working at full speed. When rumors reached us that gas might be used, I stopped its production in 11/1944. I stopped it by the following means. I blocked the so-called preliminary production, that is, the chemical supplies for the making of gas, so that the gas production, as the Allied authorities themselves ascertained, after the end of December or the beginning of January, actually slowed down and finally came to a standstill. Beginning with a letter which is still in existence and which I wrote to Hitler in 10/1944, I tried through legal methods to obtain his permission to have these gas factories stop their production. The reason I gave him was that on account of air raids the preliminary products, primarily cyanide, were needed urgently for other purposes. Hitler informed me that the gas production would have to continue whatever happened, but I gave instructions for the preliminary products not to be supplied any more.

MR. JUSTICE JACKSON: Can you identify others of the group that were advocating gas warfare?

SPEER: In military circles there was certainly no one in favor of gas warfare. All sensible Army people turned gas warfare down as being utterly insane since, in view of your superiority in the air, it would not be long before it would bring the most terrible catastrophe upon German cities, which were completely unprotected.

MR. JUSTICE JACKSON: The group that did advocate it, however, consisted of the political group around Hitler, didn't it?

SPEER: A certain circle of political people, certainly very limited. It was mostly Ley, Goebbels and Bormann, always the same three, who by every possible means wanted to increase the war effort; and a man like Fegelein certainly belonged to a group like that too. Of Himmler I would not be too sure, for at that time Himmler was a little out of favor with Hitler because he allowed himself the luxury of directing an army group without being qualified.

MR. JUSTICE JACKSON: Now, one of these gases was the gas which you proposed to use on those who were proposing to use it on others, and I suppose your motive was...

SPEER: I must say quite frankly that my reason for these plans was the fear that under certain circumstances gas might be used, and the association of ideas in using it myself led me to make the whole plan.

MR. JUSTICE JACKSON: And your reasons, I take it, were the same as the military's, that is to say, it was certain Germany would get the worst of it if Germany started that kind of warfare: That is what was worrying the military, wasn't it?

SPEER: No, not only that. It was because at that stage of the war it was perfectly clear that under no circumstances should any international crimes be committed which could be held against the German people after they had lost the war. That was what decided the issue.

MR. JUSTICE JACKSON: Now, what about the bombs, after the war was plainly lost, aimed at England day after day; who favored that?

SPEER: You mean the rockets?

MR. JUSTICE JACKSON: Yes.

SPEER: From the point of view of their technical production the rockets were a very expensive affair for us, and their effect compared to the cost of their output was negligible. In consequence we had no particular interest in developing the affair on a bigger scale. The person who kept urging it was Himmler, in this case. He gave one Obergruppenfuhrer Kammler the task of firing off these rockets over England. In Army circles they were of the same opinion as I, namely, that the rockets were too expensive; and in Air Force circles, the opinion was the same, since for the equivalent of one rocket one could almost build a fighter. It is quite clear that it would have been much better for us if we had not gone in for this nonsense.

MR. JUSTICE JACKSON: Going back to the characteristics of this gas, was one of the characteristics of this gas an exceedingly high temperature? When it was exploded it created exceedingly high temperature, so that there could be no defense against it?

SPEER: No, that is an error. Actually, ordinary gas evaporates at normal atmospheric temperature. This gas would not evaporate until very high temperatures were reached and such very high temperatures could only be produced by an explosion; in other words, when the explosives detonated, a very high temperature set in, as you know, and then the gas evaporated. The solid substance turned into gas, but the effects had nothing to do with the high temperature.

MR. JUSTICE JACKSON: Experiments were carried out with this gas, were they not, to your knowledge?

SPEER: That I can tell you. Experiments must certainly have been carried out with it.

MR. JUSTICE JACKSON: Who was in charge of the experimentations with the gases?

SPEER: As far as I know it was the research and development department of the OKH in the Army ordnance office. I cannot tell you for certain.

MR. JUSTICE JACKSON: And certain experiments were also conducted and certain researches conducted in atomic energy, were they not?

SPEER: We had not got as far as that, unfortunately, because the finest experts we had in atomic research had emigrated to America, and this had thrown us back a great deal in our research, so that we still needed another year or two in order to achieve any results in the splitting of the atom.

MR. JUSTICE JACKSON: The policy of driving people out who didn't agree with Germany hadn't produced very good dividends, had it?

SPEER: Especially in this sphere it was a great disadvantage to us.

MR. JUSTICE JACKSON: Now, I have certain information, which was placed in my hands, of an experiment which was carried out near Auschwitz and I would like to ask you if you heard about it or knew about it. The purpose of the experiment was to find a quick and complete way of destroying people without the delay and trouble of shooting and gassing and burning, as it had been carried out, and this is the experiment, as I am advised. A village, a small village was provisionally erected, with temporary structures, and in it approximately 20000 Jews were put. By means of this newly invented weapon of destruction, these 20000 people were eradicated almost instantaneously, and in such a way that there was no trace left of them; that it developed, the explosive developed, temperatures of from 400 to 500 centigrade and destroyed them without leaving any trace at all.

Do you know about that experiment?

SPEER: No, and I consider it utterly improbable. If we had had such a weapon under preparation, I should have known about it. But we did not have such a weapon. It is clear that in chemical warfare attempts were made on both sides to carry out research on all the weapons one could think of, because one did not know which party would start chemical warfare first.

MR. JUSTICE JACKSON: The reports, then, of a new and secret weapon were exaggerated for the purpose of keeping the German people in the war?

SPEER: That was the case mostly during the last phase of the war. From August, or rather June or 7/1944 on I very often went to the front. I visited about 40 frontline divisions in their sectors and could not help seeing that the troops, just like the German people, were given hopes about a new weapon coming, new weapons and wonder-weapons which, without requiring the use of soldiers, without military forces, would guarantee victory. In this belief lies the secret why so many people in Germany offered their lives, although common sense told them that the war was over. They believed that within the near future this new weapon would arrive. I wrote to Hitler about it and also tried in different speeches, even before Goebbels' propaganda leaders, to work against this belief. Both Hitler and Goebbels told me, however, that this was no propaganda of theirs but that it was a belief which had grown up amongst the people. Only in the dock here in Nuremberg, I was told by Fritzsche that this propaganda was spread systematically among the people through some channels or other, and that SS Standartenfuhrer Berg was responsible for it. Many things have become clear to me since, because this man Berg, as a representative of the Ministry of Propaganda, had often taken part in meetings, in big sessions of my Ministry, as he was writing articles about these sessions. There he heard of our future plans and then used this knowledge to tell the people about them with more imagination than truth.

MR. JUSTICE JACKSON: When did it become apparent that the war was lost? I take it that your attitude was that you felt some responsibility for getting the German people out of it with as little destruction as possible. Is that a fair statement of your position?

SPEER: Yes, but I did not only have that feeling with regard to the German people. I knew quite well that one should equally avoid destruction taking place in the occupied territories. That was just as important to me from a realistic point of view, for I said to myself that after the war the responsibility for all these destructions would no longer fall on us, but on the next German Government, and the coming German generations.

MR. JUSTICE JACKSON: Where you differed with the people who wanted to continue the war to the bitter end, was that you wanted to see Germany have a chance to restore her life. Is that not a fact? Whereas Hitler took the position that if he couldn't survive, he didn't care whether Germany survived or not?

SPEER: That is true, and I would never have had the courage to make this statement before this Tribunal if I had not been able to prove it with the help of some documents, because such a statement is so monstrous. But the letter which I wrote to Hitler on 29 March, in which I confirmed this, shows that he said so himself.

MR. JUSTICE JACKSON: Well, if I may comment, it was not a new idea to us that that was his viewpoint. I think it was expressed in most of the other countries that that was his viewpoint.

Now, were you present with Hitler at the time he received the telegram from Goering, suggesting that Goering take over power?

SPEER: On 23 April I flew to Berlin in order to take leave of several of my associates, and, I should like to say this quite frankly, after all that had happened, also in order to place myself at Hitler's disposal. Perhaps this will sound strange here, but the conflicting feelings I had about the action I wanted to take against him and about the way he had handled things, still did not give me any clear grounds or any clear inner conviction as to what my relations should be toward him, so I flew over to see him. I did not know whether he knew of my plans, and I did not know whether he would order me to remain in Berlin. Yet I felt that it was my duty not to run away like a coward, but to stand up to him again. It was on that day that Goering's telegram to Hitler arrived. This telegram was not to Hitler, but from Goering to Ribbentrop; it was Bormann who submitted it to him.

MR. JUSTICE JACKSON: Submitted it to Hitler?

SPEER: Yes, to Hitler.

MR. JUSTICE JACKSON: What did Hitler say on that occasion?

SPEER: Hitler was unusually excited about the contents of the telegram, and said quite plainly what he thought about Goering. He said that he had known for some time that Goering had failed, that he was corrupt, and that he was a drug addict. I was extremely shaken, because I felt that if the head of the State had known this for such a long time, then it showed a lack of responsibility on his part to leave such a man in office, when the lives of countless people depended on him. It was typical of Hitler's attitude towards the entire problem, however, that he followed his statement up by saying: "But let him negotiate the capitulation all the same."

MR. JUSTICE JACKSON: Did he say why he was willing to let Goering negotiate the capitulation?

SPEER: No. He said in an offhand manner: "It doesn't matter anyway who does it." He expressed all his disregard for the German nation in the way he said this.

MR. JUSTICE JACKSON: That is, his attitude was that there was nothing left worth saving, so let Goering work it out. Is that a fair statement of his position?

SPEER: That was my impression, yes.

MR. JUSTICE JACKSON: Now, this policy of driving Germany to destruction after the war was lost had come to weigh on you to such a point that you were a party to several plots, were you not, in an attempt to remove the people who were responsible for the destruction, as you saw it, of your country?

SPEER: Yes. But I want to add...

MR. JUSTICE JACKSON: There were more plots than you have told us about, weren't there?

SPEER: During that time it was extremely easy to start a plot. One could accost practically any man in the street and tell him what the situation was, and then he would say: "This is insane"; and if he had any courage he would place himself at your disposal. Unfortunately, I had no organization behind me which I could call upon and give orders to, or designate who should have done this or that. That is why I had to depend on personal conversations to contact all kinds of people. But I do want to say that it was not as dangerous as it looks here because actually the unreasonable people who were still left only amounted perhaps to a few dozen. The other 80 million were perfectly sensible as soon as they knew what it was all about.

MR. JUSTICE JACKSON: Perhaps you had a sense of responsibility for having put the 80 million completely in the hands of the Fuhrer Principle. Did that occur to you, or does it now, as you look back on it?

SPEER: May I have the question repeated, because I did not understand its sense.

MR. JUSTICE JACKSON: You have 80 million sane and sensible people facing destruction; you have a dozen people driving them on to destruction and they are unable to stop it. And I ask if you have a feeling of responsibility for having established the Fuhrer Principle, which Goering has so well described for us, in Germany?

SPEER: I, personally, when I became Minister in 2/1942, placed myself at the disposal of this Fuhrer Principle. But I admit, that in my organization I soon saw that the Fuhrer Principle was full of tremendous mistakes, and so I tried to weaken its effect. The terrible danger of the authoritarian system, however, became really clear only at the moment when we were approaching the end. It was then that one could see what the principle really meant, namely, that every order should be carried out without criticism. Everything that has become known during this Trial in the way of orders carried out without any consideration, finally proved, for example the carrying out of the order to destroy the bridges in our own country, to be a mistake or a consequence of this authoritarian system. The authoritarian system, or let me put it like this, upon the collapse of the authoritarian system it became clear what tremendous dangers there are in a system of that kind, quite apart from the personality of Hitler. The combination of Hitler and this system, then, brought about these terrible catastrophes in the world.

MR. JUSTICE JACKSON: Well, now, Hitler is dead; I assume you accept that, and we ought to give the devil his due. Isn't it a fact that in the circle around Hitler there was almost no one who would stand up and tell him that the war was lost, except yourself?

SPEER: That is correct to a certain extent. Among the military leaders there were many who, each in his own sphere, told Hitler quite clearly what the situation was. Many commanders of army groups, for instance, made it clear to him how catastrophic developments were, and there were often fierce arguments during the discussions on the situation. Men like Guderian and Jodl, for instance, often talked openly about their sectors in my presence, and Hitler could see quite well what the general situation was like. But I never observed that those who were actually responsible in the group around Hitler, ever went to him and said, "The war is lost." Nor did I ever see these people who had responsibility endeavor to unite in undertaking some joint step with Hitler. I did not attempt it for my part either, except once or twice, because it would have been useless, since at this stage, Hitler had so intimidated his closest associates that they no longer had any wills of their own.

MR. JUSTICE JACKSON: Well, let us take the Number 2 man, who has told us that he was in favor of fighting to the very finish. Were you present at a conversation between Goering and General

Galland, in which Goering, in substance, forbade Galland to report the disaster that was overtaking Germany?

SPEER: No; in that form, that is not correct. That was another conference.

MR. JUSTICE JACKSON: Well, tell us what there is about General Galland's conversation with Goering, as far as you know it.

SPEER: It was at the Fuhrer's headquarters in East Prussia in front of Goering's train. Galland had reported to Hitler that enemy fighter planes were already escorting bomber squadrons as far as Liege and that it was to be expected that in the future the bomber units would travel still farther from their bases escorted by fighters. After a discussion with Hitler on the military situation Goering upbraided Galland and told him with some excitement that this could not possibly be true, that the fighters could not go as far as Liege. He said that from his experience as an old fighter pilot he knew this perfectly well. Thereupon Galland replied that the fighters were being shot down, and were lying on the ground near Liege. Goering would not believe this was true. Galland was an outspoken man who told Goering his opinion quite clearly and refused to allow Goering's excitement to influence him. Finally Goering, as Supreme Commander of the Air Force, expressly forbade Galland to make any further reports on this matter. It was impossible, he said, that enemy fighters could penetrate so deeply in the direction of Germany, and so he ordered him to accept that as being true. I continued to discuss the matter afterward with Galland and Galland was actually later relieved by Goering of his duties as Commanding General of Fighters. Up to this time Galland had been in charge of all the fighter units in Germany. He was the general in charge of all the fighters within the High Command of the Air Force.

THE PRESIDENT: What is the date of that?

MR. JUSTICE JACKSON: I was going to ask.

SPEER: It must have been toward the end of 1943.

MR. JUSTICE JACKSON: If it please the Tribunal, I wanted to ask you whether it was known in the days when you were struggling for manpower enough to make armaments for Germany, that Goering was using manpower to collect art and transport art for his own purposes. Was that known to you at the time?

SPEER: He did not need many workers for that purpose.

MR. JUSTICE JACKSON: Well, very few were very valuable, were they not?

SPEER: The art treasures were valuable, not the workers.

MR. JUSTICE JACKSON: To him?

MR. JUSTICE JACKSON: Well, let me ask you about your efforts in producing, and see how much difficulty you were having. Krupp's was a big factor in the German armament production, was it not?

SPEER: Yes.

MR. JUSTICE JACKSON: The biggest single unit, wouldn't you say?

SPEER: Yes, but not just to the extent I said yesterday. It produced few guns and armaments, but it was a big concern, one of the most respected ones in the armament industry.

MR. JUSTICE JACKSON: But you had prevented, as far as possible, the use of resources and manpower for the production of things that were not useful for the war, is not that true?

SPEER: That is true.

MR. JUSTICE JACKSON: And the things which were being created, being built in Krupp's, whether they were guns or other objects, were things which were essential to carrying on the economy or to conducting the war? That would be true, would it not?

SPEER: Generally speaking one can say that in the end every article which in wartime is produced in the home country, whether it is a pair of shoes for the workers, or clothing, or coal is, of course, is made to assist in the war effort. That has nothing to do with the old conception, which has long since died out, and which we find in the Geneva Prisoner of War Convention.

MR. JUSTICE JACKSON: Well, at the moment I am not concerned with the question of the application of the Geneva Convention. I want to ask you some questions about your efforts to produce essential goods, whether they were armament or not armament, and the conditions that this regime was imposing upon labor and adding, as I think, to your problem of production. I think you can give us some information about this. You were frequently at the Krupp plant, were you not?

SPEER: I was at the Krupp plant five or six times.

MR. JUSTICE JACKSON: You had rather close information as to the progress of production in the Krupp plant, as well as others?

SPEER: Yes, when I went to visit these plants, it was mostly in order to see how we could do away with the consequences of air attacks. It was always shortly after air raids, and so I got an idea of the production. As I worked hard I knew a lot about these problems, right down to the details.

MR. JUSTICE JACKSON: Krupp also had several labor camps, did they not?

SPEER: Of course, Krupp had labor camps.

MR. JUSTICE JACKSON: Krupp was a very large user of both foreign labor and prisoners of war?

SPEER: I cannot give the percentage, but no doubt Krupp did employ foreign workers and prisoners of war.

MR. JUSTICE JACKSON: Well, I may say to you that we have investigated the Krupp labor camps, and from Krupp's own charts it appears that in 1943 they had 39,245 foreign workers and 11,234 prisoners of war, and that this steadily increased until in 9/1944 Krupp had 54,990 foreign workers and 18,902 prisoners of war.

Now, would that be somewhere near what you would expect from your knowledge of the industry?

SPEER: I do not know the details. I do not know the figures of how many workers Krupp employed in all. I am not familiar with them at the moment. But I believe that the percentage of foreign workers at Krupp was about the same as in other plants and in other armament concerns.

MR. JUSTICE JACKSON: And what would you say that percentage was?

SPEER: That varied a great deal. The old established industries which had their old regular personnel had a much lower percentage of foreign workers than the new industries which had just grown up and which had no old regular personnel. The reason for this was that the young age groups were drafted into the Armed Forces and therefore the concerns which had a personnel of older workers still retained a large percentage of the older workers. Therefore the percentage of foreign workers in Army armaments, if you take it as a whole and as one of the older industries, was lower than the percentage of foreign workers in air armaments, because that was a completely new industry which had no old regular personnel.

MR. JUSTICE JACKSON: Now, the foreign workers who were assigned to Krupp—let us use Krupp as an example—were housed in labor camps and under guard, were they not?

SPEER: I do not believe that they were under guard, but I cannot say. I do not want to dodge giving information here, but I had no time to worry about such things on my visits. The things I was concerned about when I went to a factory were in an entirely different sphere. In all my activities as Armament Minister I never once visited a labor camp, and cannot, therefore, give any information about them.

MR. JUSTICE JACKSON: Well now, I am going to give you some information about the labor camp at Krupp's, and then I am going to ask you some questions about it. And I am not attempting to say that you were personally responsible for these conditions. I merely give you the indications as to what the regime was doing and I am going to ask you certain questions as to the effect of this sort of thing on your work of production.

Are you familiar with Document D – 288, which is United States Exhibit 202, the affidavit of Dr. Jager, who was later brought here as a witness?

SPEER: Yes, but I consider that somewhat exaggerated.

MR. JUSTICE JACKSON: You don't accept that?

SPEER: No.

MR. JUSTICE JACKSON: Well, you have no personal knowledge of the conditions. What is the basis of your information that Dr. Jager's statement is exaggerated?

SPEER: If such conditions had existed, I should probably have heard of them, since when I visited plants the head of the plant naturally came to me with his biggest troubles. These troubles occurred primarily after air raids when, for example, both the German workers and foreign workers had no longer any proper shelter. This state of affairs was then described to me, so that I know that what is stated in the Jager affidavit cannot have been a permanent condition. It can only have been a condition caused temporarily by air raids, for a week or a fortnight, and which was improved later on. It is clear that after a severe air raid on a city all the sanitary installations, the water supply, gas supply, electricity, and so on, were out of order and severely damaged, so that temporarily there were very difficult conditions.

MR. JUSTICE JACKSON: I remind you that Dr. Jager's affidavit relates to the time of 10/1942, and that he was a witness here. And, of course, you are familiar with his testimony.

SPEER: Yes.

MR. JUSTICE JACKSON: Well now, I call your attention to a new document, which is D – 361, and would become United States Exhibit 893, a document signed by the office chief of the locomotive construction works, describing conditions of his labor supply, foreign labor.

And I am not suggesting, I repeat I am not suggesting, that this was your responsibility. I am suggesting it is the responsibility of the regime. I should like to read this despite its considerable length. This is dated at the boilermaking shop, 2/25/1942, addressed to Hupe by way of Winters and Schmidt.

"I received the enclosed letter of the 18th of this month from the German Labor Front, sent to my private address, inviting me to the Office of the German Labor Front. I tried to settle the business, which I did not know about, by telephone. The answer from the German Labor Front was that the matter was very important and called for my personal appearance. Thereupon I asked Herr Jungerich of the Department for Social Labor Matters whether I had to go. He answered, 'You probably do not have to, but it would be better if you went.' About 9:50 I went to Room 20 at the place indicated and met Herr Prior.

"The following provided the subject of this conversation, which Herr Prior carried on in a very excited manner, and which lasted about half an hour:

"On the 16th, 23 Russian prisoners of war were assigned to Number 23 Boiler Shop. The people came in the morning without bread and tools. During both breaks the prisoners of war crept up to the German workers and begged for bread, pitifully pointing out their hunger. For lunch on the first day the factory was able to distribute among the Russians rations which remained over from French POW's. In order to alleviate these conditions, I went to the Weidkamp kitchen on the 17th, on instructions from Herr Theile, and talked to the head of the kitchen, Fraulein Block, about the provision of the midday meal. Fraulein Block promised me the food immediately, and also lent me the 22 sets of eating utensils which I asked for. At the same time I asked Fraulein Block to give any food left over by the 800 Dutchmen messing there to our Russian POW's at noon until further notice. Fraulein Block promised to do this too, and the following noon she sent down a container of milk soup as an extra. The following noon the ration was short in quantity. Since a few Russians had collapsed already, I telephoned Fraulein Block and asked for an increase in the food, as the special ration had ceased from the second day onwards. As my telephone conversation was unsuccessful, I again visited

Fraulein Block personally. Fraulein Block refused in a very abrupt manner to give any further special ration.

"Now, regarding the discussion in detail, Herr Prior, two other gentlemen of the DAF and Fraulein Block, head of the Weidkamp kitchen, were present in the room. Herr Prior commenced and accused me, gesticulating, and in a very insulting manner, of having taken the part of the Bolsheviks in a marked way. He referred to the law paragraphs of the Reich Government which spoke against it. I was unfortunately not clear about the legal position, otherwise I would have left the conference room immediately. I then tried to make it clear to Herr Prior, with special emphasis, that the Russian POW's were assigned to us as workers and not as Bolsheviks; the people were starved and not in a position to perform the heavy work with us in the boiler shop which they were supposed to do; sick people are a dead weight to us and not a help to production. To this remark Herr Prior stated that if one was no good, then another was; that the Bolsheviks were a soulless people; and if 100,000 of them died, another 100,000 would replace them. On my remarking that with such a coming and going we would not attain our goal, namely the delivery of locomotives to the Reichsbahn, who were continually cutting down the time limit, Herr Prior said, 'Deliveries are only of secondary importance here.'

"My attempts to get Herr Prior to understand our economic needs were not successful. In closing, I can only say that as a German I know our relations to the Russian prisoners of war exactly, and in this case I acted only on behalf of my superiors and with the view to the increase in production which is demanded from us."

It is signed, "Sohling, Office Chief, Locomotive Construction Works."

And there is added this letter as a part of the communication, signed by Theile:

"I have to add the following to the above letter:

"After the Russian POW's had been assigned to us on the 16th of this month by labor supply, I got into touch with Dr. Lehmann immediately about their food. I learned from him that the prisoners received 300 gr. of bread each between 0400 and 0500 hours. I pointed out that it was impossible to last until 1800 hours on this ration of bread, whereupon Dr. Lehmann said that the Russians must not be allowed to get used to western European feeding. I replied that the POW's could not do the work required of them in the boiler shop on that food, and that it was not practical for us to have these people in the works any longer under such conditions. At the same time I demanded that if the Russians continued to be employed, they should be given a hot midday meal, and that if possible the bread ration should be split so that onehalf was distributed early in the morning and the second half during our breakfast break. My suggestion has already been carried out by us with the French POW's and has proved to be very practicable and good.

"Unfortunately, however, Dr. Lehmann took no notice of my suggestion, and on this account I naturally had to take matters into my own hands and therefore told Herr Sohling to get the feeding of the Russian POW's organized on exactly the same lines as for the French POW's, so that the Russians could as soon as possible carry out the work they were supposed to do. For the whole thing concerns an increase in production such as is demanded from us by the Minister of munitions and armaments and by the DAF."

Now, I ask you, in the first place, if the position of the chief of the locomotive construction works was not entirely a necessary position in the interests of production?

SPEER: It is clear that a worker who has not enough food cannot achieve a good work output. I already said yesterday that every head of a plant, and I too at the top, was naturally interested in having well-fed and satisfied workers, because badly fed, dissatisfied workers make more mistakes and produce poor results.

I should like to comment on this document. The document is dated 2/25/1942. At that time there were official instructions that the Russian workers who came to the Reich should be treated worse than the western prisoners of war and the western workers. I learned of this through complaints from the heads of concerns. In my document book, there is a Fuhrer protocol which dates from the middle of 3/1942, that is, 3 or 4 weeks after this document, in which I called Hitler's attention to the fact that the feeding both of Russian prisoners of war and of Russian workers was absolutely insufficient and that they would have to be given an adequate diet, and that moreover the Russian workers were being kept behind barbed wire like prisoners of war and that that would have to be stopped also. The protocol shows that in both cases I succeeded in getting Hitler to agree that conditions should be changed and they were changed.

I must say furthermore that it was really to Sauckel's credit that he fought against a mountain of stupidity and did everything so that foreign workers and prisoners of war should be treated better and receive decent food.

MR. JUSTICE JACKSON: Well, we will go on with the conditions later. Because I am going to ask you, if you are not responsible and Sauckel is not responsible, who is responsible for these conditions, and you can keep it in mind that is the question that we are coming up to here.

I will show you a new document, which is a statement, D – 398, which would be Exhibit USA 894 – A, taken by the British-American team in the investigation of this work camp at Krupp's.

Well, D – 321. I can use that just as well. We will use Document D – 321, which becomes 893.

THE PRESIDENT: 894 was the last number you gaze us. What number is this document that you are now offering?

MR. JUSTICE JACKSON: 398 was 894. 321 will be 895.

Now, this relates to the — this is an employee of the Reich Railways. None of our investigation, I may say, is based upon the statements of the prisoners themselves.

"I, the undersigned, Adam Schmidt, employed as *Betriebswart* on the Essen-West Railway Station and residing . . . state voluntarily and on oath:

"I have been employed by the Reich Railways since 1918 and have been at Essen-West Station since 1935. In the middle of 1941 the first workers arrived from Poland, Galicia, and the Polish Ukraine. They came to Essen in trucks in which potatoes, building materials and also cattle had been transported, and were brought to perform work at Krupp's. The trucks were jammed full with people. My personal view was that it was inhuman to transport people in such a manner. The people were packed closely together and they had no room for free movement. The Krupp overseers laid special value on the speed with which the slave workers got in and out of the trucks. It was enraging for every decent German who had to watch this to see how the people were beaten and kicked and generally maltreated in a brutal manner. In the very beginning when the first transport arrived we could see how inhumanly these people were treated. Every truck was so overfilled that it was incredible that such a number of people could be jammed into one. I could see with my own eyes that sick people who could scarcely walk (they were mostly people with foot trouble, or with injuries, and people with internal trouble) were nevertheless taken to work. One could see that it was sometimes difficult for them to move. The same can be said of the Eastern Workers and POW's who came to Essen in the middle of 1942."

He then describes their clothing and their food. In the interest of time, I will not attempt to read the entire thing.

Do you consider that that, too, is an exaggerated statement?

SPEER: When the workers came to Germany from the East, their clothing was no doubt bad, but I know from Sauckel that while he was in office a lot was done to get them better clothes, and in Germany many of the Russian workers were brought to a considerably better condition than they had previously been in in Russia. The Russian workers were quite satisfied in Germany. If they arrived here in rags, that does not mean that that was our fault. We could not use ragged workers with poor shoes in our industry, so conditions were improved.

MR. JUSTICE JACKSON: Well, now, I would like to call your attention to D – 398.

THE PRESIDENT: Well, before you pass from that, what do you say about the conditions of the transports? The question you were asked was whether this was an exaggerated account. You have not answered that except in reference to clothing.

SPEER: Mr. President, I cannot give any information about this transport matter. I received no reports about it.

MR. JUSTICE JACKSON: Well, I will ask you about Exhibit 398, which becomes USA – 894. I mean Document 398, which becomes Exhibit 894, a statement by Homer, living in Essen:

"From 4/1943 I worked with Lowenkamp every day in Panzer Shop 4. Lowenkamp was brutal to the foreigners. He confiscated food which belonged to the POW's and took it home. Every day he maltreated Eastern Workers, Russian POW's, French, Italian, and other foreign civilians. He had a steel cabinet built which was so small that one could hardly stand in it. He locked up foreigners in the box, women too, for 48 hours at a time without giving the people food.

"They were not released even to relieve nature. It was forbidden for other people, too, to give any help to the persons locked in, or to release them. While clearing a concealed store he fired on escaping Russian civilians without hitting any of them.

"One day, while distributing food, I saw how he hit a French civilian in the face with a ladle and made his face bleed. Further, he delivered Russian girls without bothering about the children afterwards. There was never any milk for them so the Russians had to nourish the children with sugar water. When Lowenkamp was arrested he wrote two letters and sent them to me through his wife. He tried to make out that he never beat people."

There is a good deal more of this, but I will not bother to put it into the record.

Is it your view that that is exaggerated?

SPEER: I consider this affidavit a lie. I would say that among German people such things do not exist, and if such individual cases occurred they were punished. It is not possible to drag the German people in the dirt in such a way. The heads of concerns were decent people too, and took an interest in their workers. If the head of the Krupp plant heard about such things, he certainly took steps immediately.

MR. JUSTICE JACKSON: Well, what about the steel boxes? The steel box couldn't have been built? Or don't you believe the steelbox story?

SPEER: No, I do not believe it; I mean I do not believe it is true. After the collapse in 1945 a lot of affidavits were certainly drawn up which do not fully correspond to the truth. That is not your fault. It is the fault of—after a defeat, it is quite possible that people lend themselves to things like that.

MR. JUSTICE JACKSON: Well, I would like to have you examine Document 258, and I attach importance to this as establishing the SS as being the guards:

"The camp inmates were mostly Jewish women and girls from Hungary and Romania. The camp inmates were brought to Essen at the beginning of 1944 and were put to work at Krupp's. The accommodation and feeding of the camp prisoners was beneath all dignity. At first the prisoners were accommodated in simple wooden huts. These huts were burned down during an air raid and from that time on the prisoners had to sleep in a damp cellar. Their beds were made on the floor and consisted of a straw-filled sack and two blankets. In most cases it was not possible for the prisoners to wash themselves daily, as there was no water. There was no possibility of having a bath. I could often observe from the Krupp factory, during the lunch break, how the prisoners boiled their underclothing in an old bucket or container over a wood fire, and cleaned themselves. An air-raid trench served as shelter, while the SS guards went to the Humboldt shelter, which was bombproof. Reveille was at 5 a. m.

There was no coffee or any food served in the morning. They marched off to the factory at 5.15 a. m. They marched for three-quarters of an hour to the factory, poorly clothed and badly shod, some without shoes, and covered with a blanket, in rain or snow.

"Work began at 6 a. m. The lunch break was from 12 to 12:30. Only during the break was it at all possible for the prisoners to cook something for themselves from potato peelings and other garbage. The daily working period was one of 10 or 11 hours. Although the prisoners were completely undernourished, their work was very heavy physically. The prisoners were often maltreated at their work benches by Nazi overseers and female SS guards. At 5 or 6 in the afternoon they were marched back to camp. The accompanying guards consisted of female SS who, in spite of protests from the civil population, often maltreated the prisoners on the way back with kicks, blows, and scarcely repeatable words. It often happened that individual women or girls had to be carried back to the camp by their comrades owing to exhaustion. At 6 or 7 p.m. these exhausted people arrived back in camp. Then the real meal was distributed. This consisted of cabbage soup. This was followed by the evening meal of water soup and a piece of bread which was for the following day. Occasionally the food on Sundays was better. As long as it existed there was never any inspection of the camp by the firm of Krupp. On 3/13/1945 the camp prisoners were brought to Buchenwald Concentration Camp, from there some were sent to work. The camp commandant was SS Oberscharfuhrer Rick. His present whereabouts is unknown."

The rest of it doesn't matter. In your estimation that, I suppose, is also an exaggeration?

SPEER: From the document...

DR. FLACHSNER: Mr. President . . .

THE PRESIDENT: May I hear the answer. I thought the defendant said something.

DR. FLACHSNER: May I call the attention of the Court to the document itself, of which I have only a copy? It is headed "Sworn on oath before a military court," and there is an ordinary signature under it. It does not say that it is an affidavit or a statement in lieu of oath, or any other such thing, it says only, "Further inquiries must be made," and it is signed by Hubert Karden. That is apparently the name of the man who was making the statement. Then there is another signature, "Kriminalassistent Z. Pr." That is a police official who is on probation and who may later have the chance of becoming a candidate in the criminal service. He has signed it. Then there is another signature, "C. E. Long, Major, President." There is not a word in this document to the effect that any of these three people want to vouch for the contents of this as an affidavit. I do not believe this document can be used as an affidavit in that sense.

THE PRESIDENT: Yes, Mr. Justice Jackson? Do you wish to say anything?

MR. JUSTICE JACKSON: The document shows for itself. I am not, as I have pointed out to this witness, I am giving him the result of an investigation. I am not prosecuting him with personal responsibility for these conditions. I intend to ask him some questions about responsibility for conditions in the camp.

THE PRESIDENT: Well, there is a statement at the top of the copy that I have got, "Sworn on oath before a military court."

MR. JUSTICE JACKSON: Yes, they were taken in Essen, in this investigation. And of course, if I were charging this particular defendant with the responsibility there might be some argument about it. They come under the head, they clearly come under the head of the Charter, which authorizes the receipt here of proceedings of other courts.

THE PRESIDENT: Have you got the original document here?

MR. JUSTICE JACKSON: Yes.

[A document was submitted to the Tribunal.]

THE PRESIDENT: The Tribunal sees no objection to the document being used in cross-examination.

Did you give it an exhibit number?

MR. JUSTICE JACKSON: I should have; it is USA – 896.

THE PRESIDENT: Yes.

MR. JUSTICE JACKSON: [Turning to the defendant.] I now want to call your attention to Exhibit Number 382.

SPEER: I wanted to comment on the document.

THE PRESIDENT: Mr. Justice Jackson, there are some photographs which have been put before us. Are they identified and do they form part of an exhibit?

MR. JUSTICE JACKSON: They form part of the exhibit which I am now offering.

THE PRESIDENT: I see.

MR. JUSTICE JACKSON: But the witness desires to comment on the last document, and I will listen to that before we go ahead.

SPEER: First I should like to say, as you have so often mentioned my non-responsibility, that if in general these conditions had been true, on the basis of my statement yesterday I should consider myself responsible. I refuse to evade responsibility. But the conditions were not what they are said to have been here. There are only individual cases which are quoted.

As for this document I should only like to say from what I have seen of it that this seems to concern a concentration camp, one of the small concentration camps near the factories. The factories could not inspect these camps. That is why the sentence is quite true where it says that no factory representative ever saw the camp. The fact that there were SS guards also shows that it was a concentration camp.

If the question which you asked me before, as to whether the labor camps were guarded, those for foreign workers, if that refers to this document, then your conclusion was wrong. For as far as I know, the other labor camps were not guarded by SS or by any other organizations.

My position is such that I feel it is my duty to protect the heads of plants from any injustice which might be done them. The head of a plant could not bother about the conditions in such a camp. I cannot say whether conditions were as described in this camp. We have seen so much material on conditions in concentration camps during the Trial.

MR. JUSTICE JACKSON: Now I will ask to have you shown Exhibit Number D – 382, I should say Document D – 382, which would be United States Exhibit 897. Now that is the statement of several persons as to one of those steel boxes which stood in the foreign workers' camp in the grounds of Number 4 Armor Shop, and of those in the Russian camp. I do not know that it is necessary to read the complete descriptions.

Is that merely an individual instance, or what is your view of that circumstance?

SPEER: What is pictured here is quite a normal locker as was used in every factory. These photographs have absolutely no value as evidence.

MR. JUSTICE JACKSON: Very well. I will ask to have you shown Exhibit D – 230. Together with D – 230 is an interoffice record of the steel switches, and the steel switches which have been found in the camp will be shown to you. Eighty were distributed, according to the reports.

SPEER: Shall I comment on this?

MR. JUSTICE JACKSON: If you wish.

SPEER: Yes. Those are nothing but replacements for rubber truncheons. We had no rubber; and for that reason, the guards probably had something like this.

MR. JUSTICE JACKSON: That is the same inference that I drew from the document.

SPEER: Yes, but the guards did not immediately use these steel switches any more than your police use their rubber truncheons. But they had to have something in their hands. It is the same thing all over the world.

MR. JUSTICE JACKSON: Well, we won't argue that point.

SPEER: I am not an expert. I only assume that that is the case. I cannot testify on oath that that was the case. That was only an argument.

THE PRESIDENT: Did you give a number to that?

MR. JUSTICE JACKSON: 898, Your Honor.

Now, 899 would be our Document D – 283, which is a 1943 report from the Krupp hospitals taken from the files of Krupp's.

"The subject:

"Cases of Deaths of Eastern Workers.

"Fifty-four Eastern Workers have died in the hospital in Lazarettstrasse, 4 of them as a result of external causes and 50 as a result of illness.

"The causes of death in the case of these 50 Eastern Workers who died of illnesses were the following: Tuberculosis, 36 (including 2 women); malnutrition, 2; internal hemorrhage, 1; disease of the bowels, 2; typhoid fever, 1 (female); pneumonia, 3; appendicitis, 1 (female); liver trouble, 1; abscess of the brain, 1. This list therefore shows that four-fifths died of tuberculosis and malnutrition."

Now, did you have any reports from time to time as to the health conditions of the labor which was engaged in your production program?

SPEER: First I should like to comment on the document. The document does not show the total number of the workers to which the number of deaths refers, so that one cannot say whether that is an unnaturally high proportion of illness. At a session of the Central Planning Board which I read here again, I observed it was said that among the Russian workers there was a high rate of tuberculosis. I do not know whether you mean that. That was a remark which Weiger made to me. But presumably through the health offices we tried to alleviate these conditions.

MR. JUSTICE JACKSON: There was an abnormally high rate of deaths from tuberculosis; there is no doubt about that, is there?

SPEER: I do not know whether that was an abnormal death rate. But there was an abnormally high rate of tuberculosis at times.

MR. JUSTICE JACKSON: Well, the exhibit does not show whether the death rate itself was abnormally high, but it shows an abnormal proportion of deaths from tuberculosis among the total deaths, does it not? Eighty percent deaths from tuberculosis is a very high incidence of tuberculosis, is it not?

SPEER: That may be. I cannot say from my own knowledge.

MR. JUSTICE JACKSON: Now I would like to have you shown . . .

THE PRESIDENT: Did you give that a number? That would be 899, would it not?

MR. JUSTICE JACKSON: 899, Your Honor.

Now, let me ask you to be shown Document D – 335. This is a report from the files of Krupp, dated at Essen on 6/12/1944, directed to the "Gau Camp Physician, Herr Dr. Jager," and signed by Stinnesbeck:

"In the middle of May I took over the medical supervision of the POW Camp 1420 in the Norggerathstrasse. The camp contains 644 French POW's.

"During the air raid on 27 April of this year the camp was largely destroyed and at the moment conditions are intolerable.

"315 prisoners are still accommodated in the camp. 170 of these are no longer in huts, but in the tunnel in Grunerstrasse on the Essen-Mulheim railway line. This tunnel is damp and is not suitable for continued accommodation of human beings. The rest of the prisoners are accommodated in 10 different factories in Krupp's works.

"Medical attention is given by a French military doctor who takes great pains with his fellow countrymen. Sick people from Krupp's factories must be brought to the sick parade too. This parade is held in the lavatory of a burned-out public house outside the camp. The sleeping accommodations of the four French medical orderlies is in what was the urinal room. There is a double tier wooden bed available for sick bay patients. In general, treatment takes place in the open. In rainy weather it has to be held in this small room. These are insufferable conditions! There are no chairs, tables, cupboards, or water. The keeping of a register of sick is impossible.

"Bandages and medical supplies are very scarce, although people badly hurt in the works are often brought here for first aid and have to be bandaged before being taken to the hospital. There are many strong complaints about food, too, which the guard personnel confirm as being justified.

"Illness and less manpower must be reckoned with under these circumstances.

"The construction of huts for the accommodation of the prisoners and the building of sick quarters for the proper treatment of the sick persons is urgently necessary.

"Please take the necessary steps.

"(Signed) Stinnesbeck."

SPEER: That is a document which shows what conditions can be after severe air raids. The conditions were the same in these cases for Germans and foreign workers. There were no beds, no cupboards, and so forth. That was because the camp in which these things had been provided had been burned down. That the food supply was often inadequate in the Ruhr district during this period was due to the fact that attacks from the air were centered on communication lines, so that food transports could not be brought into the Ruhr to the necessary extent. These were temporary conditions which we were able to improve when the air raids ceased for a time. When conditions became even worse after September or October of 1944, or rather after November of 1944, we made every effort to give food supplies the priority for the first time over armament needs, so that in view of these difficulties the workers would be fed first of all, while armaments had to stand back somewhat.

MR JUSTICE JACKSON: Well, then you did make it your business to get food and to see to the conditions of these workers? Do I understand that you did it, that you took steps?

SPEER: It is true that I did so, and I am glad that I did, even if I am to be reproached for it. For it is a universal human obligation when one hears of such conditions to try to alleviate them, even if it is somebody else's responsibility. But the witness Riecke testified here that the whole of the food question was under the direction of the Food Ministry.

MR. JUSTICE JACKSON: And it was an essential part of production, was it not, to keep workers in proper condition to produce? That is elementary, is it not?

SPEER: No. That is wrongly formulated.

MR. JUSTICE JACKSON: Well, you formulate it for me as to what the relation is between the nourishment of workers and the amount of production produced.

SPEER: I said yesterday that the responsibility for labor conditions was divided up between the Food Ministry, the Health Office in the Reich Ministry of the Interior, the Labor Trustee in the office of the Plenipotentiary General for the Allocation of Labor, and so on. There was no comprehensive authority in my hands. In the Reich, because of the way in which our state machine was built up, we lacked a comprehensive agency in the form of a Reich Chancellor, who would have gathered all these departments together and held joint discussions. But I, as the man responsible for production, had no responsibility in these matters. However, when I heard complaints from factory heads or from my deputies, I did everything to remove the cause of the complaints.

MR. JUSTICE JACKSON: I think perhaps, Your Honor, the photographs in evidence are left a little unintelligible, if the record does not show the description of them. I shall read it briefly.

"Torture cabinets which were used in the foreign workers' camp in the grounds of Number 4 Armor Shop and those in the dirty neglected Russian Camp were shown to us, and we depose the following on oath:

"Photograph 'A' shows an iron cupboard which was specially manufactured by the firm of Krupp to torture Russian civilian workers to an extent that cannot possibly be described by words. Men and women were often locked into a compartment of the cupboard, in which hardly any man could stand up for long periods. The measurements of this compartment are: Height 1.52 meters; breadth and depth 40 to 50 centimeters each. Frequently even two people were kicked and pressed into one compartment. The Russian..."

I will not read the rest of that.

"Photograph 'B' shows the same cupboard as it looks when it is locked.

"Photograph 'C' shows the cupboard open.

"In Photograph 'D' we see the camp that was selected by the Krupp Directorate to serve as living quarters for the Russian civilian workers. The individual rooms were 2 to 2.5 meters wide, 5 meters long, and 2 meters high. In each room up to 16 persons were accommodated in double tier beds." (Document USA – 897)

I think that covers it.

THE PRESIDENT: Mr. Justice Jackson, one moment. I think you ought to read the last three lines of the second paragraph, beginning, "At the top of the cupboard..."

MR. JUSTICE JACKSON: Oh yes, I am sorry.

"At the top of the cupboard there are a few sievelike air holes through which cold water was poured on the unfortunate victims during the ice-cold winter."

THE PRESIDENT: I think you should read the last three lines of the penultimate paragraph in view of what the defendant said about the evidence.

MR. JUSTICE JACKSON: "We are enclosing two letters which Camp Commandant Lowenkamp had smuggled out of prison in order to induce the undersigned Hofer to give evidence favorable to him."

And perhaps I should read the last:

"The undersigned, Dahm," one of the signers, "personally saw how three Russian civilian workers were locked into the cupboard, two in one compartment, after they had first been beaten on New Year's Eve 1945. Two of the Russians had to stay the whole of New Year's Eve locked in the cupboard, and cold water was poured on them as well."

I may say to the Tribunal that we have upwards of a hundred different statements and depositions relating to the investigation of this camp. I am not suggesting offering them, because I think they would be cumulative, and I shall be satisfied with one more, D – 313, which would become Exhibit USA – 901, which is a statement by a doctor.

THE PRESIDENT: Mr. Justice Jackson, was this camp that you are referring to a concentration camp?

MR. JUSTICE JACKSON: Well, it was, as I understand it, a prisoner-of-war camp and a labor camp. There were labor camps and prisoner-of-war camps at Essen. I had not understood that it was a concentration camp, but I admit the distinction is a little thin at times.

This document reads:

"I, the undersigned, Dr. Apolinary Gotowicki, a physician in the Polish Army, was taken prisoner by the Germans on 1/3/1941 and remained as such until the entry of the Americans. I gave medical attention to the Russian, Polish, and French prisoners of war who were forced to work in various places of Krupp's factories. I personally visited the Russian POW camp in the Raumastrasse in Essen, which contained about 1,800 men. There was a big hall in the camp which could house about 200 men comfortably, in which 300 to 400 men were thrown together in such a catastrophic manner that no medical treatment was possible. The floor was cement and the mattresses on which the people slept were full of lice and bugs. Even on cold days the room was never heated and it seemed to me, as a doctor, unworthy of human beings that people should find themselves in such a position. It was impossible to keep the place clean because of the overcrowding of these men who had hardly room to move about normally Every day at least 10 people were brought to me whose bodies were covered with bruises on account of the continual beatings with rubber tubes, steel switches, or sticks. The people were often writhing with agony and it was impossible for me to give them even a little medical aid. In spite of the fact that I protested, made complaints and petitions, it was impossible for me to protect the people or see that they got a day off from work. It was difficult for me to watch how such suffering people could be dragged to do heavy work. I visited personally, with danger to myself, gentlemen of the Krupp administration, as well as gentlemen from the Krupp Directorate, to try to get help. It was strictly forbidden, as the camp was under the direction of the SS and Gestapo; and according to well-known directives I had to keep silent, otherwise I might have been sent to a concentration camp. I have brought my own bread innumerable times to the camp in order to give it to the prisoners, as far as it was possible, although bread was scarce enough for me. From the beginning in 1941 conditions did not get better, but worse. The food consisted of a watery soup which was dirty and sandy, and often the prisoners of war had to eat cabbage which was bad and stank. I could notice people daily who, on account of hunger or ill-treatment, were slowly dying. Dead people often lay for 2 or 3 days on the beds until their bodies stank so badly that fellow prisoners took them outside and buried them somewhere. The dishes out of which they ate were also used as toilets because they were too tired or too weak from hunger to get up and go outside. At 3 o'clock they were wakened. The same dishes were then used to wash in and later for eating out of. This matter was generally known. In spite of this it was impossible for me to get even elementary help or facilities in order to get rid of these epidemics, illnesses, or cases of starvation.

There can be no mention of medical aid for the prisoners. I never received any medical supplies myself. In 1941 I alone had to look after these people from a medical point of view; but it is quite understandable that it was impossible for me as the only one to look after all of these people, and apart from that, I had scarcely any medical supplies. I could not think what to do with a number of 1,800 people who came to me daily crying and complaining. I myself often collapsed daily, and in spite of this I had to take everything upon myself and watch how people perished and died. A report was never made as to how the prisoners of war died.

"I have seen with my own eyes the prisoners coming back from Krupp's and how they collapsed on the march and had to be wheeled back on barrows or carried by their comrades. It was in such a manner that the people came back to the camp. The work which they had to perform was very heavy and dangerous and many cases happened where people had cut their fingers, hands or legs. These accidents were very serious and the people came to me and asked me for medical help. But it was not even possible for me to keep them from work for a day or two, although I had been to the Krupp Directorate and asked for permission to do so. At the end of 1941, two people died daily, and in 1942 the deaths increased to three and four per day.

"I was under Dr. May and I was often successful in getting him to come to the camp to see the terrible conditions and listen to the complaints, but it was not possible for him to get medical aid from the Medical Department of the Armed Forces or Krupp's, or to get better conditions, treatment, or food. I was a witness during a conversation with some Russian women who told me personally that they were employed in Krupp's factory and that they were beaten daily in the most bestial manner. The food consisted of watery soup which was dirty and inedible and its terrible smell could be perceived from a distance. The clothing was ragged and torn and on their feet they had rags and wooden shoes. Their treatment, as far as I could make out, was the same as that of the prisoners of war. Beating was the order of the day. The conditions lasted for years, from the very beginning until the day the American troops entered. The people lived in great anxiety and it was dangerous for them to describe to anyone anywhere the conditions which reigned in their camps. The directions were such that they could have been murdered by any one of the guards, the SS, or Gestapo if they noticed it. It was possible for me as a doctor to talk to these people; they trusted me and knew that I was a Pole and would never betray them to anyone.

"Signed: Dr. Apolinary Gotowicki."

[Turning to the defendant.] Now you have explained that some of these conditions were due, in your judgment, to the fact that bombing took place and the billets of the prisoners and workers were destroyed.

SPEER: That is true, but I should like to point out that the conditions described in this affidavit cannot be considered as general; apart from that, I do not believe that this description is correct, but I cannot speak about these things since you will not expect me to be intimately acquainted with what happened in the camps of the firm of Krupp.

MR. JUSTICE JACKSON: Well, in the first place, was it considered proper by you to billet forced workers and prisoners of war so close to military targets as these prisoners were?

SPEER: I would rather not tell you here things which every German has at heart. No military targets were attacked, and the camps, therefore, could not be near military targets.

MR. JUSTICE JACKSON: You would not consider the Krupp plants proper targets?

SPEER: The camps were not in the Krupp works, they were near the city of Essen. On principle, we did not construct camps near the works which we expected would be bombed; and we did not want the camps to be destroyed.

MR. JUSTICE JACKSON: Did you notice that one of the photographs in evidence shows the camp directly against the works?

SPEER: May I see it again, please?

[A photograph was shown to the defendant.]

Some large factory is recognizable in the background of this photograph, but that does not affect my statement that in almost all cases we constructed the camps outside the cities. I do not know why this particular instance is different, and I cannot even say whether this is a camp or just a hut for changing clothes, or anything which had to be near the camp. I still believe that these cabinets were cabinets for clothes, and this is one of the many huts which were necessary so that the workers could change clothes before and after their work. Any expert in Germany can tell you that these are wardrobes and not some special cabinets, because they are mass-produced articles; this is also confirmed by the fact that there are air vents at the top, for every wardrobe has these ventilation holes at the top and bottom.

MR. JUSTICE JACKSON: As production Minister, you were vitally interested in reducing the sickness rate among workers, were you not?

SPEER: I was interested in a high output of work, that is obvious, and in addition, in special cases. . .

MR. JUSTICE JACKSON: Well, special cases—part of production is in all cases, is it not, dependent upon the sickness rate of our labor force, and is it not a fact, as a man engaged in production you will know this, that the two greatest difficulties in manpower and production are sickness and rapid turnover, and that those factors reduce production?

SPEER: These two factors were disturbing for us, but not as extensively as your words might suggest. Cases of sickness made up a very small percentage which in my opinion was normal. However, propaganda pamphlets dropped from aircraft were telling the workers to feign illness, and detailed instructions were given to them on how to do it. And to prevent that, the authorities concerned introduced certain measures, which I considered proper.

MR. JUSTICE JACKSON: What were those measures?

SPEER: I cannot tell you in detail, because I myself did not institute these penalties, nor did I have the power to do so; but as far as I know, they were ordered by the Plenipotentiary General for the Allocation of Labor in collaboration with the Police or State authorities; but the jurisdiction in this connection was with the authorities responsible for legal action.

MR. JUSTICE JACKSON: Now, if you did not know what they were, how can you tell us that you approved of them? We always get to this blank wall that nobody knew what was being done. You knew that they were at least penalties of great severity, did you not?

SPEER: When I say that I approved I am only expressing my wish not to dodge my responsibility in this respect. But you must understand that a minister of production, particularly in view of the air attacks, had a tremendous task before him and that I could only take care of matters outside my own field if some particularly important factor forced me to do so. Otherwise, I was glad if I could finish my own work and, after all, my task was by no means a small one.

I think that if during the German air attacks on England you had asked the British Minister of Production whether he shared the worries of the Minister of Labor and whether he was dealing with them, then he would with justification have told you that he had something else to do at that time, that he had to keep up his production and that he expected the Minister of Labor to manage affairs in his sector; and no one would have raised a direct accusation against the British Minister of Production on that account.

MR. JUSTICE JACKSON: Well, production was your enterprise, and do you mean to tell me that you did not have any records or reports on the condition of the manpower which was engaged in production, which would tell you if there was anything wrong in the sick rate or anything wrong in the general conditions of the labor?

SPEER: What I knew is contained in the reports of the Central Planning Board; there you will get a picture of what I was told. Although there were many other meetings I cannot tell you in detail what I knew, because these were things outside my sphere of activity. Naturally, it is a matter of course that anyone closely concerned with the affairs of State will also hear of matters not immediately connected with his own sphere, and of unsatisfactory conditions existing in other sectors; but one is not obliged to deal with these conditions and later on one will not remember them in detail. You cannot expect that of me. But if you have any particular passage, I shall be glad to give you information on it.

MR. JUSTICE JACKSON: All right; assume that these conditions had been called to your attention and that they existed. With whom would you have taken it up to have them corrected? What officer of the Government?

SPEER: Normally, a minister would send a document to the Government authorities responsible for such conditions. I must claim for myself that when I heard of such deficiencies I tried to remedy them by establishing direct contact with the authority responsible, in some cases the German Labor Front, where I had a liaison officer, or in other cases my letter was transmitted to Sauckel through my office of manpower deployment. My practice in this respect was that if I did not receive a return report I considered the matter settled; for I could not then again pursue those things and make further inquiries whether they had been dealt with or not.

MR. JUSTICE JACKSON: With Krupp's, then, you would not have taken it up? You think they had no responsibility for these conditions?

SPEER: During visits to Krupp's discussions certainly took place on the conditions which generally existed for workers after air attacks; this was a source of great worry for us, particularly with regard to Krupp. I knew this well, but the reports from Krupp were not different from — I cannot remember ever being told that foreign workers or prisoners of war were in a particularly bad position. Temporarily they all lived under very primitive conditions; German workers lived in cellars during those days, and six or eight people were often quartered in a small basement room.

MR. JUSTICE JACKSON: Your statement some time ago that you had a certain responsibility as a Minister of the Government for the conditions — I should like to have you explain what responsibility you referred to when you say you assume a responsibility as a member of the Government.

SPEER: Do you mean the declaration I made yesterday that I . . .

MR. JUSTICE JACKSON: Your common responsibility, what do you mean by your common responsibility along with others?

SPEER: Oh, yes. In my opinion, a state functionary has two types of responsibility. One is the responsibility for his own sector and for that, of course, he is fully responsible. But above that I think that in decisive matters there is, and must be, among the leaders a common responsibility, for who is to bear responsibility for developments, if not the close associates of the head of State?

This common responsibility, however, can only be applied to fundamental matters, it cannot be applied to details connected with other ministries or other responsible departments, for otherwise the entire discipline in the life of the State would be quite confused, and no one would ever know who is individually responsible in a particular sphere. This individual responsibility in one's own sphere must, at all events, be kept clear and distinct.

MR. JUSTICE JACKSON: Well, your point is, I take it, that you as a member of the Government and a leader in this period of time acknowledge a responsibility for its large policies, but not for all the details that occurred in their execution. Is that a fair statement of your position?

SPEER: Yes, indeed.

MR. JUSTICE JACKSON: I think that concludes the crossexamination.

Summation for the Prosecution

by Justice Robert Jackson

MR. JUSTICE ROBERT H. JACKSON (Chief of Counsel for the United States): Mr. President and Members of the Tribunal: An advocate can be confronted with few more formidable tasks than to select his closing arguments where there is great disparity between his appropriate time and his available material. In 8 months a short time as state trials gow have introduced evidence which embraces as vast and varied a panorama of events as has ever been compressed within the framework of a litigation. It is impossible in summation to do more than outline with bold strokes the vitals of this Trial's mad and melancholy record, which will live as the historical text of the twentieth century's shame and depravity.

It is common to think of our own time as standing at the apex of civilization, from which the deficiencies of preceding ages may patronizingly be viewed in the light of what is assumed to be "progress." The reality is that in the long perspective of history the present century will not hold an admirable position, unless its second half is to redeem its first. These two-score years in the twentieth century will be recorded in the book of years as one of the most bloody in all annals. Two World Wars have left a legacy of dead which number more than all the armies engaged in any way that made ancient or medieval history. No half-century ever witnessed slaughter on such a scale, such cruelties and inhumanities, such wholesale deportations of peoples into slavery, such annihilations of minorities. The terror of Torquemada pales before the Nazi Inquisition. These deeds are the overshadowing historical facts by which generations to come will remember this decade. If we cannot eliminate the causes and prevent the repetition of these barbaric events, it is not an irresponsible prophecy to say that this twentieth century may yet succeed in bringing the doom of civilization.

Goaded by these facts, we were moved to redress the blight on the record of our era. The defendants complain that our pace is too fast. In drawing the Charter of this Tribunal, we thought we were recording an accomplished advance in international law. But they say we have outrun our times, that we have anticipated an advance that should be, but has not yet been made. The Agreement of London, whether it originates or merely records, at all events marks a transition in international law which roughly corresponds to that in the evolution of local law when men ceased to punish crime by "hue and cry" and began to let reason and inquiry govern punishment. The society of nations has emerged from the primitive "hue and cry," the law of "catch and kill." It seeks to apply sanctions to enforce international law, but to guide their application by evidence, law, and reason instead of outcry. The defendants denounce the law under which their accounting is asked. Their dislike for the law which condemns them is not original. It has been remarked before that: "No thief e'er felt the halter draw with good opinion of the law."

I shall not labor the law of this case. The position of the United States was explained in my opening statement. My distinguished colleague, the Attorney General of Great Britain, will reply on behalf of all the chief prosecutors to the defendants' legal attack. At this stage of the proceedings, I shall rest upon the law of these crimes as laid down in the Charter. The defendants, who except for the Charter would have no right to be heard at all, now ask that the legal basis of this Trial be nullified. This Tribunal, of course, is given no power to set aside or modify the agreement between the Four Powers, to which 18 other nations have adhered. The terms of the Charter are conclusive upon every party to these proceedings.

In interpreting the Charter, however, we should not overlook the unique and emergent character of this body as an International Military Tribunal. It is no part of the constitutional mechanism of internal justice of any of the signatory nations. Germany has unconditionally surrendered, but no peace treaty has been signed or agreed upon. The Allies are still technically in a state of war with Germany, although the enemy's political and military institutions have collapsed. As a military tribunal, this Tribunal is a continuation of the war effort of the Allied nations. As an International Tribunal, it is not bound by the procedural and substantive refinements of our respective judicial or constitutional systems, nor will its rulings introduce precedents into any country's internal system of civil justice. As an International Military Tribunal, it rises above the provincial and transient and seeks guidance not only from international law but also from the basic principles of jurisprudence which are assumptions of civilization and which long have found embodiment in the codes of all nations.

Of one thing we may be sure. The future will never have to ask, with misgiving, what could the Nazis have said in their favor. History will know that whatever could be said, they were allowed to say. They have been given the kind of a Trial which they, in the days of their pomp and power, never gave to any man.

But fairness is not weakness. The extraordinary fairness of these hearings is an attribute of our strength. The Prosecution's case, at its close, seemed inherently unassailable because it rested so heavily on German documents of unquestioned authenticity. But it was the weeks upon weeks of pecking at this case, by one after another of the defendants, that has demonstrated its true strength. The fact is that the testimony of the defendants has removed any doubt of guilt which, because of the extraordinary nature and magnitude of these crimes, may have existed before they spoke. They have helped write their own judgment of condemnation.

But justice in this case has nothing to do with some of the arguments put forth by the defendants or their counsel. We have not previously and we need not now discuss the merits of all their obscure and tortuous philosophy. We are not trying them for the possession of obnoxious ideas. It is their right, if they choose, to renounce the Hebraic heritage in the civilization of which Germany was once a part. Nor is it our affair that they repudiated the Hellenic influence as well. The intellectual bankruptcy and moral perversion of the Nazi regime might have been no concern of international law had it not been utilized to goosestep the Herrenvolk across international frontiers. It is not their thoughts, it is their overt acts which we charge to be crimes. Their creed and teachings are important only as evidence of motive, purpose, knowledge, and intent.

We charge unlawful aggression but we are not trying the motives, hopes, or frustrations which may have led Germany to resort to aggressive war as an instrument of policy. The law, unlike politics, does not concern itself with the good or evil in the status quo, nor with the merits of the grievances against it. It merely requires that the status quo be not attacked by violent means and that policies be not advanced by war. We may admit that overlapping ethnological and cultural groups, economic barriers, and conflicting national ambitions created in the 1930's, as they will continue to create, grave problems for Germany as well as for the other peoples of Europe. We may admit too that the world had failed to provide political or legal remedies which would be honorable and acceptable alternatives to war. We do not underwrite either the ethics or the wisdom of any country, including my own, in the face of these problems. But we do say that it is now, as it was for sometime prior to 1939, illegal and criminal for Germany or any other nation to redress grievances or seek expansion by resort to aggressive war.

Let me emphasize one cardinal point. The United States has no interest which would be advanced by the conviction of any defendant if we have not proved him guilty on at least one of the Counts charged against him in the Indictment. Any result that the calm and critical judgment of posterity would pronounce unjust would not be a victory for any of the countries associated in this Prosecution. But in summation we now have before us the tested evidences of criminality and have heard the flimsy excuses and paltry evasions of the defendants. The suspended judgment with which we opened this case is no longer appropriate. The time has come for final judgment and if the case I present seems hard and uncompromising, it is because the evidence makes it so.

I perhaps can do no better service than to try to lift this case out of the morass of detail with which the record is full and put before you only the bold outlines of a case that is impressive in its simplicity. True, its thousands of documents and n;ore thousands of pages of testimony deal with an epoch and cover a continent, and touch almost every branch of human endeavor. They illuminate specialities, such as diplomacy, naval development and warfare, land warfare, the genesis of air warfare, the politics of the Nazi rise to power, the finance and economics of totalitarian war, sociology, penology, mass psychology, and mass pathology. I must leave it to experts to comb the evidence and write volumes on their specialities, while I picture in broad strokes the offenses whose acceptance as lawful could threaten the continuity of civilization. I must, as Kipling put it, "splash at a 10-league canvas with brushes of comet's hair."

The Crimes of the Nazi Regime.

The strength of the case against these defendants under the conspiracy Count, which it is the duty of the United States to argue, is in its simplicity. It involves but three ultimate inquiries: First, have the acts defined by the Charter as crimes been committed; second, were they committed pursuant to a Common Plan or Conspiracy; third, are these defendants among those who are criminally responsible?

The charge requires examination of a criminal policy, not of a multitude of isolated, unplanned, or disputed crimes. The substantive crimes upon which we rely, either as goals of a common plan or as means for its accomplishment, are admitted. The pillars which uphold the conspiracy charge may be found in five groups of overt acts, whose character and magnitude are important considerations in appraising the proof of conspiracy.

1. The Seizure of Power and Subjugation of Germany to a Police State.

The Nazi Party seized control of the German State in 1933. "Seizure of power" is a characterization used by defendants and defense witnesses, and so apt that it has passed into both history and everyday speech.

The Nazi junta in the early days lived in constant fear of overthrow. Goering, in 1934, pointed out that its enemies were legion and said:

"Therefore, the concentration camps have been created, where we have first confined thousands of Communists and social democrat functionaries"

In 1933 Goering forecast the whole program of purposeful cruelty and oppression when he publicly announced:

"Whoever in the future raises a hand against a representative of the National Socialist movement or of the State must know that he will lose his life in a very short while" (2494 – PS).

New political crimes were created to this end. It was made a treason, punishable with death, to organize or support a political party other than the Nazi Party (2548 – PS). Circulating a false or exaggerated statement, or one which would harm the State or even the Party, was made a crime (1652 – PS). Laws were enacted of such ambiguity that they could be used to punish almost any innocent act. It was, for example, made a crime to provoke "any act contrary to the public welfare" (1390 – PS).

The doctrine of punishment by analogy was introduced to enable conviction for acts which no statute forbade (1962 – PS). Minister of Justice Gurtner explained that National Socialism considered every violation of the goals of life which the community set up for itself to be a wrong per se, and that the acts could be punished even though it was not contrary to existing "formal law" (2549 – PS).

The Gestapo and the SD were instrumentalities of an espionage system which penetrated public and private life (1680 – PS). Goering controlled a personal wire-tapping unit. All privacy of communication was abolished (1390 – PS). Party Blockleiter appointed over every 50 householders spied continuously on all within their ken (1893 – PS).

Upon the strength of this spying individuals were dragged off to "protective custody" and to concentration camps without legal proceedings of any kind (1956 – PS) and without statement of any reason therefor (2533 – PS). The partisan Political Police were exempted from effective legal responsibility for their acts (2347 – PS).

With all administrative offices in Nazi control and with the Reichstag reduced to impotence, the judiciary remained the last obstacle to this reign of terror (2469 – PS). But its independence was soon overcome and it was reorganized to dispense a venal justice (784 – PS) Judges were ousted for political or racial reasons and were spied upon and put under pressure to join the Nazi Party (2967 – PS). After the Supreme Court had acquitted three of the four men whom the Nazis accused of setting the Reichstag fire, its jurisdiction over treason cases was transferred to a newly established "People's Court" consisting of two judges and five Party officials (2967 – PS). The German film of this "People's Court" in operation, which we showed in this chamber, revealed its presiding judge pouring partisan abuse on speechless defendants (3054 – PS). Special courts were created to try political crimes, only Party members were appointed judges (2065 – PS), and "judges' letters" instructed the puppet judges as to the "general lines" they must follow (D – 229).

The result was the removal of all peaceable means either to resist or to change the Government. Having sneaked through the portals of power, the Nazis slammed the gate in the face of all others who might also aspire to enter. Since the law was what the Nazis said it was, every form of opposition was rooted out and every dissenting voice throttled. Germany was in the clutch of a police state, which used the fear of the concentration camp as a means to enforce nonresistance. The Party was the State, the State was the Party, and terror by day and death by night were the policy of both.

2. The Preparation and Waging of Wars of Aggression.

From the moment the Nazis seized power, they set about feverish but stealthy efforts, in defiance of the Versailles Treaty, to arm for war. In 1933 they found no air force. By 1939 they had 21 squadrons, consisting of 240 echelons or about 2,400 first-line planes, together with trainers and transports. In 1933 they found an army of 3 infantry and 3 cavalry divisions. By 1939 they had raised and equipped an army of 51 divisions, 4 of which were fully motorized and 4 of which were Panzer divisions. In 1933 they found a navy of 1 cruiser and 6 light cruisers. By 1939 they had built a navy of 4 battleships, 1 aircraft carrier, 6 cruisers, 22 destroyers, and 54 submarines. They had also built up in that period an armament industry as efficient as that of any country in the world (EC – 28).

These new weapons were put to use, commencing in September 1939, in a series of undeclared wars against nations with which Germany had arbitration and nonaggression treaties, and in violation of repeated assurances. On 9/1/1939, this rearmed Germany attacked Poland. The following April witnessed the invasion and occupation of Denmark and Norway, and May saw the overrunning of Belgium, the Netherlands, and Luxembourg. Another spring saw Yugoslavia and Greece under attack, and in June 1941 came the invasion of Soviet Russia. Then Japan, which Germany had embraced as a partner, struck without warning at Pearl Harbor in December 1941 and 4 days later Germany declared war on the United States.

We need not trouble ourselves about the many abstract difficulties that can be conjured up about what constitutes aggression in doubtful cases. I shall show you, in discussing the conspiracy, that by any test ever put forward by any responsible authority, by all the canons of plain common sense, these were unlawful wars of aggression in breach of treaties and in violation of assurances.

The third group of crimes was: Warfare in Disregard of International Law.

It is unnecessary to labor this point on the facts. Goering asserts that the Rules of Land Warfare were obsolete, that no nation could fight a total war within their limits. He testified that the Nazis would have denounced the conventions to which Germany was a party, but that General Jodl wanted captured German soldiers to continue to benefit from their observance by the Allies.

It was, however, against the Soviet people and Soviet prisoners that Teutonic fury knew no bounds, in spite of a warning by Admiral Canaris that the treatment was in violation of international law.

We need not, therefore, for the purposes of the conspiracy Count, recite the revolting details of starving, beating, murdering, freezing, and mass extermination admittedly used against the Eastern soldiery. Also, we may take as established or admitted that the lawless conduct such as shooting British and American airmen, mistreatment of Western prisoners of war, forcing French prisoners of war into German war work, and other deliberate violations of the Hague and Geneva Conventions, did occur, and in obedience to highest levels of authority (R – 110).

The fourth group of crimes is: Enslavement and Plunder of Populations in Occupied Countries.

The Defendant Sauckel, Plenipotentiary General for the Utilization of Labor (1666 – PS), is authority for the statement that "out of 5,000,000 foreign workers who arrived in Germany, not even 200,000 came voluntarily" (R – 124). It was officially reported to Defendant Rosenberg that in his territory "recruiting methods were used which probably have their origin in the blackest period of the slave trade" (294 – PS). Sauckel himself reported that male and female agents went hunting for men, got them drunk, and "shanghaied' them to Germany (220 – PS). These captives were shipped in trains without heat, food, or sanitary facilities. The dead were thrown out at stations, and the newborn were thrown out the windows of moving trains (054 – PS).

Sauckel ordered that "all the men must be fed, sheltered, and treated in such a way as to exploit them to the highest possible extent at the lowest conceivable degree of expenditure" (054 – PS). About two million of these were employed directly in the manufacture of armaments and munitions (016 – PS). The director of the Krupp locomotive factory in Essen complained to the company that Russian forced laborers were so underfed that they were too weakened to do their work (D – 316), and the Krupp doctor confirmed their pitiable condition (D – 288). Soviet workers were put in camps under Gestapo guards, who were allowed to punish disobedience by confinement in a concentration camp or by hanging on the spot (3040 – PS).

Populations of occupied countries were otherwise exploited and oppressed unmercifully. Terror was the order of the day. Civilians were arrested without charges, committed without counsel, executed without hearing. Villages were destroyed, the male inhabitants shot or sent to concentration camps, the women sent to forced labor, and the children scattered abroad (3012 – PS). The extent of the slaughter in Poland alone was indicated by Frank, who reported, and I quote:

"If I wanted to have a poster put up for every seven Poles who were shot, the forests of Poland would not suffice for producing the paper for such posters" (2032 – PS).

Those who will enslave men cannot be expected to refrain from plundering them. Boastful reports show how thoroughly and scientifically the resources of occupied lands were sucked into the German war economy, inflicting shortage, hunger, and inflation upon the inhabitants (EC – 317). Besides this grand plan to aid the German war effort there were the sordid activities of the Rosenberg *Einsatzstab* which pillaged art treasures for Goering and his fellow bandits (014 – PS). It is hard to say whether the spectacle of Germany's Number 2 leader urging his people to give up every comfort and strain every sinew on essential war work while he rushed around confiscating art by the trainload should be cast as tragedy or comedy. In either case it was a crime.

International law at all times before and during this war spoke with precision and authority respecting the protection due civilians of an occupied country and the slave trade and plunder of occupied countries was at all times flagrantly unlawful.

And the fifth group of crimes is: Persecution and Extermination of Jews and Christians.

The Nazi movement will be of evil memory in history because of its persecution of the Jews, the most far-flung and terrible racial persecution of all time. Although the Nazi Party neither invented nor monopolized anti-Semitism, its leaders from the very beginning embraced it, incited it, and exploited it. They used it as "the psychological spark that ignites the mob." After the seizure of power it became an official state policy. The persecution began in a series of discriminatory laws eliminating the Jews from the civil service, the professions, and economic life. As it became more intense it included segregation of Jews in ghettos, and exile. Riots were organized by Party leaders to loot Jewish business places and to burn synagogues. Jewish property was confiscated and a collective fine of a billion marks was imposed upon German Jewry. The program progressed in fury and irresponsibility to the "final solution." This consisted of sending all Jews who were fit to work to concentration camps as slave laborers, and all who were not fit, which included children under 12 and people over 50, as well as any others judged unfit by an SS doctor, to concentration camps for extermination (2605 – PS).

Adolf Eichmann, the sinister figure who had charge of the extermination program, has estimated that the anti-Jewish activities resulted in the killing of 6 million Jews. Of these, 4 million were killed in extermination institutions, and 2 million were killed by *Einsatzgruppen*, mobile units of the Security Police and SD which pursued Jews in the ghettos and in their homes and slaughtered them by gas wagons, by mass shooting in antitank ditches and by every device which Nazi ingenuity could conceive. So thorough and uncompromising was this program that the Jews of Europe as a race no longer exist, thus fulfilling the diabolic "prophecy" of Adolf Hitler at the beginning of the war (2738 – PS).

Of course, any such program must reckon with the opposition of the Christian Church. This was recognized from the very beginning. Defendant Bormann wrote all Gauleiters in 1941 that "National Socialism and Christian concepts are irreconcilable," and that the people must be separated from the churches and the influence of the churches totally removed (D – 75). Defendant Rosenberg even wrote dreary treatises advocating a new and weird Nazi religion (2349 – PS).

The Gestapo appointed "Church specialists" who were instructed that the ultimate aim was "destruction of the confessional churches" 1815 – PS). The record is full of specific instances of the persecution of clergymen (1164 – PS, 1521 – PS, 848 – PS, 849 – PS), the confiscation of Church property (1481 – PS), interference with religious publications (1498 – PS), disruption of religious education (121 – PS) and suppression of religious organizations (1481 – PS, 1482 – PS, R – 145).

The chief instrumentality for persecution and extermination was the concentration camp, sired by the Defendant Goering and nurtured under the overall authority of Defendants Frick and Kaltenbrunner.

The horrors of these iniquitous places have been vividly disclosed by documents (2309 – PS, 3870 – PS) and testified to by witnesses.

The Tribunal must be satiated with ghastly verbal and pictorial portrayals. From your records it is clear that the concentration camps were the first and worst weapon of Nazi oppression used by the

National Socialist State, and that they were the primary means utilized for the persecution of the Christian Church and the extermination of the Jewish race. This has been admitted to you by some of the defendants from the witness stand. In the words of Defendant Frank: "A thousand years will pass and this guilt of Germany will still not be erased."

These, then, were the five great substantive crimes of the Nazi regime. Their commission, which cannot be denied, stands admitted. The Defendant Keitel, who is in a position to know the facts, has given the Tribunal what seems to be a fair summation of the case on the facts:

"The defendant has declared that he admits the contents of the general Indictment to be proved from the objective and factual point of view (that is to say, not every individual case) and this in consideration of the law of procedure governing the Trial. It would be senseless, despite the possibility of refuting several documents or individual facts, to attempt to shake the Indictment as a whole."

I pass now to the inquiry as to whether these groups of criminal acts were integrated in a Common Plan or Conspiracy.

The Prosecution submits that these five categories of premeditated crimes were not separate and independent phenomena but that all were committed pursuant to a Common Plan or Conspiracy. The Defense admits that these classes of crimes were committed but denies that they are connected one with another as parts of a single program.

The central crime in this pattern of crimes, the kingpin which holds them all together, is the plot for aggressive wars. The chief reason for international cognizance of these crimes lies in this fact. Have we established the Plan or Conspiracy to make aggressive war?

Certain admitted or clearly proven facts help answer that question. First is the fact that such war of aggression did take place. Second, it is admitted that from the moment the Nazis came to power, every one of them and every one of the defendants worked like beavers to prepare for some war. The question therefore comes to this: Were they preparing for the war which did occur, or were they preparing for some war which never has happened? It is probably true that in their early days none of them had in mind what month of what year war would begin, the exact dispute which would precipitate it, or whether its first impact would be Austria, Czechoslovakia, or Poland. But I submit that the defendants either knew or were chargeable with knowledge that the war for which they were making ready would be a war of German aggression. This is partly because there was no real expectation that any power or combination of powers would attack Germany. But it is chiefly because the inherent nature of the German plans was such that they were certain sooner or later to meet resistance and that they could then be accomplished only by aggression.

The plans of Adolf Hitler for aggression were just as secret as *Mein Kampf*, of which over six million copies were published in Germany. He not only openly advocated overthrowing the Treaty of Versailles, but made demands which went far beyond a mere rectification of its alleged injustices (GB – 128). He avowed an intention to attack neighboring states and seize their lands, which he said would have to be won with "the power of a triumphant sword." Here, for every German to hearken to, were the "ancestral voices prophesying war."

Goering has testified in this courtroom that at his first meeting with Hitler, long before the seizure of power, quoting:

"I noted that Hitler had a definite view of the impotency of protest and, as a second point, that he was of the opinion that Germany should be freed of the peace of Versailles. We did not say we shall have to have a war and defeat our enemies; this was the aim, and the methods had to be adapted to the political situation." When asked if this goal were to be accomplished by war if necessary, Goering did not deny that eventuality but evaded a direct answer by saying, "We did not even debate about those things at that time." He went on to say that the aim to overthrow the Treaty of Versailles was open and notorious and that, I quote again, "every German in my opinion was for its modification, and there was no doubt that this was a strong inducement for joining the Party." Thus, there can be no possible excuse for any person who aided Hitler to get absolute power over the German people, or who took a part in his regime, to fail to know the nature of the demands he would make on Germany's neighbors.

Immediately after the seizure of power the Nazis went to work to implement these aggressive intentions by preparing for war. They first enlisted German industrialists in a secret rearmament program. Twenty days after the seizure of power Schacht was host to Hitler, Goering, and some 20 leading industrialists. Among them were Krupp von Bohlen of the great Krupp armament works and representatives of I. G. Farben and other Ruhr heavy industries. Hitler and Goering explained their program to the industrialists, who became so enthusiastic that they set about to raise 3 million Reichsmark to strengthen and confirm the Nazi Party in power (EC – 433). Two months later Krupp was working to bring a reorganized association of German industry into agreement with the political aims of the Nazi Government (D – 157). Krupp later boasted of the success in keeping the German war industries secretly alive and in readiness despite the disarmament clauses of the Versailles Treaty, and recalled the industrialists' enthusiastic acceptance of "the great intentions of the Fuhrer in the rearmament period of 1933-39" (D – 317).

Some 2 months after Schacht had sponsored his first meeting to gain the support of the industrialists, the Nazis moved to harness industrial labor to their aggressive plans. In April 1933 Hitler ordered Dr. Ley "to take over the trade unions," numbering some six million members. By Party directive Ley seized the unions, their property and their funds. Union leaders, taken into "protective custody" by the SS and SA, were put into concentration camps (2283 – PS, 2271 – PS, 2335 – PS, 2334 – PS, 2928 – PS, 2277 – PS, 2332 – PS 2333 – PS). The free labor unions were then replaced by a Nazi organization known as the German Labor Front, with Dr. Ley at its head. It was expanded until it controlled over 23 million members (2275 – PS). Collective bargaining was eliminated, the voice of labor could no longer be heard as to working conditions and the labor contract was prescribed by "trustees of labor" appointed by Hitler (405 – PS). The war purpose of this labor program was clearly acknowledged by Robert Ley 5 days after war broke out, when he declared in a speech that:

"We National Socialists have monopolized all resources and all our energies during the past 7 years so as to be able to be equipped for the supreme effort of battle" (1939 – PS).

The Nazis also proceeded at once to adapt the Government to the needs of war. In April 1933 the Cabinet formed a Defense Council, the working committee of which met frequently thereafter. In the meeting of 5/23/1933 at which Defendant Keitel presided the members were instructed that:

"No document must be lost since otherwise the enemy propaganda would make use of it. Matters communicated orally cannot be proven; they can be denied by us in Geneva" (EC – 177).

In January 1934, and, Your Honors, dates in this connection are important, with Defendant Jodl present, the Council planned a mobilization calendar and mobilization order for some 240,000 industrial plants. Again it was agreed that nothing should be in writing so that "the military purpose may not be traceable" (EC – 404).

On 5/21/1935, the top secret Reich Defense Law was enacted. Defendant Schacht was appointed Plenipotentiary for War Economy with the task of secretly preparing all economic forces for war and in the event of mobilization, of financing the war (2261 – PS).

Schacht's secret efforts were supplemented in October 1936 by the appointment of Defendant Goering as commissioner of the Four Year Plan, with the duty of putting the entire economy in a state of readiness for war within 4 years (EC – 408).

A secret program for the accumulation of the raw materials and foreign credits necessary for extensive rearmament was also set on foot immediately upon seizure of power. In September of 1934, the Minister of Economics was already complaining that:

"The task of stockpiling is being hampered by the lack of foreign currency; the need for secrecy and camouflage also is a retarding influence" (EC – 128).

Foreign currency controls were at once established. Financing was delegated to the wizard Schacht, who conjured up the bill to serve the dual objectives of tapping the shortterm money market for rearmament purposes while concealing the amount of these expenditures (EC – 436).

The spirit of the whole Nazi administration was summed up by Goering at a meeting of the Council of Ministers, which included Schacht, on 5/27/1936, when he said,

"All measures are to be considered from the standpoint of an assured waging of war" (1301 – PS).

The General Staff, of course, also had to be enlisted in the war plan. Most of the generals, attracted by the prospect of rebuilding their armies, became willing accomplices. The holdover Minister of War Von Blomberg and the Chief of Staff General Von Fritsch, however, were not cordial to the increasingly belligerent policy of the Hitler regime, and by vicious and obscene plotting they were discredited and removed in January 1938. Thereupon, Hitler assumed for himself Supreme Command of the Armed Forces and the positions of Blomberg and of Von Fritsch were filled by others who became, as Blomberg said of Keitel, "a willing tool in Hitler's hands for every one of his decisions." The generals did not confine their participation to merely military matters. They participated in all major diplomatic and political maneuvers, such as the Obersalzberg meeting where Hitler, flanked by Keitel and other top generals, issued his virtual ultimatum to Schuschnigg (1780 – PS).

As early as 11/5/1937 the plan to attack had begun to take definiteness as to time and victim. In a meeting which included the Defendants Raeder, Goering, and Von Neurath, Hitler stated the cynical objective: "The question for Germany is where the greatest possible conquest could be made at the lowest possible cost." He discussed various plans for the invasion of Austria and Czechoslovakia, indicating clearly that he was thinking of these territories not as ends in themselves, but as means for further conquest. He painted out that considerable military and political assistance could be afforded by possession of these lands and discussed the possibility of constituting from them new armies up to a strength of about 12 divisions. The aim he stated boldly and baldly as the acquisition of additional living space in Europe, and recognized that "the German question can be solved only by way of force" (386 – PS).

Six months later, emboldened by the bloodless Austrian conquest, Hitler, in a secret directive to Keitel, stated his "unalterable decision to smash Czechoslovakia by military action in the near future" (388 – PS).

On the same day, Jodl noted in his diary that the Fuhrer had stated his final decision to destroy Czechoslovakia soon and had initiated military preparations all along the line (1780 – PS). By April the plan had been perfected to attack Czechoslovakia "with lightning swift action as the result of an incident" (388 – PS).

All along the line preparations became more definite for a war of expansion on the assumption that it would result in a worldwide conflict. In September 1938 Admiral Carls officially commented on a "Draft Study of Naval Warfare against England": "There is full agreement with the main theme of the study. "

"1. If according to the Fuhrer's decision Germany is to acquire a position as a world power, she needs not only sufficient colonial possessions but also secure naval communications and secure access to the ocean.

"2. Both requirements can only be fulfilled in opposition to Anglo-French interests and will limit their positions as world powers. It is unlikely that they can be achieved by peaceful means. The decision to make Germany a world power therefore forces upon us the necessity of making the corresponding preparations for war.

"3. War against England means at the same time war against the Empire, against France, probably against Russia as well, and a large number of countries overseas; in fact, against one-half to one-third of the whole world.

"It can only be justified and have a chance of success if it is prepared economically as well as politically and militarily and waged with the aim of conquering for Germany an outlet to the ocean" (C – 23).

This Tribunal knows what categorical assurances were given to an alarmed world after the *Anschluss*, after Munich, after the occupation of Bohemia and Moravia, that German ambitions were realized and that Hitler had "no further territorial demands to make in Europe." The record of this Trial shows that those promises were calculated deceptions and that those high in the bloody brotherhood of Nazidom knew it.

As early as 4/15/1938 Goering pointed out to Mussolini and Ciano that the possession of those territories would make possible an attack on Poland (1874 – PS). Ribbentrop's Ministry on 8/26/1938 was writing:

"After the settlement of the Czechoslovakian question, it will be generally assumed that Poland will be next in turn" (TC – 76).

Hitler, after the Polish invasion, boasted that it was the Austrian and Czechoslovakian triumphs by which "the basis for the action against Poland was laid" (789 – PS). Goering suited the act to the purpose and gave immediate instructions to exploit for the further strengthening of the German war potential, first the Sudetenland, and then the whole Protectorate (R – 133).

By May of 1939 the Nazi preparations had ripened to the point that Hitler confided to the Defendants Goering, Raeder, Keitel, and others his readiness "to attack Poland at the first suitable opportunity," even though he recognized that "further successes cannot be attained without the shedding of blood." The larcenous motives behind this decision he made plain in words that echoed the covetous theme of *Mein Kampf*:

"Circumstances must be adapted to aims. This is impossible without invasion of foreign states or attacks upon foreign property. Living space in proportion to the magnitude of the state is the basis of all powerfurther successes cannot be attained without expanding our living space in the East..." (L – 79).

While a credulous world slumbered, snugly blanketed with perfidious assurances of peaceful intentions, the Nazis prepared not as before for a war but now for the war. The Defendants Goering, Keitel, Raeder, Frick, and Funk, with others, met as the Reich Defense Council in June of 1939. The minutes, authenticated by Goering, are revealing evidences of the way in which each step of Nazi planning dovetailed with every other. These five key defendants, 3 months before the first Panzer unit had knifed into Poland, were laying plans for "employment of the population in wartime," and had gone so far as to classify industry for priority in labor supply after "5 million servicemen had been called up." They decided upon measures to avoid "confusion when mobilization takes place," and declared a purpose "to gain and maintain the lead in the decisive initial weeks of a war." They then planned to use in production prisoners of war, criminal prisoners, and concentration camp inmates. They then decided on "compulsory work for women in wartime." They had already passed on applications from 1,172,000 specialist workmen for classification as indispensable, and had approved 727,000 of them. They boasted that orders to workers to report for duty "are ready and tied up in bundles at the labor offices." And they resolved to increase the industrial manpower supply by bringing into Germany "hundreds of thousands of workers" from the Protectorate to be "housed together in hutments" 3787 – PS).

It is the minutes of this significant conclave of many key defendants which disclose how the plan to start the war was coupled with the plan to wage the war through the use of illegal sources of labor to maintain production. Hitler, in announcing his plan to attack Poland, had already foreshadowed the slave-labor program as one of its corollaries when he cryptically pointed out to the Defendants Goering, Raeder, Keitel, and others that the Polish population "will be available as a source of labor" (L – 79). This was part of the plan made good by Frank, who as Governor General notified Goering that he would supply "at least one million male and female agricultural and industrial workers to the Reich" (1374 – PS), and by Sauckel, whose impressments throughout occupied territory aggregated numbers equal to the total population of some of the smaller nations of Europe.

Here also comes to the surface the link between war labor and concentration camps, a manpower source that was increasingly used and with increasing cruelty. An agreement between Himmler and the Minister of Justice Thierack in 1942 provided for "the delivery of antisocial elements from the execution of their sentence to the Reichsfuhrer SS to be worked to death" (654 – PS). An SS directive provided that bedridden prisoners be drafted for work to be performed in bed (1395 – PS). The Gestapo ordered 46,000 Jews arrested to increase the "recruitment of manpower into the concentration camps" (1472 – PS). One hundred thousand Jews were brought from Hungary to augment the camps' manpower (R – 124). On the initiative of the Defendant Donitz, concentration camp labor was used in the construction of submarines (C – 195). Concentration camps were thus geared into war production on the one hand, and into the administration of justice and the political aims of the Nazis on the other.

The use of prisoner-of-war labor as then planned in that meeting also grew with German needs. At a time when every German soldier was needed at the front and forces were not available at home, Russian prisoners of war were forced to man anti-aircraft guns against Allied planes. Field Marshal Milch reflected the Nazi merriment at this flagrant violation of international law, saying: ". . . this is an amusing thing, that the Russians must work the guns" (R – 124).

The orders for the treatment of Soviet prisoners of war were so ruthless that Admiral Canaris, pointing out that they would "result in arbitrary mistreatments and killing," protested to the OKW against them as breaches of international law. The reply of Keitel was unambiguous. He said:

"The objections arise from the military conception of chivalrous warfare! This is the destruction of an ideology! Therefore, I approve and back the measures" (C – 338).

The Geneva Convention would have been thrown overboard openly except that Jodl objected because he wanted the benefits of Allied observance of it while it was not being allowed to hamper the Germans in any way.

Other crimes in the conduct of warfare were planned with equal thoroughness as a means of insuring victory of German arms. In October 1938, almost a year before the start of the war, the large scale violation of the established rules of warfare was contemplated as a policy, and the Supreme Command circulated a "most secret" list of devious explanations to be given by the Propaganda Minister in such cases (C – 2). Even before this time commanders of the Armed Forces were instructed to employ any means of warfare so long as it facilitated victory (L – 211). After the war was in progress the orders increased in savagery. A typical Keitel order, demanding the use of the"most brutal means," provided that: ". . . It is the duty of the troops to use all means without restriction, even against women and children, so long as it insures success."

The German naval forces were no more immune from the infection than the land forces. Raeder ordered violations of the accepted rules of warfare wherever necessary to gain strategic successes (C – 157). Donitz urged his submarine crews not to rescue survivors of torpedoed enemy ships in order to cripple merchant shipping of the Allied Nations by decimating their crews (D – 642).

Thus, the war crimes against Allied forces and the crimes against humanity committed in occupied territories are incontestably part of the program for making the war because, in the German calculations, they were indispensable to its hope of success.

Similarly, the whole group of prewar crimes, including the persecutions within Germany, fall into place around the plan for aggressive war like stones in a finely wrought mosaic. Nowhere is the whole catalog of crimes of Nazi oppression and terrorism within Germany so well integrated with the crime of war as in that strange mixture of wind and wisdom which makes up the testimony of Hermann Goering. In describing the aims of the Nazi program before the seizure of power, Goering said:

"The first question was to achieve and establish a different political structure for Germany which would enable Germany to obtain against the dictate (of Versailles) not only a protest but an objection of such a nature that it would actually be considered."

With these purposes, Goering admitted that the plan was made to overthrow the Weimar Republic to seize power, and to carry out the Nazi program by whatever means were necessary, whether legal or illegal.

From Goering's cross-examination we learn how necessarily the whole program of crime followed. Because they considered a strong state necessary to get rid of the Versailles Treaty, they adopted the *Fuhrerprinzip*. Having seized power, the Nazis thought it necessary to protect it by abolishing parliamentary government and suppressing all organized opposition from political parties (L – 83). This was reflected in the philosophy of Goering that the opera was more important than the Reichstag. Even the "opposition of each individual was not tolerated unless it was a matter of unimportance." To insure the suppression of opposition a secret police force was necessary. In order to eliminate incorrigible opponents, it was necessary to establish concentration camps and to resort to the device of protective custody. Protective custody, Goering testified, meant that:

"People were arrested and taken into protective custody who had committed no crime but who one might expect, if they remained in freedom, would do all sorts of things to damage the German State."

The same war purpose was dominant in the persecution of the Jews. In the beginning, fanaticism and political opportunism played a principal part, for anti-Semitism and its allied scapegoat, mythology, was a vehicle on which the Nazis rode to power. It was for this reason that the filthy Streicher and the blasphemous Rosenberg were welcomed at Party rallies and made leaders and officials of the State or Party. But the Nazis soon regarded the Jews as foremost among the opposition to the police state with which they planned to put forward their plans of military aggression. Fear of their pacifism and their opposition to strident nationalism was given as the reason that the Jews had to be driven from the political and economic life of Germany. Accordingly, they were transported like cattle to the concentration camps, where they were utilized as a source of forced labor for war purposes.

At a meeting held on 11/12/1938, 2 days after the violent anti-Jewish pogroms instigated by Goebbels and carried out by the Party Leadership Corps and the SA, the program for the elimination of Jews from the German economy was mapped out by Goering, Funk, Heydrich, Goebbels, and the other top Nazis. The measures adopted included confinement of the Jews in ghettos, cutting off their food supply, "Aryanizing" their shops, and restricting their freedom of movement (1816 – PS). Here another purpose behind the Jewish persecutions crept in, for it was the wholesale confiscation of their property which helped finance German rearmament. Although Schacht's plan to have foreign money ransom the entire race within Germany was not adopted, the Jews were stripped to the point where Goering was able to advise the Reich Defense Council that the critical situation of the Reich exchequer, due to rearmament, had been relieved "through the billion Reichsmark fine imposed on Jewry, and through profits accrued to the Reich in the Aryanization of Jewish enterprises" (3575 – PS).

A glance over the dock will show that, despite quarrels among themselves, each defendant played a part which fitted in with every other, and that all advanced the common plan. It contradicts experience that men of such diverse backgrounds and talents should so forward each other's aims by coincidence.

The large and varied role of Goering was half militarist and half gangster. He stuck his pudgy finger in every pie. He used his SA musclemen to help bring the gang into power. In order to entrench that power he contrived to have the Reichstag burned, established the Gestapo, and created the concentration camps. He was equally adept at massacring opponents and at framing scandals to get rid of stubborn generals. He built up the Luftwaffe and hurled it at his defenseless neighbors. He was among the foremost in harrying Jews out of the land. By mobilizing the total economic resources of Germany he made possible the waging of the war which he had taken a large part in planning. He was, next to Hitler, the man who tied the activities of all the defendants together in a common effort.

The parts played by the other defendants, although less comprehensive and less spectacular than that of the Reichsmarshal, were nevertheless integral and necessary contributions to the joint undertaking, without any one of which the success of the common enterprise would have been in jeopardy. There are many specific deeds of which these men have been proven guilty. No purpose would be servednor indeed is time availableto review all the crimes which the evidence has charged up to their names. Nevertheless, in viewing the conspiracy as a whole and as an operating mechanism, it may be well to recall briefly the outstanding services which each of the men in the dock rendered to the common cause.

The zealot Hess, before succumbing to wanderlust, was the engineer tending the Party machinery, passing orders and propaganda down to the Leadership Corps, supervising every aspect of Party activities, and maintaining the organization as a loyal and' ready instrument of power. When apprehensions abroad threatened the success of the Nazi regime for conquest, it was the duplicitous Ribbentrop, the salesman of deception, who was detailed to pour wine on the troubled waters of suspicion by preaching the gospel of limited and peaceful intentions. Keitel, the weak and willing tool, delivered the Armed Forces, the instrument of aggression, over to the Party and directed them in executing its felonous designs.

Kaltenbrunner, the grand inquisitor, took up the bloody mantle of Heydrich to stifle opposition and terrorize compliance, and buttressed the power of National Socialism on a foundation of guiltless corpses. It was Rosenberg, the intellectual high priest of the "master race," who provided the doctrine of hatred which gave the impetus for the annihilation of Jewry, and who put his infidel theories into practice against the Eastern Occupied Territories. His woolly philosophy also added boredom to the long list of Nazi atrocities. The fanatical Frank, who solidified Nazi control by establishing the new order of authority without law, so that the will of the Party was the only test of legality, proceeded to export his lawlessness to Poland, which he governed with the lash of Caesar and whose population he reduced to sorrowing remnants. Frick, the ruthless organizer, helped the Party to seize power, supervised the police agencies to insure that it stayed in power, and chained the economy of Bohemia and Moravia to the German war machine.

Streicher, the venomous vulgarian, manufactured and distributed obscene racial libels which incited the populace to accept and assist the progressively savage operations of "race purification." As Minister of Economics Funk accelerated the pace of rearmament and as Reichsbank president banked for the SS the gold teeth fillings of concentration camp victims, probably the most ghoulish collateral in banking history. It was Schacht, the facade of starched respectability, who in the early days provided the window dressing, the bait for the hesitant, and whose wizardry later made it possible for Hitler to finance the colossal rearmament program, and to do it secretly.

Donitz, Hitler's legatee of defeat, promoted the success of the Nazi aggressions by instructing his pack of submarine killers to conduct warfare at sea with the illegal ferocity of the jungle. Raeder, the political admiral, stealthily built up the German Navy in defiance of the Versailles Treaty, and then put it to use in a series of aggressions which he had taken a leading part in planning. Von Schirach, poisoner of a generation, initiated the German youth in Nazi doctrine, trained them in legions for service in the SS and Wehrmacht, and delivered them up to the Party as fanatic, unquestioning executors of its will.

Sauckel, the greatest and cruelest slaver since the Pharaohs of Egypt, produced desperately needed manpower by driving foreign peoples into the land of bondage on a scale unknown even in the ancient days of tyranny in the kingdom of the Nile. Jodl, betrayer of the traditions of his profession, led the Wehrmacht in violating its own code of military honor in order to carry out the barbarous aims of Nazi policy. Von Papen, pious agent of an infidel regime, held the stirrup while Hitler vaulted into the saddle, lubricated the Austrian annexation, and devoted his diplomatic cunning to the service of Nazi objectives abroad.

Seyss-Inquart, spearhead of the Austrian fifth column, took over the government of his own country only to make a present of it to Hitler, and then, moving north, brought terror and oppression to the Netherlands and pillaged its economy for the benefit of the German juggernaut. Von Neurath, the old-school diplomat, who cast the pearls of his experience before Nazis, guided Nazi diplomacy in the early years, soothed the fears of prospective victims, and, as Reich Protector of Bohemia and Moravia, strengthened the German position for the coming attack on Poland. Speer, as Minister of Armaments and Production, joined in planning and executing the program to dragoon prisoners of war and foreign workers into German war industries, which waxed in output while the laborers waned in starvation. Fritzsche, radio propaganda chief, by manipulation of the truth goaded German public opinion into frenzied support of the regime and anesthetized the independent judgment of the population so that they did without question their masters' bidding. And Bormann, who has not accepted our invitation to this reunion, sat at the throttle of the vast and powerful engine of the Party, guiding it in the ruthless execution of Nazi policies, from the scourging of the Christian Church to the lynching of captive Allied airmen.

The activities of all these defendants, despite their varied backgrounds and talents, were joined with the efforts of other conspirators not now in the dock, who played still other essential roles. They blend together into one consistent and militant pattern animated by a common objective to reshape the map of Europe by force of arms. Some of these defendants were ardent members of the Nazi movement from its birth. Others, less fanatical, joined the common enterprise later, after success had made participation attractive by the promise of rewards. This group of latter-day converts remedied a crucial defect in the ranks of the original true believers, for as Dr. Siemers has pointed out in his summation:

". . .There were no specialists among the National Socialists for the particular tasks. Most of the National Socialist collaborators did not previously follow a trade requiring technical education."

It was the fatal weakness of the early Nazi band that it lacked technical competence. It could not from among its own ranks make up a government capable of carrying out all the projects necessary to realize its aims. Therein lies the special crime and betrayal of men like Schacht and Von Neurath, Speer and Von Papen, Raeder and Donitz, Keitel and Jodl. It is doubtful whether the Nazi master plan could have succeeded without their specialized intelligence which they so willingly put at its command. They did so with knowledge of its announced aims and methods, and continued their services after practice had confirmed the direction in which they were tending. Their superiority to the average run of Nazi mediocrity is not their excuse. It is their condemnation.

The dominant fact which stands out from all the thousands of pages of the record of this Trial is that the central crime of the whole group of Nazi crimesthe attack on the peace of the world was clearly and deliberately planned. The beginning of these wars of aggression was not an unprepared and spontaneous springing to arms by a population excited by some current indignation. A week before the invasion of Poland Hitler told his military commanders:

"I shall give a propagandist cause for starting warnever mind whether it be plausible or not. The victor shall not be asked later on whether we told the truth or not. In starting and making a war, it is not the right that matters, but victory (1014 – PS).

The propagandist incident was duly provided by dressing concentration camp inmates in Polish uniforms, in order to create the appearance of a Polish attack on a German frontier radio station (2751 – PS). The plan to occupy Belgium, Holland, and Luxembourg first appeared as early as August 1938 in connection with the plan for attack on Czechoslovakia (375 – PS). The intention to attack became a program in May 1939, when Hitler told his commanders that "the Dutch and Belgian air bases must be occupied by armed forces. Declarations of neutrality must be ignored" (L – 79).

Thus, the follow-up wars were planned before the first was launched. These were the most carefully plotted wars in all history. Scarcely a step in their terrifying succession and progress failed to move according to the master blueprint or the subsidiary schedules and timetables until long after the crimes of aggression were consummated.

Nor were the war crimes and the crimes against humanity unplanned, isolated, or spontaneous offenses. Aside from our undeniable evidence of their plotting, it is sufficient to ask whether 6 million people could be separated from the population of several nations on the basis of their blood and birth, could be destroyed and their bodies disposed of, except that the operation fitted into the general scheme of government. Could the enslavement of 5 millions of laborers, their impressment into service, their transportation to Germany, their allocation to work where they would be most useful, their maintenance, if slow starvation can be called maintenance, and their guarding have been accomplished if it did not fit into the common plan? Could hundreds of concentration camps located throughout Germany, built to accommodate hundreds of thousands of victims, and each requiring labor and materials for construction, manpower to operate and supervise, and close gearing into the economycould such efforts have been expended under German autocracy if they had not suited the plan? Has the Teutonic passion for organization suddenly become famous for its toleration of nonconforming activity? Each part of the plan fitted into every other. The slave-labor program meshed with the needs of industry and agriculture, and these in turn synchronized with the military machine. The elaborate propaganda apparatus geared with the program to dominate the people and incite them to a war their sons would have to fight. The armament industries were fed by the concentration camps. The concentration camps were fed by the Gestapo. The Gestapo was fed by the spy system of the Nazi Party. Nothing was permitted under the Nazi iron rule that was not in accordance with the program. Everything of consequence that took place in this regimented society was but a manifestation of a premeditated and unfolding purpose to secure the Nazi State a place in the sun by casting all others into darkness.

The defendants meet this overwhelming case, some by admitting a limited responsibility, some by putting the blame on others, and some by taking the position in effect that while there have been enormous crimes there are no criminals. Time will not permit me to examine each individual and particular defense, but there are certain lines of defense common to so many cases that they deserve some consideration.

Counsel for many of the defendants seek to dismiss the conspiracy or common planning charge on the ground that the pattern of the

Nazi plan does not fit into the concept of conspiracy applicable in German law to the plotting of a highway robbery or a burglary. Their concept of conspiracy is in the terms of a stealthy meeting in the dead of night, in a secluded hideout, in which a small group of felons plot every detail of a specific crime. The Charter forestalls resort to such parochial and narrow concepts of conspiracy taken from local law by using the additional and nontechnical term, "common plan." Omitting entirely the alternative term of "conspiracy," the Charter reads that "leaders, organizers, instigators, and accomplices participating in the formulation or execution of a common plan to commit any of the described crimes are responsible for all acts performed by any persons in execution of such plan."

The Charter concept of a common plan really represents the conspiracy principle in an international context. A common plan or conspiracy to seize the machinery of a state, to commit crimes against the peace of the world, to blot a race out of existence, to enslave millions, and to subjugate and loot whole nations cannot be thought of in the same terms as the plotting of petty crimes, although the same underlying principles are applicable. Little gangsters may plan which will carry a pistol and which a stiletto, who will approach a victim from the front and who from behind, and where they will waylay him. But in planning a war, the pistol becomes a Wehrmacht, the stiletto, a Luftwaffe. Where to strike is not a choice of dark alleys, but a matter of world geography. The operation involves the manipulation of public opinion, the law of the state, the police power, industry, and finance. The baits and bluffs must be translated into a nation's foreign policy. Likewise the degree of stealth which points to a guilty purpose in a conspiracy will depend upon its object. The clandestine preparations of a state against international society, although camouflaged to those abroad, might be quite open and notorious among its own people. But stealth is not an essential ingredient of such planning. Parts of the common plan may be proclaimed from the housetops, as anti-Semitism was, and parts of it kept under cover s rearmament for a long time was. It is a matter of strategy how much of the preparation shall be made public, as was Goering's announcement in 1935 of the creation of an air force, and how much shall be kept covert, as in the case of the Nazis' use of shovels to teach "labor corps" the manual of arms (3054 – PS). The forms of this grand type of conspiracy are amorphous, the means are opportunistic, and neither can divert the law from getting at the substance of things.

The defendants contend, however, that there could be no conspiracy involving aggressive war because: (1) None of the Nazis wanted war; (2) rearmament was only intended to provide the strength to make Germany's voice heard in the family of nations and (3) the wars were not in fact aggressive wars but were defensive against a "Bolshevik menace."

When we analyze the argument that the Nazis did not want war it comes down, in substance, to this: "The record looks bad indeed objectively, but when you consider the state of my mind, subjectively I hated war. I knew the horrors of war. I wanted peace." I am not so sure of this. I am even less willing to accept Goering's description of the General Staff as pacifist. However, it will not injure our case to admit that as an abstract proposition none of these defendants liked war. But they wanted things which they knew they could not get without war. They wanted their neighbors' lands and goods. Their philosophy seems to be that if the neighbors would not acquiesce, then they are the aggressors and are to blame for the war. The fact is, however, that war never became terrible to the Nazis until it came home to them, until it exposed their deceptive assurances to the German people that German cities, like the ruined one in which we meet, would be invulnerable. From then on, war was terrible.

But again the defendants claim, "To be sure, we were building guns. But not to shoot. They were only to give us weight in negotiating." At its best this argument amounts to a contention that the military forces were intended for blackmail, not for battle. The threat of military invasion which forced the Austrian *Anschluss*, the threats which preceded Munich, and Goering's threat to bomb the beautiful city of Prague if the President of Czechoslovakia did not consent to a Protectorate, are examples of what the defendants have in mind when they talk of arming to back negotiation.

But from the very nature of German demands, the day was bound to come when some country would refuse to buy its peace, would refuse to pay danegelt, "for the end of that game is oppression and shame, and the nation that plays it is lost."

Did these defendants then intend to withdraw German demands, or was Germany to enforce them and manipulate propaganda so as to place the blame for the war on the nation so unreasonable as to resist? Events have answered that question, and documents such as Admiral

Carl's memorandum, earlier quoted, leave no doubt that the events occurred as anticipated.

But some of the defendants argue that the wars were not aggressive and were only intended to protect Germany against some eventual danger from the "menace of Communism," which was something of an obsession with many Nazis.

At the outset this argument of self-defense falls because it completely ignores this damning combination of facts clearly established in the record: First, the enormous and rapid German preparations for war; second, the repeatedly avowed intentions of the German leaders to attack, which I have previously cited; and third, the fact that a series of wars occurred in which German forces struck the first blows, without warning, across the borders of other nations. Even if it could be shown, which it cannot, that the Russian war was really defensive, such is demonstrably not the case with those wars which preceded it. It may also be pointed out that even those who would have you believe that Germany was menaced by Communism also compete with each other in describing their opposition to the disastrous Russian venture. Is it reasonable that they would have opposed that war if it were undertaken in good-faith self-defense? The frivolous character of the self-defense theory on the facts it is sought to compensate, as advocates often do, by resort to a theory of law. Dr. Jahrreiss, in his scholarly argument for the defense, rightly points out that no treaty provision and no principle of law denied Germany, as a sovereign nation, the right of self-defense. He follows with the assertion for which there is authority in classic international law, that ". . . every state is alone judge of whether in a given case it is waging a war of self-defense."

It is not necessary to examine the validity of an abstract principle which does not apply to the facts of our case. I do not doubt that if a nation arrived at a judgment that it must resort to war in self-defense, because of conditions affording reasonable grounds for such an honest judgment, any tribunal would accord it great and perhaps conclusive weight, even if later events proved that judgment mistaken. But the facts in this case call for no such deference to honest judgment because no such judgment was ever pretended much less honestly made.

In all the documents which disclose the planning and rationalization of these attacks, not one sentence has been or can be cited to show a good-faith fear of attack. It may be that statesmen of other nations lacked the courage forthrightly and fully to disarm. Perhaps they suspected the secret rearmament of Germany. But if they hesitated to abandon arms, they did not hesitate to neglect them. Germany well knew that her former enemies had allowed their armaments to fall into decay, so little did they contemplate another war. Germany faced a Europe that not only was unwilling to attack, but was too weak and pacifist even adequately to defend, and went to the very verge of dishonor, if not beyond, to buy its peace. The minutes we have shown you of the Nazis' secret conclaves identify no potential attacker. They bristle with the spirit of aggression and not of defense. They contemplate always territorial expansion, not the maintenance of territorial integrity.

Minister of War Von Blomberg, in his 1937 directive prescribing general principles for the preparation for war of the Armed Forces has given the lie to these feeble claims of self-defense. He stated at that time:

"The general political situation justifies the supposition that Germany need not consider an attack on any side. Grounds for this are, in addition to the lack of desire for war in almost all nations, particularly the Western Powers, the deficiencies in the preparedness for war in a number of states and of Russia in particular."

Nevertheless, he recommended:

". . . a continuous preparation for war in order to (a) counterattack at any time, and (b) to enable the military exploitation of politically favorable opportunities should they occur."

If these defendants may now cynically plead self-defense, although no good-faith need of self-defense was asserted or contemplated by any responsible leader at that time, it reduces nonaggression treaties to a legal absurdity. They become additional instruments of deception in the hands of the aggressor, and traps for well-meaning nations. If there be in nonaggression pacts an implied condition that each nation may make a bona fide judgment as to the necessity for self-defense against imminent threatened attack, it certainly cannot be invoked to shelter those who never made any such judgment at all.

In opening this case I ventured to predict that there would be no serious denial that the crimes charged were committed, and that the issue would concern the responsibility of particular defendants. The defendants have fulfilled that prophecy. Generally, they do not deny that these things happened, but it is contended that they "just happened," and that they were not the result of a common plan or conspiracy.

One of the chief reasons the defendants say there was no conspiracy is the argument that conspiracy was impossible with a dictator. The argument runs that they all had to obey Hitler's orders, which had the force of law in the German State, and hence obedience could not be made the basis of an original charge. In this way it is explained that while there have been wholesale killings, there have been no murderers.

This argument is an effort to evade Article 8 of the Charter, which provides that the order of the Government or of a superior shall not free a defendant from responsibility but can only be considered in mitigation. This provision of the Charter corresponds with the justice and with the realities of the situation, as indicated in Defendant Speer's description of what he considered to be the common responsibility of the leaders of the German nation:

". . . with reference to utterly decisive matters, there is total responsibility. There must be total responsibility insofar as a person is one of the leaders, because who else could assume responsibility for the development of events, if not the immediate associates who work with and around the head of the State?"

Again he told the Tribunal:

". . . it is impossible after the catastrophe to evade this total responsibility. If the war had been won, the leaders would also have assumed total responsibility."

Like much of Defense Counsel's abstract arguments, the contention that the absolute power of Hitler precluded a conspiracy crumbles in the face of the facts of record. The *Fuhrerprinzip* of absolutism was itself a part of the common plan, as Goering has pointed out. The defendants may have become the slaves of a dictator, but he was their dictator. To make him such was, as Goering has testified, the object of the Nazi movement from the beginning. Every Nazi took this oath:

"I pledge eternal allegiance to Adolf Hitler. I pledge unconditional obedience to him and the Fuhrers appointed by him" (1893 – PS).

Moreover, they forced everybody else in their power to take it This oath was illegal under German law, which made it criminal to become a member of an organization in which obedience to "unknown superiors or unconditional obedience to known superiors is pledged." These men destroyed free government in Germany and now plead to be excused from responsibility because they became slaves. They are in the position of the fictional boy who murdered his father and mother and then pleaded for leniency because he was n orphan.

What these men have overlooked is that Adolf Hitler's acts are their acts. It was these men among millions of others, and it was these men leading millions of others, who built up Adolf Hitler and vested in his psychopathic personality not only innumerable lesser decisions but the supreme issue of war or peace. They intoxicated him with power and adulation. They fed his hates and aroused his fears. They put a loaded gun in his eager hands. It was left to Hitler to pull the trigger, and when he did they all at that time approved. His guilt stands admitted, by some defendants reluctantly, by some vindictively. But his guilt is the guilt of the whole dock, and of every man in it.

But it is urged that these defendants could not be in agreement on a common plan or in a conspiracy because they were fighting among themselves or belonged to different factions or cliques. Of course, it is not necessary that men should agree on everything in order to agree on enough things to make them liable for a criminal conspiracy. Unquestionably there were conspiracies within the conspiracy, and intrigues and rivalries and battles for power. Schacht and Goering disagreed, but over which of them should control the economy, not over whether the economy should be regimented for war. Goering claims to have departed from the plan because through Dahlerus he conducted some negotiations with men of influence in England just before the Polish war. But it is perfectly clear that this was not an effort to prevent aggression against Poland but to make that aggression successful and safe by obtaining English neutrality (TC – 90). Rosenberg and Goering may have had some differences as to how stolen art should be distributed but they had none about how it should be stolen. Jodl and Goering may have disagreed about whether to denounce the Geneva Convention, but they have never disagreed about violating it. And so it goes through the whole long and sordid story. Nowhere do we find a single instance where any one of the defendants stood up against the rest and said: "This thing is wrong and I will not go along with it." Wherever they differed, their differences were as to method or disputes over jurisdiction, but always within the framework of the common plan.

Some of the defendants also contend that in any.event there was no conspiracy to commit war crimes or crimes against humanity because cabinet members never met with the military to plan these acts. But these crimes were only the inevitable and incidental results of the plan to commit the aggression for *Lebensraum* purposes. Hitler stated, at a conference with his commanders, that: "The main objective in Poland is the destruction of the enemy and not the reaching of a certain geographical line" (1014 – PS). Frank picked up the tune and suggested that when their usefulness was exhausted, ". . . then, for all I care, mincemeat can be made of the Poles and Ukrainians and all the others who run around here, it does not matter what happens" (2233 – PS).

Reichskommissar Koch in the Ukraine echoed the refrain: "I will draw the very last out of this country. I did not come to spread bliss..." (1130 – PS).

This was *Lebensraum* on its seamy side. Could men of their practical intelligence expect to get neighboring lands free from the claims of their tenants without committing crimes against humanity? The last stand of each defendant is that even if there was a conspiracy, he was not in it. It is therefore important in examining their attempts at avoidance of responsibility to know, first of all, just what it is that a conspiracy charge comprehends and punishes. In conspiracy we do not punish one man for another man's crime. We seek to punish each for his own crime of joining a common criminal plan in which others also participated. The measure of the criminality of the plan and therefore of the guilt of each participant is, of course, the sum total of crimes committed by all in executing the plan. But the gist of the offense is participation in the formulation or execution of the plan. These are rules which every society has found necessary in order to reach men, like these defendants, who never get blood on their own hands but who lay plans that result in the shedding of blood. All over Germany today, in every zone of occupation, little men who carried out these criminal policies under orders are being convicted and punished. It would present a vast and unforgivable caricature of justice if the men who planned these policies and directed these little men should escape all penalty. These men in this dock, on the face of this record, were not strangers to this program of crime, nor was their connection with it remote or obscure. We find them in the very heart of it. The positions they held show that we have chosen defendants of self evident responsibility. They are the very top surviving authorities in their respective fields and in the Nazi State. No one lives who, at least until the very last moments of the war, outranked Goering in position, power, and influence. No soldier stood above Keitel and Jodl, and no sailor above Raeder and Donitz. Who can be responsible for the diplomacy of duplicity if not the Foreign Ministers, Von Neurath and Ribbentrop, and the diplomatic handy man Von Papen? Who should be answerable for the oppressive administration of occupied countries if Gauleiters, protectors, governors and Kommissars such as Frank, Seyss-Inquart, Frick, Von Schirach, Von Neurath, and Rosenberg are not? Where shall we look for those who mobilized the economy for total war if we overlook Schacht and Speer and Funk? Who was the master of the great slaving enterprise if it was not Sauckel? Where shall we find the hand that ran the concentration camps if it was not the hand of Kaltenbrunner? And who whipped up the hates and fears of the public, and manipulated the Party organizations to incite these crimes, if not Hess, Von Schirach, Fritzsche, Bormann, and the unspeakable Julius Streicher? The list of defendants is made up of men who played indispensable and reciprocal parts in this tragedy. The photographs and the films show them again and again together on important occasions. The documents show them agreed on policies and on methods, and all working aggressively for the expansion of Germany by force.

Each of these men made a real contribution to the Nazi plan. Each man had a key part. Deprive the Nazi regime of the functions performed by a Schacht, a Sauckel, a Von Papen, or a Goering and you have a different regime. Look down the rows of fallen men and picture them as the photographic and documentary evidence shows them to have been in their days of power. Is there one who did not substantially advance the conspiracy along its bloody path toward its bloody goal? Can we assume that the great effort of these men's lives was directed toward ends they never suspected?

To escape the implications of their positions and the inference of guilt from their activities, the defendants are almost unanimous in one defense. The refrain is heard time and again: These men were without authority, without knowledge, without influence without importance. Funk summed up the general self-abasement of the dock in his plaintive lament that: "I always, so to speak, came up to the door, but I was not permitted to enter."

In the testimony of each defendant, at some point there was reached the familiar blank wall: Nobody knew anything about what was going on. Time after time we have heard the chorus from the dock: "I only heard about these things here for the first time."

These men saw no evil, spoke none, and none was uttered in their presence. This claim might sound very plausible if made by one defendant. But when we put all their stories together, the impression which emerges of the Third Reich, which was to last a thousand years, is ludicrous. If we combine only the stories of the front bench, this is the ridiculous composite picture of Hitler's Government that emerges. It was composed of:

A Number 2 man who knew nothing of the excesses of the Gestapo which he created, and never suspected the Jewish extermination program although he was the signer of over a score of decrees which instituted the persecutions of that race;

A Number 3 man who was merely an innocent middleman transmitting Hitler's orders without even reading them, like a postman or delivery boy;

A foreign minister who knew little of foreign affairs and nothing of foreign policy;

A field marshal who issued orders to the Armed Forces but had no idea of the results they would have in practice;

A security chief who was of the impression that the policing functions of his Gestapo and SD were somewhat on the order of directing traffic;

A Party philosopher who was interested in historical research and had no idea of the violence which his philosophy was inciting in the twentieth century;

A governor general of Poland who reigned but did not rule;

A Gauleiter of Franconia whose occupation was to pour forth filthy writings about the Jews, but who had no idea that anybody would read them;

A minister of interior who knew not even what went on in the interior of his own office, much less the interior of his own department, and nothing at all about the interior of Germany;

A Reichsbank president who was totally ignorant of what went in and out of the vaults of his bank;

And a plenipotentiary for the war economy who secretly marshaled the entire economy for armament, but had no idea it had anything to do with war.

This may seem like a fantastic exaggeration, but this is what you would actually be obliged to conclude if you were to acquit these defendants.

They do protest too much. They deny knowing what was common knowledge. They deny knowing plans and programs that were as public as *Mein Kampf* and the Party program. They deny even knowing the contents of documents they received and acted upon.

Nearly all the defendants take two or more conflicting positions. Let us illustrate the inconsistencies of their positions by the record of one defendant who, if pressed, would himself concede that he is the most intelligent, honorable, and innocent man in the dock. That is Schacht. And this is the effect of his own testimony, but let us not forget that I recite it not against him alone, but because most of its self-contradictions are found in the testimony of several defendants:

Schacht did not openly join the Nazi movement until it had won, nor openly desert it until it had lost. He admits that he never gave it public opposition, but asserts that he never gave it private loyalty. When we demand of him why he did not stop the criminal course of the regime in which he was a minister, he says he had not a bit of influence. When we ask why he remained a member of the criminal regime, he tells us that by sticking on he expected to moderate its program. Like a Brahmin among untouchables, he could not bear to mingle with the Nazi socially, but never could he afford to separate from them politically. Of all the Nazi aggressions by which he now claims to have been shocked there is not one that he did not support before the world with the weight of his name and prestige. Having armed Hitler to blackmail a continent, his answer now is to blame England and France for yielding.

Schacht always fought for his position in a regime he now affects to despise. He sometimes disagreed with his Nazi confederates about what was expedient in reaching their goal, but he never dissented from the goal itself. When he did break with, them in the twilight of the regime, it was over tactics, not principles. From then on he never ceased to urge others to risk their positions and their necks to forward his plots, but never on any occasion did he hazard either of his own. He now boasts that he personally would have shot Hitler if he had had the opportunity, but the German newsreel shows that even after the fall of France, when he faced the living Hitler, he stepped out of line to grasp the hand he now claims to loathe and hung upon the words of the man he now says he thought unworthy of belief. Schacht says he steadily "sabotaged" the Hitler Government. Yet the most relentless secret service in the world never detected him doing the regime any harm until long after he knew the war to be lost and the Nazis doomed. Schacht, who dealt in hedges all his life, always kept himself in a position to claim that he was in either camp. The plea for him is as specious on analysis as it is persuasive on first sight. Schacht represents the most dangerous and reprehensible type of opportunism, that of the man of influential position who is ready to join a movement that he knows to be wrong because he thinks it is winning.

These defendants, unable to deny that they were the men in the very top ranks of power, and unable to deny that the crimes I have outlined actually happened, know that their own denials are incredible unless they can suggest someone who is guilty.

The defendants have been unanimous, when pressed, in shifting the blame on other men, sometimes on one and sometimes on another. But the names they have repeatedly picked are Hitler, Himmler, Heydrich, Goebbels, and Bormann. All of these are dead or missing. No matter how hard we have pressed the defendants on the stand, they have never pointed the finger at a living man as guilty. It is a temptation to ponder the wondrous workings of a fate which has left only the guilty dead and only the innocent alive. It is almost too remarkable.

The chief villain on whom blame is placed — some of the defendants vie with each other in producing appropriate epithets — is Hitler. He is the man at whom nearly every defendant has pointed an accusing finger.

I shall not dissent from this consensus, nor do I deny that all these dead and missing men shared the guilt. In crimes so reprehensible that degrees of guilt have lost their significance they may have played the most evil parts. But their guilt cannot exculpate the defendants. Hitler did not carry all responsibility to the grave with him. All the guilt is not wrapped in Himmler's shroud. It was these dead men whom these living chose to be their partners in this great conspiratorial brotherhood, and the crimes that they did together they must pay for one by one.

It may well be said that Hitler's final crime was against the land he had ruled. He was a mad messiah who started the war without cause and prolonged it without reason. If he could not rule he cared not what happened to Germany. As Fritzsche has told us from the stand, Hitler tried to use the defeat of Germany for the self-destruction of the German people. He continued to fight when he knew it could not be won, and continuance meant only ruin. Speer, in this courtroom, has described it as follows:

" . . . The sacrifices which were made on both sides after January 1945 were without sense. The dead of this period will be the accusers of the man responsible for the continuation of that fight, Adolf Hitler, just as much as the destroyed cities, destroyed in that last phase, who had lost tremendous cultural values and tremendous numbers of dwellings.... The German people," he said, "remained faithful to Adolf Hitler until the end. He has betrayed them knowingly. He has tried to throw them into the abyss. . ."

Hitler ordered everyone else to fight to the last and then retreated into death by his own hand. But he left life as he lived it, a deceiver; he left the official report that he had died in battle. This was the man whom these defendants exalted to a Fuhrer. It was they who conspired to get him absolute authority over all of Germany. And in the end he and the system they created for him brought the ruin of them all. As stated by Speer on cross-examination:

". . . the tremendous danger, however, contained in this totalitarian system only became abundantly clear at the moment when we were approaching the end. It was then that one could see what the meaning of the principle was, namely, that every order should be carried out without any criticism. Everything . . . you have seen in the way of orders which were carried out without any consideration, did after all turn out to be mistakes . . . This system, let me put it like this, to the end of the system it had become clear what tremendous dangers are contained in any such system, as such quite apart from Hitler's principle. The combination of Hitler and this system, then, brought about this tremendous catastrophe to this world."

But let me for a moment turn devil's advocate. I admit that Hitler was the chief villain. But for the defendants to put all blame on him is neither manly nor true. We know that even the head of the state has the same limits to his senses and to the hours of his days as do lesser men. He must rely on others to be his eyes and ears as to most that goes on in a great empire. Other legs must run his errands; other hands must execute his plans. On whom did Hitler rely for such things more than upon these men in the dock? Who led him to believe he had an invincible air armada if not Goering? Who kept disagreeable facts from him? Did not Goering forbid Field Marshal Milch to warn Hitler that in his opinion Germany was not equal to the war upon Russia? Did not Goering, according to Speer, relieve General Galland of his air force command for speaking of the weaknesses and bungling of the air forces? Who led Hitler, utterly untraveled himself, to believe in the indecision and timidity of democratic peoples if not Ribbentrop, Von Neurath, and Von Papen? Who fed his illusion of German invincibility if not Keitel, Jodl, Raeder, and Donitz? Who kept his hatred of the Jews inflamed more than Streicher and Rosenberg? Who would Hitler say deceived him about conditions in concentration camps if not Kaltenbrunner, even as he would deceive us? These men had access to Hitler and often could control the information that reached him and on which he must base his policy and his orders. They were the Praetorian Guard, and while they were under Caesar's orders, Caesar was always in their hands.

If these dead men could take the witness stand and answer what has been said against them, we might have a less distorted picture of the parts played by these defendants. Imagine the stir that would occur in the dock if it should behold Adolf Hitler advancing to the witness box, or Himmler with an armful of dossiers, or Goebbels, or Bormann with the reports of his Party spies, or the murdered Rohm or Canaris. The ghoulish defense that the world is entitled to retribution only from the cadavers is an argument worthy of the crimes at which it is directed. We have presented to this Tribunal an affirmative case based on incriminating documents which are sufficient, if unexplained, to require a finding of guilt on Count One against each defendant. In the final analysis, the only question is whether the defendant's own testimony is to be credited as against the documents and other evidence of their guilt. What, then, is their testimony worth? The fact is that the Nazi habit of economizing in the use of truth pulls the foundations out from under their own defenses. Lying has always been a highly approved Nazi technique. Hitler, in *Mein Kampf*, advocated mendacity as a policy. Von Ribbentrop admits the use of the "diplomatic lie." Keitel advised that the facts of rearmament be kept secret so that they could be denied at Geneva (EC – 177). Raeder deceived about rebuilding the German Navy in violation of Versailles. Goering urged Ribbentrop to tell a "legal lie" to the British Foreign Office about the *Anschluss*, and in so doing only marshaled him the way he was going (2947 – PS). Goering gave his word of honor to the Czechs and proceeded to break it (TC – 27).

Even Speer proposed to deceive the French into revealing the specially trained among their prisoners (R – 124). Nor is the lie direct the only means of falsehood. They all speak with a Nazi double talk with which to deceive the unwary. In the Nazi dictionary of sardonic euphemisms "final solution" of the Jewish problem was a phrase which meant extermination; "special treatment" of prisoners of war meant killing; "protective custody" meant concentration camp; "duty labor" meant slave labor; and an order to "take a firm attitude" or "take positive measures" meant to act with unrestrained savagery. Before we accept their word at what seems to be its face, we must always look for hidden meanings. Goering assured us, on his oath, that the Reich Defense Council never met "as such." When we produced the stenographic minutes of a meeting at which he presided and did most of the talking, he reminded us of the "as such" and explained this was not a meeting of the Council "as such" because other persons were present. Goering denies "threatening" Czechoslovakia; he only told President Hacha that he would "hate to bomb the beautiful city of Prague." Besides outright false statements and double talk, there are also other circumventions of truth in the nature of fantastic explanations and absurd professions. Streicher has solemnly maintained that his only thought with respect to the Jews was to resettle them on the island of Madagascar. His reason for destroying synagogues, he blandly said, was only because they were architecturally offensive. Rosenberg was stated by his counsel to have always had in mind a "chivalrous solution" to the Jewish problem. When it was necessary to remove Schuschnigg after the *Anschluss*, Ribbentrop would have had us believe that the Austrian Chancellor was resting at a "villa." It was left to cross-examination to reveal that the "villa" was Buchenwald Concentration Camp. The record is full of other examples of dissimulations and evasions. Even Schacht showed that he, too, had adopted the Nazi attitude that truth is any story which succeeds. Confronted on cross-examination with a long record of broken vows and false words, he declared in justification, and I quote from the record:

"I think you can score many more successes when you want to lead someone if you don't tell them the truth than if you tell them the truth."

This was the philosophy of the National Socialists. When for years they have deceived the world, and masked falsehood with plausibilities, can anyone be surprised that they continue their habits of a lifetime in this dock? Credibility is one of the main issues of this Trial. Only those who have failed to learn the bitter lessons of the last decade can doubt that men who have always played on the unsuspecting credulity of generous opponents would not hesitate to do the same, now.

It is against such a background that these defendants now ask this Tribunal to say that they are not guilty of planning, executing, or conspiring to commit this long list of crimes and wrongs. They stand before the record of this Trial as bloodstained Gloucester stood by the body of his slain king. He begged of the widow, as they beg of you: "Say I slew them not." And the Queen replied, "Then say they were not slain. But dead they are..." If you were to say of these men that they are not guilty, it would be as true to say that there has been no war, there are no slain, there has been no crime.

CPSIA information can be obtained at www.ICGtesting.com
Printed in the USA
LVOW101926151212

311779LV00004B/555/P